W9-CCD-265

California Dreams and Realities

Readings for Critical Thinkers and Writers

California Dreams and Realities

Readings for Critical Thinkers and Writers

Second Edition

Sonia Maasik
University of California, Los Angeles

Jack Solomon
California State University, Northridge

Bedford/St. Martin's   Boston ◆ New York

For Sadie

For Bedford/St. Martin's
Developmental Editor: Stephen A. Scipione
Production Editor: Bridget Leahy
Production Supervisor: Joseph Ford
Marketing Manager: Charles Cavaliere
Editorial Assistant: Maura Shea
Copyeditor: Rosemary Winfield
Text Design: Claire Seng-Niemoeller
Cover Design: Hannus Design Associates
Cover Art: David Hockney, *Pearblossom Highway, 11–18th April 1986* #2 (detail).
Photographic collage, 78″ × 111″. Copyright © David Hockney.
Composition: Pine Tree Composition, Inc.
Printing and Binding: R.R. Donnelley and Sons

President: Charles H. Christensen
Editorial Director: Joan E. Feinberg
Director of Editing, Design, and Production: Marcia Cohen
Managing Editor: Elizabeth M. Schaaf

Library of Congress Catalog Card Number: 98–87535

Copyright © 1999 by Bedford/St. Martin's

All rights reserved. No part of this book may be reproduced, stored in a retrieval system, or transmitted by any form or by any means, electronic, mechanical, photocopying, recording, or otherwise, except as may be expressly permitted by the applicable copyright statutes or in writing by the Publisher.

Manufactured in the United States of America.

3 2 1 0
f e d c b

For information, write: Bedford/St. Martin's, 75 Arlington Street, Boston, MA
02116 (617-426-7440)

ISBN: 0–312–19419–6

Acknowledgments
Susan E. Brown, "The ZIP-Code Route into UC" from the *Los Angeles Times* (May 3, 1989). Copyright © 1989. Reprinted with the permission of Pacific News Service.
Matthew A. Cahn and H. Eric Schockman, "Political Culture in California" from *California: An Owner's Manual.* Copyright © 1997 by Prentice-Hall, Inc. Reprinted with the permission of Prentice-Hall, Inc., Upper Saddle River, New Jersey 07458.
John Cassidy, "The Comeback" from *The New Yorker* (February 23 and March 2, 1998). Copyright © 1998 by John Cassidy. Reprinted with the permission of the author.
Cesar Chavez, "The Organizer's Tale" from Jonathan Eisen and David Fine (eds.), *Unknown California.* Originally published in *Ramparts* (July 1966). Copyright © 1966 by Ramparts Magazine, Inc. Reprinted with the permission of the Cesar Chavez Foundation.

Acknowledgments and copyrights are continued at the back of the book on pages 357–59, which constitute an extension of the copyright page. It is a violation of the law to reproduce these selections by any means whatsoever without the written permission of the copyright holder.

Preface for Instructors

In 1997, the population of California grew to over thirty-three million people. At the same time, California's economy, which lagged behind the rest of the nation in the first half of the decade, dramatically reversed itself in a sudden surge that restored much of the Golden State's tarnished luster. Such growth, both demographic and economic, propelled California once again to the forefront of the national imagination, where it now stands as a testing ground for the social and economic policies that will carry America into the twenty-first century.

That is why we have prepared the second edition of *California Dreams and Realities* — why California, in our view, merits and even invites a composition textbook all its own. It is not that we believe that California is superior to any other part of the country; rather, we believe that the special nature of the California experience offers unique opportunities to students enrolled in California's many public and private colleges and universities. The state's rich history, along with the mythic promise of the California dream, presents California's students with a wide range of writing subjects that can be personally as well as intellectually felt, while its social and political challenges and controversies offer a host of provocative topics on which to hone critical thinking and argumentation skills. But more than anything else, what California has to offer as a theme for a composition reader is its very familiarity, its closeness to the lives of California instructors and students alike. We write best when we write about topics close to us, and students beginning their training in college-level writing and critical thinking can accordingly find in their home state a secure place from which to launch themselves into their collegiate futures.

The readings themselves were chosen to allow students both to take advantage of their knowledge of California and to explore issues from a range of styles and perspectives. The readings are designed to be culturally and geographically diverse, reflecting a broad range of the people who populate our state and the places where they live. In addition, we've included a diverse range of discourses, such as academic writing, journalism, oral history, an interview, personal narratives, and literature. By learning to read and navigate these different sorts of texts, students can learn how a writer's rhetorical choices shape a reader's view of the world — an important step in developing critical judgment.

To help your students in this endeavor, we include a general introduction, which situates California both historically and within the American imagination as a place of continual reinvention — the place where immigrants from all over America and the world come to reinvent themselves, generation after generation. At the same time, the general introduction establishes the dual nature of the California experience: alongside all the glamorous dreams are gritty realities that Californians, too, must address.

Individual chapter introductions provide background for the topics raised in the book's six chapters, along with frameworks for critical thinking and evaluation. Since many of the issues your students will confront in these chapters are controversial, it is important to note that our chapter introductions are designed to stimulate lively class discussion, not to dictate the terms of that discussion. But the neutrality of our contextualizations does not mean that your students should be neutral: the point is for them to learn how to construct powerful arguments to defend what may be passionately held positions on many of the most controversial issues of the day.

The purpose of the readings, then, is to encourage your students to think and write critically about issues that are likely to strike very close to home for them — issues like affirmative action in university admission policies and bilingual education in the schools. Some of the readings are op-ed pieces that appear to provide solutions to the problems they address, but we do not intend them as ready-made answers to the dilemmas your students will be considering. Indeed, in some cases we have paired diametrically opposed opinion pieces to show how arguments can be constructed for different sides of a controversy. In other cases, the selections present striking arguments that invite rebuttal or further support.

There are no easy answers to the questions the readings raise, and the exercises and assignments we provide in the editorial apparatus of *California Dreams and Realities* are not intended to supply such answers. Rather, they are designed to guide your students in analytical thinking and argumentation, leading them to devise their own solutions to complex problems and, more important, reasoned justifications for those solutions. Some assignments call for in-class debates, others for formal essays and research, and others still for informal journal entries. At the close of each chapter, we propose topics for further research as well as projects that suggest that students visit their own communities to explore further the issues their reading assignments will raise.

Not all of the readings and assignments are analytic or argumentative, however. Sometimes they are intended to stimulate personal reflection and exploration. Poems and selections from novels offer opportunities for both literary analysis and creative expression. And some readings, especially in Chapter 6, "Of Work and Wealth: The Economics of the Dream," invite students to contemplate their own economic futures as California residents and employees.

What's New in the Second Edition

When the first edition of *California Dreams and Realities* was published, Californians were still reeling from a veritable plague of social ills and natural disasters. The state was mired in the worst economic recession since the Great Depression, the wounds from the L.A. riots were still fresh, and rubble from the Northridge earthquake still littered the ground. Since then, things have improved, and the second edition of our text has been revised in response to these changes. Though the underlying causes of the riots have by no means been resolved, the riots themselves are receding into history and no longer require a chapter of their own. Instead, we have prepared a new chapter on California's political realities — "Governing California: Democracy, Demography, and the Politics of the Dream" — to explore the larger political issues in the state where the riots occurred. This new chapter includes not only readings on California's racial climate but also texts on the dynamics of California's participatory democracy, especially the tendency of California's citizens to decide controversial issues by way of ballot initiatives and amendments to the state constitution.

Similarly, while our run of natural disasters has by no means come to an end, the catastrophic earthquakes and fires of the late 1980s and early 1990s are also receding into history. Accordingly, we have removed our chapter on natural disasters and instead prepared a new chapter, prompted by the striking upturn in the California economy in the late 1990s. "Of Work and Wealth: The Economics of the Dream" focuses on the new promises and old unsolved problems presented by the California economy, especially by its high-tech and entertainment industries.

We have kept four chapters from the first edition whose relevance is as keen today as it was in 1994. These chapters, whose readings have been substantially updated, include our chapters on the California dream, immigration, education, and land use. Since the publication of the first edition of *California Dreams and Realities*, the passage of Propositions 187, 209, and 227 has kept immigration and education in the public spotlight, and we have accordingly included new readings that reflect the impact of the initiative system on California's immigrants and students.

In a departure from the first edition, we now present literary texts in the second edition of *California Dreams and Realities*. These texts include selections from such California writers as Nathanael West, John Steinbeck, Gary Soto, and Anna Deavere Smith and appear in the chapters to which they bear the most thematic relevance. We have also included new personal narratives, such as Jack Lopez's "Of *Cholos* and Surfers." In another change from the first edition, we have added to the research topics included with every chapter new Internet-related assignments, "California on the Web," which are designed for use whether or not your class is formally "wired up." And finally, we have revised the tone of our second edition to reflect the more promising tenor of California life today, without, however, sacrificing the critical edge that is necessary to the development of critical thinking.

Resources for Teaching

We have written a supplementary instructor's manual, *Editor's Notes to Accompany California Dreams and Realities,* to provide a context for the book's selections and to highlight what we believe to be the essential issues it raises. Because many of the readings in the book are controversial, calling for classroom debate and argumentation, we have not attempted in the manual to give the "right answers" to the suggested assignments. But we do discuss each chapter and selection, suggest ways of presenting the readings to your class, and include assignments ranging from in-class debates to private journal entries, from extended research exercises to community-based exploration and service.

Acknowledgments

We are grateful to our California colleagues who chose to use the first edition of *California Dreams and Realities* in their classes. With no other book quite like this one, selecting it may well have been something of an adventure. We are especially grateful to those who took the time and trouble to suggest improvements for the second edition. Those instructors include Lisa Alvarez, Irvine Valley College; Marcia Corcoran, Evergreen Valley College; Mona Field, Glendale Community College; Trudi Fields, Las Positas College; Annette Fruehan, Orange Coast College; Dorothy Gilbert, California State University–Hayward; Jennifer Morrow, University of Southern California; Kathy Parrish, Southwestern College; Kimberly Reina, Sierra College; Margaret E. Riley, Las Positas College; Josephine (Joan) Riordan, Evergreen Valley College; John Rosewall, California State University–Dominguez Hills; Herbert Shapiro, Stanford University; Paul Staver, Santa Clara University; Scott Stevens, California State University–Fresno; Marie Wilson, Laney College. We thank as well Janet Gardner of the University of Massachusetts for her gracious suggestions.

Yet once more we find ourselves indebted to Bedford/St. Martin's for enabling us to bring a book into the world. Chuck Christensen and Joan Feinberg contributed the vision and leadership necessary to our project, while Steve Scipione served (for the fourth time now!) as our editor. We also wish to thank Maura Shea, Bridget Leahy, and Rosemary Winfield, without whose efforts all of the rest of our work would have been in vain. Thank you all, folks. We're glad to be a part of the Bedford/St. Martin's team.

Contents

which had been wedged into the dirt. Trash spilled down a steep slope below it. The bushes smelled of urine."

4. Developing the Dream: Issues in California Land Use   **167**

"Gray Line buses do not linger in Bakersfield or Oildale or Taft. Movie stars and sports celebrities seldom buy homes there, though they might well invest in the land. People don't visit, as a rule, unless they have business there, or relatives, or have come searching for Oildorado."

"But the truth is that I went through a lot of hell, and a lot of people did. If we can even the score a little for the workers, then we are doing something."

"And with the passing/of each season/human life knows little/ change."

California Dreams and Realities

Readings for Critical Thinkers and Writers

Introduction
Reinventing the Dream

For a while, things looked pretty bleak for the California dream. A devastating earthquake, an economic depression, and a wrenching controversy over immigration all seemed to team together to knock the Golden State to its knees. What many once had regarded as a kind of Promised Land looked more and more like a staging ground for the apocalypse.

You might think we are referring here to the calamities of the mid-1990s, but we're not. Rather, the social, economic, and natural afflictions we have named all belonged to the California of the 1930s, when the Great Depression flattened the state's economy, and the controversy over immigration included not only migrant laborers from Mexico, who during that decade were repatriated back to Mexico in large numbers, but emigrants from the Dust Bowl states as well, the so-called Okies. And the earthquake struck in Long Beach, not in Northridge.

So you see, Californians have been through rough times before. And just as California bounced back from the reversals of the 1930s, it now is bouncing back from the setbacks of the early 1990s. There's a lesson in that—both for those of us who call ourselves Californians and for the many others who seem both to take satisfaction in watching California's tribulations and to envy us during our good times.

The lesson is that California is a remarkably resilient place, a land of constant reinvention. Once a sparsely populated land inhabited by such Native American peoples as the Chumash, the Modocs, and the Hupas, California has been reinvented many times since the Spanish conquest. From the days of the Mexican rancheros, through the era of U.S. annexation and Anglo-Saxon settlement, to today, when immigrants from all over the globe are once again changing the face of the Golden State, California has seen many profound changes.

Another way of putting this is that there is no single California. Not only is California divided into many geographical regions—the north coast, the interior valleys, the Bay Area, the southern coast, the mountains of the southern Cascades, the Sierra, the desert—inhabited by the most diversified population in the nation, but there is also no single California story. California is neither the sun-drenched land of glitter and glamour that many outsiders imagine when they think of the Golden State, nor is it the war zone that has recently captured the national imagination. Certainly we have our share of sunshine, glitter, and glamour, as well as poverty, violence, and social tension, but our character is much more complex than that.

At present, the one constant in California life is that of change. Once again, California is in a state of transformation, reinventing its economy, its demography, and its politics. As students in California's system of higher education—the largest and most distinguished of such state systems in the nation—you are well aware of many of the changes now occurring in the Golden State, as well as the social controversies that change can bring. From Proposition 187 (the ballot measure that attempted to ban public services for illegal immigrants), to Proposition 209 (the measure that ended public affirmative action programs), to Proposition 227 (the proposition aimed at bilingual education), Californians have faced the sometimes wrenching effects of reinvention. But there's another way of looking at the matter. The fact that California can endure change and even prosper in its wake can stand as a model for the rest of America, which will also be reinventing itself in the years to come.

And you can be certain that the rest of the country is watching us. It is often said that whatever happens in America happens first in California, and with over 10 percent of the nation's population and roughly one-eighth of the nation's gross domestic output, it is understandable that California holds such a prominent place in the national imagination.

We have written *California Dreams and Realities* both to help make you aware of the many changes and challenges that face Californians today and to prepare you to contribute to the ongoing reinvention of our state. Given the crucial role that California's system of higher education plays in the social, cultural, and economic environment of our state, we believe that one of its responsibilities should be to prepare you for a future that you yourselves will make. The readings and assignments in this text are all designed to help you take stock of the transformations now going on in California and to lead you to the kind of thinking from which a new California may be born, all while you develop your skills in college-level writing and critical thinking.

Writing the Future

Think for a moment of what your vision of a future California might be. Do you envision a place where California's many peoples find a common ground for cooperation rather than interracial strife? Where urban and suburban development accommodates the needs of our social and natural ecologies? We would all probably share such a California dream, but the question is: how can we achieve such goals? What obstacles stand in our way to a better future? What social conflicts divide us, and how might those divisions be resolved? Are you prepared to argue for your vision and your solutions in a manner that would persuade someone with a different point of view?

Learning how to construct persuasive arguments is one of the goals of your first-year composition class. Another goal is to enhance your confidence in self-expression—in the articulation of your own thoughts and experiences. Your composition class is also designed to train you in the careful close reading and comprehension of texts, both expository and literary, as well as to prepare you to engage in collaborative learning and research. *California Dreams and Realities* will help you achieve all of these goals. Each chapter focuses on a current California issue, presenting background information and conflicting views that can help you shape your own arguments, as well as literary selections that can help you explore the issues in more personal and poetic ways.

To start you on your project of rewriting California, the first chapter, "California Dreaming: Myths of the Golden Land," presents readings that invite you to explore the ways in which California has traditionally figured in our cultural imagination. Here you will find reflections on the California promise written from such diverse viewpoints as that of a fourth-generation Sacramento aristocrat and a first-generation Chicano surfer. The lures of gold rush–era San Francisco and of postwar Southern California are also explored, as well as a glimpse of Hollywood in the golden age of the movies. Together, these readings are designed to provide an imaginative and historical background for the issues that appear in the book's subsequent chapters.

Chapter 2, "The Great Migration: Immigrants in California History," accordingly focuses on the people whom the California dream has attracted through the years, especially those twentieth-century immigrants who have come from Latin America and Asia. These readings explore not only the lives and personal histories of the new immigrants but also the political controversies surrounding immigration and its impact on our culture and economy.

Chapter 3, "The Best-Laid Plans: Education and the California Dream," extends the discussion of many of the issues explored in Chapter 2 by focusing on the statewide debates over affirmative action and bilingual education. Other educational issues explored in this chapter include the question of access to higher education in California and the growing shortage of instructors available to teach the state's burgeoning school enrollments.

Chapter 4, "Developing the Dream: Issues in California Land Use," looks at the state's environment and its place in our lives and history. Here you will find readings on the history of California water policy, as well as alternative visions of land-use policy that include organic farming and the sustainability movement. To provide a cultural contrast to current land-use issues and policies, we have also included readings on the attitudes and practices of the first Californians, the Native American peoples who inhabited the land for thousands of years without significantly altering it.

Chapter 5, "Governing California: Democracy, Demography, and the Politics of the Dream," explores the complex political spectrum of contemporary California, focusing on demographic change and the tendency of

Californians to tackle their most devisive political problems through the use of ballot initiatives. These readings often address the racial tensions that have come with demographic change, but they also include visions of resolving those tensions peacefully, so that diversity might be coupled with social harmony rather than political controversy.

The final chapter of this book, "Of Work and Wealth: The Economics of the Dream," considers some of the leading industries that define California's economy, both present and future. Here you will find readings on Silicon Valley and the Hollywood film industry, the two great engines of the current California economy, as well as texts on the drawbacks of high-tech prosperity. Readings from the point of view of farm workers are also included, as well as a reflection on the Central Valley's oil economy, to balance the coastal viewpoints presented in selections on Silicon Valley and Hollywood.

In each chapter you will find various viewpoints and arguments that are intended to stimulate the formation of your own arguments in both your writing assignments and class discussions. Each reading is accordingly accompanied by sets of questions designed to encourage careful close reading and to provide prompts for argumentative essays, journal entries, and in-class discussions and debates. Some questions encourage further individual or group research into the topics raised by a particular reading, and every chapter concludes with special "Researching the Issues" and "California on the Net" sections that suggest topics for expanded research into the issues raised by that chapter, encouraging you to make use of community, library, and Internet resources in conducting your research.

We have written *California Dreams and Realities,* then, to serve two purposes: to help train you in college-level writing and critical thinking and to make you an informed citizen of the state of California, one who will be prepared to share in the reshaping of our state. As you learn the techniques that you will need to succeed in your college course work, you will also be gaining the understanding necessary to help California succeed in the future. California has always been a place of dreams: this book asks you to help keep it that way.

1 California Dreaming
Myths of the Golden Land

After the Gold Rush

The words are almost always the same: *paradise, the golden land, the dream.* Whenever writers try to describe the place of California in the national imagination, such terms and phrases inevitably appear. Whether referring to the climate, the spectacular scenery, or the economic opportunities California has offered to Americans since the 1849 gold rush, the words *paradise* and *dream* sum up California's unique significance in American history. Indeed, with the help of Hollywood and a century of effective real estate promotion, California has long figured as a special case of the American dream: a more promising version dreamed under ever-sunny skies.

Those of us who live in California, of course, know better. The sun does not always shine. The streets are not paved with gold (and never were). And paradise was marked with fault lines long before the great San Francisco quake of 1906 awakened us to the instability within the California earth. Still, here we are. And for most of us, native born and immigrant alike, we are here because California offered us, or our ancestors, something special, something no other state in the union had to offer.

Perhaps your grandparents came to California to escape New England winters or Midwestern provinciality. Or perhaps your family came during the war to work in the shipyards of Richmond or maybe afterward to take advantage of California's postwar economic expansion. Perhaps you yourself came because this is where the most exciting opportunities were. Perhaps you and your family arrived along with the thousands who fled Vietnam in the aftermath of the war, or perhaps you were fleeing civil war in Central America, poverty in Mexico, revolution in Iran, or persecution in the Soviet Union. One way or another, most of our families have arrived in California relatively recently, looking for a new beginning.

Of course, if you are descended from one of California's many Native American tribes, you may have a different point of view. The dream that has attracted so many immigrants — European, Asian, and Latin American — may look to you like a nightmare: the long night of your people's dispossession. And for Chicanos, the California promise, too, may look less like an offer than a seizure, for California was once a part of the Republic of

Mexico, seized by the United States during the Mexican-American War. But for the millions of other Californians who have arrived since the Spanish and the American conquests, the myth of California defines this place as a land of renewal and opportunity, an earthly paradise blessed with perpetual sunshine.

To test the power of the myth of the golden land, just think for a moment about leaving California. Where would you go? Would you seek one of those places like Colorado, Washington, Oregon, Arizona, or even Las Vegas, where thousands of Californians in the early 1990s sought what then appeared to be shinier, less tarnished versions of the traditional California dream? Or would you look for some place completely different, like New England, New York, the South, or the Midwest, regions whose images contrast sharply with that of California? Or, finally, does the thought of leaving California leave you cold? Do you think you'd rather stay after all because this is still California, the place where the continent ends and the dreams still begin?

The Way We Were

In this chapter we look at the traditional vision of the California good life. This will be our touchstone, the standard against which we may compare some more contemporary versions of California life. The general rosiness of the traditional vision may strike you as being a little unrealistic — especially if you or your family has suffered in any way from one of California's recent reversals — but then it might also strike you with a shock of recognition, a feeling that, yes, that's what California has always meant to you.

Consider for a moment of the images that spring to mind when you think of California. Do you see hot tubs set on redwood decks suspended over steep canyons or Malibu villas overlooking the Pacific? Is it Hollywood that you see, glamorous names inscribed along the Walk of Fame, Beverly Hills mansions, and the trendy crowds sauntering along Rodeo Drive and the Sunset Strip? Maybe you see the redwoods on the Mendocino coast, the salt flats of Death Valley, or the razor edge of the Sierra Nevada's eastern escarpment. Or perhaps you see the hills of San Francisco, the blue waters of the Bay, the Golden Gate Bridge and Mount Tamalpais beyond. Maybe you have a Valley view — not the San Fernando Valley but the seemingly endless plain of the Central Valley with its rows on rows of irrigated fields and orchards flashing in the sun like spokes on a wheel as you drive on by. And then again, perhaps no image as such comes to mind at all, but only a feeling, an expectation, that this is the place where desires are satisfied, where freeways take you wherever you want to go, and where there are no limits to what you can do.

If all this sounds a little corny — and just a few years ago it might have sounded more than corny — it is still a part of California's legacy. Since the nineteenth century, California has been sold to America as a paradise, a place of perpetual sunshine, orange groves, and opportunity. This image has burned like a beacon for generations of immigrants from all over the nation and the world, drawing them here to test its validity. Once drawn by land and gold, they're still coming, attracted today by a reinvigorated and reinvented economy, as well as by that special quality of life that non-Californians have often joked about but have never ignored.

The Readings

James J. Rawls begins our survey of the traditional California dream with an essay on the vision of the good life that California has always represented. Though fundamentally a glowing tribute to California, Rawls's essay still sounds a warning note as it explores the "paradox of expectations" that California's inordinate promise presents whenever it fails. Malcolm J. Rohrbough's portrait of gold rush–era San Francisco illustrates the notorious inhibition-busting effects of California on traditional American Puritanism, while Denise S. Spooner follows with an historical survey of the Midwestern emigration to California in the years immediately after World War II, often in search of the kinds of freedom that the forty-niners found in San Francisco. Richard Rodriguez's essay "Proofs" offers a journalistic and yet poetic meditation on the complex meaning of the "promised land" for Mexican immigrants, a place of Border Patrolmen and economic opportunity where "you can be anything you want to be" if you can get past *la migra*. Next, Jack Lopez offers a personal memoir of what it was like to grow up as the child of immigrants in southern California, at once attracted to the Anglo world of surfing and yet loyal too to the *cholos* of East L.A. Charlie Stoddard, a graduate of Claremont McKenna College, follows with an op-ed article on the need to formulate a new California dream in an era of diminishing expectations. Nathanael West's satirical look at the way Californians, especially in Hollywood, express their desires through elaborate sartorial and architectural charades provides a glimpse of California's eternal promise of self-invention, while Joan Didion's classic essay "Notes from a Native Daughter" concludes the chapter with an exploration of the California that non-Californians and coastal Californians alike tend to neglect: the Sacramento Valley, home to families like Didion's, made up of the descendants of the Anglo pioneers who came to California in the mid-nineteenth century.

JAMES J. RAWLS

California: A Place, A People, A Dream

"In the imagination of the twentieth century, California is the quintessential Promised Land," **James J. Rawls** (b. 1945) writes as he explores the California dream and its place in American mythology. But though the dream "is simply a vision of the good life," Rawls cautions, it also contains a paradox: With the high promise of its glittering reputation, can California always deliver? And if it can't, what disillusionment may follow? A long-time interpreter and chronicler of the California experience, Rawls teaches history at Diablo Valley College, is the author of several books, including *Indians of California: The Changing Image* (1984) and, with Walter Bean, *California: An Interpretive History* (1998), and is editor of *New Directions in California History* (1988) and *California: A Place, A People, A Dream* (1986), from which this essay is taken.

The California Dream — you can sense it in the crisp air of the High Sierra, taste it in the ocean spray at Malibu, feel it in the sun-drenched skies of the Central Valley, glimpse it in the mist and fog of Muir Woods. It surrounds and envelops you, engaging your senses, permeating your soul. The California Dream is a love affair with an idea, a marriage to a myth, a surrender to a collective fantasy. Unbounded by time or space, the California Dream is transcendent, creating a unity, a whole, a merging of past, present, and future in the total California experience. It's quite impossibly everything — and quite possibly nothing at all.

I suppose that there are as many versions of the California Dream as there are dreamers — or as there are essayists who try to capture its essence on paper. For most of us, the California Dream is simply a vision of the good life. It once was seen glittering in the California gold fields. Today it may be fashioned from images of California ranch houses, redwood decks and patios, outdoor barbecues and kidney-shaped swimming pools. The California Dream — whatever its present form — draws its power from universal human needs. Founded on expectation and hope, the California Dream promises to fulfill our deepest longings for opportunity and success, warmth, sunshine and beauty, health and long life, freedom, and even a foretaste of the future.

Opportunity and success — these promises are at the heart of the California Dream. When Stephen Wozniak and Steven Jobs launched Apple Computers a decade ago, they were acting in a long tradition of visionary California entrepreneurs. Forty years earlier, two young Stanford graduates named William Hewlett and David Packard founded in a Palo Alto garage a company destined soon to become one of the nation's premier electronics firms. The list of California successes is embarrassingly rich and endless. Before high technology and aerospace, there were motion pictures, oil fields, citrus groves, real estate, railroads, and, of course, gold. It's as though a special deity watches over California, for in each generation a new resource or new industry develops, reaffirming once again the identity of California with opportunity. California is America's own New World, a land of incredible enterprise, fortune, and good luck.

Warmth and sunshine — more glowing promises of the California Dream. The image of California as a land of perpetual sun — "It Never Rains in Southern California" so the song goes — has an obvious appeal to snowbound Easterners and Midwesterners. It's easy to identify with the sentiments of one Midwestern newcomer who wrote in the 1930s: "I'd get letters from friends that had settled here. . . . I'd hear about the orange groves and palms, . . . sunny days and cool nights, and how the only snow you saw was miles off in the mountains, and — well, I was sick of the prairie landscape and stoking the fire all winter and frying all summer, and first chance I got, I boarded a train to find out if this country came up to the brag." I've always suspected that the annual New Year's Day telecast of the Rose Parade in Pasadena — cameras panning healthy, tanned men and women sauntering in shirt sleeves under palm trees and clear skies — accounts for a sizeable share of the yearly migration to California. As if the seductive climate weren't enough, the mere mention of California conjures up images of stunning natural beauty. Endless blue skies and spectacular seacoasts, magnificent groves of giant sequoia, gentle hills and soaring mountains — all are part of the overwhelming vision of Beautiful California.

With such a salubrious climate, so it's said, California is also a particu-   5
larly healthy place to live. Today's "fat farms," tanning booths, and longevity institutes are modern expressions of the same fitness impulse that was evident in the sanitoriums and health resorts of the nineteenth century. During the 1880s, southern California welcomed thousands of invalids who erroneously believed that the region's warm, clean air would cure their tuberculosis and ensure them a long and healthy life. Such healthfulness even brought on predictions that a new and superior "California race" was emerging here. As early as 1866, Charles Loring Brace claimed to have seen evidence of positive physical changes among those who had arrived in California. The superiority of *homo sapiens Californium* seemed to be confirmed by the 1984 Summer Olympics in Los Angeles. Under sunny blue skies, young Californians won the gold, silver, and bronze in vastly disproportionate numbers. A product of their own environment, how could they do less?

With visions of healthy, attractive, fit Californians in mind, it's easy to recall another suggestive promise of the California Dream — romance. "Sex and California," declared a recent *Los Angeles Times* article — "the two seem to go together." The identification of California and romance has taken many forms over the years. Malibu Barbie became, for a time, a popular icon for half the preteen population of America. Meanwhile, a line of cosmetics called California Girls offered the chance for older sisters to achieve at least the surface glow of a genuine Californian. And of course for everyone, there's Hollywood. Its glitter and allure have added an unmistakable glamour to the image of the Golden State. Romantic opportunity is the theme of countless Hollywood films, from *San Francisco* to the *Bikini Beach* series, where bronzed and nubile youths frolic to the music of Frankie Avalon. The lyrics and pulsating rhythms of the California Sound, pioneered by the Beach Boys in the early 1960s, capture the sensuous simplicity of life on the California beaches. And what did the Beach Boys write about? "They wrote about the beach and girls and cars, and that was it," remembers David Crosby. "All we really cared about was girls in the first place, and cars were a way to get from your parents and get the girls — and the beach was the place to go. And those were the main elements of our consciousness." Freedom, outdoor living, and romance — those are also the bright lights of the California Dream.

Freedom — in California it's a promise that allows unconventional political movements, personal eccentricities, and unusual fads and fashions to bloom unmolested. "Almost anything might work in California," Carey McWilliams once observed, "you never know." Free from the restraints of tradition and history, California seems uniquely able to shape the nature of things to come. A leader in adopting progressive reforms early in the century, California has altered the national political scene with such innovations as the use of professional campaign management firms, the techniques of image management, and the use of Hollywood celebrities as campaign fundraisers — or as candidates themselves. The idea of California as the harbinger of the American future — from campus turmoil and tax revolts to community colleges, freeways, and shopping malls — is by now a popular cliché.

Promising so much to so many, California is forever being described in superlatives. In the imagination of the twentieth century, California is the quintessential Promised Land. "Why *should* anybody die out here?" asked a character in Steward Edward White's 1920 novel, *The Rose Dawn.* "They'll never get any closer to heaven." And forty years later, Brian Wilson, one of the founding brothers of the Beach Boys, explained: "All good teenagers go to California when they die."

It's tempting to stop here, having neatly summarized and categorized the promises of the California Dream. But that would leave the great misimpression that the California Dream is somehow static and fixed. It would ignore the very essence, excitement, and energy of the dream. The California Dream can't be contained by neat categories. Like California and its people, the dream is alive, an ever-changing and turbulent dynamic. It's made not only of promises but also of paradoxes, the joining of seeming opposites. The paradoxes are what give the dream its dynamism, for in California there is an ongoing dialectic in which new syntheses are born from the paradoxes of the past.

We see this dialectic at work in what might be called the paradox of expectations. The promises of the California Dream raise the expectations of the millions who come to California, hoping that their lives here will be better than what they leave behind. California is to them their best — or perhaps their last — chance for success. "There is no more new frontier," the

10

Eagles have told us. "We have got to make it here." Many of those who come find what they are looking for. They become enthusiastic boosters of the Golden State, recruiting friends and relatives to join them. Yet California doesn't fulfill the expectations of all those who come. Many find that life here isn't at all what they had hoped or dreamed that it would be. Despair, isolation, and disillusionment arise out of the newcomers' experience, turning would-be dreamers into bitter antagonists who denounce the false promises of the California Dream.

Obviously there is a paradox here, for California is at once a land of great expectation and disappointment, lauded and damned with equal intensity. While the major chords in the California Dream have been affirmative and celebratory, audible too, usually in the background, are the minor chords of doubt and disillusionment. If only because California promises so much, its failure to live up to expectations has been especially vivid, conspicuous, and dramatic.

The gold rush experience itself was forged on this paradox of expectation. Hundreds of diaries and reminiscences extoll the charms of the golden land, but others speak of the painful contrast between California's vaunted promises and its actual conditions. "I really hope that no one will be deterred from coming here," wrote one disappointed argonaut in 1850. "The more fools the better — the fewer to laugh when we get home." And a popular gold rush ballad ended with the bitter refrain, "Oh land of gold you did me deceive, and I intend in thee my bones to leave."

California's writers have often provided a counterpoint to the myth of California as the land of boundless opportunity, success, and romance. The alleged failure of the myth became a major preoccupation for the writers of the 1930s, powerfully expressed in the works of Nathanael West, Aldous Huxley, and John Steinbeck. Today's California writers are still using the California Dream as a foil for their work. Much of the appeal of their work lies in the fact that the dream is always there, if only to be denied. In "Some Dreamers of the Golden Dream," Joan Didion tells the pathetic story of a desperate woman, living in the San Bernardino Valley, who is convicted of the murder of her husband. "Of course she came from somewhere else, came off the prairie in search of something she had seen in a movie or heard on the radio, for this is a Southern California story."

A new genre of anti-California literature — the minor chords now in concert — appeared in gloomy force in the late 1960s and 1970s. "California — Has Dream Gone Sour?" ran a headline in the *Los Angeles Times,* and the Pacific News Service syndicated an article captioned "Shades of the Sunbelt Shift: California Dream in a Body Bag." Books appeared with titles such as *Anti-California* and *California: The Vanishing Dream.* California seemed to be its own worst enemy as the impulse to debunk was powerfully stimulated by a bizarre set of "California events" — the Berkeley FSM,[1] the Watts riot, the

---

[1]Free Speech Movement. [Eds.]

flowering of Haight-Ashbury, the Manson cult murders, the Patty Hearst kidnapping, the People's Temple mass murder-suicide, and the assassinations of San Francisco mayor George Moscone and supervisor Harvey Milk.

In this dire outpouring of pop commentary, the promises of the California Dream are still present, but they have been turned inside out, frisked for clues as to what went wrong. The image of California as the land of opportunity becomes a *cause* of California's multiple tragedies. The gold rush syndrome — high hopes, soon dashed — makes California especially susceptible to the appeal of crackpot schemes of self-proclaimed messiahs. Even California's climate is at fault — all that warmth and sunshine attracts "emotionally unwrapped" people to the state. In these bleak analyses of the 1960s and 1970s, California is no longer seen as a land of health but as a dark precinct of social pathology. Wide publicity is given to the state's rate of alcoholism, drug abuse, and suicide — clear evidence that California is now the land of failed dreams and broken promises. California, land of romance, becomes California, land of rampant immorality and sexual deviance. As for California's social freedom — by clear consensus — it is a case of too much of a good thing. America take heed! Freedom from tradition leads to disorientation and rootlessness, tolerance attracts the unbalanced and antisocial.

The minor chords in the California Dream, always present, reached a crescendo in the early 1970s. Then, just as this climax was passing, we began to hear something new. California came to be the subject of a remarkable new body of descriptive literature, what James D. Houston elsewhere calls the New Anatomy of California. Finally we began to see a clear-sighted portrait of California, a balanced appraisal of the state's virtues and accomplishments as well as its faults and failures. Kevin Starr's *Americans and the California Dream* (1973) signaled the emergence of this new perception, identifying the "best possibilities" of the state's regional culture rather than dwelling on the half-truths of contemporary cliché and stereotype. Five years later James D. Hart's *A Companion to California* was published. This encyclopedic work neither boosts the California myth nor belabors the state's excesses. It is a straightforward catalogue of California people, places, and things, from Abalone to Zukor. . . .

Another paradox in the California Dream is the paradox of growth. Here too we see the dynamic quality of the dream — the workings of a dialectic and the emergence of new forms. After more than a century of phenomenal growth, California became the nation's most populous state at the end of 1962. Today it leads New York, its closest rival, by more than eight million people. Throughout California history, growth has been thought of as the greatest good. We happily measure our success by it, for it reassures us that faith in the California Dream remains strong, that its promises are being fulfilled. Yet as the California Dream succeeds in attracting ever greater numbers of people, the ability of California to fulfill its promises diminishes.

This paradox of growth isn't just a phenomenon of our own times; it cuts across the state's history. With news of gold in California, "the world rushed in." By the end of 1848 some six thousand miners in California had wrested $10 million worth of gold from the foothills of the Sierra. By 1852, the peak year, the output was $80 million but the number of miners had risen to a hundred thousand. In just four years, the per capita yield of the California mines had been cut in half. Quick and easy wealth was the promise of California, yet as more and more hopeful miners arrived, the prospects for the promise being fulfilled dimmed accordingly. . . .

It's only been in recent years that Californians generally have come to appreciate the nature of this paradox. When California became the most populous state late in 1962, many residents joined in a statewide celebration of "Population Day," but it was apparent even then that growth had its price. In great rings around the state's cities, the geometry and monotomy of tract development were replacing open space, green fields, and orchards. The state's parklands, hopelessly overcrowded, were in danger of being loved to death by vacationing Californians. Urban freeways, built as pathways for automobility, were becoming monuments to immobility.

Out of this paradox of growth — in which the ultimate success of the   20
California Dream would mean its utter demise — there emerged a new synthesis. California, the most populous state, dedicated itself to the control of growth. Starting with a Petaluma ordinance in 1973, communities across the state began to take steps to limit further growth. Cities as diverse as Stockton and Belmont, Saratoga and Santa Cruz, passed ordinances controlling growth, and growth-control candidates were elected in such rapidly growing counties as Santa Clara, Orange, and San Diego. The growth-control movement represents a radical reversal of traditional values. California, once so proud of its phenomenal growth, is now home to the movement to limit growth. Apparently Californians have come at last to appreciate the wisdom of former governor Earl Warren. "Mere numbers," Warren remarked upon the occasion of California's emergence as the most populous state, "do not mean happiness."

Still there's another paradox in the California Dream — the paradox of plenty. From the gold rush to the present, fulfillment of the dream has most often meant getting rich. Money-making is a kind of fixed mania for many Californians, and the evidence of California's riches is plain enough. A stroll down Rodeo Drive in Beverly Hills should convince the most skeptical — stretch limousines at the curb, haberdashers offering their four-hundred-dollar cotton shirts, display windows adorned with bedspreads made from the fur of the Mongolian gray fox. Today California ranks third among the states in personal income, a full 13 percent above the national average. If California were a separate nation, it would be one of the world's major economic powers, ranking twelfth in the value of international trade and eighth in gross national product.

Yet the pursuit of wealth in California has not been unopposed. California has long been a battleground between the forces of economic development and environmental protection. Here, where the environment is so magnificent and the drive to achieve economic success is so strong, the impulse to protect and defend the environment has been most powerfully aroused.

Whenever the state's environment has been threatened, from the days of John Muir to the present, Californians have risen in its defense. In 1969 an offshore well of the Union Oil Company sprang a leak and smeared the beaches of Santa Barbara with oil. Two years later, a pair of Standard Oil tankers collided in the fog just inside the Golden Gate, spilling their cargo of oil into San Francisco Bay. Both of these incidents, and countless others, provoked an impassioned and vigorous response from outraged Californians. The sight of beaches littered with the oil-soaked bodies of dead seagulls and dying marine mammals added tremendous emotional fuel to the environment movement.

Out of this intensely charged struggle between the forces of economic development and environmental protection has come the search for non-polluting, renewable sources of energy. Solar, wind, and geothermal power represent ways in which economic development may proceed with a minimum of environmental damage. (They also are ways, of course, of reducing dependence on foreign oil.) Here again is evidence of the California dialectic at work. From opposing forces a new synthesis is being formed. Today California is *the* solar state in the union, containing more than 40 percent of the total United States solar collector capacity. San Diego, Santa Barbara, and Santa Clara counties are the first in the country to require solar water heating in new residential construction. California also leads the nation in the harnessing of wind and geothermal power. The world's largest wind energy project is being built by PG&E in the rolling hills of Solano County, while Sonoma County is the home of the nation's first commercial geothermal power plant. All are new solutions, born of the paradox of plenty. . . .

Promise and paradox are at the center of the California Dream. In spite of the withering analyses of the past, the promises of California remain undiminished, bringing new generations of newcomers from around the world. The paradoxes find resolution through a dialectic in which new perceptions, relations, and ways of life are forever being created. The emerging syntheses are informed by the virtues of balance, control, restraint, and the willingness to experiment and seek innovation. It is through the pursuit of these virtues that we ensure the survival of California — a place, a people, a dream.

Understanding the Text

1. Summarize in your own words the classic image of the California dream as Rawls describes it.
2. How does Rawls see popular culture as contributing to the image of California?

3. What does Rawls mean by the "paradox of expectations" (paras. 10–12) created by the California dream?

4. How, according to Rawls, do the slow-growth and environmental movements relate to the "paradox of growth" (paras. 17–20)?

Exploring and Debating the Issues

1. In your journal, brainstorm your own version of the California dream. Share your entry with your class, and discuss how the class's versions compare with Rawls's description of the dream.

2. Rawls wrote this essay in 1986. Write an essay in which you argue whether his description of the California good life is still valid, supporting your position with current evidence.

3. Does Rawls's version of the California dream apply to all residents of this state? In class, discuss whether there are any groups of individuals who may be excluded from this version. Then, drawing on your class discussion, write an essay in which you argue the extent to which the California dream includes all its residents.

4. Write an essay in which you support, refute, or modify Rawls's statement in the concluding paragraph that "the promises of California remain undiminished." To develop your essay, consult the other selections in this chapter, Chapter 2 on immigration, or Chapter 6 on California's economy.

MALCOLM J. ROHRBOUGH

Days of Gold

"Don't call it Frisco," San Franciscans will tell you when speaking of their beloved city by the Bay, preferring simply to call their home "the City." But as **Malcolm J. Rohrbough** suggests in his historical portrait of San Francisco at the height of the gold rush, "the City" may be too tame a label for this raucous, unconventional town, which still is unlike any other major city in America. An historian whose many works include *Aspen* (1988) and *Trans Appalachian Frontier* (1989), Rohrbough is also the author of *Days of Gold: The California Gold Rush and the American Nation* (1997), from which this selection is taken.

(*1*) **E**xperiences on shipboard or on the California Trail that sometimes called on the forty-niners to come to terms with their values and standards of behavior and conduct were only a prelude to the range of choices and temptations that began at the docks in San Francisco, on the streets in Placerville (or Hangtown, as it was called in those days), and in the diggings along the Feather or American Rivers. From the moment of their arrival, the forty-niners acknowledged that California was different. It was different in its opportunities; it was different in its standards of doing business and of personal behavior; it was different in its wide range of attractions. The most dramatic introduction to these differences lay in San Francisco itself. Here, the dynamic town that was turning into a city met the ambitions of the forty-niners who had traveled so far and who now landed with such high hopes. "The land of promise," wrote Charles Buckingham as he sailed into the great harbor: "Every heart beats high as we near the Golden Shore. All is speculation, expectation & anticipation."[1]

Gold brought together people from the distant reaches of the Western Hemisphere, and by the fall of 1849, San Francisco was booming. In December 1849, Rinaldo Taylor of Boston wrote of the City on the Bay, "It is now a great place, such a one as the world never produced before. Crowded with people from all parts of the world, the Yankees & the Chinaman jostling each other in the streets, while French, Germans, Sandwich Islands, Chillians, Malays, Mexicans, &c &c in all their varieties of costume and language go to form a 'congrommoration' of humanity, such as the world never saw before."[2] Here, the arriving Americans, a provincial and local people whose tolerance level was further limited by the sense of the search for gold as a competition, came face to face with one another and with peoples whose varieties they could not have imagined.

John C. Collbreath wrote in the summer of 1849, "The city of San Francisco presents the strangest state of society I ever saw or heard of."[3] This sense of differentness began in the harbor, where the Argonauts saw for the first time the masts of hundreds of idle craft, deserted by their crews stampeding to the gold fields. Arriving forty-niners had not been ashore for ten minutes or gone more than ten feet from their landing site before they experienced a flood of powerful impressions.

For the newly arrived forty-niner, more impressive than the varieties of peoples and cultures were the opportunities to make money. From the streets at the edge of the harbor to the crests of the distant Sierra, California was a new economic experience. Even more than the display of goods, the ostentatious flaunting of money jolted the new arrivals. What had begun as incomparable riches in the imaginations of men in small towns and on farms seemed to receive the most dramatic kind of confirmation in California. Forty-niners from all places and of whatever previous economic condition again and again expressed astonishment at the quantities of hard money visible, passing from hand to hand. William Daingerfield wrote on his arrival in California, "Gold is measured here by bushels and shovel full."[4]

[1]Charles Buckingham, diary, October 31, 1849, Henry E. Huntington Library, San Marino, CA (HEH).

[2]Rinaldo Taylor to his wife, December 30, 1849, Letters, Massachusetts Historical Society, Boston (MASS).

[3]John Collbreath to parents, brother, and sister, June 30, 1849, Letters, Bancroft Library, University of California, Berkeley (BAN).

[4]William Daingerfield to his mother, August 10, 1850, Letters, BAN. The *Nantucket Enquirer* quoted a correspondent, "money never looked of so little consequence as it does here." April 8, 1849. See also the Newburyport *Daily Herald*, December 19, 1848.

5 The large quantity of money in circulation dramatically inflated prices and wages. Gold, the standard currency, was plentiful, the property of everyone. Albert Osbun reflected his astonishment at the widespread holding of wealth when he wrote that gold was as common as sands in the seas. He concluded: "Money here seems to be of little value, & every person has plenty."[5]

6 The forty-niners could not help but observe that gold was most visible in connection with activities of questionable morality. The gambling houses that lined the streets of San Francisco were its most prominent and opulent buildings. They paid the highest rents; they were, from all accounts, the most profitable; they were the first structures rebuilt after a fire. The widespread presence of gambling and other leisure time activities — from prostitution to billiards and bowls — shocked the newly arrived Argonauts. "If any persons wants to convince himself that money is the root of evil let them come here," wrote John Craven to his wife. "Nearly every other house is a gambling hole many that come down in the money from the *placer* — independent & rich are forced to lie down at night in the open air for want of means to pay their lodging."[6] That hard-earned money should be risked and so spent provoked astonishment — and the more so after the forty-niners worked in the mines and realized first hand how dearly bought by labor were such sums.

7 The range of the entertainment industry — gambling, drinking, prostitution, music, and variety shows — and its universal presence and success, even on the Sabbath, testified to new kinds of beliefs and spending habits. In the gambling halls of San Francisco, "you may see a dozen tables in a room on which are displayed thousands of dollars in gold, and silver surrounded by a crowd of eager victims, betting from 25 cts to many doubloons or ounces as they are called," wrote Lafayette Fish. Rinaldo Taylor commented of the gambling houses with reference to images from home: "I could not help thinking today (Sunday) what our staid New Englanders would think could they have stood with me, about the time of church opening at home, in the door of one of these places in the most public street in the city, & cast their eyes over the scene." Taylor's comments capture the sense of displacement from family, community, and a lifetime of accepted patterns and standards of behavior. In California, from one end of the gold camps to the other, these values seemed turned upside down. "Here are to be found two extremes, good and bad, and here it is that vice predominates," Milo Goss told his wife.[7]

8 The riches of San Francisco extended beyond its displays of gold to its streets, where goods of every description lay discarded and rotting. The city — if so it might be called in the summer of 1849 — was a hodgepodge of tents

[5]Edward Abbe, diary, July 9, 1849, HEH; Albert G. Osbun, diary, June 16, 1849, HEH.
[6]John J. Craven to his wife, September 18, 1849, Letters, HEH.
[7]Lafayette Fish, journal, January 11, 1849, HEH; Taylor to his wife, December 30, 1849, Letters, MASS; Goss to his wife, June 29, 1851, Letters, BAN.

and wooden shacks where "millions of dollars worth of goods of every description from Canton silks & toys to Yankee 'nick-nacks' lie stacked up in the streets or strewn about the vacant lots, for want of buildings to store them in."[8] Lafayette Fish commented in early 1849, "The destruction and loss of property is astonishing . . . thousands upon thousands of dollars worth of every kind rotting in the streets. This arises partly from the unsaleableness of some kinds, and the difficulty of getting storage when the rainy season first commenced."[9] This profligacy of resources testified to the city's central position in outfitting and trading, in which the arrival of a few shiploads of goods would drive down the price of woolen shirts or pants and make stocks of these goods worth only a fraction of their original value.

⑨ This treatment of trade goods as expendable extended to the treatment of the landscape in the mining camps of the Sierra. California's mining areas were rapidly transformed into a vast public dump. Transient miners filled the placers with unused, unneeded, or depleted goods. Men bought clothes, wore them until they literally disintegrated, and then threw them away and bought others. The devastated landscape of the California Sierra was soon littered with the debris of tens of thousands of miners who considered time more important than possessions and surplus clothing or food of insufficient value to save. This expenditure of raw materials seemed justified by the high rewards awaiting them and by the temporary nature of their stay.

⑩ How did the new arrivals from New England and upstate New York and Pennsylvania, from the Middle West and the South, react to the presence of these different values, so strange and contrary to their beliefs, and yet seemingly accepted by all? Some simply could not resolve the strife between the conflicting standards of value. Immediately on arriving, they looked around, did not like what they saw, and took the next boat back. (Most of the return travel was by sea.) Those who stayed were a self-selected group who were willing to adapt to the new moral climate they found. They wished to pursue wealth in California and were willing to make the concessions of principle necessary in order to succeed. To succeed in this world, they realized, they must be prepared to deal with it on terms and under conditions already set by others.

⑪ They did not have to accept the gambling of San Francisco, the drinking of the camps, or loose spending habits so visible around them, but they did have to adjust to the extent of putting moral differences behind them in the interest of profiting from economic opportunity. To this end, they bought what was necessary to mine at the inflated prices demanded for these goods. Most forty-niners also accepted the new habits associated with Sun-

10

---

[8]John C. Collbreath to his parents, June 30, 1849, Letters, BAN; Taylor to his wife, August 22, 1849, Letters, MASS. Alexander Spear, journal, April 9, 1850, HEH, is an observation by a man of limited education.

[9]Lafayette Fish, journal, January 11, 1849, HEH.

day, a day into which was crowded the miners' errands, leisure, business, and recreation. The degree of adaptation varied, of course, from individual to individual and group to group. It was simply easier to do business on Sunday, and in a world of intense work and competition, to make things easier was an important consideration. Isaac Owen, a missionary, observed that a man who considered himself "a good Methodist" routinely sold goods on Sunday, to Owen's great distress and presumably to the other man's profit. The longer someone stayed in California and worked in the placers, probably the more complete was the change. Indeed, one of the striking qualities associated with the gold rush was the degree to which each arriving annual wave of forty-niners adapted to this new world.[10]

The presence of gold and its widespread availability forced the forty-niners to modify their views about a wide range of subjects. Among the first they had to confront was the issue of new patterns of earning and spending, investment and return. The newly arrived Argonauts soon discovered that the prices of goods and services were high beyond anything imaginable for people coming from the East, such as a dinner at a San Francisco hotel for two gentlemen, two ladies, and four children for which the bill was ninety dollars.[11]

The forty-niners also found that before washing the first pan of dirt in the streams of the Sierra, they had to invest capital in tools for mining and equipment and supplies for daily subsistence and shelter. Those who arrived in California with the right equipment (as opposed to one of the useless goldometers and gold-digging machines advertised in the East) had to land it and move it a hundred miles overland. Those who bought the proper tools and supplies in California itself — shovel, pan, pick, tent, blankets, cradle — also had to purchase food and transport everything to the placers. Procuring supplies for the mines — salt pork, flour, sugar, tea, and coffee — might involve the outlay of one hundred dollars per miner, plus transportation costs of another one hundred. It was appropriate to the expense involved that when Argonauts later described their financial condition to interested parties back home, they listed foodstuffs as among their assets. Allan Varner wrote to his brother from the diggings in late 1849, "I have got one thousand dollars in gold dust and three hundred pounds of provisions which are worth five hundred dollars here."[12]

For the forty-niners, the California gold rush also raised the larger question of what something was worth. This issue first emerged in the decision of what to take to California, in most stark terms for those who went overland and who found what they could take severely limited. Money had no value on the overland trail to California, for there was nothing to buy. James Wilkins noted the question of value after only four weeks on the trail when

[10]Isaac Owen, journal, November 16, 1850, HEH.
[11]Delaware *Wilmington Weekly Commercial,* August 10, 1849, Bieber Coll., HEH.
[12]Allen to Elias Varner, December 16, 1849, Letters, HEH.

he wrote, "Money does not here represent the value of property. If one man has a thing that another wants he will give twenty times its value in something he does not want. There is a great deal of trading done in this way at this point."[13] The issue of value soon became more concentrated on a few items as the journey stretched on toward the West. Livestock, food, and water were necessary and irreplaceable items. All else was expendable.

In the mines, the necessary tools for work were the items of greatest value. A grand piano was useless in the diggings, whereas a half-dozen shovels were immensely valuable. The list of items valued for providing comfort and well-being was precise and short: a sack of flour, tools, newspapers from home, and especially mail. These took precedence and commanded the highest possible price, or were literally beyond price. As prospective miners moved farther into the diggings, money was worth less and vital goods and services more. The forty-niners newly arrived in the gold camps were astonished that bearded men would emerge from tents and offer them fifty dollars, say three ounces of gold, for the pair of boots they were wearing, for which they had paid three dollars in St. Louis. What they would come to realize quickly is that in the isolation of the gold camps, items necessary to wear, to eat, and to work with were much more valuable than gold dust.

Another major adjustment to the conceptions of value that the forty-niners brought with them was in the range of work that men were willing to perform. Thousands mined, but others flocked into the mining camps and the towns and took the other available jobs. Farmers from Illinois did day labor on the streets and in construction; lawyers from Philadelphia unloaded ships and transported goods around the city; doctors from St. Louis waited table in restaurants and dealt cards in gambling houses. California society had a dramatic openness about it. It was an unformed world in which men took new work identities, just as they might well take new personal identities. Richard Cowley of New York City noted that "a man can Work at anything here and need not be ashamed." William Daingerfield knew a Philadelphia lawyer who worked in a circus and lawyers and editors with jobs as auctioneers. Daingerfield himself had mined, auctioneered, clerked, and practiced law since his arrival in California, and he concluded that "all classes engage in anything that may present itself."[14]

What the forty-niners would not do was work as a servant class. In a world outwardly characterized by independence, by movement from place to place and from occupation to occupation, even the most marginal of laborers valued a sense of his own work. One forty-niner noted on his arrival in San Francisco, "One hates to ask even a servant to do any service much less an equal as it is so reluctantly performed." He concluded,

[13]James Wilkins, journal, June 26, 1849, HEH.
[14]Richard Cowley, journal, October 8, 1849, HEH; Daingerfield, letter of November 14, 1850, Letters, BAN.

"It seems as if the usual habits & actions of men were subverted."[15] These attitudes represented one of the many differences found in the land of gold.

These adaptations to varying standards of value began on the dock and extended to the most distant camps. Coming to California, and coming to terms with the emerging values and allegiances it offered, now placed the forty-niners in a new and different world, a world with new values that demanded that they form new bonds and allegiances with those around them, even as they struggled in the name of their duties to the world they had left behind.

Understanding the Text

1. What changes in values did the forty-niners experience when they arrived in San Francisco? *Pg 20*

2. What was the gold miners' attitude toward natural resources? *Pg 18*

3. Explain in your own words how the forty-niners' attitudes toward monetary values adjusted during the gold rush.

4. In what ways was San Francisco considered a "strange" (para. 3) and "different" (para. 1) sort of American city?

Exploring and Debating the Issues

1. Compare the forty-niners' expectations for their future with those of Mexican immigrants to California in the late twentieth century. How does each group understand the California dream? Can you account for any differences in their views? To develop your ideas, read or reread Richard Rodriguez's "Proofs" (p. 34), Ramón "Tianguis" Pérez's "Ripon" (p. 108), or William Langewiesche's "Invisible Men" (p. 99).

2. Rohrbough describes the image of gold rush–era San Francisco as a city where traditional moral values were suspended. Write an essay in which you describe and analyze today's image of San Francisco. To what extent has the gold rush image remained the same or changed?

3. Write an essay discussing the ways in which the forty-niners' treatment of the environment set the stage for future environmental exploitation and degradation. Consult Chapter 4, "Developing the Dream: Issues in California Land Use," to develop your ideas.

4. Compare the forty-niners' assumptions about money and prosperity with those now prevailing in Silicon Valley. See Michael J. Mandel's "Silicon Valley: Taking Its Place in the Pantheon" (p. 285) and John Cassidy's "The Comeback" (p. 274) for discussions of the current spirit in California's high-tech industries.

[15]William to Charlotte Prince, December 15, 1849, Letters, BAN.

DENISE S. SPOONER

A New Perspective on the Dream

When we think of today's newcomers to the Golden State, we usually imagine immigrants from Latin America, Asia, Persia, and even post-Soviet Russia. But as **Denise S. Spooner** shows in this essay, originally published in *California History,* an enormous number of migrants from the Midwest flocked to California in the years following World War II seeking not only opportunity and glamour but also freedom from the rigid social conventions of the Midwestern towns and villages they were fleeing. Spooner is coeditor of *H-California* and teaches California and U.S. history at California State University, Northridge.

C alifornia. For over a century it has been a name that has evoked vivid images in the minds of Americans. Sunshine, oranges, beaches, Hollywood — the pursuit of a life defined by these images has long been thought to have been the primary motivation for the migration of millions of Americans to southern California from the late 1880s through the twentieth century. Indeed, as a number of California historians have noted, in the late nineteenth and early twentieth centuries a series of promotional campaigns sponsored by corporations and institutions with an economic stake in the region's growth used many of these symbols as a means of generating migration to southern California.[1]

The Midwest was specially targeted by turn-of-the-century promoters, a marketing scheme that provided returns certainly beyond the grandest projections of the sponsors. Recorded as the largest stream by early 1900, the flow of migrants from the Midwest to California continued as such until it was interrupted by the Great Depression and World War II. In the postwar decades it resumed. The 1960 census recorded the West North Central and East North Central census divisions, which make up the Midwest, as the numbers one and three contributors to California's population.[2]

---

[1]Carey McWilliams was first to write on this subject in *Southern California Country: An Island on the Land* (New York: Duell, Sloan & Pierce, 1946; reprint Santa Barbara, Calif.: Peregrine Smith, Inc., 1979), chaps. 6 and 7. See also John Bauer, *Health Seekers of Southern California* (San Marino, Calif.: Huntington Library Publications, 1959), chaps. 1 and 2; John L. Phillips, "Crating Up the California Dream," *American Heritage* (April 1977): 88–93; Alfred Runte, "Promoting the Golden West: Advertising and the Railroad," *California History* 70 (Spring 1991): 62–75; Kevin Starr, *Inventing the Dream: California through the Progressive Era* (New York: Oxford University Press, 1985); Richard S. Street, "Marketing California Crops at the Turn of the Century," *Southern California Quarterly* 61 (1979): 239–53; T. H. Watkins, "The Social History of a Singular Fruit," *American Heritage* (April 1977): 94–95; Oscar O. Winther, "The Use of Climate as a Means of Promoting Migration to Southern California," *Mississippi Valley Historical Review* 33 (1946): 411–24; Tom Zimmerman, "Paradise Promoted: Boosterism and the Los Angeles Chamber of Commerce," *California History* 64 (Winter 1985): 22–23.

[2]Margaret S. Gordon, *Employment Expansion and Population Growth: The California Experience, 1900–1950* (Berkeley: University of California Press, 1954), table A-2, p. 162; U.S.

Considering that change is the one constant in life, it would be quite peculiar to find that the dream that inspired post–World War II Midwestern migrants was the same as that that motivated those who came earlier in the century. As Robert Fogelson pointed out almost thirty years ago, southern California was sold to late-nineteenth- and early-twentieth-century Midwesterners, and initially developed, as a place like the Midwest, but better. The citrus groves, sunshine, and ocean were to serve as a more congenial backdrop for the same type of community as the one they had left, one Fogelson described as "embodied in single-family houses, located on large lots, surrounded by landscaped lawns, and isolated from business activities."[3] Today when you visit many of the cities in the region that developed between approximately 1870 and 1920, especially in Orange County and the San Gabriel Valley of Los Angeles County, you find many townscapes that appear to be realizations of the Midwesterners' desire for a new setting for their former communities.[4]

In the post–World War II years, however, some migrants had a different vision of what life in southern California promised. While many still imagined it as a place of exceptional physical beauty, some also envisioned it as an opportunity to escape from a type of community common throughout the Midwest, one that judged people on the basis of the degree to which they adhered to various locally determined norms. For these people, southern California in the postwar years represented a place where their lives could be different, where they would be free to express their individuality as openly or privately as they wished.[5] Examining the images migrants held prior to leaving the Midwest, and investigating the conditions that produced them, deepens our understanding of the culture of post–World War II southern California.

From the start of the boosters' program in the late nineteenth century through much of this one, a special relationship grew between southern California and one Midwestern state in particular, Iowa. The creators of the marketing plan recognized early that the profitability of Iowa's agriculture made for a relatively well-off, retirement-age population ready to remove themselves to a place with a far more temperate climate. Such was partly

5

Bureau of the Census, *U.S. Census of Population: 1960, Subject Reports, State of Birth*, Final Report PC (2) 2-A (Washington, D.C.: U.S. Government Printing Office, 1963), table 18.

[3]Robert Fogelson, *The Fragmented Metropolis: Los Angeles, 1850–1930* (Cambridge, Mass.: Harvard University Press, 1967), 144–45.

[4]Here I am thinking of cities such as Orange and Tustin in Orange County and Claremont and Monrovia in the San Gabriel Valley.

[5]These conclusions are based on responses to questionnaires I sent to, and interviews I conducted with, migrants whose names, addresses, and places of birth I took from records maintained by the registrars of voters for Los Angeles and Orange counties. The sample I compiled consisted of 982 respondents, 407 from Los Angeles County and 574 from Orange County. Of the 982 questionnaires sent out, 277, or approximately 28 percent were returned. Of those 277, I netted 106 who had migrated within the time frame of my study, 1946–1964.

the motivation behind the California Fruit Growers' special promotional trains to Iowa between 1907 and 1911, which used some of the symbols noted above, especially those related to citrus and sunshine, to encourage people to settle in southern California. The seeds of that effort took root, grew beautifully, and continued to bear fruit throughout much of the next fifty years. In every census taken between 1910 and 1930, Iowa ranked among the top ten state contributors to California's population, along with far more populous states such as New York, Illinois, and Pennsylvania. Mirroring the trend of Midwestern migration in general, the flow of migrants from Iowa to southern California slowed considerably during the Depression and war years, and then resumed its pre-Depression course during the great population boom of the post–World War II decades. For example, in 1960, when the West North Central census division was recorded as the number one contributor to California's population at the division level, among the states in that division, only Iowa and Missouri were also on the list of the top ten states contributing to California's population.[6] It is no wonder that one of the myths popular in southern California for years was that the region was largely made up of former Iowans. That exaggeration aside, the census figures suggest that by using Iowans as a case study group we might extend our understanding of the California Dream as it was envisioned by Midwestern migrants in the post–World War II years.

The premigration images of California held by the migrants I surveyed and interviewed are depicted in Diagram 1.[7] Images I have labeled "traditional" were reported by 81 percent of my subjects. Those symbols, many of which were devised by the early promoters, portrayed the region as a physically wondrous place. Visions of sunshine, palm trees, citrus, mountains, and ocean contrasted sharply with many migrants' experience of Iowa as a climate of extremes, in a landscape of sameness: sweltering summers and long, cold, gray winters, across gently, but relentless, rolling hills. Nancy Rutherford was one who envisioned southern California as a place fantastically different from Iowa. As a youngster, bed-ridden with rheumatic fever, she began writing to an uncle in southern California who was recovering from a heart attack:

> He would talk about those huge palm trees and I had this wonderful vision. It wasn't really Beverly Hills, but a beautiful place with palm trees and swimming pools and blue sky all year 'round. When I was younger I used to do a lot of day dreaming in the midst of the snowstorms in January and

---

[6]McWilliams, *Southern California Country*, 129, 161, 163–64; Gordon, *Employment Expansion and Population Growth*, table A-3, 163; U.S. Bureau of the Census, *U.S. Census of Population: 1960, State of Birth*, table 18.

[7]Together the percentages equal more than 100 percent because most people reported more than one image that they associated with southern California. The percentages depicted in the diagram are as follows: weather = 38 percent; palm trees = 5 percent; Hollywood = 31 percent; citrus = 23 percent; ocean = 19 percent; mountains/desert = 12 percent.

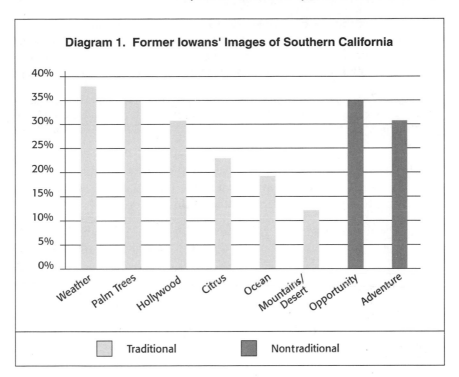

Diagram 1. Former Iowans' Images of Southern California

Legend: ☐ Traditional   ■ Nontraditional

February, and I would hear from my uncle. Just think! He was getting to look out at the sun and trees and green grass and all that.[8]

To this list of images that depicted southern California as a place with a balmy climate and a more varied landscape, some postwar migrants added images of the entertainment industry, which I have labeled "Hollywood."[9] Of course, the movies played a central role in creating this image for many, including Don Fromknecht:

> We used to go down to the Capitol Theater in Sioux City, Iowa, and sit there and watch Bing Crosby movies, and I said, "Man, is that what it's like out there? I got to get out there!" See how naive we were. Why, hey. They could paint those palm trees in the back of those movie sets as fast as you could leave.[10]

[8]Nancy Rutherford, interview with the author, 21 September 1988, Carlsbad, California, tape recording and transcript, California State University, Fullerton: Oral History Collection, 21–22 (hereinafter OHC).

[9]Carey McWilliams mentions the addition of entertainment to the images of the California Dream in *Southern California Country*, 135–36. Kevin Starr gives the topic a thorough examination in the final two chapters of *Inventing the Dream: California through the Progressive Era*.

[10]Don Fromknecht, interview with the author, 8 October 1988, Fullerton, California, tape recording and transcipt, OHC, 11–12.

With the establishment of the television and pop music industries in southern California in the postwar decades, younger migrants such as Priscilla Eckert, who was in her early twenties when she left Iowa, were influenced by the impressions of the region they received through those media:

> That's when the Beach Boys were a large part of the teenage life, as far as music went; and [they] had a connotation of the beach and the bikinied girls and the tans, the blonds, the water.... I did figure that California looked like that.[11]

And then there were migrants like William Powell, who imagined southern California as the entertainment capital of the world, as well as the balmy paradise captured in images the industry produced:

> [Southern California was] all glamorous: the palm trees and the movie stars and everything. Back in those days [the 1950s], it was the place to go.[12]

In addition to these traditional images, 58 percent of the migrants had a somewhat different view of southern California, one I have labeled "nontraditional" on the diagram. They still imagined it as a place, but rather than emphasizing the environmental characteristics that distinguished it from the places where they had grown up, their vision of southern California was as a place of adventure and opportunity, a place where their lives could be different.[13]

Associating California with adventure and opportunity was not a new phenomenon. The Spanish settlers of the eighteenth century, as well as the American infiltrators and gold rushers of the mid-nineteenth century, identified California with risk, danger, excitement, and the chance of acquiring a fortune. This was exactly what some of the migrants had in mind when they imagined southern California as a land of adventure and opportunity. For example, when Dee Ann Shaw dreamed of southern California, she thought of the many exciting things there would be to do for fun, and all the different sorts of businesses there would be in which a person could find a job.[14] Don Cameron equated southern California with opportunity, which he described strictly in terms of the chance to make more money. In Iowa, where he was born and raised, he worked as a salesman for a wholesale produce company, but his goal was to get into the origination end of that business.

[11]Priscilla Eckert, interview with the author, 29 October 1988, Irvine, California, tape recording and transcript, OHC, 9–10.

[12]William Powell, interview with the author, 10 October 1988, Anaheim, California, tape recording and transcript, OHC, 7.

[13]Thirty-five percent identified California with opportunity; 31 percent associated it with adventure.

[14]Dee Ann Shaw, interview with the author, 10 December 1988, Laguna Beach, California, tape recording and transcript, OHC, 10.

As garden to so much of the United States, California was the best place to live in order to achieve that goal, he decided.[15]

But there were other migrants who give a unique twist to the southern California-as-adventure-and-opportunity image. Seventy-three percent of those who identified the region in this way used *adventure* and *opportunity* as code words for "escape from community." In the towns and rural neighborhoods of Iowa in which they lived, community was created through cooperation and judgment. In essence, both were used to measure who was a part of the group and who was not. Some migrants found this aspect of community repressive. Martha Celmer was one. Throughout her life she held a variety of images of southern California, but the one that motivated her migration was envisioning southern California as a chance for a different, freer life:

> As a young teenager girl, it was just all Hollywood at its best; but I never got out here when I was a young girl. So I never got to see if that was really true. By the time I finally got out here, I was already maybe twenty-six, twenty-five. I had matured a little. My perception of things wasn't quite the same as it had been as a teenager. I came out with my sister-in-law and brother-in-law the first time and I guess while I was here, I developed an idea that I could make it out here and I went from there. I don't want to say that it was land of milk and honey, because I wasn't that far off in my perception of things past at that point, but I also realized that it was an opportunity to live a different kind of lifestyle, and maybe one that I thought might be a little better for me than living in the Midwest.[16]

The lifestyle Martha Celmer and some of the other migrants wanted was one where they were free to be whomever and whatever they wanted to be, without limitations on individuality imposed by community in the cities, towns, and rural neighborhoods they lived in through cooperation and judgment.

As Kenneth Jackson has written, "the term *community* implies cooperation," and in much of the Midwest from the time of settlement through the first half of the twentieth century, cooperation between neighbors in work and social life was essential to success, if not survival.[17] For instance, Collins Roe's father got his start as an independent farmer through the money he made one season when he and a neighbor worked together to try to harvest more corn than anyone else in Iowa.[18] Moreover, the financial health of businesses in many Iowa communities was directly tied to the profitability of farming.

[15]Don Cameron, interview with the author, 27 September 1988, Anaheim, California, tape recording and transcript, OHC, 26.

[16]Martha Ann Celmer, interview with the author, 14 November 1988, Rancho Palos Verdes, California, tape recording and transcript, OHC, 13–14.

[17]Kenneth T. Jackson, *Crabgrass Frontier: The Suburbanization of the United States* (New York: Oxford University Press, 1985), 272.

[18]Collins Roe, interview with the author, 22 September 1988, Garden Grove, California, tape recording and transcript, OHC, 4.

In addition, the isolation of farm families and lack of entertainment opportunities in small towns made neighbors dependent on one another for their social life. Typically, Saturday nights brought farm families to town. During those visits farmers purchased supplied and talked prices and politics with other men while women gathered in automobiles to visit with one another.[19] Other factors that brought country and town people together were those that maintained shared institutions, such as churches, schools, the local chapters of the Farm Bureau, various fraternal organizations, including the Masons and Odd-fellows, and the community memory of important events, like the Civil War and World War I.[20]

For those who grew up and lived in larger cities and towns, the presence of movie houses, amusement parks, and such made neighbors somewhat less reliant on one another for a social life. Still, people from cities recalled their neighborhoods as warm, open, nurturing places. For example, Lynn Achak described her Davenport neighborhood as a place without fences, where neighbors roasted hot dogs and marshmallows together in the autumn over bonfires built from fallen leaves they had all raked out to the curb. Robert Allison explained the widespread participation in community by saying that "back in Des Moines, or in small towns in Iowa, you knew everybody in town. It took everybody in town to make it a town."[21]

Together, the interaction between people in spheres of work and leisure created cohesiveness and interdependence. But there was that other activity that helped create community: judgment. The Midwestern tendency to judge people, a theme prevalent in the writings of Hamlin Garland, Sherwood Anderson, and Sinclair Lewis, and inferred in Grant Wood's famous painting, *American Gothic*, was reflective of many aspects of Midwestern culture, including the predominance of small towns throughout the region and its heritage from the mid-nineteenth century, when nativism was a force throughout the nation. Viewing anyone or anything different as a threat to the prevailing order was characteristic of both. Thus, judging people across a wide spectrum of characteristics and according to a restrictive moral code was common in Iowa communities. In this way, judging emphasized likeness as a basis for community. It isolated those who did not conform to

[19]Kenneth Bauermeister, interview with the author, 6 October 1988, Newport Beach, California, tape recording and transcript, OHC, 3–5; Robert Littschwager, interview with the author, 23 September 1988, Newport Beach, California, tape recording and transcript, OHC, 5; Collins Roe, interview with the author, 22 September 1988, Garden Grove, California OHC, 5–6.

[20]All of the interviewees, except two, recalled that they and/or their family participated in these sorts of groups. Church was the most often mentioned, followed by the Farm Bureau or coop; social groups such as square dance, card club, or lodge; and a variety of other groups. Memorial Day was remembered by Margaret Pille as a special celebration that brought town and rural folks together. Lynn Achak and Margaret Pille, interview with the author, 22 October 1988, El Toro, California, tape recording and transcript, OHC, 23–24.

[21]Lynn Achak and Margaret Pille, interview with the author, 22 October 1988, El Toro, California, OHC, 7–9; Robert Allison, interview with the author, 17 October 1988, Redondo Beach, California, tape recording and transcript, OHC, 30.

various criteria, including the community norms of class, ethnicity, and religion.

Class divisions within communities were drawn along two nonexclusive lines: farm versus town, and the more usual manner, according to social group based largely on income. According to Irene Molloy, farm kids such as herself were one step down from "the kids on the other side of the track," at least in the eyes of people who lived in town.[22] Growing up in the 1940s and 1950s in Burlington, Iowa, Priscilla Eckert, the daughter of an electrical engineer and a school teacher, recalled her awareness of the existence and importance of class:

> I think I was [aware of it] in high school. I wasn't before that, but I think I was in high school because, when I started dating, there were boys who couldn't come to the golf club for things that were going on there. I couldn't understand that, because everyone went there, I thought. But, in fact, everyone didn't go there.[23]

Ethnicity was also a characteristic by which individuals were judged within and between communities. Dee Ann Shaw explained that, in the area of Iowa where she grew up, communities were organized based on where in Scandinavia a family had originated. Norwegians and Swedes populated her hometown, Calendar, while fifteen miles away, was a town that was primarily Danish. Tension between the towns was so intense that when the Lutheran church burned down in the Danish community, some people in Callendar balked at the idea of Danes coming to Callendar to go to their Lutheran church.[24]

People were also judged by their religious identification. Discrimination against those not belonging to the dominant Protestant churches was common, especially in the form of anti-Catholicism. Not only did religious discrimination divide even people with the same national heritage, it also denied participation in social life to those not belonging to the dominant religion, and it helped determine who shared work with whom.[25]

[22]Irene Molloy, interview with the author, 12 September 1988, Los Angeles, California, tape recording and transcript, OHC, 9–10.

[23]Priscilla Eckert, interview with the author, 29 September 1988, Irvine, California, OHC, 42.

[24]Dee Ann Shaw, interview with the author, 10 December 1988, Laguna Beach, California, OHC, 27–28. Deborah Fink reported the existence of geographically consolidated, or isolated, depending on how you choose to look at it, ethnic groups in Iowa as late as the 1980s in her study *Open Country, Iowa: Rural Women, Tradition, and Change* (Albany: State University of New York Press, 1986), 91. Carl Hamilton also noted its presence in his reminiscences of farm life in Iowa, 1914–1940, in *No Time At All* (Ames: Iowa State University Press, 1974), 28–29.

[25]Kenneth Bauermeister, interview with the author, 6 October 1988, Newport Beach, California, OHC, 23; Joseph Conway, interview with the author, 5 December 1988, Tustin California, tape recording and transcript, OHC, 20–21; Doris Headrick, interview with the author, 20 October 1988, La Habra, California, tape recording and transcript, OHC, 32; Irene Molloy, interview with the author, 12 September 1988, Los Angeles, California, OHC, 26; Helen Perez, interview with the author, 11 October 1988, Burbank, California, tape recording and transcript, OHC, 10; Dee Ann Shaw, interview with the author, 10 December 1988, Laguna Beach, California, OHC, 27–28.

In addition to classification according to class and culture, a second type of judging also was prevalent: the judging of conduct. The tendency to judge conduct, rather than adherence to specific moral rules, has seemed to sociologist Robin Williams to be the basis of Americans' moral orientation.[26] This sort of moral orientation did not go unnoticed by the former Iowans I studied. Eighty-four percent reported it as an aspect of life in Iowa that they remembered most vividly. However, contrary to Williams's belief, it is evident throughout my conversations with the Iowa migrants that there was a moral code against which conduct was appraised. The degree to which a person could be judged a hard worker, and adherence to traditional morals such as honesty, were central elements of that code.

That many Iowans were not far removed from a farming past where survival, not to mention prosperity, depended on everyone doing their part probably accounts for much of the emphasis on being a good, hard worker. Of those I studied, 62 percent were either the children or grandchildren of farmers. But respect for hard work was a value held by city people too. In talking about which Iowa qualities he tried to impart to his children, Don Fromknecht, who was born and raised in Sioux City and Des Moines, noted that one of the values he took from his upbringing was the idea that people get paid what their labor warrants. "I'm still carrying that [motto] the old man [his father] taught us. I still believe that value earned is value received."[27]

Adherence to traditional morals was another standard against which   20
conduct was judged in Iowa. Honesty was cited most frequently as an eminent value. Kenneth Bauermeister explained its importance:

> [There was a] tremendous belief that all people had that they should be as fair and honest with their neighbors as they possibly could because everybody knew everybody. If you started telling a little white lie or whatever it was, it was soon to catch up with you, no matter what it was. It wasn't like the big city where you could hide in an atmosphere of anonymity.[28]

In essence, honesty and being a hard worker were essential components of a good reputation in Iowa's small towns. In larger cities, the size of the population made it difficult to make those sorts of assessments about everyone. Instead, other methods were used. For example, Don Fromknecht reported that, in the section of Des Moines where he lived, those who tried to win respect by displaying all that their money could buy were considered not quite trustworthy.[29]

[26]Robin M. Williams, *American Society: A Sociological Interpretation* (New York: Knopf, 1961), 424, quoted by Scott G. McNall and Sally Allen McNall in *Plains Families: Exploring Sociology through Social History* (New York: St. Martin's Press, 1983), 71–72.

[27]Don Fromknecht, interview with the author, 8 October 1988, Fullerton, California, OHC, 63–65.

[28]Kenneth Bauermeister, interview with the author, 6 October 1988, Newport Beach, California, OHC, 13.

[29]Don Fromknecht, interview with the author, 8 October 1988, Fullerton, California, OHC, 65.

The migrants had mixed feelings about the dynamic of community that I have just described. Generally, all had fond memories of sharing work and social life, but their feelings about judgment varied. Fifty-four percent had decidedly negative feelings on the subject, while the rest were neutral. Common throughout the statements of those in the first group was the sense that judging limited self-expression. It determined the sort of work individuals could pursue, the friendships and marriage bonds that were formed, and even what people did for fun and relaxation. As a result, community proved too restrictive for many.

The consequences for these individuals and for California were significant. Sixty-seven percent of those who were dissatisfied with the judging that went on in Iowa communities held images of southern California as a place of adventure and opportunity. Not coincidentally, the reasons many of them gave for moving to southern California also reflect the adventure and opportunity theme. . . . Of those who stated that they moved in search of greater economic opportunity and/or the desire for more autonomy, anonymity, and adventure than existed in Iowa, 50 percent held images of southern California as a place where life could be different. In short, many of these were the people who defined the California Dream, in part, as an escape from community.

Several questions remain. First, how did the migrants come to associate southern California with escape from community? Second, after they moved to the region, did they like it? Were they satisfied with the level and kind of community that existed in southern California? The first question is difficult to answer definitively because I did not collect any information on how migrants came by their vision of the dream. Still, it is possible to speculate. Many of the migrants who held images of southern California as an escape from community were people looking for something different from what they had in Iowa. And the traditional images portrayed a place not just different, but wonderfully so. The sun, palm trees, citrus, and ocean all depicted a climate where there was greater freedom of movement and dress than was found in Iowa. In addition, the never-ending stories of music, film, and television personalities rising from obscurity to stardom, plus the likewise incessant tales of celebrities' marital peccadillos might have communicated the message that in southern California there was more social freedom as well. To people yearning for greater freedom of self-expression, these traditional images might have conveyed the idea that southern California was just the place for them.

Another way people might have come to associate southern California with escape from the limitations of community is suggested in comments made by Lois Smith. When she was a child in Iowa, her family was desperately poor. During those years, she had an uncle who had moved to California and who occasionally brought his family back to Iowa to visit. It seemed to Smith that her uncle and his family had far more money than her family *because* they had moved to California. She believed that her uncle, who had grown up in the same circumstances in Iowa as her mother, where

community imposed restrictions on upward mobility, had been able to escape those conditions in California.[30] So perhaps some migrants came to
imagine southern California as an escape from the limitations imposed by
community, based on contact with friends and relatives who seemed to
have made that escape themselves. Indeed, 65 percent of the migrants had
networks of family and friends who had made the trek to California before
them.

The migration of Americans who defined the California Dream in part   25
as an escape from community must have had some influence on the nature
of that institution in southern California in the post–World War II era. At
this time, it is not possible to say when the weak state of community evident
today in many suburban neighborhoods of southern California became
prevalent. The history of community in southern California has yet to be
written. But there is little doubt that the migration of people whose experiences caused them to flee close-knit communities must have had some role
in the development of the kind of community that exists today. When asked
if they missed the closeness of community they had experienced in Iowa,
not surprisingly, some of those who had envisioned southern California as
an escape from community replied that they did not. What is surprising,
however, is that others, who did not leave Iowa because they were dissatisfied with community life there, also said that they did not long for a more
closely knit community life once they settled in the region. For example,
Richard Mongar says:

> Out here in California people have a lot of things going on in their own
> [lives.] They don't really pay too much attention to other people. I kind of
> like that though. I like neighbors, but I don't like to have them come in and
> have a drink in the afternoon, or coffee in the morning. I like to live an inde-
> pendent [life].[31]

Perhaps Mongar's preference for the greater autonomy that life in southern
California provided was a result of his adaption to the culture of the region.
Or perhaps the cause was his feelings about the closeness of community in
Iowa, which he did not reveal. . . .

Throughout the immediate post–World War II decades, the California
Dream continued to lure Midwesterners to the Golden State. Portraits of a
land of movie stars, palm trees, the ocean, oranges, and a place for a sun-
kissed life continued to be central images of the dream. But this examination of the lives of a group of postwar migrants from one state suggests that
there was another set of images attached to southern California; that, in
fact, the dream was more complex than most of us realize. Images of southern California as an escape from community in the Midwest, where judg-

[30]Lois Smith, interview with the author, 10 September 1988, Lakewood, California,
tape recording and transcript, OHC, 14–16.

[31]Richard Mongar, interview with the author, 19 October 1988, Seal Beach, California,
tape recording and transcript, OHC. Overall, 31 percent said they did not miss the closeness of the neighborhoods they had left in Iowa.

ments made about people on the basis of class, ethnicity, religion, and adherence to traditional morals seemed to limit individuality, also were a part of the dream, for some.

By understanding these images, and the conditions that created them, we achieve two things. First, we have identified one piece of the puzzle of community in postwar suburban southern California. Through the attitudes and lives of people such as those I studied, we find that the weak sense of community that prevails in many suburban areas of the region is not a fluke. It is the result of probably a number of factors, including the one I have explored here, the new residents' negative experiences of more intimate community elsewhere. And second, for people interested in studying California, these images lend a new perspective to the California Dream, a feature unique to the state, as it was envisioned by some in the postwar decades.

Understanding the Text

1. What were the traditional images and industries that attracted Midwesterners to California, according to Spooner?

2. In addition to the traditional images of California, Spooner claims, the state offered a special, unusual attraction. What was it, and why did it appeal particularly to Midwesterners?

3. Why, in Spooner's view, did California promotional campaigns target Iowans?

4. What are the positive and negative connotations that Spooner believes the Midwestern migrants attached to the word *community*? How did their attitudes toward community influence their interest in California?

5. According to Spooner, in what ways did Midwesterners judge each other?

Exploring and Debating the Issues

1. Spooner claims that, because some migrants to California sought to "escape from community" (para. 23), there is a "weak state of community evident today in many suburban neighborhoods of southern California" (para. 25). Write an essay in which you agree, challenge, or modify this claim, being sure to focus your discussion on specific neighborhoods or towns.

2. Spooner writes that southern California was publicized to Midwesterners "as a place like the Midwest, but better" (para. 3). Write an essay in which you test her assertion on a city that she mentions, such as Orange, Tustin, or Claremont. If you are unfamiliar with those locations, you alternately could analyze the ways in which the Sacramento community that Joan Didion describes in "Notes from a Native Daughter" (p. 51) resembles a Midwestern community.

3. Interview several friends or relatives who migrated to California from another region in the United States during the post–World War II decades. What were their reasons for moving to this state, and what were their

expectations? Did their experiences live up to their expectations? Use your findings to write your own analysis of the images and values that attracted people to California.

4. In class, debate whether the ability to reinvent oneself, which Spooner describes as a motivation for Midwesterners to migrate to this California, is a reality for today's newcomers to this state.

RICHARD RODRIGUEZ

Proofs

California, like America, is a land of immigrants, but getting here isn't always easy. As **Richard Rodriguez** (b. 1944) describes in this selection, for many Mexican immigrants "you trip, you fall" on the way to *el norte.* You try to avoid *la migra,* or U.S. Border Patrol officers, who seek to thwart your journey to San Diego, San Joaquin, Sacramento. And "you run." Born to an immigrant family in the Bay Area, Rodriguez is an editor for the Pacific News Service who has written for the *Los Angeles Times, Harper's, Saturday Review, Nuestro,* and the *New York Times,* among other publications. He is the author of *Hunger of Memory: The Education of Richard Rodriguez* (1982), an autobiography, and *Days of Obligation: An Argument with My Mexican Father* (1992).

Y ou stand around. You smoke. You spit. You are wearing your two shirts, two pants, two underpants. Jesús says if they chase you, throw that bag down. Your plastic bag is your mama, all you have left: the yellow cheese she wrapped has formed a translucent rind; the laminated scapular of the Sacred Heart nestles, flame in its cleft. Put it in your pocket. Inside. Put it in your underneath pants' pocket. The last hour of Mexico is twilight, the shuffling of feet. Jesús says they are able to see in the dark. They have X rays and helicopters and searchlights. Jesús says wait, just wait, till he says. Though most of the men have started to move. You feel the hand of Jesús clamp your shoulder, fingers cold as ice. *Venga, corre.* You run. All the rest happens without words. Your feet are tearing dry grass, your heart is lashed like a mare. You trip, you fall. You are now in the United States of America. You are a boy from a Mexican village. You have come into the country on your knees with your head down. You are a man.

Papa, what was it like?

I am his second son, his favorite child, his confidant. After we have polished the DeSoto, we sit in the car and talk. I am sixteen years old. I fiddle with the knobs of the radio. He is fifty.

He will never say. He was an orphan there. He had no mother, he remembered none. He lived in a village by the ocean. He wanted books and he had none.

You are lucky, boy.

In the nineteenth century, American contractors reached down into Mexico for cheap labor. Men were needed to build America: to lay track, to mine, to dredge, to harvest. It was a man's journey. And, as a year's contract was extended, as economic dependence was established, sons followed their fathers north. When American jobs turned scarce — during the Depression, as today — Mexicans were rounded up and thrown back over the border. But for generations it has been the rite of passage for the poor Mexican male.

I will send for you or I will come home rich.

In the fifties, Mexican men were contracted to work in America as *braceros,* farm workers. I saw them downtown in Sacramento. I saw men my age drunk in Plaza Park on Sundays, on their backs on the grass. I was a boy at sixteen, but I was an American. At sixteen, I wrote a gossip column, "The Watchful Eye," for my school paper.

Or they would come into town on Monday nights for the wrestling matches or on Tuesdays for boxing. They worked over in Yolo county. They were men without women. They were Mexicans without Mexico.

On Saturdays, they came into town to the Western Union office where   10
they sent money — money turned into humming wire and then turned back into money — all the way down into Mexico. They were husbands, fathers, sons. They kept themselves poor for Mexico.

Much that I would come to think, the best I would think about male Mexico, came as much from those chaste lonely men as from my own father who made false teeth and who — after thirty years in America — owned a yellow stucco house on the east side of town.

The male is responsible. The male is serious. A man remembers.

Fidel, the janitor at church, lived over the garage at the rectory. Fidel spoke Spanish and was Mexican. He had a wife down there, people said; some said he had grown children. But too many years had passed and he didn't go back. Fidel had to do for himself. Fidel had a clean piece of linoleum on the floor, he had an iron bed, he had a table and a chair. He had a coffee pot and a frying pan and a knife and a fork and spoon, I guess. And everything else Fidel sent back to Mexico. Sometimes, on summer nights, I would see his head through the bars of the little window over the garage at the rectory.

The migration of Mexico is not only international, south to north. The epic migration of Mexico, and throughout Latin America, is from the village to the city. And throughout Latin America, the city has ripened, swollen with the century. Lima. Caracas. Mexico City. So the journey to Los Angeles is much more than a journey from Spanish to English. It is the journey from *tu* — the familiar, the erotic, the intimate pronoun — to the repellent *usted* of strangers' eyes.

Most immigrants to America came from villages. The America that   15
Mexicans find today, at the decline of the century, is a closed-circuit city of ramps and dark towers, a city without God.

It is 1986 and I am a journalist. I am asking questions of a Mexican woman in her East L.A. house. She is watchful and pretty, in her thirties, she wears an apron. Her two boys — Roy and Danny — are playing next door. Her husband is a tailor. He is sewing in a bright bedroom at the back of the house. His feet work the humming treadle of an old Singer machine as he croons Mexican love songs by an open window.

For attribution, mama says she is grateful for America. This country has been so good to her family. They have been here ten years and look, already they have this nice house. Outside the door is Mexican Los Angeles; in the distance, the perpetual orbit of traffic. Here old women walk slowly under lace parasols. The Vietnam vet pushes his tinkling ice cream cart past little green lawns. Teenagers in this neighborhood have scorpions tattooed onto their biceps.

The city is evil. Turn. Turn.

At 16th and Mission in San Francisco, young Mexican Americans in dark suits preach to the passing city from Perfectbound Bibles. They pass leaflets for Victory Outreach — "the junkie church."

In Latin America, Catholicism remains the religion of the village. But in the city now, in Lima as in Los Angeles, more and more souls rap upon the skin of the tambourine for the promise of evangelical Protestantism: You can be cleansed of the city, you can become a new man, you can be born again.

The raven-haired preacher with a slash on his neck tells me his grandmother is from Jalisco, Mexico. His mother understood Spanish but she couldn't speak it. She couldn't do anything right. She was a junkie. She had him when she was seventeen. She disappeared.

"I lived out on the streets. Didn't go past seventh grade. Grass, crack, dust — I've had it all; messed up with gangs, rolled queers. I've stabbed people, man, I've stuck the blade all the way in and felt a heart flutter like a pigeon.

"I was a sinner, I was alone in the city. Until I found Jesus Christ. . . ."

The U.S. Border Patrol station at Chula Vista has a P.R. officer who handles journalists; he says he is glad to have us — "helps in Washington if the public can get a sense of the scope of the problem."

Right now he is occupied with a West German film crew. They were promised a helicopter. Where is the helicopter? Two journalists from a Tokyo daily — with five canvas bags of camera equipment between them — lean against the wall, arms folded. One of them brings up his wrist to look at his watch. A reporter from Chicago catches my sleeve, says, Did I hear about the other night? What? There was a carload of Yugoslavians caught coming over.

The Japanese reporter who is not looking at his watch is popping Cheezits into his mouth. The Border Patrol secretary has made some kind of mistake. She has me down as a reporter for *American Farmer*. Fat red steer in clover. Apologies. White-out. "I . . . agree to abide by any oral directions given to me during the operation by the officer in charge of the unit. . . ." Having signed the form, I am soon assigned a patrolman with whom I will spend the night.

We stop for coffee at a donut shop along the freeway. The patrolman tells me about growing up Tex-Mex in Dallas. After City College, he worked with an antipoverty agency. Then he was a probation officer. He got married, needed money, moved to California, and took this job with the *migra*.

Once into the dark, I cannot separate myself from the patrolman's intention. We ride through the dark in a Ram Charger, both intent upon finding people who do not want to be found.

We come upon a posse of Border Patrolmen preparing to ride into the canyon on horseback. I get out of the truck; ask the questions; pet the horses in the dark, prickly, moist, moving in my hand. The officers call me sir. It is as though I am being romanced at some sort of cowboy cotillion. "Here," says one, "have a look." He invites me so close to his chin I can smell cologne as I peer through his night-vision scope.

Mexico is on the phone — long distance. 30

A crow alights upon a humming wire, bobs up and down, needles the lice within his vest, surveys with clicking eyes the field, the cloud of mites, then dips into the milky air and flies away.

Juanito killed! My mother shrieks, drops the phone in the dark. She cries for my father. For light.

The earth quakes. The peso flies like chaff in the wind. The police chief purchases his mistress a mansion on the hill.

The doorbell rings. I split the blinds to see three nuns standing on our front porch.

Mama. Mama. 35

Monsignor Lyons has sent three Mexican nuns over to meet my parents. The nuns have come to Sacramento to beg for Mexico at the eleven o'clock Mass. We are the one family in the parish that speaks Spanish. As they file into our living room, the nuns smell pure, not sweet, pure like candles or like laundry.

The nun with a black mustache sighs at the end of each story the other two tell. Orphan. Leper. Crutch. Dry land. One eye. Casket.

¡Que lastima!

But the Mexican poor are not bent. They are proof of a refining fire.

The Mexican nuns smile with dignity as they stand after Mass with their 40
baskets extended, begging for Mexico.

A dusty black car pulls up in front of our house. My uncle has brought his family all the way from Ciudad Juarez. During their visit, my mother keeps trying to give them things to take back. There is a pair of lamps in the living room with porcelain roses. My aunt's eyes demur with pleasure to my uncle. My uncle says no. My uncle says his sister's children (I am the only one watching) would get the wrong impression of Mexico.

Mexico is poor. But my mama says there are no love songs like the love songs of Mexico. She hums a song she can't remember. The ice cream there is creamier than here. Someday we will see. The people are kinder — poor, but kinder to each other.

My mother's favorite record is *"Mariachis de Mexico y Pepe Villa con Orchestra."* Every Sunday she plays her record *("Rosas de Plata"; "Madrecita Linda")* while she makes us our pot roast dinner.

Men sing in Mexico. Men are strong and silent. But in song the Mexican male is granted license he is otherwise denied. The male can admit longing, pain, desire.

HAIII — EEEE — a cry like a comet rises over the song. A cry like mock weeping tickles the refrain 'of Mexican love songs. The cry is meant to encourage the balladeer — it is the raw edge of his sentiment. HAIII-EEEE. It is the man's sound. A ticklish arching of semen, a node wrung up a guitar string, until it bursts in a descending cascade of mockery. HAI. HAI. HAI. The cry of a jackal under the moon, the whistle of the phallus, the maniacal song of the skull.   45

Tell me, Papa.
What?
About Mexico.
I lived with the family of my uncle. I was the orphan in the village. I used to ring the church bells in the morning, many steps up in the dark. When I'd get up to the tower I could see the ocean.
The village, Papa, the houses too. . . .   50
The ocean. He studies the polished hood of our beautiful blue DeSoto.

Mexico was not the past. People went back and forth. People came up for work. People went back home, to mama or wife or village. The poor had mobility. Men who were too poor to take a bus walked from Sonora to Sacramento.

Relatives invited relatives. Entire Mexican villages got recreated in three stories of a single house. In the fall, after the harvest in the Valley, families of Mexican adults and their American children would load up their cars and head back to Mexico in caravans, for weeks, for months. The school teacher said to my mother what a shame it was the Mexicans did that — took their children out of school.

Like wandering Jews. They carried their home with them, back and forth; they had no true home but the tabernacle of memory.

Each year the American kitchen takes on a new appliance.   55
The children are fed and grow tall. They go off to school with children from Vietnam, from Kansas, from Hong Kong. They get into fights. They come home and they say dirty words.

The city will win. The city will give the children all the village could not — VCRs, hairstyles, drum beat. The city sings mean songs, dirty songs. But the city will sing the children a great Protestant hymn.
You can be anything you want to be.

We are parked. The patrolman turns off the lights of the truck — "back in a minute" — a branch scrapes the door as he rolls out of the van to take a piss.

The brush crackles beneath his receding steps. It is dark. Who? Who is out there? The faces I have seen in San Diego — dishwashers, janitors, gardeners. They come all the time, no big deal. There are other Mexicans who tell me the crossing is dangerous.

The patrolman returns. We drive again. I am thinking of epic migrations in history books — pan shots of orderly columns of paleolithic peoples, determined as ants, heeding some trumpet of history, traversing miles and miles . . . of paragraph. 60

The patrolman has turned off the headlights. He can't have to piss again? Suddenly the truck accelerates, pitches off the rutted road, banging, slamming a rock, faster, ignition is off, the truck is soft-pedaled to a stop in the dust; the patrolman is out like a shot. The cab light is on. I sit exposed for a minute. I can't hear anything. Cautiously, I decide to follow — I leave my door open as the patrolman has done. There is a boulder in the field. Is that it? The patrolman is barking in Spanish. His flashlight is trained on the boulder like a laser, he weaves it along the grain as though he is untying a knot. He is: Three men and a woman stand up. The men are young — sixteen, seventeen. The youngest is shivering. He makes a fist. He looks down. The woman is young too. Or she could be the mother? Her legs are very thin. She wears a man's digital wristwatch. They come from somewhere. And somewhere — San Diego, Sacramento — somebody is waiting for them.

The patrolman tells them to take off their coats and their shoes, throw them in a pile. Another truck rolls up.

As a journalist, I am allowed to come close. I can even ask questions.

There are no questions.

You can take pictures, the patrolman tells me. 65

I stare at the faces. They stare at me. To them I am not bearing witness; I am part of the process of being arrested. I hold up my camera. Their eyes swallow the flash, a long tunnel, leading back.

Your coming of age. It is early. From your bed you watch your mama moving back and forth under the light. The bells of the church ring in the dark. Mama crosses herself. From your bed you watch her back as she wraps the things you will take.

You are sixteen. Your father has sent for you. That's what it means: He has sent an address in Nevada. He is there with your uncle. You remember your uncle remembering snow with his beer.

You dress in the shadows. You move toward the table, the circle of light. You sit down. You force yourself to eat. Mama stands over you to make the sign of the cross on your forehead with her thumb. You are a man. You smile. She puts the bag of food in your hands. She says she has told *La Virgin*.

Then you are gone. It is gray. You hear a little breeze. It is the rustle of your old black *Dueña*, the dog, taking her short-cuts through the weeds, crazy *Dueña*, her pads on the dust. She is following you. 70

You pass the houses of the village, each window is a proper name. You pass the store. The bar. The lighted window of the clinic where the pale medical student from Monterrey lives alone and reads his book full of sores late into the night.

You want to be a man. You have the directions in your pocket: an address in Tijuana, and a map with a yellow line that leads from the highway to an "X" on a street in Reno. You are afraid, but you have never seen snow.

You are just beyond the cemetery. The breeze has died. You turn and throw a rock back at *La Dueña,* where you know she is — where you will always know where she is. She will not go past the cemetery. She will turn in circles like a *loca* and bite herself.

The dust takes on gravel, the path becomes a rutted road which leads to the highway. You walk north. The sky has turned white overhead. Insects click in the fields. In time, there will be a bus.

I will send for you or I will come home rich.   75

Understanding the Text

1. According to Rodriguez, what expectations about California do Mexicans have when they first come to this state?

2. Why does Rodriguez say that the journey from Mexico or Latin America to Los Angeles "is the journey from *tu* . . . to the repellent *usted*" (para. 14)?

3. What is Rodriguez's attitude toward the U.S. Border Patrol?

4. Why does Rodriguez conclude his essay with the statement *"I will send for you or I will come home rich"* (para. 75)?

5. Rodriguez combines first-, second-, and third-person points of view in this selection. Write an outline that charts the shifts in narrative point of view.

Exploring and Debating the Issues

1. Write a letter to a prospective Mexican immigrant in which you attempt to prepare him or her for life in your part of California. As you compose your letter, take Rodriguez's characterizations of the goals and interests of Mexican immigrants into account.

2. Rodriguez focuses as much on Mexico as he does on the destination of the immigrants he describes. In class, discuss the significance of that focus and what it suggests about the immigrants' attitudes toward the California dream.

3. Working in small groups, write a version of the California dream that addresses the interests and desires of the Mexican immigrants Rodriguez describes. Share your work with the class.

4. Write an essay in which you support, refute, or modify Rodriguez's assertion that the Mexicans he discusses "had no true home but the tabernacle of memory" (para. 54).

5. Assume the role of the U.S. Border Patrol officer whom Rodriguez describes, and compose a letter to Rodriguez in which you respond to his characterization of you and your professional activities.

JACK LOPEZ

Of *Cholos* and Surfers

On the West Side of L.A., where the population has traditionally been Anglo, lies the ocean. On the East Side, far from the beach but close to the original center of Mexican Los Angeles, dwell the descendants of the first Angelinos, as well as many new arrivals from Mexico. Born into the East L.A. community, **Jack Lopez** (b. 1950) writes here of the loyalties he feels for his birth community, even as he feels the lure of assimilation, of joining the world of surfing that has come to symbolize white culture and privilege. A fiction writer and essayist whose works include *Cholos and Surfers: A Chicano Family Album* (1998), Jack Lopez is a professor of English at California State University, Northridge.

T he only store around that had this new magazine was a Food Giant on Vermont Avenue, just off Imperial. *Surfer Quarterly*, it was then called. Now it's *Surfer Magazine* and they've celebrated their thirtieth anniversary. Sheldon made the discovery by chance when he'd gone shopping with his mother, who needed something found only at Food Giant. Normally we didn't go that far east to shop; we went west toward Crenshaw, to the nicer part of town.

We all wanted to be surfers, in fact called ourselves surfers even though we never made it to the beach, though it was less than ten miles away. One of the ways you could become a surfer was to own an issue of *Surfer Quarterly*. Since there had been only one prior issue, I was hot to get the new one. To be a surfer you also had to wear baggy shorts, large Penney's Towncraft T-shirts, and go barefoot, no matter how much the hot sidewalks burned your soles.

That summer in the early sixties I was doing all sorts of odd jobs around the house for my parents: weeding, painting the eaves, baby-sitting during the daytime. I was earning money so that I could buy Lenny Muelich's surfboard, another way to be a surfer. It was a Velzy-Jacobs, ten feet six inches long, twenty-four inches wide, and it had the coolest red oval decal. Lenny was my across-the-street neighbor, two years older than I, the kid who'd taught me the facts of life, the kid who'd taught me how to wrestle, the kid who'd played army with me when we were children, still playing in the dirt.

Now we no longer saw much of each other, though he still looked out for me. A strange thing happened to Lenny the previous school year. He grew. Like the Green Giant or something. He was over six feet tall and the older guys would let him hang out with them. So Lenny had become sort of a hood, wearing huge Sir Guy wool shirts, baggy khaki pants with the cuffs rolled, and French-toed black shoes. He drank wine, even getting drunk in the daytime with his hoodlum friends. Lenny was now respected, feared, even, by some of the parents, and no longer needed or desired to own a surfboard — he was going in the opposite direction. There were two distinct paths in my neighborhood: hood or surfer.

41

I was entering junior high school in a month, and my best friends were   5
Sheldon Cohen and Tom Gheridelli. They lived by Morningside Heights,
and their fathers were the only ones to work, and their houses were more
expensive than mine, and they'd both been surfers before I'd aspired toward such a life. Sheldon and Tom wore their hair long, constantly cranking
their heads back to keep their bangs out of their eyes. They were thirteen
years old. I was twelve. My parents wouldn't let hair grow over my ears no
matter how much I argued with them. But I was the one buying a surfboard.
Lenny was holding it for me. My parents would match any money I saved
over the summer.

Yet *Surfer Quarterly* was more tangible since it only cost one dollar.
Lenny's Velzy Jacobs was forty-five dollars, quite a large sum for the time.
The issue then became one of how to obtain the object of desire. The Food
Giant on Vermont was reachable by bike, but I was no longer allowed to
ride up there. Not since my older brother had gone to the Southside Theatre
one Saturday and had seen a boy get knifed because he wasn't colored. Vermont was a tough area, though some of the kids I went to school with lived
up there and they weren't any different from us. Yet none of them wished to
be surfers, I don't think.

What was needed was for me to include my father in the negotiation. I
wasn't allowed to ride my bike to Vermont, I reasoned with him. Therefore,
he should drive me. He agreed with me and that was that. Except I had to
wait until the following Friday when he didn't have to work.

My father was a printer by trade. He worked the graveyard shift. I
watched my younger brother and sister during the day (my older brother,
who was fifteen years old, was around in case anything of consequence
should arise, but we mostly left him alone) until my mother returned from
work — Reaganomics had hit my family decades before the rest of the
country. Watching my younger sister and brother consisted of keeping
them quiet so my father could sleep.

In the late afternoons I'd go to Sportsman's Park, where I'd virtually
grown up. I made the all-stars in baseball, basketball, and football. Our first
opponent on the path to the city championships was always Will Rogers
Park in Watts. Sheldon and Tom and I had been on the same teams. Sometimes I'd see them in the afternoons before we'd all have to return home for
dinner. We'd pore over Sheldon's issue of *Surfer* while sitting in the bleach-
ers next to the baseball diamond. If it was too hot we'd go in the wading
pool, though we were getting too old for that scene, since mostly women
and kids used it.

When Friday afternoon arrived and my father had showered and my   10
mother had returned from work, I reminded my father of our agreement. We
drove the neighborhood streets up to Vermont, passing Washington High
School, Normandie Avenue, Woodcrest Elementary School, and so on. We
spoke mostly of me. Was I looking forward to attending Henry Clay Junior
High? Would I still be in accelerated classes? My teachers and the principal
had talked with my parents about my skipping a grade but my parents said no.

Just as my father had exhausted his repertoire of school questions, we arrived at the Food Giant. After parking in the back lot, we entered the store and made for the liquor section, where the magazines were housed. I stood in front of the rack, butterflies of expectation overtaking my stomach while my father bought himself some beer. I knew immediately when I found the magazine. It looked like a square of water was floating in the air. An ocean-blue cover of a huge wave completely engulfing a surfer with the headline BANZAI PIPELINE. I held the magazine with great reverence, as if I were holding something of spiritual value, which it was.

"Is that it?" my father asked. He held a quart of Hamm's in each hand, his Friday night allotment.

"Yes." I beamed.

At the counter my father took the magazine from me, leafing through it much too casually, I thought. I could see the bulging veins in his powerful forearms, and saw too the solid bumps that were his biceps.

"Looks like a crazy thing to do," he said, finally placing the magazine   15
on the counter next to the beer. My father, the practical provider, the person whose closet was pristine for lack of clothes — although the ones he did own were stylish, yet not expensive. This was why he drank beer from quart bottles — it was cheaper that way. I know now how difficult it must have been raising four children on the hourly wages my parents made.

The man at the counter rang up the purchases, stopping for a moment to look at the *Surfer*. He smiled.

"*¿Eres mexicano?*" my father asked him.

"*Sí, ¿cómo no?*" the man answered.

Then my father and the store clerk began poking fun at my magazine in Spanish, nothing too mean, but ranking it as silly adolescent nonsense.

When we got back in the car I asked my father why he always asked cer-   20
tain people if they were Mexican. He only asked men who obviously were, thus knowing in advance their answers. He shrugged his shoulders and said he didn't know. It was a way of initiating conversation, he said. Well, it was embarrassing for me, I told him. Because I held the magazine in my lap, I let my father off the hook. It was more important that I give it a quick thumb-through as we drove home. The *Surfer* was far more interesting for me as a twelve-year-old than larger issues of race.

I spent the entire Friday evening holed up in my room, poring over the magazine, not even interested in eating popcorn or watching *77 Sunset Strip*, our familial Friday-night ritual. By the next morning I had almost memorized every photo caption and their sequence. I spoke with Sheldon on the phone and he and Tom were meeting me later at Sportsman's Park. I did my chores in a self-absorbed trance, waiting for the time when I could share my treasure with my friends. My mother made me eat lunch before I was finally able to leave.

Walking the long walk along Western Avenue toward Century and glancing at the photos in the magazine, I didn't pay attention to the *cholo* whom I passed on the sidewalk. I should have been more aware, but was too preoccupied. So there I was, in a street confrontation before I knew what had happened.

"You a surfer?" he said with disdain. He said it the way you start to say *chocolate. Ch,* like in *choc — churfer.* But that didn't quite capture it, either.

I stopped and turned to face him. He wore a wool watch cap pulled down onto his eyebrows, a long Sir Guy wool shirt with the top button buttoned and all the rest unbuttoned, khaki pants so long they were frayed at the bottoms and so baggy I couldn't see his shoes. I wore Bermuda shorts and a large Towncraft T-shirt. I was barefoot. My parents wouldn't let hair grow over my ears. *Cholo* meets surfer. Not a good thing. As he clenched his fists I saw a black cross tattooed onto the fleshy part of his hand.

His question was *not* like my father's. My father, I now sensed, wanted a 25 common bond upon which to get closer to strangers. This guy was Mexican American, and he wanted to fight me because I wore the outfit of a surfer.

I rolled the magazine in a futile attempt to hide it, but the *cholo* viewed this action as an escalation with a perceived weapon. It wasn't that I was overly afraid of him, though fear can work to your advantage if used correctly. I was big for my age, athletic, and had been in many fights. The problem was this: I was hurrying off to see my friends, to share something important with them, walking on a summer day, and I didn't feel like rolling on the ground with some stranger because *he'd* decided we must do so. Why did he get to dictate when or where you would fight? There was another consideration, one more utilitarian: Who knew what sort of weapons he had under all that baggy clothing? A rattail comb, at the least. More likely a knife, because in those days guns weren't that common.

At Woodcrest Elementary School there was a recently arrived Dutch Indonesian immigrant population. One of the most vicious fights I had ever seen was the one when Victor VerHagen fought his own cousin. And the toughest fight I'd ever been in was against Julio, something during a baseball game. There must be some element of self-loathing that propels us to fight those of our own ethnicity with a particular ferocity.

Just before the *cholo* was going to initiate the fight, I said, "I'm Mexican." American of Mexican descent, actually.

He seemed unable to process this new information. How could someone be Mexican and dress like a surfer? He looked at me again, this time seeing beyond the clothes I wore. He nodded slightly.

This revelation, this recognition verbalized, molded me in the years to 30 come. A surfer with a peeled nose and a Karmann Ghia with surf racks driving down Whittier Boulevard in East L.A. to visit my grandparents. The charmed life of a surfer in the midst of *cholos.*

When I began attending junior high school, there was a boy nicknamed Niño, who limped around the school yard one day. I discovered the reason for his limp when I went to the bathroom and he had a rifle pointed at boys and was taking their money. I fell in love with a girl named Shirley Pelland, the younger sister of a local surfboard maker. I saw her in her brother's shop after school, but she had no idea I loved her. That fall the gang escalation in my neighborhood became so pronounced my parents decided to move. We sold our house very quickly and moved to Huntington Beach, and none of us could sleep at night for the quiet. We were surrounded by cornfields and strawberry fields and tomato fields. As a bribe for our sudden move my parents chipped in much more than matching funds so I could buy Lenny Muelich's surfboard. I almost drowned in the big waves of a late-autumn south swell, the first time I went out on the Velzy-Jacobs. But later, after I'd surfed for a few years, I expertly rode the waves next to the pier, surfing with new friends.

But I've got ahead of myself. I must return to the *cholo* who is about to attack. But there isn't any more to tell about the incident. We didn't fight that summer's day over thirty years ago. In fact, I never fought another of my own race and don't know if this was a conscious decision or if circumstances dictated it. As luck would have it, I fought only a few more times during my adolescence and did so only when attacked.

My father's question, which he'd asked numerous people so long ago, taught me these things: The reason he had to ask was because he and my mother had left the safe confines of their Boyle Heights upbringing. They had thrust themselves and their children into what was called at the time the melting pot of Los Angeles. They bought the post–World War II American dream of assimilation. I was a pioneer in the sociological sense that I had no distinct ethnic piece of geography on which my pride and honor depended. Cast adrift in the city streets. Something gained, something lost. I couldn't return to my ethnic neighborhood, but I could be a surfer. And I didn't have to fight for ethnic pride over my city street. The neighborhood kids did, however, stick together, though this was not based upon race. It was a necessity. The older guys would step forward to protect the younger ones. That was how it was done.

The most important thing I learned was that I could do just about anything I wished, within reason. I could be a surfer, if I chose, and even *cholos* would respect my decision. During my adolescence I went to my grandparents' house for all the holidays. They lived in East Los Angeles. When I was old enough to drive I went on my own, sometimes with a girlfriend. I was able to observe my Los Angles Mexican heritage, taking a date to the *placita* for Easter service and then having lunch at Olvera Street. An Orange County girl who had no idea this part of Los Angeles existed. I was lucky; I got the best of both worlds.

Understanding the Text

1. What symbolic significance did being a surfer hold for Lopez and his friends?

2. How did Lopez's attitude toward his Mexican heritage compare with that of his father?

3. Why does the *cholo* object to Lopez's surfer clothing?

4. How did Lopez eventually reconcile his surfer and his Mexican American identities?

5. What did Lopez gain and lose through assimilation into mainstream California culture?

Exploring and Debating the Issues

1. In your journal, reflect on your own aspirations as they are shaped by California's open invitation to be whatever you want to be. If you do not see signs of that invitation, discuss instead the obstacles you believe you face.

2. In an essay, explain the extent to which Lopez's experiences demonstrate that California is a place where one can reinvent oneself.

3. A generational gap separated Lopez's and his father's attitudes toward assimilation. Compare that gap in attitude with that of the Vietnamese immigrants that Nancy Wride describes in "Vietnamese Youths No Longer Look Homeward" (p. 113). Be sure to keep in mind that Lopez is writing about the 1960s while Wride is discussing the 1990s.

4. The surfer image is still a strong one in contemporary youth codes. What is that image today, and how does it compare to the surfer image of the 1960s, when this narrative takes place?

CHARLIE STODDARD

An Age of Limits and Definitions

What's waiting for you when you graduate from college? In this op-ed piece written for the *Los Angeles Times,* **Charlie Stoddard** (b. 1972) describes her thoughts on graduating from Claremont McKenna College in 1994 only to find that the standard of living she had always taken for granted was no longer within her reach. Having chosen to redefine her expectations rather than give up on the Golden State, Stoddard resides in southern California, where she works in an electronics publications firm.

Two weeks ago, I left college behind to traverse Los Angeles in an exhausting search for a place to live. For the better part of daylight, I ricocheted throughout Santa Monica, bouncing from address to address, hoping to find the ideal apartment. Eventually I hoped to find *any* apartment, as building after building was eliminated: earthquake damage, too small, too dingy, olive-green shag carpeting. Building eliminations soon led to neighborhood and then regional exclusions: The area looked too run-down, "suspicious" cars drove by just a little too slowly, shady characters hung around outside the local supermarket. It occurred to me that the California in which I grew up was a California not available to most people; in fact, it was a California not now available to me.

Exhausted and depressed, I turned a corner to consult my map and found myself in a neighborhood not unlike my hometown of Claremont: quaint bungalows, mowed lawns, palms, and picket fences. Now this was California — the California that exists in many people's minds and the California that existed in my reality, the California ideal, the California of my expectations. The options looked brighter and I continued my search with renewed vigor. But this vigor was not to last long. There was not an apartment building to be found, and the cost of the occasional duplex made me reel. Nothing to rent, lease, or even buy within this housing oasis. There was no room in this area for those with only aspirations of upward mobility and certainly no room for those with no such ambition. Living within the environment of the California ideal in which I grew up is no longer an expectation, but part of a dream.

California's history comprises the dream, by arrivals from all directions, of [people seeking] a better quality of life for themselves and their families. But that quality has become more difficult to attain, and many of those who have achieved it now believe they must escape just to maintain it. Those of us who can afford to now seem to perpetually run from those now following the same California vision that allowed our own success. We form exclusive communities, without looking back, hoping never to catch a glimpse of the reality that would require us to see these communities as the anachronism that they are rapidly becoming.

The reality of California occupies more than the occasional glimpse that we catch on our way to the airport or the Laker game, when we step outside our sheltered bubble. The reality of California is not the microcosm of palms and bungalows. The reality of California is what we try to escape. That escape is what keeps the California ideal from becoming reality.

Rather than define ourselves according to a dream available only to the few, we need to include in our definition characteristics that make all aspects of California and Californians unique: our ability to adapt to the constant and unexpected changes in our definition; our ability to rumble, roll, shift, and shake without warning and still manage to come out standing. It is this resilience that defines California, a resilience on which we have always stood and on which we should continue to rely.

With the taste of graduation still lingering and the scent of the working world wafting in a bit too quickly, I set out with a new vision of California. For me, it is no longer a leisurely ride down tree-lined streets toward the park and not yet a frenzied commute down crowded highways toward corporate headquarters. While many people see mine as an age of limitless options, it is also a time in which seeking limits and definitions is the most important option.

I now set off to define what it means to be a Californian. I may not get my own bungalow; more likely, a studio in a multi-unit apartment complex. But maybe I'll have a palm outside my window.

Understanding the Text

1. How, according to Stoddard, has the California dream changed for today's college graduate?
2. What lessons does Stoddard draw from her frustrating search for an apartment?
3. What "new vision" (para. 6) of California does Stoddard suggest?
4. Is Stoddard ultimately optimistic or pessimistic about her future?

Exploring and Debating the Issues

1. In class, discuss how realistic you find Stoddard's expectations after leaving college. Do you share similar expectations, and do you predict you will be able to fulfill them?
2. What racial and social presuppositions does Stoddard reveal when she speaks of the "we" who "perpetually run from those now following the same California vision that allowed our own success" (para. 3)?
3. Since Stoddard wrote this essay, the California economy has improved substantially. Write an essay in which you support, challenge, or modify her suggestion that Californians need to seek "limits" (para. 6).
4. In what ways is Stoddard's ideal vision for her future a Midwestern one? To develop your ideas, consult Denise S. Spooner, "A New Perspective on the Dream" (p. 22).

NATHANAEL WEST

FROM

The Day of the Locust

Nathanael West (1903–1940) was on his way to becoming one of America's most daring and influential writers when his life was cut short suddenly in a car accident near El Centro, California. Beginning as an East Coast novelist, West (born Nathan Weinstein) reinvented himself as a Hollywood screenwriter in the 1930s. West's own experience enabled him to write with scathing insight into the dreams and desires of the men and women who came to Hollywood during the golden age of the movies, as can be seen in this excerpt from what is probably the first great Hollywood novel, *The Day of the Locust* (1939). West's other novels include *The Dream Life of Balso Snell* (1931), *Miss Lonelyhearts* (1933), and *A Cool Million* (1934).

A round quitting time, Tod Hackett heard a great din on the road outside his office. The groan of leather mingled with the jangle of iron and over all beat the tattoo of a thousand hooves. He hurried to the window.

An army of cavalry and foot was passing. It moved like a mob; its lines broken, as though fleeing from some terrible defeat. The dolmans of the hussars, the heavy shakos of the guards, Hanoverian light horse, with their flat leather caps and flowing red plumes, were all jumbled together in bobbing disorder. Behind the cavalry came the infantry, a wild sea of waving sabre-taches, sloped muskets, crossed shoulder belts and swinging cartridge boxes. Tod recognized the scarlet infantry of England with their white shoulder pads, the black infantry of the Duke of Brunswick, the French grenadiers with their enormous white gaiters, the Scotch with bare knees under plaid skirts.

While he watched, a little fat man, wearing a cork sun-helmet, polo shirt and knickers, darted around the corner of the building in pursuit of the army.

"Stage Nine — you bastards — Stage Nine!" he screamed through a small megaphone.

The cavalry put spur to their horses and the infantry broke into a   5
dogtrot. The little man in the cork hat ran after them, shaking his fist and cursing.

Tod watched until they had disappeared, behind half a Mississippi steamboat, then put away his pencils and drawing board, and left the office. On the sidewalk outside the studio he stood for a moment trying to decide whether to walk home or take a streetcar. He had been in Hollywood less than three months and still found it a very exciting place, but he was lazy and didn't like to walk. He decided to take the streetcar as far as Vine Street and walk the rest of the way.

A talent scout for National Films had brought Tod to the Coast after seeing some of his drawings in an exhibit of undergraduate work at the Yale School of Fine Arts. He had been hired by telegram. If the scout had met Tod, he probably wouldn't have sent him to Hollywood to learn set and costume designing. His large sprawling body, his slow blue eyes and sloppy grin made him seem completely without talent, almost doltish in fact.

Yes, despite his appearance, he was really a very complicated young man with a whole set of personalities, one inside the other like a nest of Chinese boxes. And *The Burning of Los Angeles,* a picture he was soon to paint, definitely proved he had talent.

He left the car at Vine Street. As he walked along, he examined the evening crowd. A great many of the people wore sports clothes which were not really sports clothes. Their sweaters, knickers, slacks, blue flannel jackets with brass buttons were fancy dress. The fat lady in the yachting cap was going shopping, not boating; the man in the Norfolk jacket and Tyrolean hat was returning, not from a mountain, but an insurance office; and the girl in slacks and sneaks with a bandanna around her head had just left a switchboard, not a tennis court.

Scattered among these masquerades were people of a different type.   10
Their clothing was somber and badly cut, brought from mail-order houses. While the others moved rapidly, darting into stores and cocktail bars, they loitered on the corners or stood with their backs to the shop windows and stared at everyone who passed. When their stare was returned, their eyes filled with hatred. At this time Tod knew very little about them except that they had come to California to die.

He was determined to learn much more. They were the people he felt he must paint. He would never again do a fat red barn, old stone wall or sturdy

Nantucket fisherman. From the moment he had seen them, he had known that, despite his race, training and heritage, neither Winslow Homer nor Thomas Ryder could be his masters and he turned to Goya and Daumier.

He had learned this just in time. During his last year in art school, he had begun to think that he might give up painting completely. The pleasures he received from the problems of composition and color had decreased as his facility had increased and he had realized that he was going the way of all his classmates, toward illustration or mere handsomeness. When the Hollywood job had come along, he had grabbed it despite the arguments of his friends who were certain that he was selling out and would never paint again.

He reached the end of Vine Street and began the climb into Pinyon Canyon. Night had started to fall.

The edges of the trees burned with a pale violet light and their centers gradually turned from deep purple to black. The same violet piping, like a Neon tube, outlined the tops of the ugly, hump-backed hills and they were almost beautiful.

But not even the soft wash of dusk could help the houses. Only dynamite would be of any use against the Mexican ranch houses, Samoan huts, Mediterranean villas, Egyptian and Japanese temples, Swiss chalets, Tudor cottages, and every possible combination of these styles that lined the slopes of the canyon.   15

When he noticed that they were all of plaster, lath and paper, he was charitable and blamed their shape on the materials used. Steel, stone and brick curb a builder's fancy a little, forcing him to distribute his stresses and weights and to keep his corners plumb, but plaster and paper know no law, not even that of gravity.

On the corner of La Huerta Road was a miniature Rhine castle with tarpaper turrets pierced for archers. Next to it was a highly colored shack with domes and minarets out of the *Arabian Nights.* Again he was charitable. Both houses were comic, but he didn't laugh. Their desire to startle was so eager and guileless.

It is hard to laugh at the need for beauty and romance, no matter how tasteless, even horrible, the results of that are. But it is easy to sigh. Few things are sadder than the truly monstrous.

Understanding the Text

1. What are the images that West uses to present Hollywood as a place of make-believe?

2. What is West's attitude toward Hollywood culture, and how do his tone and diction convey that attitude?

3. Why would Tod's friends consider his leaving art school to work in Hollywood to be "selling out" (para. 12)?

Exploring and Debating the Issues

1. The architecture that West describes represents a desire to invent an exotic and romantic personal environment. Write an essay in which you analyze contemporary architecture in California. To what extent do Californians still use architecture to express their desire for romance and adventure? Be sure to focus your comments on specific buildings or neighborhoods.

2. James J. Rawls claims that West explored the "failure of the myth" of the California dream in his writings (see "California: A Place, A People, A Dream," p. 8). Write an essay in which you explain whether this passage demonstrates Rawls's claim.

3. West's description of the make-believe army marching through the streets exemplifies Hollywood's ability to invent fantasies for millions of Americans throughout this century. Referring to specific films or television programs, argue whether Hollywood today does more to spin fantasies, as West believed, or to depict reality.

4. Rent a videotape of the film *The Day of the Locust,* and write an analysis of its image of Hollywood and, more broadly, of California.

JOAN DIDION

Notes from a Native Daughter

Few Californians have distinguished themselves as such prominent interpreters of the California scene as **Joan Didion** (b. 1934). The author of numerous essays, short stories, and novels — many of them set in her home state — Didion here presents her perspective as a descendant of Sacramento Valley pioneers, for whom the California dream has a special, even rather exclusive, resonance. In this selection excerpted from her renowned collection of essays *Slouching Towards Bethlehem* (1968), Didion admonishes those for whom California ends a few miles east of the coastline not to forget the interior valleys and their place in the California vision. Didion's many books include *Play It as It Lays* (1970), *The White Album* (1979), *Salvador* (1983), *Democracy* (1984), *After Henry* (1992), and *The Last Thing He Wanted* (1996).

It is very easy to sit at the bar in, say, La Scala in Beverly Hills, or Ernie's in San Francisco, and to share in the pervasive delusion that California is only five hours from New York by air. The truth is that La Scala and Ernie's are only five hours from New York by air. California is somewhere else.

Many people in the East (or "back East," as they say in California, although not in La Scala or Ernie's) do not believe this. They have been to Los Angeles or to San Francisco, have driven through a giant redwood and have seen the Pacific glazed by the afternoon sun off Big Sur, and they naturally tend to believe that they have in fact been to California. They have not been, and they probably never will be, for it is a longer and in many ways a more difficult trip than they might want to undertake, one of those trips on which the destination flickers chimerically on the horizon, ever receding, ever diminishing. I happen to know about that trip because I come from California, come from a family, or a congeries of families, that has always been in the Sacramento Valley.

You might protest that no family has been in the Sacramento Valley for anything approaching "always." But it is characteristic of Californians to speak grandly of the past as if it had simultaneously begun, *tabula rasa,* and reached a happy ending on the day the wagons started west. *Eureka* — "I Have Found It" — as the state motto has it. Such a view of history casts a certain melancholia over those who participate in it; my own childhood was suffused with the conviction that we had long outlived our finest hour. In fact that is what I want to tell you about: what it is like to come from a place like Sacramento. If I could make you understand that, I could make you understand California and perhaps something else besides, for Sacramento *is* California, and California is a place in which a boom mentality and a sense of Chekhovian loss meet in uneasy suspension; in which the mind is troubled by some buried but ineradicable suspicion that things had better work here, because here, beneath that immense bleached sky, is where we run out of continent.

In 1847 Sacramento was no more than an adobe enclosure, Sutter's Fort, standing alone on the prairie; cut off from San Francisco and the sea by the Coast Range and from the rest of the continent by the Sierra Nevada, the Sacramento Valley was then a true sea of grass, grass so high a man riding into it could tie it across his saddle. A year later gold was discovered in the Sierra foothills, and abruptly Sacramento was a town, a town any moviegoer could map tonight in his dreams — a dusty collage of assay offices and wagonmakers and saloons. Call that Phase Two. Then the settlers came — the farmers, the people who for two hundred years had been moving west on the frontier, the peculiar flawed strain who had cleared Virginia, Kentucky, Missouri; they made Sacramento a farm town. Because the land was rich, Sacramento became eventually a rich farm town, which meant houses in town, Cadillac dealers, a country club. In that gentle sleep Sacramento dreamed until perhaps 1950, when something happened. What happened was that Sacramento woke to the fact that the outside world was moving in, fast and hard. At the moment of its waking Sacramento lost, for better or for worse, its character, and that is part of what I want to tell you about.

But the change is not what I remember first. First I remember running a boxer   5
dog of my brother's over the same flat fields that our great-great-grandfather had found virgin and had planted; I remember swimming (albeit nervously, for I was a nervous child, afraid of sinkholes and afraid of snakes, and perhaps that was the beginning of my error) the same rivers we had swum for a century: the Sacramento, so rich with silt that we could barely see our hands a few inches beneath the surface; the American, running clean and fast with melted Sierra snow until July, when it would slow down, and rattlesnakes would sun

themselves on its newly exposed rocks. The Sacramento, the American, sometimes the Cosumnes, occasionally the Feather. Incautious children died every day in those rivers; we read about it in the paper, how they had miscalculated a current or stepped into a hole down where the American runs into the Sacramento, how the Berry Brothers had been called in from Yolo County to drag the river but how the bodies remained unrecovered. "They were from away," my grandmother would extrapolate from the newspaper stories. "Their parents had no *business* letting them in the river. They were visitors from Omaha." It was not a bad lesson, although a less than reliable one; children we knew died in the rivers too.

When summer ended — when the State Fair closed and the heat broke, when the last green hop vines had been torn down along the H Street road and the tule fog began rising off the low ground at night — we would go back to memorizing the Products of Our Latin American Neighbors and to visiting the great-aunts on Sunday, dozens of great-aunts, year after year of Sundays. When I think now of those winters I think of yellow elm leaves wadded in the gutters outside the Trinity Episcopal Pro-Cathedral on M Street. There are actually people in Sacramento now who call M Street Capitol Avenue, and Trinity has one of those featureless new buildings, but perhaps children still learn the same things there on Sunday mornings:

Q. In what way does the Holy Land resemble the Sacramento Valley?
A. In the type and diversity of its agricultural products.

And I think of the rivers rising, of listening to the radio to hear at what height they would crest and wondering if and when and where the levees would go. We did not have as many dams in those years. The bypasses would be full, and men would sandbag all night. Sometimes a levee would go in the night, somewhere upriver; in the morning the rumor would spread that the Army Engineers had dynamited it to relieve the pressure on the city.

After the rains came spring, for ten days or so; the drenched fields would dissolve into a brilliant ephemeral green (it would be yellow and dry as fire in two or three weeks) and the real estate business would pick up. It was the time of year when people's grandmothers went to Carmel; it was the time of year when girls who could not even get into Stephens or Arizona or Oregon, let alone Stanford or Berkeley, would be sent to Honolulu, on the *Lurline.* I have no recollection of anyone going to New York, with the exception of a cousin who visited there (I cannot imagine why) and reported that the shoe salesmen at Lord & Taylor were "intolerably rude." What happened in New York and Washington and abroad seemed to impinge not at all upon the Sacramento mind. I remember being taken to call upon a very old woman, a rancher's widow, who was reminiscing (the favored conversational mode in Sacramento) about the son of some contemporaries of hers. "That Johnston boy never did amount to much," she said. Desultorily, my mother protested: Alva Johnston, she said, had won the Pulitzer Prize, when he was working for the *New York Times.* Our hostess looked at us impassively. "He never amounted to anything in Sacramento," she said.

Hers was the true Sacramento voice, and, although I did not realize it then, one not long to be heard, for the war was over and the boom was on and the voice of the aerospace engineer would be heard in the land. Vets no down! Executive living on low FHA!

Later, when I was living in New York, I would make the trip back to Sacramento four and five times a year (the more comfortable the flight, the more obscurely miserable I would be, for it weighs heavily upon my kind that we could perhaps not make it by wagon), trying to prove that I had not meant to leave it all, because in at least one respect California — the California we are talking about — resembles Eden: It is assumed that those who absent themselves from its blessings have been banished, exiled by some perversity of heart. Did not the Donner-Reed Party,[1] after all, eat its own dead to reach Sacramento?

I have said that the trip back is difficult, and it is — difficult in a way   10
that magnifies the ordinary ambiguities of sentimental journeys. Going back to California is not like going back to Vermont, or Chicago; Vermont and Chicago are relative constants, against which one measures one's own change. All that is constant about the California of my childhood is the rate at which it disappears. An instance: On Saint Patrick's Day of 1948 I was taken to see the legislature "in action," a dismal experience; a handful of florid assemblymen, wearing green hats, were reading Pat-and-Mike jokes into the record. I still think of the legislators that way — wearing green hats, or sitting around on the veranda of the Senator Hotel fanning themselves and being entertained by Artie Samish's emissaries. (Samish was the lobbyist who said, "Earl Warren may be the governor of the state, but I'm the governor of the legislature.") In fact there is no longer a veranda at the Senator Hotel — it was turned into an airline ticket office, if you want to embroider the point — and in any case the legislature has largely deserted the Senator for the flashy motels north of town, where the tiki torches flame and the steam rises off the heated swimming pools in the cold Valley night.

It is hard to *find* California now, unsettling to wonder how much of it was merely imagined or improvised; melancholy to realize how much of anyone's memory is no true memory at all but only the traces of someone else's memory, stories handed down on the family network. I have an indelibly vivid "memory," for example, of how Prohibition affected the hop growers around Sacramento: The sister of a grower my family knew brought home a mink coat from San Francisco, and was told to take it back, and sat on the floor of the parlor cradling that coat and crying. Although I was not born until a year after Repeal, that scene is more "real" to me than many I have played myself.

---

[1]California pioneers who committed cannibalism while trapped in the snow of the High Sierras during the winter of 1846. [Eds.]

I remember one trip home, when I sat alone on a night jet from New York and read over and over some lines from a W. S. Merwin poem I had come across in a magazine, a poem about a man who had been a long time in another country and knew that he must go home:

> . . . But it should be
> Soon. Already I defend hotly
> Certain of our indefensible faults,
> Resent being reminded; already in my mind
> Our language becomes freighted with a richness
> No common tongue could offer, while the mountains
> Are like nowhere on earth, and the wide rivers.

You see the point. I want to tell you the truth, and already I have told you about the wide rivers.

It should be clear by now that the truth about the place is elusive, and must be tracked with caution. You might go to Sacramento tomorrow and someone (although no one I know) might take you out to Aerojet-General, which has, in the Sacramento phrase, "something to do with rockets." Fifteen thousand people work for Aerojet, almost all of them imported; a Sacramento lawyer's wife told me, as evidence of how Sacramento was opening up, that she believed she had met one of them, at an open house two Decembers ago. ("Couldn't have been nicer, actually," she added enthusiastically. "I think he and his wife bought the house next *door* to Mary and Al, something like that, which of course was how *they* met him.") So you might go to Aerojet and stand in the big vendors' lobby where a couple of thousand components salesmen try every week to sell their wares and you might look up at the electrical wallboard that lists Aerojet personnel, their projects and their location at any given time, and you might wonder if I have been in Sacramento lately. MINUTEMAN, POLARIS, TITAN, the lights flash, and all the coffee tables are littered with airline schedules, very now, very much in touch.

But I could take you a few miles from there into towns where the banks still bear names like The Bank of Alex Brown, into towns where the one hotel still has an octagonal-tile floor in the dining room and dusty potted palms and big ceiling fans; into towns where everything — the seed business, the Harvester franchise, the hotel, the department store and the main street — carries a single name, the name of the man who built the town. A few Sundays ago I was in a town like that, a town smaller than that, really, no hotel, no Harvester franchise, the bank turned out, a river town. It was the golden anniversary of some of my relatives and it was 110 degrees and the guests of honor sat on straight-backed chairs in front of a sheaf of gladioluses in the Rebekah Hall. I mentioned visiting Aerojet-General to a cousin I saw there, who listened to me with interested disbelief. Which is the true California? That is what we all wonder.

Let us try out a few irrefutable statements, on subjects not open to interpretation. Although Sacramento is in many ways the least typical of the Valley

15

towns, it *is* a Valley town, and must be viewed in that context. When you say "the Valley" in Los Angeles, most people assume that you mean the San Fernando Valley (some people in fact assume that you mean Warner Brothers), but make no mistake: We are talking not about the valley of the sound stages and the ranchettes but about the real Valley, the Central Valley, the fifty thousand square miles drained by the Sacramento and the San Joaquin Rivers and further irrigated by a complex network of sloughs, cutoffs, ditches, and the Delta-Mendota and Friant-Kern Canals.

A hundred miles north of Los Angeles, at the moment when you drop from the Tehachapi Mountains into the outskirts of Bakersfield, you leave Southern California and enter the Valley. "You look up the highway and it is straight for miles, coming at you, with the black line down the center coming at you and at you . . . and the heat dazzles up from the white slab so that only the black line is clear, coming at you with the whine of the tires, and if you don't quit staring at that line and don't take a few deep breaths and slap yourself hard on the back of the neck you'll hypnotize yourself."

Robert Penn Warren wrote that about another road, but he might have been writing about the Valley road, U.S. 99, three hundred miles from Bakersfield to Sacramento, a highway so straight that when one flies on the most direct pattern from Los Angeles to Sacramento one never loses sight of U.S. 99. The landscape it runs through never, to the untrained eye, varies. The Valley eye can discern the point where miles of cotton seedlings fade into miles of tomato seedlings, or where the great corporation ranches — Kern County Land, what is left of DiGiorgio — give way to private operations (somewhere on the horizon, if the place is private, one sees a house and a stand of scrub oaks), but such distinctions are in the long view irrelevant. All day long, all that moves is the sun, and the big Rainbird sprinklers.

Every so often along 99 between Bakersfield and Sacramento there is a town: Delano, Tulare, Fresno, Madera, Merced, Modesto, Stockton. Some of these towns are pretty big now, but they are all the same at heart, one- and two- and three-story buildings artlessly arranged, so that what appears to be the good dress shop stands beside a W. T. Grant store, so that the big Bank of America faces a Mexican movie house. *Dos Peliculas, Bingo Bingo Bingo.* Beyond the downtown (pronounced *down*town, with the Okie accent that now pervades Valley speech patterns) lie blocks of old frame houses — paint peeling, sidewalks cracking, their occasional leaded amber windows overlooking a Foster's Freeze or a five-minute car wash or a State Farm Insurance office; beyond those spread the shopping centers and the miles of tract houses, pastel with redwood siding, the unmistakable signs of cheap building already blossoming on those houses which have survived the first rain. To a stranger driving 99 in an air-conditioned car (he would be on business, I suppose, any stranger driving 99, for 99 would never get a tourist to Big Sur or San Simeon, never get him to the California he came to see), these towns must seem so flat, so impoverished, as to drain the imagination. They hint at evenings spent hanging around gas stations, and suicide pacts sealed in drive-ins.

But remember:

Q. In what way does the Holy Land resemble the Sacramento Valley?

A. In the type and diversity of its agricultural products.

U.S. 99 in fact passes through the richest and most intensely cultivated 20
agricultural region in the world, a giant outdoor hothouse with a billion-
dollar crop. It is when you remember the Valley's wealth that the mono-
chromatic flatness of its towns takes on a curious meaning, suggests
a habit of mind some would consider perverse. There is something in
the Valley mind that reflects a real indifference to the stranger in his air-
conditioned car, a failure to perceive even his presence, let alone his
thoughts or wants. An implacable insularity is the seal of these towns. I
once met a woman in Dallas, a most charming and attractive woman accustomed to the hospitality and social hypersensitivity of Texas, who told
me that during the four war years her husband had been stationed in
Modesto, she had never once been invited inside anyone's house. No one
in Sacramento would find this story remarkable ("She probably had no
*rel*atives there," said someone to whom I told it), for the Valley towns understand one another, share a peculiar spirit. They think alike and they look
alike. *I* can tell Modesto from Merced, but I have visited there, gone to
dances there; besides, there is over the main street of Modesto an arched
sign which reads:

WATER — WEALTH

CONTENTMENT — HEALTH

There is no such sign in Merced.

I said that Sacramento was the least typical of the Valley towns, and it is —
but only because it is bigger and more diverse, only because it has had the
rivers and the legislature; its true character remains the Valley character, its
virtues the Valley virtues, its sadness the Valley sadness. It is just as hot in
the summertime, so hot that the air shimmers and the grass bleaches white
and the blinds stay drawn all day, so hot that August comes on not like a
month but like an affliction; it is just as flat, so flat that a ranch of my family's with a slight rise on it, perhaps a foot, was known for the hundred-
some years which preceded this year as "the hill ranch." (It is known this
year as a subdivision in the making, but that is another part of the story.)
Above all, in spite of its infusions from outside, Sacramento retains the
Valley insularity.

To sense that insularity a visitor need do no more than pick up a copy
of either of the two newspapers, the morning *Union* or the afternoon *Bee*.
The *Union* happens to be Republican and impoverished and the *Bee* Democratic and powerful ("The Valley of the Bees!" as the McClatchys, who own
the Fresno, Modesto, and Sacramento *Bees,* used to headline their adver-
tisements in the trade press. "Isolated from All Other Media Influence!"),
but they read a good deal alike, and the tone of their chief editorial

concerns is strange and wonderful and instructive. The *Union,* in a county heavily and reliably Democratic, frets mainly about the possibility of a local takeover by the John Birch Society; the *Bee,* faithful to the letter of its founder's will, carries on overwrought crusades against phantoms it still calls "the power trusts." Shades of Hiram Johnson, whom the *Bee* helped elect governor in 1910. Shades of Robert La Follette, to whom the *Bee* delivered the Valley in 1924. There is something about the Sacramento papers that does not quite connect with the way Sacramento lives now, something pronouncedly beside the point. The aerospace engineers, one learns, read the San Francisco *Chronicle.*

The Sacramento papers, however, simply mirror the Sacramento peculiarity, the Valley fate, which is to be paralyzed by a past no longer relevant. Sacramento is a town which grew up on farming and discovered to its shock that land has more profitable uses. (The chamber of commerce will give you crop figures, but pay them no mind — what matters is the feeling, the knowledge that where the green hops once grew is now Larchmont Riviera, that what used to be the Whitney ranch is now Sunset City, thirty-three thousand houses and a country-club complex.) It is a town in which defense industry and its absentee owners are suddenly the most important facts; a town which has never had more people or more money, but has lost its *raison d'être.* It is a town many of whose most solid citizens sense about themselves a kind of functional obsolescence. The old families still see only one another, but they do not see even one another as much as they once did; they are closing ranks, preparing for the long night, selling their rights-of-way and living on the proceeds. Their children still marry one another, still play bridge and go into the real-estate business together. (There is no other business in Sacramento, no reality other than land — even I, when I was living and working in New York, felt impelled to take a University of California correspondence course in Urban Land Economics.) But late at night when the ice has melted there is always somebody now, some Julian English, whose heart is not quite in it. For out there on the outskirts of town are marshaled the legions of aerospace engineers, who talk their peculiar condescending language and tend their dichondra and plan to stay in the promised land; who are raising a new generation of native Sacramentans and who do not care, really do not care, that they are not asked to join the Sutter Club. It makes one wonder, late at night when the ice is gone; introduces some air into the womb, suggests that the Sutter Club is perhaps not, after all, the Pacific Union or the Bohemian; that Sacramento is not *the city.* In just such self-doubts do small towns lose their character.

I want to tell you a Sacramento story. A few miles out of town is a place, six or seven thousand acres, which belonged in the beginning to a rancher with one daughter. That daughter went abroad and married a title, and when she brought the title home to live on the ranch, her father built them a vast house — music rooms, conservatories, a ballroom. They needed a ballroom because they entertained: people from abroad, people from San Francisco, house parties that lasted weeks and involved special trains. They are long dead, of course, but their only son, aging and unmarried, still lives on the place. He does not live in the house, for the house is no longer there. Over the years it burned, room by room, wing by wing. Only the chimneys of the great house are still standing, and its heir lives in their shadow, lives by himself on the charred site, in a house trailer.

That is a story my generation knows; I doubt that the next will know it, the children of the aerospace engineers. Who would tell it to them? Their grandmothers live in Scarsdale, and they have never met a great-aunt. "Old" Sacramento to them will be something colorful, something they read about in *Sunset*. They will probably think that the Redevelopment has always been there, that the Embarcadero, down along the river, with its amusing places to shop and its picturesque fire houses turned into bars, has about it the true flavor of the way it was. There will be no reason for them to know that in homelier days it was called Front Street (the town was not, after all, settled by the Spanish) and was a place of derelicts and missions and itinerant pickers in town for a Saturday-night drunk: VICTORIOUS LIFE MISSION, JESUS SAVES, BEDS 25¢ A NIGHT, CROP INFORMATION HERE. They will have lost the real past and gained a manufactured one, and there will be no way for them to know, no way at all, why a house trailer should stand alone on seven thousand acres outside town.

But perhaps it is presumptuous of me to assume that they will be missing something. Perhaps in retrospect this has been a story not about Sacramento at all, but about the things we lose and the promises we break as we grow older; perhaps I have been playing out unawares the Margaret in the poem:

> Margaret, are you grieving
> Over Goldengrove unleaving? . . .
> It is the blight man was born for,
> It is Margaret you mourn for.

Understanding the Text

1. Why does Didion say that "California is somewhere else" (para. 1), not just Los Angeles and San Francisco?

2. How has Didion's Sacramento changed since her girlhood?

3. Explain in your own words why Didion feels that "Sacramento *is* California" (para. 3).

4. What are the most striking features of the Central Valley, according to Didion?

5. What tone does Didion adopt in this essay, and how does it affect your response as a reader?

Exploring and Debating the Issues

1. Considering that coastal California is home to the majority of the state's population, write an argument in which you support, challenge, or complicate Didion's contention that the Central Valley is the true California.

2. In class, form groups and discuss the class implications of Didion's celebration of Sacramento's "old families" (para. 24). How would someone from Aerojet-General or a farmworker be likely to respond to her essay?

3. To what extent does Didion's description of the Central Valley support, challenge, or qualify James J. Rawls's vision of the California dream ("California: A Place, A People, A Dream," p. 8)? To support your argument, you may draw on your own observations or experiences and any of the selections in this chapter.

4. Didion sees U.S. 99 as symbolic of the Central Valley and, thus, of California. Using Didion's essay as a model, propose an alternative freeway or road as a symbol of the state, being sure to explain how its features are characteristically Californian.

5. Write an essay arguing for or against the proposition that the state capitol be moved from Sacramento to a city closer to California's economic and population centers.

Researching the Issues

1. To what extent do students at your school believe in the traditional California dream? Interview at least half a dozen students about their aspirations and expectations for the future. Write a report detailing and evaluating your findings.

2. Research the California gold rush of 1849. In an essay, explain how it contributed to the formation of the California dream. Be sure to consider the costs as well as the rewards of the gold rush in your analysis.

3. Read Helen Hunt Jackson's novel *Ramona,* and analyze the way it presents California's Spanish mission culture.

4. Brainstorm in class a list of television programs or movies that prominently feature California as a setting for the action (e.g., *Falling Down, Blade Runner, Beverly Hills 90210, American Graffiti, L.A. Story, Boyz N the Hood, L.A. Confidential,* and *San Francisco*) and then pick one to analyze, showing the ways in which it reflects California mythology.

5. Interview some recent immigrants to California, either from other states or from other nations, and then use your findings to write an essay on why people still come to the Golden State.

6. California has figured prominently in many popular songs, including "Hotel California," "California Dreaming," "San Francisco," "L.A.

CALIFORNIA ON THE NET

1. Visit a California web site devoted to tourism, and analyze the language and images used to depict the state. To what extent do the images reflect those discussed by James J. Rawls in "California: A People, A Place, A Dream" (p. 8)? You might try http://www.gocalif.ca.gov/gallery or http://www.ca.gov/s/history/scrapbook.html.
2. What is the current view of the culture and impact of the California gold rush? Consult http://www.museumca.org/goldrush.html or http://www.sjmercury.com/goldrush/goldrush_story.shtml.
3. Kevin Starr, the State Librarian of California, is one of the leading experts on the California dream. Visit the web site "California: The Dream and the Challenge" at http://www.ca.gov/s/history/cahdream.html. Compare his history of the California dream with those discussions in this chapter.

Woman," "California Girls," "I Left My Heart in San Francisco," "Do You Know the Way to San Jose?" and "Lodi," to name a few. Choose several songs that feature California, and write an analysis of the image that they project.

7. Interview some members of a California Indian tribe, and ask them what they think of the California dream. Report your findings to the class. You may want to consult *The Earth Is Our Mother: A Guide to the Indians of California, Their Locales, and Historic Sites* by Dolan H. Eargle, Jr. (San Francisco: Tress Company Press, 1986).

8. Research the history of Spanish exploration in California, and write a report on the views of such explorers as Gaspar de Portolá and Juan Rodriguez Cabrillo. Consider how the Spanish vision of California differed from, or agreed with, the American vision.

9. Read Joan Didion's novel *Play It as It Lays,* and write an analysis of its interpretation of the southern California dream.

2 The Great Migration
Immigrants in California History

Into the Promised Land

The first North American settlers migrated here thousands of years ago across an Ice Age land bridge stretching between the regions now called Siberia and Alaska. Coming south, they eventually entered a rich land empty of humans but teeming with game, where they spread out, settled down, and became the first Californians. Why they came, no one really knows for sure, but if they were at all like the immigrants who followed them to California thousands of years later, they probably came in search of better lives as they scanned the horizon for greener pastures.

In this chapter, you will read and write about immigration, a topic that might be the most controversial issue in California today. On the one side are those who believe that California has no room for more immigrants, while on the other are those who believe that, since California has always been a land of immigrants, it is hypocritical to close the door now. During the 1990s, two hotly contested ballot initiatives that have put immigration on the front burner of California politics passed—Proposition 187 in 1994 and Proposition 227 in 1998—and the future promises further controversy.

The controversy is all the more bitter because of its racial overtones. For unlike the massive migrations that transformed America in the late nineteenth century, the overwhelming majority of today's immigrants are not European. To be sure, Europeans who immigrated to America a century ago brought their own languages and cultures with them, but their racial similarities with those who were already here enabled them to blend relatively smoothly into what has become known as the American melting pot. But immigrants from Latin America and Asia face a different racial reality, and, as the controversy over Proposition 227—the ballot measure designed to eliminate bilingual education from California's schools—demonstrates, such immigrants often wish to preserve the language and culture they brought with them as well.

The result has been a political polarization in California that presents what may be the greatest challenge that the state must face in the coming years. It will not be long before California has no racial majority at all; ideally, this might lead us to stop identifying ourselves in racial terms and instead unite together simply as Californians. But if we are not careful, there is also the possibility that we may fracture further into warring groups, each one pursuing its own interests in opposition to all of the others and so, in the end, destroying the California dream itself.

The More Things Change, the More They Stay the Same

The history of California's immigration controversy is a long one, and in it we may find yet another instance of the special place that California has always occupied in the American dream. For if California has long stood as a brighter, more golden version of the dream, it has also played a crucial role in the flip side of the American promise, the nativistic hostility toward non–Anglo-Saxon immigrants that Americans have often harbored. In the 1840s, for example, Irish immigrants to Boston and New York faced significant hostility ("No Irish Need Apply" was a sign commonly seen in windows of businesses seeking employees), while Jews, Italians, Greeks, and other eastern and southern European immigrants at the turn of the century also faced discrimination and oppression. It is significant that California helped inaugurate a history of anti-immigration legislation in America by pushing for the passage of the Chinese Exclusion Act by Congress in 1882, the first of many immigration restrictions in U.S. law designed to keep out not only Chinese immigrants but also all immigrants not from northern Europe.

Nor was California a hospitable place for the Okies who fled the Midwestern Dust Bowl in the 1930s—a migration immortalized in John Steinbeck's *The Grapes of Wrath*—or the African Americans who came during World War II to work in California's shipyards and munitions factories. For the Japanese immigrants who were rounded up and sent to detention camps like Manzanar during the war, the history of California's response to immigrants has an especially painful dimension. And for many Mexican immigrants, the bitter irony is that they must be identified as immigrants at all, for California was once a part of the Republic of Mexico.

In short, immigration has long divided Californians even as it has enlarged the meaning of being a Californian. If you are like most residents of the state, you are likely to have some strong feelings, one way or the other, about immigration. And as students in California's system of higher education, you are experiencing the issue directly in the form of curricula that are being restructured to reflect the multicultural diversity that immigration has fostered. Perhaps you attended a high school where English was not the language spoken by the majority of students—indeed, where you, like the majority of your classmates, spoke English as a second language. And while it has not been primarily an immigration-related issue, the controversy over affirmative action in California's schools has certainly affected you, and there, too, immigration has played its part.

A Diverse Future

Here, too, America will be following California's lead. For just as by the year 2000 immigration will result in a demographic shift by which whites will become a minority group in the state, so too is the demography of America changing. Just as the arrival of millions of eastern and southern European immigrants to U.S. shores at the turn of the century transformed a largely Anglo-Saxon and Scots-Irish nation into a more broadly European culture, so too is the late–twentieth-century arrival of millions of Latin Americans, Asians, Middle Easterners, and so on, transforming the American demographic landscape. Will that transformation lead to social conflict? Or will it lead to a social and cultural enrichment that all Americans can enjoy? The answers will have a great deal to do with the way that California handles its current immigration controversies. Will we lead the nation to a new sense of American identity? It may well be your generation that will decide.

The Readings

An excerpt from John Steinbeck's classic novel *The Grapes of Wrath* begins this chapter, showing how the current controversies over immigration are nothing new and how refugees from such Dust Bowl states as Kansas, Texas, and Oklahoma once faced the same kind of reception that refugees from Central America and Asia sometimes face today. Yeh Ling-Ling, a first-generation immigrant from Vietnam, follows with an editorial arguing for restrictions on immigration both to California and the United States based on her perception that there is no more room for immigrants in America. Next, Rubén Martinez presents a contrasting argument supporting an open-door policy on immigration, basing his position on a survey of immigration history in California and America. Connie Yu's family saga documenting the lives of Chinese immigrants, especially Chinese women, to California in the early years of the century is followed by an interview with Sue Kunitomi Embrey, an American citizen who, like most prewar Japanese immigrants, was rounded up in 1942 to spend the war in detention camps like California's Manzanar. Next, William Langewiesche explores the hidden canyons of San Diego County, where undocumented laborers live bleak lives in cardboard shanties, while Ramón "Tianguis" Pérez provides a more hopeful firsthand account of his experiences as an undocumented farm worker in the Central Valley. Nancy Wride's newspaper article on the children of Vietnamese immigrants in Southern California concludes the chapter with a report on the mixed emotions such immigrants feel when they contemplate their parents' homeland and the new world in which they live.

JOHN STEINBECK

FROM
The Grapes of Wrath

Arguably California's most distinguished writer, **John Steinbeck** (1902–1968) made California the setting for many of his novels and stories. Unlike previous novelists who romanticized California, such as Helen Hunt Jackson, Steinbeck often wrote about the gritty underside of the California dream—of the migrant workers who harvested California's crops and the labor strife that erupted when they tried to improve their lives. In *The Grapes of Wrath* (1939), his most famous novel, Steinbeck dramatized the lives of the Okie farm laborers who came to California in the 1930s, fleeing abandoned farms in the Dust Bowl states in the hopes of finding a better life but finding, as Steinbeck shows in this selection, suspicion and hostility instead. Other novels in which Steinbeck wrote, often controversially, of the lives of farm laborers include *In Dubious Battle* (1936) and *Of Mice and Men* (1937). John Steinbeck was awarded the Nobel Prize for Literature in 1962.

Once California belonged to Mexico and its land to Mexicans; and a horde of tattered feverish Americans poured in. And such was their hunger for land that they took the land—stole Sutter's land, Guerrero's land, took the grants and broke them up and growled and quarreled over them, those frantic hungry men; and they guarded with guns the land they had stolen. They put up houses and barns, they turned the earth and planted crops. And these things were possession, and possession was ownership.

The Mexicans were weak and fled. They could not resist, because they wanted nothing in the world as frantically as the Americans wanted land.

Then, with time, the squatters were no longer squatters, but owners; and their children grew up and had children on the land. And the hunger was gone from them, the feral hunger, the gnawing, tearing hunger for land, for water and earth and the good sky over it, for the green thrusting grass, for the swelling roots. They had these things so completely that they did not know about them any more. They had no more the stomach-tearing lust for a rich acre and a shining blade to plow it, for seed and a windmill beating its wings in the air. They arose in the dark no more to hear the sleepy birds' first chittering, and the morning wind around the house while they waited for the first light to go out to the dear acres. These things were lost, and crops were reckoned in dollars, and land was valued by principal plus interest, and crops were bought and sold before they were planted. Then crop failure, drought, and flood were no longer little deaths within life, but simple losses of money. And all their love was thinned with money, and all their fierceness dribbled away in interest until they were no longer farmers at all, but little shopkeepers of crops, little manufacturers who must sell before they can make. Then those farmers who were not good shopkeepers lost their land to good shopkeepers. No matter how clever, how loving a man might be with earth and growing things, he could not survive if he were not also a good shopkeeper. And as time went on, the business men had the farms, and the farms grew larger, but there were fewer of them.

Now farming became industry, and the owners followed Rome, although they did not know it. They imported slaves, although they did not call them slaves: Chinese, Japanese, Mexicans, Filipinos. They live on rice and beans, the business men said. They don't need much. They wouldn't know what to do with good wages. Why, look how they live. Why, look what they eat. And if they get funny—deport them.

And all the time the farms grew larger and the owners fewer. And there were pitifully few farmers on the land any more. And the imported serfs were beaten and frightened and starved until some went home again, and some grew fierce and were killed or driven from the country. And the farms grew larger and the owners fewer.

And the crops changed. Fruit trees took the place of grain fields, and vegetables to feed the world spread out on the bottoms: lettuce, cauliflower, artichokes, potatoes—stoop crops. A man may stand to use a scythe, a plow, a pitchfork; but he must crawl like a bug between the rows of lettuce, he must bend his back and pull his long bag between the cotton rows, he must go on his knees like a penitent across a cauliflower patch.

And it came about that owners no longer worked on their farms. They farmed on paper; and they forgot the land, the smell, the feel of it, and remembered only that they owned it, remembered only what they gained and lost by it. And some of the farms grew so large that one man could not even conceive of them any more, so large that it took batteries of book-keepers to keep track of interest and gain and loss; chemists to test the soil, to replenish; straw bosses to see that the stooping men were moving along the rows as swiftly as the material of their bodies could stand. Then such a farmer really became a storekeeper, and kept a store. He paid the men, and sold them food, and took the money back. And after a while he did not pay the men at all, and saved bookkeeping. These farms gave food on credit. A man might work and feed himself; and when the work was done, he might find that he owed money to the company. And the owners not only did not work the farms any more, many of them had never seen the farms they owned.

And then the dispossessed were drawn west—from Kansas, Oklahoma, Texas, New Mexico; from Nevada and Arkansas families, tribes, dusted out, tractored out. Carloads, caravans, homeless and hungry; twenty thousand and fifty thousand and a hundred thousand and two hundred thousand. They streamed over the mountains, hungry and restless—restless as ants, scurrying to find work to do—to lift, to push, to pull, to pick, to cut—anything, any burden to bear, for food. The kids are hungry. We got no place to live. Like ants scurrying for work, for food, and most of all for land.

We ain't foreign. Seven generations back Americans, and beyond that Irish, Scotch, English, German. One of our folks in the Revolution, an' they was lots of our folks in the Civil War—both sides. Americans.

They were hungry, and they were fierce. And they had hoped to find a home, and they found only hatred. Okies—the owners hated them because the owners knew they were soft and the Okies strong, that they were fed and the Okies hungry; and perhaps the owners had heard from their grandfathers how easy it is to steal land from a soft man if you are fierce and hungry and armed. The owners hated them. And in the towns, the store-keepers hated them because they had no money to spend. There is no shorter path to a storekeeper's contempt, and all his admirations are exactly opposite. The town men, little bankers, hated Okies because there was nothing to gain from them. They had nothing. And the laboring people hated Okies because a hungry man must work, and if he must work, if he has to work, the wage payer automatically gives him less for his work; and then no one can get more.

And the dispossessed, the migrants, flowed into California, two hundred and fifty thousand, and three hundred thousand. Behind them new tractors were going on the land and the tenants were being forced off. And new waves were on the way, new waves of the dispossessed and the home-less, hardened, intent, and dangerous.

And while the Californians wanted many things, accumulation, social success, amusement, luxury, and a curious banking security, the new bar-barians wanted only two things—land and food; and to them the two were one. And whereas the wants of the Californians were nebulous and unde-fined, the wants of the Okies were beside the roads, lying there to be seen and coveted: the good fields with water to be dug for, the good green fields, earth to crumble experimentally in the hand, grass to smell, oaten stalks to chew until the sharp sweetness was in the throat. A man might look at a fal-low field and know, and see in his mind that his own bending back and his own straining arms would bring the cabbages into the light, and the golden eating corn, the turnips and carrots.

And a homeless hungry man, driving the roads with his wife beside him and his thin children in the back seat, could look at the fallow fields which might produce food but not profit, and that man could know how a fallow field is a sin and the unused land a crime against the thin children. And such a man drove along the roads and knew temptation at every field, and knew the lust to take these fields and make them grow strength for his children and a little comfort for his wife. The temptation was before him always. The fields goaded him, and the company ditches with good water flowing were a goad to him.

And in the south he saw the golden oranges hanging on the trees, the little golden oranges on the dark green trees; and guards with shotguns pa-trolling the lines so a man might not pick an orange for a thin child, oranges to be dumped if the price was low.

He drove his old car into a town. He scoured the farms for work. Where can we sleep the night? 15

Well, there's Hooverville on the edge of the river. There's a whole raft of Okies there.

He drove his old car to Hooverville. He never asked again, for there was a Hooverville on the edge of every town.

The rag town lay close to water; and the houses were tents, and weed-thatched enclosures, paper houses, a great junk pile. The man drove his family in and became a citizen of Hooverville—always they were called Hooverville. The man put up his own tent as near to water as he could get; or if he had no tent, he went to the city dump and brought back cartons and built a house of corrugated paper. And when the rains came the house melted and washed away. He settled in Hooverville and he scoured the countryside for work, and the little money he had went for gasoline to look for work. In the evening the men gathered and talked together. Squatting on their hams they talked of the land they had seen.

There's thirty thousan' acres, out west of here. Layin' there. Jesus, what I could do with that, with five acres of that! Why, hell, I'd have ever'thing to eat.

Notice one thing? They ain't no vegetables nor chickens nor pigs at the farms. They raise one thing—cotton, say, or peaches, or lettuce. 'Nother place'll be all chickens. They buy the stuff they could raise in the dooryard.

Jesus, what I could do with a couple pigs!

Well, it ain't yourn, an' it ain't gonna be yourn.

What we gonna do? The kids can't grow up this way.

In the camps the word would come whispering, There's work at Shafter. And the cars would be loaded in the night, the highways crowded—a gold rush for work. At Shafter the people would pile up, five times too many to do the work. A gold rush for work. They stole away in the night, frantic for work. And along the roads lay the temptations, the fields that could bear food.

That's owned. That ain't our'n.

Well, maybe we could get a little piece of her. Maybe—a little piece. Right down there—a patch. Jimson weed now. Christ, I could git enough potatoes off'n that little patch to feed my whole family!

It ain't our'n. It got to have Jimson weeds.

Now and then a man tried; crept on the land and cleared a piece, trying like a thief to steal a little richness from the earth. Secret gardens hidden in the weeds. A package of carrot seeds and a few turnips. Planted potato skins, crept out in the evening secretly to hoe in the stolen earth.

Leave the weeds around the edge—then nobody can see what we're a-doin'. Leave some weeds, big tall ones, in the middle.

Secret gardening in the evenings, and water carried in a rusty can.

And then one day a deputy sheriff: Well, what you think you're doin'?

I ain't doin' no harm.

I had my eye on you. This ain't your land. You're trespassing.

The land ain't plowed, an' I ain't hurtin' it none.

You goddamned squatters. Pretty soon you'd think you owned it. You'd be sore as hell. Think you owned it. Get off now.

And the little green carrot tops were kicked off and the turnip greens trampled. And then the Jimson weed moved back in. But the cop was right. A crop raised—why, that makes ownership. Land hoed and the carrots eaten—a man might fight for land he's taken food from. Get him off quick! He'll think he owns it. He might even die fighting for the little plot among the Jimson weeds.

Did ya see his face when we kicked them turnips out? Why, he'd kill a fella soon's he'd look at him. We got to keep these here people down or they'll take the country. They'll take the country.

Outlanders, foreigners.

Sure, they talk the same language, but they ain't the same. Look how they live. Think any of us folks'd live like that? Hell, no!

In the evenings, squatting and talking. And an excited man: Whyn't   40
twenty of us take a piece of lan'? We got guns. Take it an' say, "Put us off if you can." Whyn't we do that?

They'd jus' shoot us like rats.

Well, which'd you ruther be, dead or here? Under groun' or in a house all made of gunny sacks? Which'd you ruther for your kids, dead now or dead in two years with what they call malnutrition? Know what we et all week? Biled nettles an' fried dough! Know where we got the flour for the dough? Swep' the floor of a boxcar.

Talking in the camps, and the deputies, fat-assed men with guns slung on fat hips, swaggering through the camps: Give 'em somepin to think about. Got to keep 'em in line or Christ only knows what they'll do! Why, Jesus, they're as dangerous as niggers in the South! If they ever get together there ain't nothin' that'll stop 'em.

Quote: In Lawrenceville a deputy sheriff evicted a squatter, and the squatter resisted, making it necessary for the officer to use force. The eleven-year-old son of the squatter shot and killed the deputy with a .22 rifle.

Rattlesnakes! Don't take chances with 'em, an' if they argue, shoot first. If a   45
kid'll kill a cop, what'll the men do? Thing is, get tougher'n they are. Treat 'em rough. Scare 'em.

What if they won't scare? What if they stand up and take it and shoot back? These men were armed when they were children. A gun is an extension of themselves. What if they won't scare? What if some time an army of them marches on the land as the Lombards did in Italy, as the Germans did on Gaul and the Turks did on Byzantium? They were land-hungry, ill-armed hordes too, and the legions could not stop them. Slaughter and terror did not stop them. How can you frighten a man whose hunger is not only in his own cramped stomach but in the wretched bellies of his children? You can't scare him—he has known a fear beyond every other.

In Hooverville the men talking: Grampa took his lan' from the Injuns.

Now, this ain't right. We're a-talkin' here. This here you're talkin' about is stealin'. I ain't no thief.

No? You stole a bottle of milk from a porch night before last. An' you stole some copper wire and sold it for a piece of meat.

Yeah, but the kids was hungry.   50

It's stealin', though.

Know how the Fairfiel' ranch was got? I'll tell ya. It was all gov'ment lan', an' could be took up. Ol' Fairfiel', he went into San Francisco to the bars, an' he got him three hunderd stew bums. Them bums took up the lan'. Fairfiel' kep' 'em in food an' whisky, an' then when they'd proved the lan', ol' Fairfiel' took it from 'em. He used to say the lan' cost him a pint of rotgut an acre. Would you say that was stealin'?

Well, it wasn't right, but he never went to jail for it.

No, he never went to jail for it. An' the fella that put a boat in a wagon an' made his report like it was all under water 'cause he went in a boat—he never went to jail neither. An' the fellas that bribed congressmen and the legislatures never went to jail neither.

All over the State, jabbering in the Hoovervilles.   55

And then the raids—the swoop of armed deputies on the squatters' camps. Get out. Department of Health orders. This camp is a menace to health.

Where we gonna go?

That's none of our business. We got orders to get you out of here. In half an hour we set fire to the camp.

They's typhoid down the line. You want ta spread it all over?

We got orders to get you out of here. Now get! In half an hour we burn   60 the camp.

In half an hour the smoke of paper houses, of weed-thatched huts, rising to the sky, and the people in their cars rolling over the highways, looking for another Hooverville.

And in Kansas and Arkansas, in Oklahoma and Texas and New Mexico, the tractors moved in and pushed the tenants out.

Three hundred thousand in California and more coming. And in California the roads full of frantic people running like ants to pull, to push, to lift, to work. For every manload to lift, five pairs of arms extended to lift it; for every stomachful of food available, five mouths open.

And the great owners, who must lose their land in an upheaval, the great owners with access to history, with eyes to read history and to know the great fact: when property accumulates in too few hands it is taken away. And that companion fact: when a majority of the people are hungry and cold they will take by force what they need. And the little screaming fact that sounds through all history: repression works only to strengthen and knit the repressed. The great owners ignored the three cries of history. The land fell into fewer hands, the number of the dispossessed increased, and every effort of the great owners was directed at repression. The money was spent for arms, for gas to protect the great holdings, and spies were sent to catch the murmuring of revolt so that it might be stamped out. The changing economy was ignored, plans for the change ignored; and only means to destroy revolt were considered, while the causes of revolt went on.

The tractors which throw men out of work, the belt lines which carry   65 loads, the machines which produce, all were increased; and more and more families scampered on the highways, looking for crumbs from the great holdings, lusting after the land beside the roads. The great owners formed associations for protection and they met to discuss ways to intimidate, to kill, to gas. And always they were in fear of a principal—three hundred thousand—if they ever move under a leader—the end. Three hundred thousand, hungry and miserable; if they ever know themselves, the land will be theirs and all the gas, all the rifles in the world won't stop them. And the great owners, who had become through their holdings both more and less than men, ran to their destruction, and used every means that in the long run would destroy them. Every little means, every violence, every raid on a Hooverville, every deputy swaggering through a ragged camp put off the day a little and cemented the inevitability of the day.

The men squatted on their hams, sharp-faced men, lean from hunger and hard from resisting it, sullen eyes and hard jaws. And the rich land was around them.

D'ja hear about the kid in that fourth tent down?

No, I jus' come in.

Well, that kid's been a-cryin' in his sleep an' a-rollin' in his sleep. Them folks thought he got worms. So they give him a blaster, an' he died. It was what they call black-tongue the kid had. Comes from not gettin' good things to eat.

Poor little fella.   70

Yeah, but them folks can't bury him. Got to go to the county stone orchard.

Well, hell.

And hands went into pockets and little coins came out. In front of the tent a little heap of silver grew. And the family found it there.

Our people are good people; our people are kind people. Pray God some day kind people won't all be poor. Pray God some day a kid can eat.

And the associations of owners knew that some day the praying would   75 stop.

And there's the end.

Understanding the Text

1. Summarize in your own words the transformation, experienced by the Americans who poured into California after it was taken from Mexico, from "squatters" to "shopkeepers" (para. 3).

2. Why did the "owners" (para. 4) of California hate and fear the Okies?

3. What natural and economic forces produced what Steinbeck calls "three hundred thousand" "dispossessed" (para. 11) Americans?

4. How does Steinbeck use repetition and parallelism to convey his ideas?

5. What, does Steinbeck predict, will be the result of the conflict between the "owners" (para. 64) and the Okies?

Exploring and Debating the Issues

1. *The Grapes of Wrath* is considered a classic exploration of the pursuit of the California dream. In this excerpt, what does the California dream mean to the Okies?

2. Today, controversy over immigration to California usually presumes racial conflict as well. How does the Okies' experience complicate the presumption that anti-immigration sentiment is necessarily racist?

3. In this selection, Steinbeck writes about the 1930s. In an essay, compare and contrast his picture of immigrant life with that presented in William Langeweische's "Invisible Men" (p. 99). Be sure to note both similarities and differences.

4. One of Steinbeck's predictions is that repression inevitably breeds revolution. In class, discuss whether the years since the 1930s have borne out his prediction.

YEH LING-LING

The Welcome Mat Is Threadbare

How spacious is the California dream? In this op-ed piece from the *Los Angeles Times,* published in 1994, **Yeh Ling-Ling** (b. 1953) argues that even the best of visions has its limits. A first-generation immigrant from Vietnam, she presents a sobering vision of an increasingly overpopulated America, focusing on immigration as a primary contributor to overcrowding in California and the rest of the nation. Ling-Ling received her B.A. from the University of Paris, with a double major in Chinese-French and law. She is the California outreach coordinator for Population-Environment Balance—a Washington, D.C.–based environmental organization—and she resides in northern California.

When the Statue of Liberty was erected in 1886, this country had 60 million people and plenty of resources. Today, the United States has 260 million residents, of whom 37 million are poor, 8.7 million unemployed, more than 35 million without health insurance, hundreds of thousands homeless. We have a $4.5 trillion national debt. Our schools are overcrowded and underfunded and our freeways more congested than ever.

Seeing this nation in distress, the Clinton administration promises that it will provide health care to all Americans, cut our welfare rolls, put our unemployed back to work, trim our national debt, and improve our public schools. Yet how can these goals be achieved without first controlling the population growth in this country?

I am a first-generation immigrant. I also have ten years' experience as an immigration paralegal. I recently joined the staff of Population-Environment Balance out of a recognition that the United States must encourage a replacement-level fertility rate of 2.1 or lower, concurrently adopt a replacement-level immigration policy of 200,000 people a year, and enforce our immigration laws. These measures are necessary to protect the quality of life of Americans of all racial backgrounds.

Immigration contributes nearly 50 percent of U.S. population growth, considering immigrants' higher-than-average fertility rates. Every year,

about 1 million immigrants enter the United States legally, while an estimated 300,000 arrive and stay illegally. The projected cost of providing universal health care to all existing Americans and legal immigrants is already
alarming. Who will finance the cost of future legal immigrants and their
U.S.-born children?

The usage of welfare by elderly resident aliens, not including natural-   5
ized citizens, increased 400 percent from 1982 to 1992. In 1992 alone, more
than 90,000 legal immigrants age fifty-five and over entered the United
States. If we continue to admit elderly immigrants at this rate, how can we
keep our welfare and Medicare rolls from soaring?

Almost every week, we hear about thousands of our workers losing their
jobs. Yet in 1992, more than 750,000 legal immigrants of working age were
admitted to this country. In addition, we admit annually more than 60,000
foreign professionals on extended work visas. Many of these "temporary
workers" enter skilled occupations, such as computer programming and
engineering, where there have been massive layoffs. If the United States
continues with an immigration policy that operates as if we had a labor
shortage, how can we expect unemployed Americans and welfare recipients
to find jobs? Donald Huddle of Rice University estimates that 2 million
American workers were displaced by 1992 as a result of immigration since
1970, at a cost of $11.9 billion paid to U.S. workers in unemployment and
other benefits. Huddle also estimates that in 1992 alone, immigrants used
services costing $42.5 billion in excess of taxes they paid.

The economy of the past two hundred years was mostly labor-
intensive. With advances in technology, our economy now requires highly
skilled workers to prosper. Yet nearly two-thirds of the legal immigrants entering this country every year are low-skilled. Half of them enter occupations that are disappearing, where they compete mostly with poor minority
workers.

This country does not even have the resources to provide an adequate
education for current residents so that they may acquire the necessary skills
to help the United States remain competitive. Where are we going to find
tax dollars to educate the hundreds of thousands of legal immigrant children we invite to this country every year?

Even if all newcomers were to bring economic assets to this country,
how can a state like California, which absorbs almost half of the U.S. immigrant population, deal with the growing problems such as water shortages
and farmland loss? Nationally, an average of 1.5 million acres of arable land
are lost annually to erosion and development due to rapid population
growth. Our underground aquifers are being depleted 25 percent faster
than the recharge rates.

Senator Alan Simpson (Republican, Wyoming) has introduced a bill[1] to   10
reduce the legal immigration ceiling to a base figure of 500,000 a year — a

---

[1]This bill was not passed into law. [Eds.]

commendable action, but the ceiling should be much lower. Given our finite fiscal and natural resources, we must aim for an all-inclusive ceiling — legal immigration, amnesty, refugees, etc. — of 200,000 a year.

In opinion polls, the majority of Americans, including 78 percent of Latino Americans, say they support a reduction in immigration, legal as well as illegal. Until our national leaders recognize that our current level of immigration far exceeds this country's carrying capacity, no real remedies to America's problems will be found.

Understanding the Text

1. Summarize Ling-Ling's case against unrestricted immigration to the United States.
2. Why, according to Ling-Ling, should California restrict immigration even if immigrants bring economic assets with them?
3. In Ling-Ling's view, how have immigrants affected American workers?
4. Why does Ling-Ling pick 200,000 as the level of immigration that she finds acceptable?

Exploring and Debating the Issues

1. Ling-Ling uses statistics and rhetorical questions throughout her essay. In class, discuss the effect of these strategies on the persuasiveness of her argument. What sorts of evidence would you need to gather to refute her position?
2. Write an essay in which you support or refute the proposition that Ling-Ling's status as a first-generation immigrant disqualifies her from arguing for immigration restrictions.
3. Assuming the validity of Ling-Ling's information, what immigration policy would you recommend for California? Write an essay explaining and defending your recommended policy. Share your essay with your class.
4. What implications does Ling-Ling's argument have for the future of the California dream? To support your position, you may draw on any of the selections in this chapter or in Chapter 1, "California Dreaming: Myths of the Golden Land."
5. Assume the role of a recent immigrant to California, and write a letter in response to Ling-Ling's argument. To develop your ideas, you may want to consult Richard Rodriguez's "Proofs" (p. 34), Nancy Wride's "Vietnamese Youths No Longer Look Homeward" (p. 113), or Ramón "Tianguis" Pérez's "Ripon" (p. 108).

RUBÉN MARTINEZ

Refine Immigration Policy to Reflect History and the Moment We Live In

America is a land of immigrants, so what's all the fuss about immigration today? To restrict immigration and to deny undocumented immigrants social welfare benefits such as health care and education, **Rubén Martinez** contends, is to deny our own history. Arguing for open borders in an era of global economics, Martinez says that Americans should embrace, not repel, the immigrant, as the immigrant has already embraced America. Born of Mexican and Salvadoran parents, Martinez is Los Angeles bureau chief for the Pacific News Service and cohost of a public affairs program, *Life and Times.* A poet, performer, and journalist, Martinez has many publications, including *The Other Side: Fault Lines, Guerilla Saints, and the True Heart of Rock 'n' Roll* (1992).

A merica, the free and democratic country whose moral strength made it the victor of the Cold War, now wants to enforce its immigration laws by the most inhumane means possible. Deny illegals health care. Deny them education. Deny them nonemergency aid after the Northridge quake. Indeed, Representative Dana Rohrbacher (Republican, Huntington Beach) even proposed that illegals be deported when they showed up at earthquake aid centers.

The debate over immigration appears all but over: Democrats and Republicans alike leap-frog over each other to propose ever more restrictionist policies. Five years after the fall of the Berlin Wall, are we on the verge of erecting a similar wall on our southern border?

The consensus that there is an "illegal" problem even includes Latino elected officials, who late last year formed Proponents for Responsible Immigration Debate and Education (PRIDE) in an attempt to counter anti-immigrant proposals. The coalition has been largely silent about the future of that portion of the Latino population who can't prove legal residency. Rather than advocate for the undocumented, a mission most consider political suicide, PRIDE officials have generally lauded the Clinton administration's new immigration policy because it appropriates money for the naturalization of "legal" residents.

Yet this obsession with "legality" in the immigration debate misses the point. Immigration policy, in practice and policy, is out of touch with both history and the moment in which we live. In an era of globalized capital, the right of people to freely move across frontiers must also be recognized.

California cannot escape the consequences of this emerging era. One day soon, the state will have an Asian and Latino majority. Those who fear a hostile takeover by a cultural "other" fail to see that immigration to America cuts both ways: The "immigrant" *and* the "native" are remade, and both become the stronger for it. The American spirit grows by embracing the "other" and by the "other" embracing it.

Immigration restrictionists would stop this acculturation. The truth is, the immigrant has already embraced us—in some cases literally. Think of

5

the Salvadoran or Mexican nannies who help working moms. Think of the food on the dinner table each night: brown hands grew and picked it from California soil. Walk city sidewalks, where vendors strive to resurrect the moribund American dream. Ride public buses, in which immigrants travel to their jobs in the predawn hours.

No, it's not some mysterious "other" that has "invaded" California. Rather, it is the immigrant come to remind us of what America really is: a land of optimism, a culture born from the cross-germination of its member cultures. To wall off the immigration from the south and from Asia would be to deny America its second great immigrant transfusion.

Not that this cultural and economic rejuvenation has ever been easy. Nativists and their immigrant-advocate counterparts have long clashed over who to allow in—and who to keep out of—the country. It is a paradox at the heart of American identity: we are a country of immigrants, yet we hate immigrants.

In the restrictionist political lexicon, the argument often comes down to this: "illegals" are in violation of the law and are thus not entitled to the rights and benefits enjoyed by "legal" citizens. But there is another—more important—factor at work here: whether or not an immigrant is called an "illegal" depends on economics—and political opportunism.

When nativist sentiments focused on Asians and non–Anglo-Saxon Europeans, the border with Mexico scarcely existed. Mexicans arrived in the Southwest in great numbers during and after the Revolution of 1910, but rarely were they divided into legals and illegals. The Border Patrol's mission was largely symbolic. Agents would ask migrants to show both hands—if no fingers were missing, you were allowed to cross into America. (Mutilated hands, it was assumed, would mean a life of begging instead of working in the fields.) It wasn't until the Great Depression that America decided there were too many Mexicans here; the repatriation sent hundreds of thousands of them back to Mexico. 10

When California agribusiness needed Mexicans during World War II, they weren't called illegals. But Mexicans deported after the war, as part of Operation Wetback, were.

Now, in the slow-growth 1990s, immigrants are again branded "illegal." The problem is that because of exploitation and the way immigration laws are enforced, Latino immigrants are often denied the upward mobility that other groups enjoy. For months, politicians have relied on a handful of studies that claim immigrants soak up more in social services than they contribute in taxes. But new research from the Urban Institute shows that immigrant labor may actually be contributing more than it is taking away.

"Immigrants in California are not the reason the economy is doing badly," says Jeffrey Passel of the Urban Institute. "It has much more to do with the defense industry cutbacks and the flow of federal money to and from California." Passel's data also show that "legal" immigrants contribute more to the overall surplus than "illegals" do, but this doesn't necessarily buttress a restrictionist immigration policy.

Legal residents, who have been in the country longer, tend to have higher levels of education and income. But these "legals" were once recently arrived—indeed, millions were once "illegals." If given half the chance, today's undocumented could become a "legal" and productive community.

"Our economy needs that labor, there's no question about it," says 15 David Hayes-Bautista of the Alta California Research Center. Of the top five economic sectors in California—agriculture, apparel, entertainment, high tech, and construction—three of the five "depend almost exclusively on immigrant labor," he says.

Just as the contributions of the undocumented-immigrant working class are absent from the immigration debate, so is a serious discussion of alternatives to the restrictionist frenzy. But there are options.

A more enlightened immigration policy must address several issues. The "illegal" problem can be dealt with by establishing a new "amnesty" similar to that implemented in 1986. It should target long-term residents, many of whom have established deep roots here. A significant portion are parents of citizen-children who identify more with America than with the old country. This would not be a "gift" to the immigrant. Rather, it would be past-due recognition of immigrants' role in our economic recovery.

But there is also the "floating" population that crosses back and forth across the border, spending several months working in the fields or in the cities, then returning to Mexico, usually at the end of the year. A new *bracero*-like program to recognize this migrant labor force is necessary. Applicants would be granted temporary residency status, which would entitle them to receive only the most basic social services, such as emergency medical care.

Political issues must be dealt with as well. Because political representation for immigrants, in general, and Latinos, in particular, is inadequate—political scientist Jorge Castañeda calls the situation in California an "electoral apartheid"—a modified electoral scheme should be instituted that would allow legal residents who are not yet citizens to vote in local elections.

Finally, we need to invest more in English-as-a-second-language and cit- 20 izenship classes so immigrants can join the political and cultural mainstream.

These programs are not merely "proimmigrant." They promote middle-class interests as well. To have a workforce that is well educated and healthy—and therefore more productive—is something that contributes to the good of all. It is an investment in our future.

It will take courage to live through this time of transition in California. But the work is already half-done: the immigrant has already embraced us.

Understanding the Text

1. How have the definitions of "legal" and "illegal" (para. 9) immigration changed over the years, according to Martinez?

2. What, according to Martinez, is the position of Proponents for Responsible Immigration Debate and Education (PRIDE)?

3. What does Martinez mean by his statement that "the American spirit grows by embracing the 'other' and by the 'other' embracing it" (para. 5)?

4. Summarize in your own words Martinez's recommendations for an enlightened immigration policy.

Exploring and Debating the Issues

1. Write an argument that supports, refutes, or complicates Martinez's statement, "We are a country of immigrants, yet we hate immigrants" (para. 8). To support your position, you may draw on any of the selections in this chapter, in addition to your own observations and experiences.

2. In your journal, explore Martinez's suggestion that noncitizens should be given the right to vote. In small groups, share your journal entries and compare your responses to his proposal.

3. Write an essay in which you argue for or against Martinez's recommendation for a new amnesty program similar to the 1986 program. To develop your ideas, you may want to consult Yeh Ling-Ling's "The Welcome Mat Is Threadbare" (p. 73).

4. Given California's recovery from the economic recession earlier in the decade, do you agree or disagree with David Hayes-Bautista's claim that "our economy needs...labor, there's no question about it" (para. 15)? Write an essay in which you defend your position. To develop your ideas, you may wish to consult Jack Miles's "Blacks vs. Browns" (p. 241) or John Cassidy's "The Comeback" (p. 274).

5. Yeh Ling-Ling ("The Welcome Mat Is Threadbare," p. 73) argues that immigration to the United States should be restricted. In class, form two teams and stage a debate between Ling-Ling and Martinez in which you address this question: Should immigration be limited or welcomed in California?

CONNIE YOUNG YU

The World of Our Grandmothers

Chinese women immigrating to California at the turn of the century often had to overcome both the restrictive traditions of Old World Chinese culture and the nativist hostility of the New World to which they came. **Connie Young Yu** tells the moving story of such women here, focusing on the experiences of her own grandmother, whose struggles to establish herself and her family in California were eventually rewarded. An historian and biographer of Chinese Americans, Yu's works include *Profiles in Excellence* (1986) and *Chinatown, San Jose USA* (1993).

In Asian America there are two kinds of history. The first is what is written about us in various old volumes on immigrants and echoed in textbooks, and the second is our own oral history, what we learn in the family chain of generations. We are writing this oral history ourselves. But as we research the factual background of our story, we face the dilemma of finding sources. Worse than burning the books is not being included in the record at all, and in American history—traditionally viewed from the white male perspective—minority women have been virtually ignored. Certainly the accomplishments and struggles of early Chinese immigrants, men as well as women, have been obscured.

Yet for a period in the development of the West, Chinese immigration was a focus of prolonged political and social debate and a subject of daily news. When I first began searching into the background of my people, I read this nineteenth-century material with curious excitement, grateful for any information on Chinese immigration.

Looking for the history of Chinese pioneer women, I began with the first glimpses of Chinese in America—newspaper accounts found in bound volumes of the *Alta California* in the basement of a university library. For Chinese workers, survival in the hostile and chaotic world of Gum San, or Gold Mountain, as California was called by Chinese immigrants, was perilous and a constant struggle, leaving little time or inclination for reflection or diary writing. So for a look into the everyday life of early arrivals from China, we have only the impressions of white reporters on which to depend.

The newspapers told of the comings and goings of "Chinamen," their mining activities, new Chinese settlements, their murders by claimjumpers, and assaults by whites in the city. An item from 17 August, 1855, reported a "disgraceful outrage": Mr. Ho Alum setting his watch under a street clock when a man called Thomas Field walked up and deliberately dashed the time-piece to the pavement. "Such unprovoked assaults upon unoffending Chinamen are not of rare occurrence...." On the same day the paper also reported the suicide of a Chinese prostitute. In this item no name, details, or commentary were given, only a stark announcement. We can imagine the tragic story behind it: the short miserable life of a young girl sold into slavery by her impoverished parents and taken to Gum San to be a prostitute in a society of single men.

An early history of this period, *Lights and Shades in San Francisco* by   5
B. E. Lloyd (1878), devoted ten chapters to the life of California Chinese, describing in detail "the subjects of the Celestial Kingdom." Chinese women, however, are relegated to a single paragraph:

> Females are little better than slaves. They are looked upon as merchantable property, and are bought and sold like any other article of traffic, though their value is not generally great. A Chinese woman never gains any distinction until after death.... Considering the humble position the women occupy in China, and the hard life they therefore lead, it would perhaps be better (certainly more merciful) were they all slain in infancy, and better still, were they never born.[1]

[1]B. E. Lloyd, *Lights and Shades in San Francisco* (San Francisco: San Francisco Press, 1878).

Public opinion, inflamed by lurid stories of Chinese slave girls, agreed with this odious commentary. The only Chinese women whose existence American society acknowledged were the prostitutes who lived miserable and usually short lives. Senate hearings on Chinese immigration in 1876 resounded with harangues about prostitutes and slave girls corrupting the morals of young white boys. "The Chinese race is debauched," claimed one lawyer arguing for the passage of the Chinese Exclusion Law: "They bring no decent women with them." This stigma on the Chinese immigrant woman remained for many decades, causing unnecessary hardship for countless wives, daughters, and slave girls.

Chinese American society finally established itself as families appeared, just as they did in the white society of the forty-niners who arrived from the East Coast without bringing "decent women" with them. Despite American laws intended to prevent the "settlement" of Chinese, Chinese women did make the journey and endured the isolation and hostility, braving it for future generations here.

Even though Chinese working men were excluded from most facets of American society and their lives were left unrecorded, their labors bespoke their existence — completed railroads, reclaimed lands, and a myriad of new industries. The evidence of women's lives seems less tangible. Perhaps the record of their struggles to immigrate and overcome discriminatory barriers is their greatest legacy. Tracing that record therefore becomes a means of recovering our history.

Our grandmothers are our historical links. As a fourth-generation Chinese American on my mother's side, and a third-generation on my father's, I grew up hearing stories about ancestors coming from China and going back and returning again. Both of my grandmothers, like so many others, spent a lot of time waiting in China.

My father's parents lived with us when I was growing up, and through   10
them I absorbed a village culture and the heritage of my pioneer Chinese family. In the kitchen my grandmother told repeated stories of coming to America after waiting for her husband to send for her. (It took sixteen years before Grandfather could attain the status of merchant and only then arrange for her passage to this country.)[2] She also told stories from the village about bandits, festivals, and incidents showing the tyranny of tradition. For example, Grandma was forbidden by her mother-in-law to return to her own village to visit her mother: A married woman belonged solely within the boundaries of her husband's world.

Sometimes I was too young to understand or didn't listen, so my mother — who knew all the stories by heart — told me those stories again later. We heard over and over how lucky Grandpa was to have come to

[2]Under the Chinese Exclusion Act of 1882, Chinese laborers could no longer immigrate to America. Until the act was repealed in 1943, only merchants, diplomats, students, and visitors were allowed to enter.

America when he was eleven—just one year before the gate was shut by the exclusion law banning Chinese laborers. Grandpa told of his many jobs washing dishes, making bricks, and working on a strawberry farm. Once, while walking outside Chinatown, he was stoned by a group of whites and ran so fast he lost his cap. Grandma had this story to tell of her anger and frustration: "While I was waiting in the immigration shed,[3] Grandpa sent in a box of *dim sum*.[4] I was still waiting to be released. I would have jumped in the ocean if they decided to deport me." A woman in her position was quite helpless, but she still had her pride and was not easily pacified. "I threw the box of *dim sum* out the window."

Such was the kind of history I absorbed. I regret deeply that I was too young to have asked the questions about the past that I now want answered; all my grandparents are now gone. But I have another chance to recover some history from my mother's side. Family papers, photographs, old trunks that have traveled across the ocean several times filled with clothes, letters, and mementos provide a documentary on our immigration. My mother—and some of my grandmother's younger contemporaries—fill in the narrative.

A year before the Joint Special Committee of Congress to investigate Chinese immigration met in San Francisco in 1876, my great-grandmother, Chin Shee, arrived to join her husband, Lee Wong Sang, who had come to America a decade earlier to work on the transcontinental railroad. Chin Shee arrived with two brides who had never seen their husbands. Like her own, their marriages had been arranged by their families. The voyage on the clipper ship was rough and long. Seasick for weeks, rolling back and forth as she lay in the bunk, Chin Shee lost most of her hair. The two other women laughed, "Some newlywed you'll make!" But the joke was on them as they mistakenly set off with the wrong husbands, the situation realized only when one man looked at his bride's normal-sized feet and exclaimed, "But the letter described my bride as having bound feet!" Chin Shee did not have her feet bound because she came from a peasant family. But her husband did not seem to care about that nor that the back of her head was practically bald. He felt himself fortunate just to be able to bring his wife to Gum San.

Chin Shee bore six children in San Francisco, where her husband assisted in the deliveries. They all lived in the rear of their grocery store, which also exported dried shrimp and seaweed to China. Great-Grandma seldom left home; she could count the number of times she went out. She and other Chinese wives did not appear in the streets even for holidays, lest they be looked upon as prostitutes. She took care of the children, made special cakes to sell on feast days, and helped with her husband's work. A photo-

[3]Between 1910 and 1940 Chinese immigrants arriving in the port of San Francisco were detained at the Angel Island Immigration Station to await physical examinations and interrogation to determine their right to enter this country. Prior to 1910 immigrants were detained in a building on the wharf known as "the shed."

[4]Chinese pastries.

graph of her shows a middle-aged woman with a kindly, but careworn face, wearing a very regal brocade gown and a long, beaded necklace. As a respectable, well-to-do Chinese wife in America, married to a successful Chinatown merchant, with children who were by birthright American citizens, she was a rarity in her day. (In contrast, in 1884 Mrs. Jew Lim, the wife of a laborer, sued in federal court to be allowed to join her husband but was denied and deported.)

In 1890 there were only 3,868 Chinese women among 103,620 Chinese males in America. Men such as Lee Yoke Suey, my mother's father, went to China to marry. He was one of Chin Shee's sons born in the rear of the grocery store, and he grew up learning the import and export trade. As a Gum San merchant, he had money and status and was able to build a fine house in Toishan. Not only did he acquire a wife but also two concubines. When his wife became very ill after giving birth to an infant who soon died, Yoke Suey was warned by his father that she was too weak to return to America with him. Reminding Yoke Suey of the harsh life in Gum San, he advised his son to get a new wife.

In the town of Foshan, not far from my grandfather's village, lived a girl who was recommended to him by his father's friend. Extremely capable, bright, and with some education, she was from a once prosperous family that had fallen on hard times. A plague had killed her two older brothers, and her heartbroken mother died soon afterwards. She was an excellent cook and took good care of her father, an herb doctor. Her name was Jeong Hing Tong, and she was pretty, with bound feet only three and a half inches long. Her father rejected the offer of the Lee family at first; he did not want his daughter to be a concubine, even to a wealthy Gum San merchant. But the elder Lee assured him this girl would be the wife, the one who would go to America with her husband.

So my maternal grandmother, bride of sixteen, went with my grandfather, then twenty-six, to live in America. Once in San Francisco, Grandmother lived a life of confinement, as did her mother-in-law before her. When she went out, even in Chinatown, she was ridiculed for her bound feet. People called out mockingly to her, "*Jhat!*" meaning bound. She tried to unbind her feet by soaking them every night and putting a heavy weight on each foot. But she was already a grown woman, and her feet were permanently stunted, the arches bent and the toes crippled. It was hard for her to stand for long periods of time, and she frequently had to sit on the floor to do her chores. My mother comments: "Tradition makes life so hard. My father traveled all over the world. There were stamps all over his passport — London, Paris — and stickers all over his suitcases, but his wife could not go into the street by herself."

Their first child was a girl, and on the morning of her month-old "red eggs and ginger party" the earth shook 8.3 on the Richter scale. Everyone in San Francisco, even Chinese women, poured out into the streets. My grandmother, babe in arms, managed to get a ride to Golden Gate Park on a horse-drawn wagon. Two other Chinese women who survived the earthquake recall the shock of suddenly being out in the street milling with thousands of people. The elderly goldsmith in a dimly lit Chinatown store had a twinkle in his eye when I asked him about the scene after the quake. "We all stared at the women because we so seldom saw them in the streets." The city was soon in flames. "We could feel the fire on our faces," recalls Lily Sung, who was seven at the time, "but my sister and I couldn't walk very fast because we had to escort this lady, our neighbor, who had bound feet." The poor woman kept stumbling and falling on the rubble and debris during their long walk to the Oakland-bound ferry.

That devastating natural disaster forced some modernity on the San Francisco Chinese community. Women had to adjust to the emergency and makeshift living conditions and had to work right alongside the men. Life in America, my grandmother found, was indeed rugged and unpredictable.

As the city began to rebuild itself, she proceeded to raise a large family, bearing four more children. The only school in San Francisco admitting Chinese was the Oriental school in Chinatown. But her husband felt, as did most men of his class, that the only way his children could get a good education was for the family to return to China. So they lived in China and my grandfather traveled back and forth to the United States for his trade business. Then suddenly, at the age of forty-three, he died of an illness on board a ship returning to China. After a long and painful mourning, Grandmother decided to return to America with her brood of now seven children. That decision eventually affected immigration history.   20

At the Angel Island immigration station in San Francisco Bay, Grandmother went through a physical examination so thorough that even her teeth were checked to determine whether she was the age stated on her passport. The health inspector said she had filariasis, liver fluke, a common ailment of Asian immigrants which caused their deportation by countless numbers. The authorities thereby ordered Grandmother to be deported as well.

While her distraught children had to fend for themselves in San Francisco (my mother, then fifteen, and her older sister had found work in a sewing factory), a lawyer was hired to fight for Grandmother's release from the detention barracks. A letter addressed to her on Angel Island from her attorney, C. M. Fickert, dated 24 March 1924, reads: "Everything I can legitimately do will be done on your behalf. As you say, it seems most inhuman for you to be separated from your children who need your care. I am sorry that the immigration officers will not look at the human side of your case."

Times were tough for Chinese immigrants in 1924. Two years before, the federal government had passed the Cable Act, which provided that any woman born in the United States who married a man "ineligible for citizenship" (including the Chinese, whose naturalization rights had been eliminated by the Chinese Exclusion Act) would lose her own citizenship. So, for example, when American-born Lily Sung, whom I also interviewed, married a Chinese citizen she forfeited her birthright. When she and her four daughters tried to reenter the United States after a stay in China, they were denied permission. The immigration inspector accused her of "smuggling little girls to sell." The Cable Act was not repealed until 1930.

The year my grandmother was detained on Angel Island, a law had just taken effect that forbade all aliens ineligible for citizenship from landing in America.[5] This constituted a virtual ban on the immigration of all Chinese, including Chinese wives of U.S. citizens.

Waiting month after month in the bleak barracks, Grandmother heard   25 many heart-rending stories from women awaiting deportation. They spoke of the suicides of several despondent women who hanged themselves in the shower stalls. Grandmother could see the calligraphy carved on the walls by other detained immigrants, eloquent poems expressing homesickness, sorrow, and a sense of injustice.

Meanwhile, Fickert was sending telegrams to Washington (a total of ten the bill stated) and building up a case for the circuit court. Mrs. Lee, after all, was the wife of a citizen who was a respected San Francisco merchant, and her children were American citizens. He also consulted a medical authority to see about a cure for liver fluke.

My mother took the ferry from San Francisco twice a week to visit Grandmother and take her Chinese dishes such as salted eggs and steamed pork because Grandmother could not eat the beef stew served in the mess hall. Mother and daughter could not help crying frequently during their short visits in the administration building. They were under close watch of both a guard and an interpreter.

After fifteen months the case was finally won. Grandmother was easily cured of filariasis and was allowed—with nine months probation—to join her children in San Francisco. The legal fees amounted to $782.50, a fortune in those days.

In 1927 Dr. Frederick Lam in Hawaii, moved by the plight of Chinese families deported from the islands because of the liver fluke disease, worked to convince federal health officials that the disease was noncommunicable. He used the case of Mrs. Lee Yoke Suey, my grandmother, as a precedent for allowing an immigrant to land with such an ailment and thus succeeded in breaking down a major barrier to Asian immigration.

My most vivid memory of Grandmother Lee is when she was in her sev-   30 enties and studying for her citizenship. She had asked me to test her on the three branches of government and how to pronounce them correctly. I was a sophomore in high school and had entered the "What American Democracy Means to Me" speech contest of the Chinese American Citizens Alliance. When I said the words "judicial, executive, and legislative," I looked directly at my grandmother in the audience. She didn't smile, and afterwards, didn't comment much on my patriotic words. She had never told me about being on

[5]The Immigration Act of 1924 affected all Asians who sought to immigrate to the United States. Congress repealed the law as to Chinese in 1943, and then in 1952 through the McCarran-Walter Act as to other Asian ethnic groups.

Angel Island or about her friends losing their citizenship. It wasn't in my textbooks either. I may have thought she wanted to be a citizen because her sons and sons-in-law had fought for this country, and we lived in a land of freedom and opportunity, but my guess now is that she wanted to avoid any possible confrontation—even at her age—with immigration authorities. The bad laws had been repealed, but she wasn't taking any chances.

I think a lot about my grandmother now and can understand why, despite her quiet, elegant dignity, an aura of sadness always surrounded her. She suffered from racism in the new country, as well as from traditional cruelties in the old. We, her grandchildren, remember walking very slowly with her, escorting her to a family banquet in Chinatown, hating the stares of tourists at her tiny feet. Did she, I wonder, ever feel like the victim of a terrible hoax, told as a small weeping girl that if she tried to untie the bandages tightly binding her feet she would grow up ugly, unwanted, and without the comforts and privileges of the wife of a wealthy man?

We seemed so huge and clumsy around her—a small, slim figure always dressed in black. She exclaimed once that the size of my growing feet were "like boats." But she lived to see some of her granddaughters graduate from college and pursue careers and feel that the world she once knew with its feudal customs had begun to crumble. I wonder what she would have said of my own daughter who is now attending a university on an athletic scholarship. Feet like boats travel far?

I keep looking at the artifacts of the past: the photograph of my grandmother when she was an innocent young bride and the sad face in the news photo taken on Angel Island. I visit the immigration barracks from time to time, a weather-beaten wooden building with its walls marked by calligraphy bespeaking the struggles of our history. I see the view of sky and water from the window out of which my grandmother gazed. My mother told me how, after visiting hours, she would walk to the ferry and turn back to see her mother waving to her from this window. This image has been passed on to me like an heirloom of pain and of love. When I leave the building, emerging from the darkness into the glaring sunlight of the island, I too turn back to look at my grandmother's window.

Understanding the Text

1. According to Yu, what are the differences between written and oral history?
2. How did American writers depict the Chinese during the nineteenth century, in Yu's view?
3. Why does Yu choose to focus on her grandmother's stories rather than on her grandfather's tales?
4. What dual predicament did Chinese women face as immigrants in the New World?
5. Why did Yu's grandmother never tell her about her experiences on Angel Island?

Exploring and Debating the Issues

1. If your family immigrated to the United States within the last century or so, write your own family's immigrant narrative. Using Yu's essay as a model, you can base your narrative on interviews with relatives, on your memories of family stories, and on other documents or photographs.

2. Chinese women not only faced racism in America but also encountered new opportunities that are implicit in Yu's account. In an essay, evaluate the drawbacks and the benefits that immigration offered women such as Yu's grandmother.

3. Compare the decision of American authorities to detain Chinese victims of liver fluke disease with the detention of Japanese Americans during World War II (see Sue Kunitomi Embrey, "Manzanar," below). What does the forced isolation of these peoples suggest about American fears and attitudes toward Asians?

4. Compare Yu's response to her grandmother's immigration experiences with the responses the students interviewed by Nancy Wride have to their parents' immigration tales ("Vietnamese Youths No Longer Look Homeward," p. 113). How do you account for any differences you may observe?

SUE KUNITOMI EMBREY

Manzanar

In 1942, most of the Japanese American population of the United States, native born and immigrant alike, were rounded up and sent to detention camps for the duration of World War II. The camp at Manzanar in the Owens Valley just east of the Sierra Nevadas is probably the best known of such camps. In this interview, **Sue Kunitomi Embrey** (b. 1923), a "Nisei," or first-generation Japanese American, tells what it was like to be suddenly taken from her Los Angeles home and interned in Manzanar, where she eventually became a journalist. Embrey is a Nisei activist who has been a part of the eventual dedication of the Manzanar Camp as a National Park site. This 1973 interview was conducted by Professors Arthur A. Hansen, David A. Hacker, and David J. Bertagnoli as part of the Oral History Program at California State University, Fullerton.

Interviewee: Sue Kunitomi Embrey
Interviewers: Arthur A. Hansen, David A. Hacker, and David J. Bertagnoli
Subject: Nisei Activist
Date: August 24, 1973, and November 15, 1973

AH: This is an interview with Sue Kunitomi Embrey for the California State University, Fullerton, Japanese American Oral History Project, on August 24, 1973, and November 15, 1973, at the Asian American Studies

Center of the University of California, Los Angeles. The interviewers are Arthur A. Hansen, David A. Hacker, and David J. Bertagnoli. Could we begin the interview, Mrs. Embrey, by finding out some information about your personal and family background?

SE: I was born in Los Angeles, California, on January 6, 1923. My parents came from the same village in Okayama, which is in the southern part of Japan.

AH: Were your parents married in Japan before immigrating to this country?

SE: No, my mother was a picture bride.   5

AH: But had he seen her before he had seen her picture?

SE: Yes, he had seen her. They were sort of related. A couple days ago, when I was visiting my mother, she sat down and for some reason started to tell me her genealogy. She said, "Your father's father came from this place and my father came from there. And originally our *hon-ke,* which is the home base, is the same." So I guess they were distant, maybe second or third, cousins. They both had the same last name; probably, she said, they came from the same family tree....

AH: Do you know approximately when [your father] came to Los Angeles?

SE: It was around 1910, 1911, or so. Then my mother came over.

AH: About when was he married to your mother?   10

SE: Let's see, my oldest brother is about fifteen years older than I am, and he was born before World War I. So they must have been married around 1907 or 1908.

AH: How many children were there in the family?

SE: There were eight altogether. I was number six. I was the second daughter. I had four brothers and one sister above me. My Japanese name is an indication of how my father felt about a big family, because the character means "last child." That was going to be the end! It turned out that I have another younger sister and brother. My mother said that was why he picked that character for my name. And Sue is an English version of Sueko.

AH: Do you have any idea what your father was doing occupationally at the time you were born?

SE: He was running a small business, which he called a transfer and mov-   15
ing company. A lot of that was involved in Little Tokyo, where they moved people from one house to another or into the city from the country. Toward the end of 1937 and 1938, many people started going back to Japan. Those who had come as immigrants worked to return home because of a real possibility of a war between the United States and Japan. So my father did a lot of packing and shipping and taking crates and boxes to San Pedro Harbor, where the Japanese ships came

in. Many people took their American-born children with them. Toward the end of 1938, a week before Christmas, in fact, my father was returning home after delivering some flowers to a wedding out in the San Fernando Valley. We never found out what happened, but evidently the panel truck he was driving overturned, and he died of a skull fracture.

AH: So he died before the war.

SE: He died toward the end of 1938. So that left my mother with all these children. My two older brothers were working. But the rest of us were all in school.

AH: So you had your finances curtailed at that point then?

SE: Oh, yes. So she had to go out.... My father was not a very good businessman. He left a lot of uncollected bills, and she went out and collected them. She would say, "You owe me this. My husband is dead. I've got to take care of my kids." This was the first time my mother actually left the house to do anything in terms of business because she had been very involved in raising the kids.

AH: You mentioned the fact that a lot of people were, owing to the urgency of war, going back to Japan. There seems to have been a heavy traffic back and forth of Japanese Americans between here and Japan during the prewar period. It seems like a long and expensive trip. I wonder how that was financed.   20

SE: I don't know. It was an expensive trip, and I don't think people had much money. We lived in a two-story house, and the people upstairs were a young couple that had come from Japan and had two daughters. When we first moved there, we didn't even know that they had any children because the two daughters were being raised in Japan. The children came back just before the war. They acted like Japanese immigrants; they spoke no English, their life-style was very strange to us. Both of the parents were working and they must have sent money back. I never asked my father how much it cost. I sometimes used to go down with him to the harbor just to watch the departing ships. They used to throw colored tapes, and the band would play. It was kind of fun.

  Toward the end of 1937 it was getting so I was going to the harbor because a lot of my friends were leaving with their parents. They didn't really want to go, but they had no choice. They took a lot of stuff with them that they thought they couldn't get in Japan. My father used to pack and crate things in the garage next to our house, and I used to watch him. You know, they'd even take things like washing machines, ironing boards, and big washtubs. You just wondered where they got the money. I don't know if all of them were in business, but they might have sold their businesses and collected the money to finance their trip, because I'm sure it cost a fortune....

AH: Where did you go to school in Los Angeles when you were a girl?

SE: Well, I lived east of Little Tokyo and there was a little grammar school, the Amelia Street School, that went from kindergarten to the eighth grade and about 90 percent were Japanese kids. The rest of the students came from a few Chinese families and some Mexican American families. It was kind of an unusual school, and I guess I have always thought of school as being such a pleasant place. My kids tell me it isn't, and I am a little surprised. But we had a very good staff, I think, and they were always doing things. People say that things like Chicano studies or black studies are innovations in education. We had all that. You know, they used to bring Indians, and they'd have dances and we'd ask them questions. This was an elementary school. On May 5 there was Cinco de Mayo and Japanese Boys' Day, and they used to have people come in from the community or have kids from the school to do these programs. We actually had a cultural program all year round that emphasized the different ethnic groups. This was something that I found very unusual. I went back and asked the principal about it after she retired. That was in 1950 or 1951, right after my husband and I were married and we were still in touch with her. She said, "Well, the school board in Los Angeles had a very progressive board member." And evidently this district was under his jurisdiction, and he was very interested in innovative things, so that by the time this principal was assigned there, she was able to do all these things. Now, her comment to me was that when she was first assigned there—I guess my brothers had already finished grammar school and were in high school—she had never seen such a group of solemn-looking kids as she saw at that school. And she went from room to room on her first day, telling stories and funny jokes, hoping she'd get some smiles out of us. She said, "You were such a serious bunch of kids." She said it was really amazing compared to another school where she had been the principal. . . .

AH: What was your particular neighborhood like? What was Little Tokyo   25
      like at the time?

SE: Well, let's see. My block had a Japanese language school which, I guess, occupied half a block from one end to the other. The rest of the families were Japanese. And across the street there was an old Japanese hospital, and most of the people who lived around there were people who worked in the hospital—nurses and administrators. There was an old American Express garage and a factory that made caskets. The rest of the blocks around us, I would say within four or five blocks, were almost all Japanese. We had the only Japanese funeral parlor, the Fukui Mortuary, two blocks away; the Japanese hospital; the Japanese language school; Amelia Street School; and then on the other side of the grammar school, I think, were some Chinese families and Mexican American families. But living in between there were Mexican families, and most of them were, I would say, maybe third-generation.

AH: Was most of your social activity, then, carried on with people from the Japanese American community?

SE: Yes, most of our social activities centered around the Japanese school that we went to. We spent an hour every day after school. For instance, the lower grades' classes started after they were out at two o'clock, and ours started around four o'clock and went on to six.

AH: Was it exclusively a language school as the name suggests, or were there other things related to it?30

SE: No, there were other things that went on. We had an annual picnic,   30
and we had other cultural activities. They had people on a visit from Japan who might come and speak to the group.

AH: Did you resent going to it like some Nisei?

SE: Well, I went all the way through, almost to the twelfth grade. My mother says I was the only one who seemed to have any interest in the school. I finally dropped out around the middle part of that year because I was very involved in high school, and I would attend maybe twice a week. But I had a teacher who was bilingual. I think I was about a year older than a lot of the other kids in that class, and he said to me that he thought that my direction in life was going different from the others, that he didn't think I would be too happy within the Japanese community. Now where he got this impression, I don't know. But he said to me, "I don't think that you are intellectually tuned in with these kids in this school."

AH: This seems ironic since you were the one who was spending so much time in this language school.

SE: So much time, right. And I still remember all the characters. We had cultural activities that were designed around the annual picnics; they would have programs at the school, and they'd have movies for the kids. Of course, a lot of the movies were American movies, not exclusively Japanese ones. But I remember they had speakers. We used to have speech contests to see how well you could speak in Japanese. We had writing with the Japanese brush, not a lot of it, but we tried.

AH: Did the Japanese language teachers have status within the com-   35
munity?

SE: Yes, they did. You see, before the war, anything that happened in the community was community business. If there were any fights between groups of kids, the Japanese school principal, the chamber of commerce people, the church groups, and the leaders always got together to try and solve it. I remember a group of Chinese kids had a fight after school with a group of Japanese kids over the war in China—I think

Japan had sent in troops—and there was an uproar in the Japanese community. I remember the language school principal and all of them getting together and having a meeting to decide who was the instigator and what they could do to prevent things like this. First of all, they didn't want the police involved, and they didn't want the kids to get the reputation that they were rowdies or the *yo-go-re* type. That was the common term that was used. One of my brothers was involved in a fight in which he was very badly cut. He had gone in to help someone else. The fight was between a Kibei, who had just come from Japan, and a young boy who was almost like a brother to us and who lived on the same block. His father was a migrant worker and his mother had died, so this old couple had adopted him and we were almost like one family. He had gone to a restaurant to eat, and this Kibei had made some crack like, "What are you staring at me for?" They went out in the street and started fighting and the Kibei pulled a knife. And my brother, in trying to pull our friend away so he wouldn't get cut, was cut himself in the process. He was taken to the hospital, and then, of course, they had to make a police report. It happened at a time when the Japanese Chamber of Commerce was having a meeting, and all the leaders were coming out of this building and found this fight going on clear out in the street. The very next morning my mother got a call from the Japanese school principal. He wanted to know all the details. They asked her if she knew the name of the boy that had pulled the knife because they were going to talk to his parents about restraining him. They even talked later on about the possibility of sending him back to Japan so he would not be a problem in the community.

AH: Did you feel that the Kibei as a whole were a problem in the community?

SE: Well, a Kibei is a person who is born in the United States of Japanese parents but sent to Japan and raised, possibly by grandparents and uncles. So basically, their education is Japanese, and, I think, their outlook is Japanese. It's kind of sad because I think a lot of them never made the adjustment, although I know some who did adjust well. I know one fellow who came here before the war who went into the Army. He was bilingual, so he served with the military intelligence, and I guess it never occurred to him to do otherwise. I don't know why unless he had experiences in Japan that made him decide that he would rather stay here.

AH: Were they frowned upon by most of the Nisei?

SE: They were considered odd, and I guess it was mostly because of their   40
language problem. They really didn't make an adjustment into the community....

AH: Now I want to get into your evacuation to Manzanar. Did you go directly to Manzanar from Los Angeles?

SE: Yes. When we signed up, we were supposed to go to Santa Anita with everyone else in the Little Tokyo area, but a couple of days before we left a notice came out that those who had relatives in Manzanar could apply to transfer to Manzanar. And my brother had been one of the thousand volunteers that had gone to Manzanar in March 1942.

AH: Do you know what his motivations were for going?

SE: Well, I think mostly the idea of adventure, for he was pretty adventuresome, and also the government did mention that those volunteering would be getting union-scale wages, which he never collected. He was, let's see, my brother right above me, so he must have been about twenty or twenty-one. And he was always the adventuresome type and very impulsive. He had a job, but he quit it and went. And I guess part of it was that he felt that if this is going to happen, he might as well get in on the ground floor to see if we could get at least some advantages out of it. So when we left in May—he had gone on March 23—we were supposed to go to Santa Anita first, and then we thought we would be transferred to Manzanar. But since we weren't really sure, we decided we would all sign up and ask to go to Manzanar. So there was a whole trainload of people that did go to Manzanar. I don't know if they were all related to the volunteers that had gone, but we went because of that.

AH: Do you know what date this was?   45

SE: It was May 9, 1942.

AH: When you got there, about how many blocks were already functioning?

SE: Well, we were assigned to Block 20, so I guess half of the camp was already filled. One whole block was filled with people from Bainbridge Island in Washington. The other block was all the people from Terminal Island in San Pedro.

AH: Do you know which blocks those were?

SE: They were in the earlier groups, so I don't know whether Block 6 may   50
have been Bainbridge Islanders.

AH: I hear the Bainbridge Islanders left the camp because the climate was too bad.

SE: They later went to the Minidoka camp in Idaho because they lived directly across the block in Manzanar where the San Pedro people were, and the two groups of people—those from Bainbridge and San Pedro—were very different. You know, if anybody wanted to do a sociological study of life-styles . . . well, these two groups were so far apart!

AH: Where was the San Pedro group in the camp? Do you recall their blocks by any chance?

SE: Gee, I don't know. They were situated sort of diagonally from Block 20, so they must have been—let's see, how many blocks there from it? You know, because 13 was directly across from 20, so it must have been 6, 13, and 20 all in a row. So they may have been in like Block 5 in the other end of camp, and then the Bainbridge Island people were almost directly across from them. I didn't know too much about them, but I understood there was a lot of bickering going on between the two groups.

AH: The Bainbridge Islanders and...   55

SE: And the San Pedro people. You see, the San Pedro group spoke almost all Japanese, and the Bainbridge Islanders spoke almost all English. The Bainbridge Islanders included a lot of college graduates and college students. They were highly intellectual type people, very artistic and rather more interested in that kind of thing. And the San Pedro people were kind of rough. They were fishermen, and they lived in their little ingrown community in San Pedro and Terminal Island, and they were almost like a Japanese village.

AH: Was it Japanesey because the culture was kept intact or because a lot of Kibei lived there, too?

SE: I don't think there were that many Kibei. I think it was because they were isolated from the rest of the Los Angeles community and the rest of the Japanese in Los Angeles.

AH: Did you become familiar with the San Pedro community in the prewar years when you went down, say, for the ship farewells? That is, when you'd go down to the harbor, did you have any relatives or associates in San Pedro to visit?

SE: No, I didn't. My father would point it out to me, but that was about it. I   60
didn't know anybody from that area until I went to Manzanar.

AH: How were the people living there looked upon by people in the Little Tokyo area?

SE: They were almost like a subgroup of Japanese.

AH: I heard there was a lot of fear of them at Manzanar.

SE: There was. Yes, I remember being at a baseball game between two teams, and one team happened to be the San Pedro group and someone in our block had just made a remark. There were some people from San Pedro standing behind her who resented the remark, and that night, after the game, a whole group of San Pedro kids—I guess they were from the San Pedro Yogores or the baseball team, I don't know—came through our block and went up to look for her barrack and specifically wanted an apology from her. And they said if she didn't give it, they really were going to go after her. "Well," she said, "what for? I don't recall that I said anything insulting." Well, to them it was insulting and to her it was nothing.

AH: It was typical ballgame banter?   65

SE: Yes. And I remember the next morning everybody was complaining that their lawn grass was really smashed down, so there must have been a large group that came wandering around the block looking for her and asking for an apology.

AH: Do you recall the activities of Terminal Islanders at the camp in terms of the jobs they had and whether they figured in the evacuee hierarchy of the camp?

SE: No, I don't. There were a few working on the paper, the *Manzanar Free Press.* I think they were younger Nisei. I guess they worked in various departments. Probably a lot of them worked in things like deliveries—driving the trucks. There were a few who were in the police department. I don't know if any of them were used for their bilingual ability.

AH: Were there some who didn't even speak English?

SE: There may have been, yes. But most of the ones I met were bilingual.   70
They spoke English fairly well, and they could also speak Japanese.

AH: Do you know if the Kibei had anything to do with the San Pedro people because of the commonality, both being, as the Nisei would describe them, Japanesey?

SE: Japanesey, yes. I don't know. I think the San Pedro people were pretty much to themselves. I know they formed their own baseball teams.

AH: Did you find that there was within the camp, then, pretty clear cultural divisions within the subculture?

SE: Yes. Yes, I found that that was even more the case after I started doing a lot of reading and talking to people, too. But I could tell it even on the strength of my own observations of people that I saw in Manzanar. I had been pretty much within Little Tokyo. I didn't get out very much as a kid, and I was very curious about the different groups in Manzanar. I guess working on the paper made me a little more aware, too, of some of the thinking of the people. So when I look back on it, I can see where the Bainbridge Islanders would have had a lot of problems with the San Pedro people because of the difference in cultural outlook. And I think this is probably one of the most tragic things of the evacuation. You don't put groups of people together because they're one race because each group, depending on where they come from, has a very different life-style. I think that in Manzanar the biggest difference was between Bainbridge Island and San Pedro, and even San Pedro from the rest of Los Angeles. The people were so different. My mother said when I asked her one time, "Well, even in Japan, fishermen are considered an entirely different group. They're rough. They have to have a lot of courage; they're fighting the seas all the time. You know, their living is very precarious. And their attitude becomes quite different from the attitude of people who work the land."

AH: Were there any other groups at Manzanar? I know that at Manzanar   75
about 85 percent of the people were from Los Angeles County and

about 70 percent were from Los Angeles city proper. You mentioned Bainbridge Island, can you think of any other areas that were included at Manzanar outside of Los Angeles, people from places other than Los Angeles?

SE: I think possibly there were a few people from central California. I don't know how they got there, unless they had relatives in the city who they moved in with....

AH: Who would you say had the power in the block with respect to leadership: Issei, Kibei, or Nisei? You've indicated that the block managers were Issei and Kibei.

SE: The two in our block were. In the beginning they wouldn't allow the Issei to take any kind of office because of the fact that they were classified as enemy aliens and the United States government was not supposed to have them do anything that might put them in jeopardy with their own country. But when the Issei began to feel they were not doing anything, the administration, the WRA [War Relocation Authority] began to change some of its policies and give some of the leadership to the Issei. But I think, generally, the camp itself, outside of the administration, was pretty much controlled by Issei.

AH: So unofficially, in any event, Issei held the real power.

SE: I think they still did. People talk a lot about the Issei not being able to   80
keep family control and all that, but I think when you come down to it the coop was run more by Issei than Nisei, and most of the block leaders eventually became Issei, partly because the young ones were leaving. In the first year, I think, there was a lot of control by the Nisei and a lot of policy making going on behind the scenes. But when furlough time came and the young men left to go work in the fields and some to enlist in the army, then there wasn't anyone left to take over except the Issei.

AH: In what capacity were you originally employed at the camp?

SE: Well, I had volunteered to help a couple of Catholic nuns who had come into camp and were going to live there and start a school because the school had not been organized. I guess I must have worked a couple of weeks without pay when I found out they were setting up this camouflage net factory and they were looking for workers. So I went and applied, and I worked there.

AH: You had to be a Nisei to work there, didn't you?

SE: Yes, you had to be a citizen to work there because we would be making camouflage nets for the United States Army and the administration had evidently signed some kind of contract. There was a lot of bickering about how much we were going to get paid and were we going to get paid, and we eventually did get paid. Then there was a lot of competition about which crew was going to make the most nets and win the watermelon or whatever they were giving away for prizes. Then the first group of furlough workers left, which meant that a lot of the staff people from the *Manzanar Free Press* were leaving, and so I thought it might be a good time for me to apply for a job there. So I applied at the *Manzanar Free Press,* and they told me that I could probably get a job there....

AH: One final question. You mentioned the book by the Houstons called   85 *Farewell to Manzanar.* You've no doubt done some thinking on this, but what exactly does it mean to say "Farewell to Manzanar"?

SE: I'm not sure, really, except that you can talk about what happened to yourself, and you can talk about what happened to others, such people as Asian immigrants. After the 1969 pilgrimage, I sort of retreated into the past because the pilgrimage had such a traumatic effect on me. I didn't realize it. I was going up there for a day, and I thought it would be adventurous—I hadn't been back to Manzanar since I left. But for about a month I would wake up in the middle of the night with nightmares. I would say to my husband, "I couldn't sleep last night." And he would reply, "You were thinking about Manzanar." And I would then say, "I guess it must be that because I can't think of anything else that would bother me."

So I started to read history, Asian American history, Japanese history, and I began to see that the internment was not just an isolated case. We blow it up so that it seems that it's the only thing that has happened to the Japanese in America. As I read over what had happened to Asians before the evacuation, I began to realize that laws had been enacted against the Chinese and that laws had been enacted against the Japanese keeping them from doing business in certain areas, like fishing and buying land. And I realized that the evacuation was only part of what had been happening to the Asian immigrant. So I could put it in better perspective, not blow it out of shape, see it as part of a continuum.

I think that the most important thing about saying "Farewell to Manzanar" is facing the fact that there is racism in America. The word *racism,* more than any other description, was what most Nisei didn't want to put on the plaque. I think once people realize that there are these things done to people and that it is due to racism, then I think they can go forward. A lot of people will say, "Oh, I've never faced that kind of prejudice. I've never been refused service. I've never been refused an apartment...." But there are cases where discrimination has taken place, and the answer from some people is, "Well, there are exceptions." They don't want to confront racism. Once you've faced it and know it's there, possibly find ways and tools to cope with it, then you can let go of the past and say, "Farewell."

Understanding the Text

1. In your own words, describe the economic and social background of the Kunitomi family.

2. Define the terms *Issei, Nisei,* and *Kibei.*

3. How does Embrey characterize the attitudes of the Kibei toward the war?

4. What, according to Embrey, were the relationships among the various Japanese groups in Manzanar?

5. What conclusions does Embrey draw about the meaning of her Manzanar experience?

Exploring and Debating the Issues

1. The forced detention of American citizens such as Embrey is an obvious case where the dream of opportunity offered by California disappeared. Given that, assess the accuracy of James J. Rawls's picture of the promises California offers its citizens ("California: A People, A Place, A Dream," p. 8). Be sure to keep in mind that Rawls does not pretend that the California dream is wholly positive.

2. In the 1940s, many Americans justified the forced detention of Japanese Americans by referring to the extraordinary tensions and fears generated by Japan's attack on Pearl Harbor. Write an essay in which you respond to this justification.

3. Today, while few people claim that the detention of Japanese Americans during World War II was constitutionally and morally just, some members of minority or underprivileged groups fear similar treatment. In class, brainstorm measures that could be taken to prevent a repeat of this chapter of American history. As you discuss this issue, consider the fear among some gay Americans that homosexuals would be quarantined because of AIDS hysteria.

4. Immigration rights activists opposed to Proposition 187 have argued that the motivations behind the initiative were similar to the racist motivations behind the detention camps like Manzanar. In an essay, agree, disagree, or modify this argument.

5. In your journal, discuss how Embrey's pre-Manzanar education resembles what we would today call a multicultural education.

WILLIAM LANGEWIESCHE

Invisible Men

Living twilight lives camped out beneath freeway underpasses and deep inside barely accessible canyons, a few thousand undocumented laborers hide out from the U.S. Border Patrol by night while seeking minimum wage work by day. In this selection, **William Langewiesche** (b. 1955) goes in search of an encampment of such workers, men and women who, in his words, "occupy the lowest place in the entire United States." Telling the story of one Jesús Ruíz, Langewiesche paints an unusual portrait of hope and despair, as Ruíz and his family find in America a life that is only marginally better than the one they left behind in Mexico. A writer and journalist, Langewiesche is a correspondant for the *Atlantic Monthly;* his work, including this essay, has also appeared in the *New Yorker.* His books include *Cutting for Sign* (1993) and *Sahara Unveiled* (1996).

F ive million people live illegally in the United States. Two million live in California alone. More than half of those are Mexican, and by the standards they left behind almost all are doing well. Many now inhabit apartments in the barrios of Los Angeles and other cities, where they can blend with the large populations of legal immigrants and walk the streets openly, without worrying about arrest and deportation. Even for those who have settled outside the safety of the barrios, it is not a bad life, warmed as it is by hard work. But there are gradations to the experience, and they are severe. At one extreme are a few thousand squatters who have scattered into the construction-torn hills of northern San Diego County. They scavenge jobs and hide in furtive groups, inhabiting cracks in the affluent suburbs and enduring ferocious new pressures from the United States Border Patrol.

There have been Mexican squatters in San Diego for at least a hundred years, and at times they have been hunted but never before so intently. Three years ago, the local authorities razed the last of the old established camps — regular shantytowns, some with shanty bars and shanty churches. And the squatters who remain in the hills today are the ones who cannot be bulldozed away. Estimates of the numbers out there range from five thousand to forty thousand. Lacking contacts and knowledge that would allow them to reach safer ground, they crouch instead in farm sheds and camouflaged scrap-wood shacks, and bear the weight of California's displeasure. There are too few of them to form an underclass, but they are the people who now occupy the lowest place in the entire United States.

They are not easy to find. I spent days in January looking for them among the colliding coastal towns — Del Mar, Encinitas, Carlsbad, Oceanside — and east across twenty miles of fractured landscape to Escondido and the craggy mountains, which rise like a wall, imposing an end to the helter-skelter of the county's development. The search was a spiral descent through the rankings of illegal immigrants. Beyond the easily found apartment dwellers, beyond the well-housed crews on big vegetable and flower farms, I was led eventually to smaller farms, where the owners were not to know of my presence, and where the workers sometimes ran from my approach. Those workers were squatters, and felt hounded and insecure, but on private farmland they enjoyed some protection from the Border Patrol, so they lived one step above the bottom.

The bottom was a place I finally found fifty miles north of the border and just inland from the coast, in a brushy ravine known loosely as Los Olvidados, which means "the forgotten ones," although the people there were living like ghosts, unseen rather than out of mind. This ravine lay like a scar through an area of expensive residential developments with more uplifting names—La Costa, Marea, Serenata—which had spread in advancing patterns of half-million-dollar houses across the hilltops overlooking it. The houses had been painted in pastels, and given cathedral ceilings and high arched windows, and seemed so light and airy that they might have been inflated. The streets were clean. Some were protected by electric gates. The ravine, by contrast, seemed merely ugly—a steep-sided gulch about half a mile long, bisected by a high-tension power line and littered with piles of illegally dumped trash—the sort of place that San Diegans pass by and hardly see. But I had been told to stop and to notice that some of those trash piles had roofs and walls, and that the wind might carry the sound of men's soft whistles, and that on gray winter days smoke rose from campfires hidden among the stunted trees.

A rain had fallen. I clambered up an embankment and started down into the ravine, moving carefully along foot trails through the brush because I was concerned that I might be mistaken for the Border Patrol. The ravine's population was said to have been about a hundred last summer but to be fewer now. About halfway down, I heard voices and spotted a patch of tin roofing through the trees below. I was cut off by a gully and forced onto another trail, which eventually led to a windowless hut with a padlocked door. The hut seemed to have been abandoned, if only temporarily. But just down the trail beyond it I came to a larger shack that I now know as the home of Jesús Ruíz. 5

I called *"Buenas tardes"* from a distance and was answered quietly from the inside. The shack perched on a narrow terrace dug into the hillside fifty feet above the floor of the ravine. It was built of plywood and corrugated plastic, patched with black plastic sheeting, and held together with nails, branches, and the frame of a wheelbarrow, which had been wedged into the dirt. Trash spilled down a steep slope below it. The bushes smelled of urine. The center of the shack was a roofed but open-sided living area, which looked out over the ravine below; it was joined at one end to a three-walled kitchen, with rough shelving and a gas burner on a plywood table, and at the other end to a windowless sleeping room about the size of a big mattress. The sleeping room had a door that could be locked with a bicycle cable.

Jesús Ruíz sat in the living area on a plastic garden chair. He was twenty-two years old—a short, Indian-looking man dressed in a windbreaker, jeans, and untied basketball shoes. He had high cheekbones, clear eyes, and a musical voice, which imparted a peculiar quizzicality to his speech. He spoke no English. His Spanish was better than mine, but crude nonetheless: he confused *he* and *she,* and had problems with the use of the past and future tenses. This was because he was a Zapotec, from the Mexican state of Oaxaca, and he spoke primarily Zapoteco. But he was not given to conversation in any language. After he invited me in, we sat mostly in silence. He did not understand my interest in his life. He said that, like the other squatters at Los Olvidados, he was a day laborer. He found jobs by knocking on doors or standing on the streets. Usually, he worked as a gardener.

During that first visit, he did not mention the Border Patrol or deportations or his long experience with coming back across the line. All that may have seemed too obvious to him. He told me that he had moved north in 1991 and had returned to Oaxaca four times since. He might have been talking about vacation travel. He said he preferred to fly from Tijuana rather than to take the bus. When I expressed surprise, he explained impatiently that the flying was faster than the driving—five hours instead of eight days. He meant that his time was worth money. Otherwise he would have stayed in Mexico.

I was more interested in why he stayed here, under siege in Los Olvidados, instead of moving on, at least to the relative safety of a farm. He would say only that he did not like hard labor. But, as I later learned, there was more to his immobility. Like other Zapotecs in the ravine, he came from a parched mountain village called Santa Ana Yareni, five hours from the city of Oaxaca in a four-wheel drive—a place so isolated and Indian that for years it had lacked any connection to the labor market of the United States. But, beginning in 1984, many of the men there were recruited by a California flower grower who needed workers for his farm, in Somis, an hour north of Los Angeles. The Zapotecs were taken by train to Tijuana and smuggled to Somis, and there they were enslaved: held in a compound in perpetual debt, frightened into submission by warnings about the Border Patrol, and forced to work sixteen hours a day. Some of the men eventually sought help. In 1990, a federal grand jury in Los Angeles indicted the grower on charges of slavery. The slavery charges were dropped in a plea bargain, but he pleaded guilty to corporate racketeering, as well as to labor and immigration violations, after a complex prosecution that navigated the difficult distinctions between safety and captivity, hard labor and servitude.

The Zapotec slaves had meanwhile fled south to the ravine at Los Olvidados, where a few villagers had already established themselves, because of the presence nearby of an aging hippyish couple who liked to drink and party with them. The couple had visited Santa Ana Yareni and had once taken a village elder to Marine World to "blow his mind." This was the closest thing the Zapotecs now had to a useful immigrant network in California, and it wasn't much. The trauma of the Somis slave camp had set them back at just the wrong time in American history—four years after the great immigration amnesty of 1986, and at a time when political sentiment had turned strongly against immigration. The attraction of Olvidados was at first the freedom it offered, the day-to-day choices to work at one job or another, or simply to rest in the ravine. But within a few years that freedom meant little.

Jesús Ruíz was too young to have been a slave, but he was affected by the Somis experience just the same. In 1991, his father fell to his death while planting corn on the precipitous mountain above Santa Ana Yareni. Jesús was sixteen. After the funeral, he decided to head north, and he knew of nowhere to go but Los Olvidados. In January, when I first met him, he faced the same lack of choice.

Outside his shack, a little stuffed elephant hung by its trunk on a string from a tree. Jesús said that he had three children. The first—a girl now four years old—was born in Mexico. After spending nearly a year alone with the baby, his young wife, Juana, had insisted on coming north to unite the family. "She wanted to see California," Jesús told me. "She thought everything would be easy."

In 1993, Juana took the baby on the bus to Tijuana and, after sneaking across the border, moved into the shack. Everything was not easy. Then, as now, water had to be hauled in yoked buckets down the steep slope from a ridge-top hydrant. But, aside from the threat of sudden deportation, the living conditions in the ravine were no worse than they had been within her memory in Oaxaca. Jesús wanted Juana to be realistic about coming north. "I told her, 'You have to work if you want to live here. That's the way it is in California.'" He got her a cleaning job three days a week. There were other women living in the ravine, and they helped with the baby.

But then she got pregnant with their second daughter and had to stop working. When she went into labor, Jesús took her to an emergency room and naively signed her in for a two-day stay at the hospital. The hospital did not ask about the couple's immigration status. The baby was born an American citizen, and Jesús was presented with a staggering bill for four thousand dollars. Slowly, he managed to pay it. By then, the family had moved into a two-bedroom apartment in Carlsbad with seven other Oaxacans and were beginning to live the urban lives of more typical illegal immigrants. At a vegetable-packing operation near the ravine, I met an old Oaxacan peasant with a pencil mustache and a straw hat, who described the horror not of such overcrowding but of the unnatural vertical stacking that is part of apartment life—the footsteps above and the quarrelling below, the distance from the sweet soil. Jesús and Juana were less attached to the land, but they realized that they were saving no money. In 1996, they returned to Los Olvidados. Jesús assured me that Juana did not mind. When she got pregnant again, she enrolled in a prenatal program, which cut the medical bill in half. The family's third child and its second American citizen, a boy, was born last September.

One rainy afternoon in November, 1997, when the new baby was two months old, the Border Patrol raided the ravine. Jesús was returning on his bicycle when he spotted the vans parked on the nearby streets. He could do nothing to help his family, and he slipped away. The Border Patrol agents closed in on the ravine, moving heavily down the trails with their radios squawking. They were preceded by a chorus of whistles and warning cries: "*La Migra!*," short for *Inmigración*. The agents were slowed by the slickness of the ground, and, as a result, almost everyone in the lowland escaped. Juana, up on the steep hillside, had her babies to think of and could not run. A cousin who also lived in the ravine was visiting her. The two women shut themselves into the darkness of the sleeping room and tried to soothe the children.

The United States Border Patrol is not a timid organization. In San Diego County, where a third of its sixty-eight hundred agents are deployed, there were more than a quarter of a million apprehensions and arrests in fiscal 1997 alone. That number is about half of what it was just two years earlier—a reduction that now seems to be undeniably the result of a tough new defensive effort initiated in October, 1994, throughout San Diego County, and especially along the critical fourteen miles of border facing Tijuana. The effort, dubbed Operation Gatekeeper, is based on an increase in fences, surveillance, and front-line patrols, and also on a new commitment to patrolling north of the border. Within the confines of San Diego County, the operation has been a success. Its national significance is harder to judge. Critics say that illegal immigrants are simply bypassing the operation by moving a few miles to the east or that, more ominously, apprehensions are down because the new defenses have forced a professionalization of the border crossing, which, in turn, means that the flow has become smarter and more difficult to stop. But Border Patrol agents are not prone to indulge in such doubts. San Diego is their sacred ground, and the success of Gatekeeper, however narrow, has at last given them a scent of victory.

In Los Olvidados, the squatters imitate the heavily burdened agents yelling "Stop running, you Mexican motherfuckers!," and they boast about their own taunting responses of "*Chinga tu madre!*" It is not just a word game. The agents do sometimes club people, and they separate families during deportation and deliver terrified peasants by the thousand to the predators who inhabit the filthy streets of the Mexican border cities. Nevertheless, the Border Patrol is not, as its critics claim, an inherently abusive organization. Its arrests are routinely softened by a grudging respect between the pursuers and the pursued. In rare cases, this may lead agents simply to let people go. I'm guessing here because no one will admit to such acts of grace. But when two rain-soaked agents finally got to Jesús' shack they found a frightened family inside, and after hearing that the babies were Americans they turned and went away. Still, Jesús had to assume that next time the outcome would be different. He had been captured twice already in 1997 and deported to Tijuana. This was not how he wanted to rear his children.

In the end, it was the talk of El Niño as much as the increasing pressure from the Border Patrol that drove the family apart. Even before the seasonal rains started, many of the women and children in the lowland had gone scurrying for shelter—some to local apartments but most back home to Mexico. After the November raid, the last of them left. The rain kept falling. Jesús reinforced the shack, but by early December the solitary living had become too hard for Juana. Jesús bought airline tickets for Mexico City and sent the family off to live there with a cousin. The departure left only two women in Los Olvidados—a toothless Chihuahuan, who slept in a tree house with a vicious little dog, and a peroxided hooker who frequented a colony of heavy drinkers on the far hillside. From Mexico City, Juana sent Jesús a note in Spanish, which he taped to the sleeping-room door: "Specially for you my love. I always want to be close to your side, but it is not easy. Night and day I think of you because I feel a coldness in my heart that you are not in my arms in order to hold you and to kiss your sweet lips. I love you and I miss you, but destiny has made us be apart from one another. The end."

I asked Jesús why Juana had not moved back to Santa Ana Yareni. He said that there was nothing for them there. I asked about their future. He said that it lay on the outskirts of Mexico City, where, with the money he would save now, he might eventually buy a piece of land and build a one-room house. It was something permanent to work toward. But I am not sure he really believed in it. He would be lucky to make three dollars a day in Mexico. His retirement plan was simply to grow old so he wouldn't have to eat much. He told me that he would visit his family in the summer of 1999, and that he would stay for two months before leaving again for California.

I said, "It's hard."   20

He said, "It's life."

Still, I wondered why he did not acknowledge his troubles. Was it politeness? Naiveté? A sense of privacy? For nearly two weeks, I kept coming back to talk to him. Only with time could I get him even to admit that within the ravine there is crime, that hard drugs are used, that men get crazy drunk and fight and set their shacks on fire, that men get sick and babies die, that the shacks are burglarized, that skinheads threaten Zapotecs on the street, that Chicano gangs attack and rob them within the ravine, that a man must be ready to run at all times, that capture by the Border Patrol is a serious setback. All this I had to learn first from other men. But Jesús had made a commitment to endure here illegally, and he insisted that it was the right commitment, and I came to realize that he described his life to himself as he described it to me. Only once, at night, over a beer that had slurred his speech, did he come close to expressing regret. He showed me a guitar, and said he was learning to play it. I asked him why, and he said, "So I'm not just hanging around crying." And even then he was not maudlin. He told me, too, that he enjoyed listening to music, especially *norteño* ballads—stories in song about love and violence and life underground in the United States. I noticed that Jesús had taken Juana's note off the door. We were not friends, but we could talk if I did not insult him with pity.

One step higher in the underground life, I found my way to a different group of squatters, who, because they had a little something to lose, were concerned that I not identify them by name. The group consisted of a dozen farmworkers who were mestizos from Michoacán. I spent several cold nights with them, huddled around a smoky wood-burning heater built of two fifty-gallon drums stacked horizontally and welded together. The men lived in a derelict chicken shed on a family farm that nestled against the steep slopes of the eastern mountains, about an hour from the coast.

The farm grew avocados. Most of the remaining farms in San Diego County are just such family operations, unable to survive without illegal workers. There are big farms, too, but, like those elsewhere in California, they tend by now to hire legal workers, often unionized, and to house them more or less correctly. The small farmers are not necessarily bad people, but they lack the economies of scale. Rather than comply with burdensome regulations pertaining to the living conditions of farmworkers (whether illegal immigrants or not), they have simply dropped out of the system. For them, the beauty of the arrangement is its deniability. Near Escondido, a flower grower said to me of his own foreman, "Manuel? Manuel? No, I don't know no Manuel. If you mean one of those wetbacks who come walking through here, I've got nothing to do with them." We understood each other perfectly. It was early evening, and he had studiously turned his back on the men who were settling into the shell of a wrecked greenhouse. Many other farmers similarly turn their backs. Their men become "trespassers," for whom they cannot be held responsible. And then, of course, every morning the farmers turn around and hire the same "trespassers," having at some point gone through the motions of checking their immigration documents.

The avocado grower who employed the workers in the chicken shed did   25
not know that I had been talking to them. I asked his permission only afterward, and he found a way to deny it. But I liked him. He was a hard, flat-bellied man of nearly seventy, a classic California grower—silver-haired, tanned, handsome, a Ronald Reagan type. He called his softer friends "puss guts." And he had a sense of humor. He said, "Fifteen pickers show up one morning, but only one's got papers, so I have to tell the others I'm real sorry but I can't use them. What happens? Two hours later, they show up again, and this time they've all got papers. There's only one problem—every one of these fellas was born on the same day, and every one of them crossed the border at the exact same time." He shrugged. The law did not require him to be an expert.

He thought of himself as a good employer. He told me he would never ask his workers to do something that he himself couldn't do. That was not necessarily a reassuring thought. He had hired college students on summer break, but they couldn't keep his pace for more than a morning. He had hired high-school athletes, but they didn't know how to dig or hammer. And that was in the past—the situation was worse today, of course. Finding Americans of any description had become practically impossible. He thanked God for the Mexicans, who came begging for the jobs and were strong pickers and knew how to dig and hammer and didn't whine or complain. He described what they went through, hour after hour, climbing the steep slopes of the groves carrying hundred-pound bags of easily bruised avocados. "You ought to try it," he said, eying me skeptically.

He said he got good work from the Mexicans by staying on them all the time. He liked Rush Limbaugh. He disliked the ACLU. But he also disapproved of the way some of the local farmers treated their men, and he included his own brother in that category. He pointed out that the chicken shed was a chicken shed no longer, and that he provided the workers there with power and running water and that when they remembered to remind him he replenished their gas, so they could have hot showers as well. He thought he treated them fairly.

The men in the chicken shed didn't exactly disagree. They said the farmer was tough and explosive, but if they went about their work correctly, he left them alone. They knew about living conditions at neighboring places, which were dark and brutishly cold. They had found this farm through their friends and had been coming here for years. The advantage of the job was the relative security it offered—an approximate assurance that there would be work on most days and that without a warrant or the farmer's permission the Border Patrol could not come onto the property and take the workers away. This farmer had mixed emotions about illegal immigrants and wanted those in the cities to be rounded up, but he did not like the Border Patrol, and for thirty years he had kept its agents off his land. So the chicken shed, however leaky its roof, was in the most important sense a good shelter.

I asked the men about the financial details of the job. They said that they made the minimum wage, but that after deductions for taxes and Social Security it amounted to less than five dollars an hour. They used phony Social Security numbers and knew they would never see that money again. They were paid by check every two weeks, and if they did well they earned about nine thousand dollars a year, of which they might mail six thousand dollars in money orders to their families in Mexico. Sometimes they carried cash when they returned to Mexico, but hemmed into their clothes because of shakedowns by the Mexican customs officials and the police. Within Mexico, they preferred to travel by air not merely for speed but for altitude: it allowed them to fly over all such risks of the road. I told them that I was familiar with the habit from traveling in Africa. They asked me if life in Africa was truly harder than in Mexico, and I answered that, yes, in general it seemed to be.

We got back to life in San Diego. The chicken shed had a Coke machine outside and a television somewhere. The men slept on wooden bunks in tangles of coats and blankets, and did their cooking on two old gas stoves. Every day, a *lonchero* drove up in an aluminum-sided catering truck to sell hot drinks and groceries and a few clothes—and also, quietly, perhaps beer, penicillin, and marijuana. *Loncheros* gain exclusive rights to farm encampments. The term, which derives from *lunch,* understates their importance to the besieged workers: by delivering the necessities (which include check-cashing and loans) to places like the chicken shed, they allow the squatters the choice of remaining within the boundaries of their refuge for weeks at a time. Later, when I talked to the farmer's wife, she expressed confusion at the men's allegiance to their *lonchero*. She had offered to do their grocery shopping for them at a store called Smart & Final, and they had refused. But, of course, grocery shopping was all she would have done for them, and they knew it.

To the men in the shed, the Border Patrol's Gatekeeper operation felt like a storm outside. One night during my stay, a man arrived after five days of crossing the border on foot. He had joined a guided group that intended to skirt the defenses by taking a bus thirty miles east from Tijuana. The group crossed the border, but within a few miles it was surprised by a roving team of Border Patrol agents. The man ran, and during the following nights he made his way north, navigating by the lights of airline flights. It hadn't always been so hard. One of his friends in the shed said, "You can tell they're looking for different ways to keep people down." I disagreed, saying, "I think they're looking for ways to keep people out." But that was an argument about intent.

The fear outside the farm was palpable. One night, I went up a dirt road into a canyon where prostitutes gather every Monday to provide the workers with sex. Because the farmers don't want prostitutes on their land, the men are forced to emerge into the open. That night, about thirty men had taken the risk. The prostitutes were Mexicans and worked in shifts arranged by age, starting with the oldest, who were perhaps in their midtwenties. The women carried cardboard to lie on and transacted their business quickly in the darkness—fifteen dollars for the basic, twenty-five without a condom. A *lonchero* had arrived to sell beer and music tapes, but it was a bad party. The canyon had been raided the night before, and the men were extremely nervous, startled by every flicker of light or unexpected footstep on gravel. *"Aguas!"* they kept hissing, which means "Look out!"

Back at the chicken shed, the squatters acknowledged the relief they felt upon returning to their refuge. I told them about Jesús Ruíz and the day laborers of Los Olvidados—people who had found no such shelter. They knew all about that kind of life. They told me about migrants who had lived nearby in a clay cave beside the Pala River until one rainy day the cave collapsed and killed them. The story was about gradations. There are two kinds of squatters in San Diego. The farmworkers did not feel privileged to live in a chicken shed, but they were glad not to have been buried alive.

Understanding the Text

1. Why does Jesús Ruíz prefer to live in a squatters' camp in Los Olvidados rather than live on one of the farms that employs laborers like him?

2. Why do the small avocado farmers continue to hire undocumented workers? How do they justify breaking the law?

3. For Jesús Ruíz and his family, how does life in Los Olvidados compare to life in their homeland, Oaxaca, Mexico?

4. Study Langewiesche's tone. What is his attitude toward the Mexican immigrants, their employers, and the U.S. Border Patrol?

Exploring and Debating the Issues

1. The farmer whom Langewiesche interviews points to his chicken shed as a sign of how good an employer he is. In an essay, evaluate the farmer's self-assessment.

2. Both Langewiesche and Richard Rodriguez ("Proofs," p. 34) describe the experiences and attitudes of Mexican immigrants who have just crossed the border illegally. Compare and contrast their depictions.

3. In class, form teams and debate whether the California dream applies to immigrants such as the Ruíz family.

4. In an essay, defend or argue against the strategies used by the U.S. Border Patrol to control illegal immigration from Mexico to California. To develop your ideas, you might consult Richard Rodriguez's "Proofs" (p. 34).

RAMÓN "TIANGUIS" PÉREZ

Ripon

It's getting dark, you've got no work, no luggage, no place to stay, and you're not in California legally anyway: What do you do? In this excerpt from *Diary of an Undocumented Immigrant* (1991), **Ramón "Tianguis" Pérez** describes what it's like to land in a small town in the Central Valley as a migrant laborer without papers. Little is known about Pérez beyond the story he tells in his *Diary*.

As the bus comes into a town called Ripon, I see five men walking on the sidewalk, men who, by their style of dress, I take to be wetbacks on their way to work. Their clothes are stained with dirt, just like their caps and tennis shoes. The bus goes into the little town's business district and stops at a little wooden building bearing the name of the bus line. Without thinking much, I grab my suitcase and get off. Estimating my route, I walk back toward the place where I'd seen the wets, but am unable to find them. On one side of the road where I'm standing, I see ahead of me houses that look like those in Hispanic neighborhoods and on the other side of the road, nicer, walled-in houses of brick, which I take to be houses where Anglos live. I walk toward the Latin settlement. It's a small place, with only one store. I run into a wetback who is leaving the store, carrying a bag of groceries, and I ask him where I can find work.

"The truth, friend, is that I don't know where," he answers me. "I'm trimming the vineyards, but we've only got work until tomorrow. The work we're doing is about to be finished."

"And you don't know where else I can ask?"

"I don't know that, either. A lot of people have come to the contractor I'm working for, and he's sent them away."

I am not worried, even though the news is not encouraging, because if   5
worst comes to worst, I can buy a ticket and go back to Los Angeles.

But I can't understand why I had stopped in such a small town and not in a city. Maybe it was because I'm from a small town and hang onto the idea that small-town people are friendly. At least that's the way my village treats outsiders, when they don't offend us. In my village, nobody refuses an outsider a bowl of beans or at least a snack. There's even a saying, "Food is sacred, and you should not refuse it to anyone." On the other hand, in a city, everyone is indifferent to everyone else. I walk up and down the neighborhood and run into other Mexicans, but they all give similar reports; work is not to be had. After a while I realize that the sun is going down, and that I've got nowhere to stay for the night.

As darkness comes, the streets clear, and I no longer find people to ask about work. I go into the store and buy a packaged hamburger. The storekeeper heats it in his microwave oven, and I go outside to eat it while walking. Now and then a car passes by. I walk back down to the bus station, but after about an hour, its caretaker locks the place to go home, and once again I'm without anywhere to stay. In the distance, I see the yellow sign of a gasoline station. I go toward it. Luckily, it's warm and I figure that I won't have to suffer from a cold night. I can lay down on a corner of the station's driveway, and the heat that the concrete has stored by day will warm me. About ten o'clock at night a station wagon pulls in to get gasoline. A short man of about twenty-five gets out. He goes into the office, comes back onto the driveway and unhooks the hose from the gas pump. Somebody inside the car hands him a key with which he opens the gas cap. Then he puts the hose in and begins pumping.

I get up from my improvised sleeping place, planning to ask the man where I might find work. I realize that asking that question at such a late hour may cause him to laugh at me, but I've got nothing to lose, after all.

On seeing me approach, the man at the pump changes his aspect from that of a self-confident man to one who is standing guard. He stares at me for a minute and then pretends not to pay any attention. When I ask him, he only shakes his head negatively. I decide not to ask any more questions because at this hour, anything one might ask gives rise to suspicions.

As I am walking away, I hear women talking and giggling inside the car.   10
They are talking in Spanish, but from my distance, I cannot understand them.

Very early the next day, I start my search again, and after a few hours, I encounter a wetback from the state of Puebla. He tells me that there is work, but there are too many workers. For the past two months, he says, he's been here, working only two or three days a week because there's not enough work for everyone. Then he directs me toward a house where a family from Puebla lives. The family has been in the United States for about ten years, he says, and its members know the contractors who take people to work in the countryside.

The house is of wood and without any fence, like all of the houses in the Hispanic neighborhood. Here and there in its yard are decorative plants. A child is riding a rusted tricycle on the lawn, and two others are making mounds of dirt with their hands. They don't pay much attention when they see me, but look at each other, as if each were expecting the others to speak. None of them says anything.

There is no closed door upon which to knock. Instead, there's a rusted and torn screen door, ajar. I say, *"Buenos días,"* to attract attention. A woman of about forty, dressed in worn, cheap clothes, comes to the door. Her hair is tied above her head with a faded red bandanna.

"Yes?" she says, leaning out the doorway.

I ask for Señor Pepe Zavala, as the wetback I encountered told me to do.   15

"Who wants to see him and how do you happen to know him?" she says, suspiciously. "He's not here right now," she adds.

I tell her how I was directed to her house and that I arrived in town the day before, looking for work.

"Well, *el señor* won't be back until about eight o'clock tonight," she tells me. Just as with others, I ask her to advise me where I might find a job, explaining that I know nobody in town. Once again, I hear the same answers.

Her mistrust eases, and she steps out onto the porch. I notice that her face is sunburned and her hands are calloused.

"I imagined that it was easier to find work," I tell her, just to have something to say to prolong the conversation.   20

"Over there in Los Angeles, you hear that in this area harvest time is due, and they say that people make good money."

"Sure, it's true, one can make a good bit when one is lucky enough to work good land," she says. "Where are you from?"

"From Oaxaca."

"And you don't know anybody here?"

"No."   25

"And you came all the way here, just trusting in God! There are a lot like you, and every year, more of them."

Behind her appears another woman, about twenty, with a rounded face, like hers. The younger woman is a little chubby. On seeing me, she opens her eyes wide.

"Mother!" she says to the older woman. "This is the guy that we ran into at the gas station!"

"Are you sure?"

"Yes! Did you spend the night at the station?" the younger one asks, incredulity in her voice.   30

"Yes," I tell them. "I spent the night there. The good thing is, the weather isn't cold."

"What a barbarity!" the older woman exclaims. "And I imagine that you haven't eaten."

"Not eating hasn't bothered me. I've just gotten into town, and I came prepared," I say.

"Well, come on in," the mother says. "Last night the girls came in and told me that they had seen a young man sleeping at the gas station. That bothered us, but we have to be careful, because you can't take risks with strangers. My husband is Señor Zavala, and he does know the contractors. Maybe he can take you on," the mother continues. "There's not much work, but at least you can earn enough to stay alive. Come on in, and when night comes, you can go across the street, where we've rented a place in which other people from Puebla are staying. There aren't any beds, but at least you'll have a roof over your head."

I tell the mother and daughter that I appreciate their attention.   35

Inside the house, beneath the peaked tin roof, are a series of small rooms. On entering, you come into a living room whose wooden walls are unadorned except for a coat of white paint. A couple of old wine-colored sofas stand against a wall, facing a low table on which a color television sits. The cement floor is covered with a dirty rug of the same color as the sofas. The living room opens onto a kitchen with all the appliances, stove, refrigerator, dish washer. On one wall of the kitchen hang several kitchen utensils and platters and some keys. Beyond the kitchen are the bath and three small bedrooms.

The mother and daughter tell me that the work available now is trimming in the vineyards and thinning in the tomato fields. They say that they came to Ripon from Puebla ten years ago as renters, but that they now own the house where they live. Since settling in, they say they've helped others from Puebla and a few disoriented people like me. Their own house grew too small for those they were aiding, so they've begun renting the house across the street for three hundred dollars a month. They say that from ten to fifteen wets usually stay there, paying two dollars a day.

The house across the street is in about the same condition as their own, except that it doesn't have as many divisions, and it has no furniture, only piles of dirty blankets and a bathroom with a commode and shower. Behind the house the grass has grown tall in the yard.

That afternoon the inhabitants of both houses arrive in two old, but big, cars. One of the cars is the one that I'd seen the night before at the gas station. Sixteen people get out of the two cars, among them two middle-aged women. Right away the mother and daughter introduce me to the father, telling him how I've come to the house. He greets me in a friendly way and says that we'll be going into the countryside to work at five in the morning.

Mr. Zavala's older son, about thirty years old, drives one of the station   40 wagons. He lives in Stockton, and he leaves shortly after arriving at the house. Mr. Zavala's daughter, her husband, also about twenty, and their two schoolchildren live in the house with Mr. Zavala and his wife. Thirteen people are living in the workers' house; I am the fourteenth. Mrs. Zavala tells me that if I'd like, she can prepare tacos for me to take to lunch tomorrow. I accept her offer with pleasure.

Understanding the Text

1. How does Pérez distinguish between immigrant and Caucasian dwellings in Ripon?
2. Why does Pérez stop in Ripon?
3. What is the social standing of the Zavala family?
4. Why does Pérez have difficulty finding work?

Exploring and Debating the Issues

1. In your journal, explore the connotations and effect of Pérez's use of the term "wetback" (para. 1).
2. Compare and contrast Ramón Pérez's experiences in Ripon with Jesús Ruíz's in San Diego (William Langewiesche, "Invisible Men," p. 99). How do you account for any differences between the two selections?
3. Which image of immigrants does Pérez more accurately illustrate: that described in Yeh Ling-Ling's "The Welcome Mat Is Threadbare" (p. 73) or Rubén Martinez's "Refine Immigration Policy to Reflect History and the Moment We Live In" (p. 76)? Defend your position in a well-supported essay.
4. Compare the conditions faced by farmworkers in Cesar Chavez's "The Organizer's Tale" (p. 345) with those faced by Ramón Pérez, and use your observations to formulate an argument about whether those conditions have improved since the 1960s.
5. How do the experiences of farmworkers such as Pérez complicate the picture of the Central Valley that Joan Didion describes in "Notes from a Native Daughter" (p. 51)? To develop your argument, you may wish to read or reread Cesar Chavez's "The Organizer's Tale" (p. 345) or Luis Omar Salinas's "My Fifty-Plus Years Celebrate Spring" (p. 353).

NANCY WRIDE

Vietnamese Youths No Longer Look Homeward

Following the Vietnam War, thousands of Vietnamese took to the high seas to escape the Communist regime that seized power in 1975. Many of these "boat people," and others who escaped by other routes, eventually made their way to California, where they continued a long tradition of immigrant assimilation into American society. In this selection, **Nancy Wride** (b. 1959) interviews a group of California high school and college students—the so-called 1.5 generation, who were born in Vietnam but raised in America—who share their thoughts about the American dream (California style), their Vietnamese ancestry, and assimilation. Wride is a staff writer for the *Los Angeles Times* who specializes in writing about people who are ordinarily ignored by the media.

Trouble seeped into Huy Tran's tranquil childhood in Vietnam like blood on sand. Coming home after a day of chasing crickets, he would overhear his parents whisper urgently in the hallway. Dispatches from the war front would flash across the TV at the town church. Then came the jailings of his father, a teacher, by the Communist regime.

Finally, when he was twelve, Tran and his father pushed off to sea and a new life in America. The boat trip was some kind of hell, he says. During the trek, a woman crazed by dehydration tried to kill herself with her fingernails. Tran finally made it to California, but it was six years before he saw his mother and siblings again.

Tran, twenty-two, will never forget his family's ordeal, yet he favors America's recent restoration of trade with the government that tormented them. He believes that doing business with Vietnam will be good for refugees in the United States and those struggling in his homeland.

"I'm still sorry our lives were disrupted by the Vietnam War. But you cannot compare my anguish or anger toward the Vietnam War to my parents'," said Tran, a computer consultant in Irvine. "They expect me to feel the same, but they also understand that, because of my age, I might not be able to remember the persecution they had to go through, and the corruption, the hardship the South had to endure once the North took over."

Vietnam-born but American-bred, Tran belongs to a generation that 5 seems detached from the war that tore apart their birthplace, forced the exodus of 1.5 million people and left up to 2 million dead.

Most are under thirty, coming of age as the twentieth anniversary of the fall of Saigon nears next year. By the end of this century, they will make up a great part of the Vietnamese American community's Establishment, from business to political leadership.

Generally, they have not inherited their parents' hatred of Communism or qualms about trading with a former enemy.

American schools do not teach them Vietnamese history. And most immigrant parents are so busy working to support their families that there is little time to review the past together—presuming they and their children can still speak the same language.

As for the children, they are trying to be a part of a society that wants to forget the Vietnam War.

"They are totally socialized into American society. I find that because there is nothing in the curriculum, even in the UC system, [about] their background, they are generally ignorant to the circumstances that brought them to the United States," said Eric Crystal, coordinator of the Center for Southeast Asia Studies at UC Berkeley.

"For these kids, first of all, their whole lives are not oriented toward what happened in South Vietnam. They've never really lived there. And then there's something vaguely negative about Vietnam to an American—it means war, soldiers, prostitutes."

It is hard to find a voice of authority about the Vietnamese American experience, Crystal said, because it has been largely ignored by U.S. universities, perhaps because it is a relatively new immigrant experience. And those who are just now approaching adulthood, Crystal said, "have been studied even less."

"But the story of this group is that their fundamental preoccupation is with the country that they know, not their parents'," Crystal said.

First-generation immigrants generally retain most of their homeland's customs and values. Their children are expected to adopt the culture of their own native country. Generational conflicts are predictable.

Straddling these worlds are young Vietnamese Americans who, like other children born in the old country but raised in the new, have been dubbed "the 1.5 generation" by academics.

Born in a country where parental authority goes unquestioned, this in-between generation is growing up in a freedom-loving society whose aggressive anthem often is "Just Do It." They are "really torn between two worlds," said a counselor at Westminster High School, home to the nation's largest Vietnamese student population.

In California, where nearly half of America's Vietnamese refugees live, many children of former political prisoners and war veterans say necessity forces them to focus not on past horrors but on their future: entering the mainstream and seeking decent jobs and the good life for their families.

"We as the younger generation expect a little bit more out of this country, and from ourself," said Helen Nguyen, twenty-one, a UC Irvine biology major who was born in Saigon and fled with her family when she was seven.

Her father was a soldier in the Vietnam War and was a prisoner for a year in the brainwashing "re-education" camps of the Communist North Vietnamese, Nguyen said. After a year of processing at a Malaysian camp, her family made its way to Ventura, where her parents live. This painful family history, she added, is seldom discussed at home.

"The first level [of immigrants], where our parents came in, were just grateful [to be here]," she said. "I can see how the younger people are just struggling to work and have a solid career. I think if you give the 1.5 generation more time, after they've established careers and families, then they later will come around to activism."

For now, though, such interest seems secondary. "My parents don't speak much about the war. My dad did serve a year in a reeducation camp; he took it as natural. [In the war], men fought, we suffered, it is past now, and we move on."

"I think the generational conflict is both universal and unique," said Yong Chen, a UC Irvine Asian American studies professor specializing in U.S. immigration history. "If you look to earlier immigrants from Europe, you will find a similar generational conflict."

More recently, new appreciation of ethnic differences and cultural diversity have reversed past patterns of abandoning heritage for the mainstream, Chen said. Those of the 1.5 generation can select what they deem the best of past and present cultures.

Dr. Duong Cao Pham has a front-row seat to the 1.5 generation. He is a visiting professor of Vietnamese history and culture at UC Irvine and UCLA and teaches high school full time. His four children were born in Vietnam. The eldest was eight when the family fled just before Saigon fell in 1975.

The Vietnamese only began immigrating en masse nineteen years ago,   25
he said. For these immigrants, technology—including radio, television, and faxes—has built unprecedented bridges between the old and new worlds. "It's easier to maintain ties and knowledge about what's going on in each country," Pham said. "We are now in another age, compared to the Chinese in the nineteenth century or the Filipinos after World War II, or the Koreans in the 1960s."

Despite the technology, Pham's twenty-one-year-old son, Vu Pham, sees greater differences between the generations. Moving from Saigon to the United States when he was three, Vu grew up in Fountain Valley and is a graduate student in UC Irvine's humanities honors program. He is writing his senior thesis on members of the 1.5 generation—particularly their lack of community involvement compared to their parents.

"In my research, I've found that there are very, very few people in the 1.5 generation who are community activists," Vu said. "Many are concentrating only on mainstreaming."

In his interviews, Vu said he found that his peers are emotionally and intellectually removed from such issues as restored trade ties because they have only considered the financial benefits and not the political reality. If many Americans seemed resigned about renewed ties with a former enemy, he noted, why wouldn't Vietnamese Americans be as well?

"More personal is that there is this alienation from Vietnam, aside from faint memories," Vu Pham said. "A lot of the 1.5 ... don't plan to return to Vietnam, they don't have any relatives in Vietnam, or if they do, they are usually relatives of their parents."

Finally, he said, there is the handicap of ignorance. "One of the major   30
reasons you don't deal with issues about Vietnam at my age is that it's not

taught in school. I had nothing taught to me in high school about the Vietnam War. We reached the late twentieth century, and it wasn't ever mentioned."

To help fellow refugees, Vietnamese student organizations have formed at numerous southern California colleges. One is Project Ngoc (pearl), which was organized in 1989 to help a new wave of refugees and asylum seekers. The groups are less political than service and social and cultural clubs such as the Vietnamese Student Association, which has chapters throughout the Southland, and the Vietnamese American Coalition, formed by four UC Irvine students, including Tran.

Out of respect, Vietnamese American students often preface their own horror stories by stressing that others have suffered much more when their country was ruined by war. "It was very hard for me, the first few years without my mom," Tran said. "I've known families that didn't reunite for ten or twelve years later."

From Vietnam, he and his father traveled to Indonesia, Texas, and finally to Los Angeles, where they were later reunited with Tran's mother and brothers. He graduated from John Marshall High School in Los Angeles, and enrolled as a biology major at UC Irvine. After one quarter he switched to political science. His parents virulently opposed the move, believing hard sciences to be a better-paying field and less discriminating against the foreign-born.

Tran had to pay his own tuition, although he was allowed to live at home. He has never regretted the decision, but he has not found work in social services and remains a full-time computer consultant. Despite all the torment, he said, coming to America "has meant I have a better life than I would have had, a better education."

At La Quinta High School in Westminster, about 60 percent of the 1,283 students are Vietnamese, the highest percentage in the country. Last year's homecoming court was Vietnamese, as was this year's queen. And all but one of the candidates for La Quinta's highest honor—Aztec boy and girl student of the year—are Vietnamese, too. The Vietnamese Club, with two hundred members, is the biggest on campus. But all meetings are in English, and it is a service group that does not focus on culture or ethnicity. Copresident Lynn Phu is Cambodian but was born after her family fled to Vietnam.

It is a sign, some experts say, of the cultural crossroads that define Generation 1.5-ers.

In the days after President Clinton announced the renewal of trade ties with Vietnam, Rita Corpin's world history honors class discussed what it all meant. A twenty-year-old bumper sticker on Corpin's lectern read "MIAs— Only Hanoi Knows." The class was celebrating the arrival of the Tet New Year. Of the thirty-six students, twelve were born in Vietnam. A show of hands revealed that the students were in agreement: they thought lifting the embargo was good. Why? Because it would make it easier to fly into Ho Chi Minh City, formerly Saigon.

Nobody mentioned the war, boat people, or concerns about doing business with a former enemy. Nobody mentioned prisoners of war.

"It will be better for two-way travel and to visit relatives now," said one student, although he added that his family had already done this. "It will be easier for us to send money there," another said.

At La Quinta, it is not just dating and curfew and report card hassles that Vietnamese-born children bring to school with them each day. There are twenty-seven English as a second language classes taught here, and the school common is visibly divided between Americanized Vietnamese and the newcomers, who speak their native language and squat Asian-style through lunch. 40

"We had a girl commit suicide the month before I came here," said principal Mitch Thomas, "and it was over one thing: assimilation.... She was a bright, beautiful, capable kid. And those kids—who say what are you talking about, what embargo?—they are interested in the here and now. Their parents know all the politics, but the kids, all of their energy is striving for assimilation."

One thing about kids is universal, say Thomas and other educators working with Vietnamese students. No matter what their nationality, they all want to fit in.

Senior Thanh Tang, seventeen, vice president of the student body and honor roll student, is something of an exception. He is among the students who seem to hold an educated opinion about the reopening of trade: He opposes it—perhaps, he says, more strongly than his parents do.

In Vietnam, his parents imported produce—mostly grapes and oranges. Before that, his father was a police officer. Here, they rise at five and work seven days a week at their Santa Ana restaurant. They lost so much to come here, he said, and Americans will lose plenty now, too.

"I think with the embargo gone we'll be losing more of the workers. Soon we'll see Sony in Vietnam; the labor is cheaper. And the environmental concerns ... people building factories without standards and destroying the rain forest there. Someone's killing your people [prisoners of war and soldiers listed as missing in action], and you're *opening trade* with them?" he said, his face turning incredulous. 45

Of those like him, born in Vietnam but raised here, he said: "Some people are too young to see or feel any of that: Why did you lift the embargo on people who hurt my parents and made me go through that?

"When I first came here, my parents talked about Communists! Communists! But they don't talk about it anymore," said Tang, who works weekends at the restaurant and has dreams of attending Harvard Business School. "When I have time to sit down and talk, it's not about Vietnam; it's more [about] what I'm doing after high school, where I'm going to school.

"I think parents don't tell them about it," Tang added. Like his family and those of his friends, "everybody is too busy trying to work to support their family."

Understanding the Text

1. Why have academics called young Vietnamese Americans "the 1.5 generation" (para. 15)?

2. Why, according to Wride, do young Vietnamese Americans have different attitudes toward their cultural background than do their parents?

3. What view do young Vietnamese Americans tend to have of the Vietnam War, according to Wride?

4. According to the selection, what is the attitude most young Vietnamese Americans have toward restoring trade ties between the United States and Vietnam, and why do they feel that way?

5. Why does La Quinta High School principal Mitch Thomas say "all of [Vietnamese American students'] energy is striving for assimilation" (para. 41)?

Exploring and Debating the Issues

1. Write an essay that supports, refutes, or modifies the proposition that California colleges and universities should include in their curricula courses on the Vietnamese American experience and on the experience of other major immigrant groups.

2. If you are an immigrant, write a journal entry in which you describe your life in your native country and the circumstances surrounding your immigration. If you are not an immigrant, write an entry in which you reflect on the experiences of the Vietnamese immigrants described in Wride's essay.

3. Interview at least five students on your campus who are immigrants (from any nation), asking them about their desire both to assimilate and to preserve their native culture. Then compare your findings with the experiences of young Vietnamese Americans as described by Wride. How can you account for the similarities or differences in attitude you may find?

4. Assuming the perspective of Huy Tran, Vu Pham, or one of the other students mentioned in Wride's essay, write a response to Yeh Ling-Ling's ("The Welcome Mat Is Threadbare," p. 73) argument for restricting immigration.

5. Assuming the role of a Vietnamese parent, write a letter to your "child" about the family's need to preserve its cultural heritage. Alternately, write a letter from the perspective of a 1.5 generation student to your Vietnamese "parent" in which you discuss your desire to assimilate.

Researching the Issues

1. Visit your college library and locate a copy of the Treaty of Guadalupe Hidalgo, which ended the Mexican-American War in 1848 with Mexico ceding California to the United States. Write a report detailing the treaty's disposition of the Mexican population in California at the time.

2. Some Chicano activists do not accept the Treaty of Guadalupe Hidalgo (see question 1), claiming that California is in fact still Mexican territory. Research this position, and then write an essay arguing for or against it. You may wish to consult Rudolfo Acuña's *Occupied America* (New York: HarperCollins, 1988) as part of your research.

3. Immigrants to California have often faced restrictive legislation. Research the Chinese Exclusion Act of 1882 and the Alien Laws of 1913 and 1924, and write a report in which you explain how these laws affected Asian immigrants.

4. Research the demographic composition of your college or university campus. To gather data, consult your admissions office or student affairs office. Share your data with your class.

5. In a research project, study the history of the Japanese detention camps during World War II. What were the social and political circumstances leading to their creation?

6. Pick an ethnic group (anything from African Americans to Cambodian refugees to Soviet Jews), and trace the history of their immigration to California. Choose from the groups discussed in this chapter, or think of a different group not included here. Why did they leave their state or land of origin, and why did they settle where they did? What did the California dream mean to this group? In addition to library research, you may want to interview some immigrants to obtain their perspective.

7. Research the history of the civil wars in Central America during the 1970s and 1980s and their effect on immigration to California. Then write an essay in which you argue for or against the proposition that U.S. support for the governments in power makes the United States morally responsible for the refugees.

8. Should the United States "seal its borders," particularly in California? Form groups, and work together to research the role of the U.S. Border Patrol, and the effects of Operation Gatekeeper, in preventing illegal immigration to California. Then stage a debate in class, supporting your group's position with research data.

9. Rent a videotape of Edward R. Murrow's *Harvest of Shame,* an exposé of conditions suffered by migrant farmworkers in the 1960s, and show it in class. Then write an essay in which you sketch what a version of the movie updated for the 1990s would look like. Base your new version on research you conduct in your college library and, if you live in an agricultural region, on visits to farms in your area.

10. Form groups to volunteer some time for a local social services agency that specializes in immigrants' needs. Then prepare a report in

CALIFORNIA ON THE NET

1. Use a search engine to identify sites devoted to Proposition 187. What arguments are used for and against the proposition, and what sort of balance do you find among supporters and opponents? You might start with sites such as Latinolink (http://www.latinolink.com), which opposes 187, and the site for the Federation for American Immigration Reform (http://www.fairus.org), which supports it.

2. What is the current status of the U.S. Border Patrol's Operation Gatekeeper, and what impact has it had on immigration? Consult the Immigration and Naturalization Service's site (http://www.ins.usdoj.gov/public_affairs/progress_reports/Gatekeeper/170.htm). For the perspective of an immigrants' rights group, check out the Mexican American Legal Defense and Education Fund's site at http://www.maldef.org.

3. Conduct further research on the history of the detention of Japanese Americans during World War II at such camps as Manzanar. Two sites to begin with are the Manzanar Project site (http://www.mvhs.srvusd.k12.ca.us/~mleck/man) and the national Manzanar Historic Park site (http://www.nps.gov/manz).

which you assess the problems immigrants face in adjusting to life in California, making specific recommendations for change. Share your project with both your class and the agency for which you have worked.

11. Research the contributions of Chinese laborers, particularly those who were required to work on railroad construction, during the nineteenth century.

12. Rent a videotape of *The Grapes of Wrath* or read the novel, and write an analysis of why it became a classic depiction of the California dream.

3 The Best-Laid Plans
Education and the California Dream

Beyond the Great Divide

In the early 1990s, as California struggled through a seemingly interminable recession and the state budget was awash in red ink, the most prominent issue facing California's public education system was funding. From the schools, where per-pupil spending fell year after year, to the colleges and universities, where ever-rising fees could not stave off the effects of massive budget cuts, the main problem was money. College students found reduced course offerings and shrinking faculty resources, while the schools ran out of such basic supplies as library books and textbooks, even as the number of students per classroom soared.

Since then things have changed a little. A statewide initiative to decrease the number of students in elementary school classrooms has been inaugurated, and state spending on public education has increased, slightly, across the board. It's not that the schools, colleges, and universities have enough money now — the losses of the early 1990s have yet to be made up — but budgets are no longer being slashed as they once were, and student fees for higher education are stable after years of double-digit growth. So while money is still a problem, it doesn't loom over the educational horizon quite the way it did just a few years ago. A new cloud has come to take its place.

The major issues in California's public education system today, and the ones that cast the longest shadows, involve the kinds of racial and cultural conflicts that are also explored in the chapters on immigration and politics in this book. These conflicts can be summed up by the often wrenching controversies over two recently passed ballot initiatives: Propositions 209 and 227. The first brought an end to all affirmative action programs in the state college and university systems, while the second, if it is upheld in the courts, will eliminate bilingual education in the schools. The effects of these initiatives on the future of California education are still not clear, but many fear that they will result in a kind of "ethnic cleansing" of the state's higher-education system and a greater failure rate in the schools among those whose primary language is not English.

It is worth pointing out — in the context of the widespread outrage that has greeted the first post–Proposition 209 reductions in the black and Latino freshman classes at UC Berkeley and UCLA — that such enrollments are likely to increase at other less popular University of California campuses. At the same time, Proposition 209 has had little impact on the California State University and community college systems, and students will still be able to transfer from these institutions into the UC system. But there is no denying the emotional impact of reduced African American and Latino enrollments in the state's most prestigious undergraduate and graduate programs in the wake of Proposition 209.

It is likely the passage of Proposition 209 will mark a kind of watershed event in California's educational history, with a distinct before and after. Before 209, the UC campuses were slowly but surely becoming more diversified in their student body populations; after 209, there are signs that the prestigious campuses will become predominantly Asian and Causasian in their demographics. And if Proposition 227 results in fewer Latino students being able to compete for slots in the UC system, this division between before and after will become even more strongly marked.

Language, Diversity, and Multiculturalism

As we write these words, the effects and even the legality of Proposition 227 are still in doubt. It may be thrown out in court and so become a moot point. If it does remain in effect, supporters claim, it might improve the educational chances of the state's many non–English-speaking students. No one really knows for sure. Though the state's educational establishment vigorously opposed the initiative, arguing that bilingual education was essential to the success of California's growing ESL population, many other educators just as sincerely believed that bilingual education was failing its students and that some other way to ensure the acquisition of the English language had to be devised.

But whatever happens to Proposition 227, the demographic forces behind the initiative will remain the same. If you are a graduate of one of California's public K–12 schools, especially of a Southern California school, you are probably well aware of these forces. As a result of a decade of worldwide immigration to the Los Angeles area, for example, a classroom in the Los Angeles Unified School District can contain students whose native tongues include Spanish, Persian, Tagalog, Hebrew, Russian, Armenian, Pakistani, Hindi, Chinese, Vietnamese, Laotian, Korean, Cambodian, and on and on. Such a mixture of languages, races, and cultures has put California in the forefront of a national debate over cultural identity. At the time of the last great immigration to the United States at the end of the nineteenth century, it was assumed that the new immigrants would all merge into a vast national melting pot that would preserve a single, monocultural American identity. But today that assumption is no longer so widely held.

For behind the debate over Proposition 227 there was a larger debate. Though both sides in the controversy agreed that all of California's students must become proficient in English if they are to have any chance at educational and economic success, they did not agree on another crucial point. This had to do with the desirability of building a multilingual, multicultural society in place of the monolingual, monocultural society that Americans have traditionally both valued and taken for granted. On the one side were those who believed that a society divided up into numerous linguistic and cultural groups runs the danger of slipping into the kind of chaos that can now be seen in the Balkans. Believing in the American motto, engraved on every coin in the currency, *e pluribus unum*, they viewed Proposition 227 as a referendum not simply on how to teach English in the schools but on how to preserve America's traditional cultural identity.

On the other side of the debate were those who passionately want to preserve the cultural and linguistic differences that immigrants bring with them, who fear that melting into a monolingual, monocultural society will rob them of their heritage and identity. Thus, one could often hear in the political debates over Proposition 227 a defense of bilingualism as a cultural possession and not only as a pedagogical means to an end. For those who held this position, 227 was really a sort of Trojan horse, an attractively packaged assault on their own version of the California dream, which holds a vision of a multilingual, multicultural society in which immigrant groups might maintain their own cultural identities.

The Politics of Education

You might think that questions pertaining to college admissions and the best way to teach English ought not to be so political, that they ought to be addressed by educators alone. But as both Propositions 209 and 227 demonstrate, there is no way to avoid the politics of education. California's educational system does not stand by itself, as if ensconced in some ivory tower: it is an integral part of a complex sociocultural mosaic in which competing interests are forever clashing. That is why educational issues can become so emotional. What takes place in the schools plays a major role in shaping the future of the California dream. It is little wonder, then, that people should take such a keen political interest in what takes place behind school doors.

Affirmative action and bilingual education, of course, are not the only highly politicized issues facing California education today. A controversy over the privatization of education through the issuance of tuition vouchers, for example, has been swirling in recent years. Californians rejected a ballot initiative in 1994 that would have inaugurated a voucher system for private school tuition, but voucher supporters have kept the issue alive and promise a new ballot measure soon. Essentially, they have given up on public education and want to turn things over to the private sector. Thus, what is at stake is the future of public education itself in California.

As Californians argue over the best way to educate California's students, the performance of those students has also become politicized. Demands for assessment procedures to make certain that students are learning the essentials are now commonly voiced in the state legislature. Similarly, politicians are demanding assessment of the state's teachers and the institution of improvements in teacher training. And in yet another politicization of teaching issues, the trustees of the CSU system have mandated an end to remedial education, even as the numbers of students requiring remediation rise year by year.

In such a climate, it is important for the major stakeholders in California education — and that means you — to be as well informed about the issues confronting California's educational system as you can be. For those of you planning to become teachers, this will be essential. Even if you're not, many of California's most potent political battles are now being fought over educational issues, which means you need to think about them as well. The readings in this chapter are designed to start you thinking about California education — for if you don't think about it yourself, someone else will do it for you. As you read the selections in this chapter, you will begin to formulate your own critical point of view over the many controversies now swirling about California education and thus be able to contribute your own arguments to the ongoing debate.

The Readings

Mike Rose's visit to a middle school in Watts opens this chapter with a vision of how things can be done right in California's inner-city schools. Sylvia S. Fox follows with a report on the challenge of getting enough teachers to educate California's burgeoning student body in a time of class-size reductions and wide-scale teacher retirements. James Richardson's report on how California's supposedly tuitionless state colleges and universities have become increasingly expensive in recent years raises questions about the future accessibility of a higher education to California students, while Susan E. Brown's statistical analysis of the demography of the UC, CSU, and the community college systems argues that each system is divided from the other by social class and racial barriers. Ward Connerly next presents the case against affirmative action in college admissions, while Nathan Glazer argues that it should be maintained, but only for African Americans. Reuben Navarrette, Jr.'s personal story of what it was like to be a Central Valley Chicano admitted to Harvard University follows. Peter Schrag's overview of the controversy over Proposition 227 presents the contentious issue of bilingual education in California, while Romesh Ratnesar's report on the conflict between African American and Hispanic parents over the question of bilingual education introduces one of the less publicized aspects of the debate. Finally, Chitra Banerjee Divakaruni's poem on the language difficulties South Asian immigrants face in California's schools offers a personal insight into the challenges of educating a multilingual population.

MIKE ROSE

A Visit to Edwin Markham Intermediate School

Inner-city schools, especially in communities like Watts, don't get very much respect these days, so **Mike Rose** (b. 1944) decided to visit one to see what was really going on. Rose found an educational environment that was neither dysfunctional nor hopeless, encountering instead dedicated teachers who were offering their students a vibrant multicultural education as well as hope for the future. Part of an ambitious project to defend public education at a time when it is coming under fire in California and America, Rose's visit to the Edwin Markham Intermediate School is documented in his book *Possible Lives: The Promise of Public Education in America* (1995). One of America's leading voices in educational circles, Rose is a professor in the Graduate School of Education at UCLA and the author of such acclaimed books as *Writer's Block: The Cognitive Dimension* (1984) and *Lives on the Boundary* (1990).

We'll start south of downtown Los Angeles, close to the geographical center of the Basin, in Watts. During the first decades of this century, Watts was a semirural junction for the Pacific Electric Railway, Henry Huntington's "Red Car," the largest urban electric railroad system in the nation. Every Red Car traveler from agricultural and beach cities to the west and south rode through Watts en route to Los Angeles. The area became a mixed-race community of Germans, Blacks, Jews, Japanese, Mexicans, and Italians. Simon Rodia, who in 1921 began his ornate and airy construction of steel, mortar, tile, glass, and shell known as the Watts Towers, was an Italian immigrant. In the late 1930s and the 1940s burgeoning manufacturing industries generated a sizable migration of blacks from the South and from Texas. Because most real estate in Los Angeles was barred to them by race-restrictive covenants, they settled in the Central and South-Central regions of the city, a settlement that was further concentrated in Watts by the building of public housing. L.A.'s heavy industries — aircraft and defense, automotive (for a time, L.A.'s auto production was second only to Detroit's), steel, rubber, metal plating — provided steady, if dirty and dangerous, work for the rapidly growing population of Watts and for a range of blue-collar communities that surrounded the industrial corridor. I remember riding buses full of workmen in oil- and soot-stained denim.

Though Watts began to feel the social effects of overcrowding and inadequate infrastructure, it became a center of African American life and culture. But as the factories began closing in the 1960s and 1970s, the community, and others like it in the corridor, lost its economic base, experienced a devastating rise in unemployment and crime, and underwent dramatic shifts in demographics. (In the last fifteen years, through immigration from Mexico and Central America, Watts has become a community that is 43 percent Latino.) There has been little reinvestment in Watts and similar communities — they are very poor now, palm tree ghettoes — and the few jobs that remain tend to be low skilled and low paying. In the last twenty years, unemployment has risen by 50 percent; in 1990, the average household income in Watts was $12,700.

Watts. Since the summer of 1965, the name conjures up images of fire and violence. Given what Angelenos read in the paper or see on television, it is hard to imagine Watts as anything other than a site of drive-by shootings, street crime, squalid projects. Few people other than residents would think of going through there. To get to Watts, you would take the Harbor Freeway, heading south out of downtown L.A. toward the harbors in San Pedro, and exit to the east at Century Boulevard. You would pass Cathy's Nails and Red's Mini-mart and Pete's Burgers, a gas station, a coin laundry, a liquor store, a place to cash checks, some apartment buildings, and a lot of people on the street. At the corner of Century and Success Avenue, a green metal sign announces WATTS. Some of the side streets you might take would reveal abandoned houses, bars on windows, old couches rotting in vacant lots. But other streets have well-kept single-family homes, trimmed lawns, flower beds. If you got back onto Century Boulevard, continued east to Compton Avenue, and took a right turn, you'd soon find Edwin Markham Intermediate School, a good school sustained by the cohesive forces in the community, by those people who, as one resident said, "try to do the right thing, are ordinary, decent folks."

There are graffiti on several of Markham's bungalows and on the windows of the snack bar. Classrooms sometimes get vandalized. But when you walk into the main courtyard, you'll find a wide stretch of deep green grass, palm and pine trees, azaleas. In the principal's office are a number of trophies for "school beautification" and for academic pentathlon victories. (In 1990, Markham was one of two L.A. schools designated a California Distinguished School.) Outside the office is a bulletin board that displays certificates for achievement. "Laureates of the Week" it announces. Each certificate bears a student's name "for attendance and academic performance at Markham Middle School." Two girls coast by on their bikes. "Hey," one says to the other, "did you see? Latisha made the honor roll."

It was three in the afternoon in Room 56, and Yvonne Divans Hutchinson   5
had just kicked off her shoes and was stretching out, spent, releasing the day. She began reflecting on her long local history.

"I grew up here, over in the projects, and went to school in the neighborhood, went to this school, in fact. And I can remember some teachers saying awful things to us. I remember one in particular who told us that we should be glad he came to Watts because no one wanted to teach here. We were always confronted with attitudes like that. Well, I took umbrage at that comment. I had wanted to be a teacher for as long as I could remember, and on that day, I decided that not only was I going to be a teacher, but I was going to teach at *this* school because we needed teachers who *believed* in us."

She was about eight when her parents moved to Los Angeles from Arkansas and settled in Exposition Park, an area close to the L.A. Coliseum. She remembers a rooming house, her sister and brother and her sleeping in one bed. And she remembers her mother's excitement when they were finally able to move into the projects called Imperial Courts: "We're going to have a house all our own!" That was in 1954. Yvonne remembers roller-skating around the neighborhood, over to the library on Grandee. She recalls walking to school along the tracks of the Red Car, playing in the courtyard of the Watts Towers, going to the Largo Theater for thirty-five cents. She entered Edwin Markham Junior High School when it opened and was in the first graduating class, in 1958. She returned to teach in 1966 and has been there ever since.

"I've been a mentor teacher and the department chair, and I've had teachers tell me, 'This class can't think; they can't do the work; I can't find anything they can do.' And I'm astounded. You can look at a child and see that brightness, that eagerness. People who come to the classroom with preconceived notions about the kids don't give them a chance. It angers me and saddens me."

Room 56 was brick and dry wall, painted light mustard, some water stains along the baseboards. A long sign over one of the blackboards reads: NOTHING IS MORE IMPORTANT THAN YOUR EDUCATION. A life-sized cut-out of Bill Cosby on the back door said the same thing. A table in the back of the class was filled with autobiographies, stood upright on display: Ernesto Galarza's *Barrio Boy*, Dick Gregory's *Nigger*, *The Autobiography of Malcolm X*, Elie Wiesel's *Night*, Russell Baker's *Growing Up*. Along the chalk tray of the blackboard was a range of novels and stories, many of them autobiographical in content: Amy Tan's *The Kitchen God's Wife*, Maya Angelou's *I Know Why the Caged Bird Sings*, John Knowles's *A Separate Peace*, Sandra Cisnero's *The House on Mango Street*. One of the themes in the district guidelines for ninth grade is "understanding ourselves," and Yvonne had selected books that, for the most part, reflected the backgrounds of her students.

"I had a young Hispanic man tell me last year that he couldn't carry   10 books because he was a homeboy — he didn't want to be a schoolboy. A lot of boys want to be cool, so they'll put their books in their lockers when they go to class. A lot of African American boys will carry Pee-Chee folders because they can roll them up and put them in their coat pockets or jam them down the back of their pants. So I give notice on the first day of school that for my class you have to have a notebook that can't be folded up. A lot of our kids, the boys especially, identify with the streets; they want to be cool. They don't want to look like nerds. But I like to tell them [laughs], 'The nerds shall inherit the Earth!' [pause] It *is* serious, though. The whole idea of being identified as a tough guy yet also doing well in school is a real dilemma for young black men — in this neighborhood especially. We have people who are scholarly types, and when they leave the school, they go to the projects and have to prove themselves. It's really difficult."

All around the classroom, student writing and student art was on display. To the right of Yvonne's desk was Mariah Legans's drawing of four very different women, sort of middle-school Cubist in style, colorful, striking: an oblong face, a full, round face, blue spiked hair, tight black hair, tiny eyes, big eyes, a smile, a frown, a nose ring. "We are all individuals," she had written under it. "We don't look alike, we don't dress the same way, but we are all humans living on the same earth. So we need to learn to get along and respect each other."

On the bulletin board by the door was a cluster of four-by-six index cards, arrayed against orange, yellow, and blue art paper. These were done in class, responses to the books the students were reading. Yvonne had asked them to select a passage that grabbed them, draw it as best they could in pencil or pen, and comment on it.

Yardenna Aaron rendered a moment from the early pages of Malcolm X's autobiography:

> The scene depicted is when the police took Mrs. Little to the hospital to see and identify her dead husband. She was very hysterical. My drawing represents my idea and Malcolm's about her. The atmosphere when she entered the room containing the dead bodies. I think the policemen were laughing when she saw her husband. I believe that having no compassion in a case like this is a sin. The police were probably happy that he was killed because he was a strong man and taught Negroes about themselves.

Evonne Santiago had this to say about page 45 of *The House on Mango Street*:

> This nun has made Esperanza embarrassed of where she lived. This reminds me of myself. I always hated where I lived (in New Jersey) because everyone in my Catholic school had beautiful houses and my house was in a bad neighborhood and had rats and roaches.

Alejandra Mendoza, who was still mastering written English, wrote about a scene in Elie Wiesel's *Night*:

> My drawing represents the German throwing the kids up in the air and killing them with a machine gun. The reason the German killed them is because the kids are Jewish. It reminds me of L.A. because every day there's a kid dying by violence.

Yvonne continued. "Teachers will say either 'We can't lower our standards' or 'This poor child is reading below grade level, so I'll need a third- or fourth-grade book.' But what you need to do is find a way to make that eighth-grade book *accessible*. You have to respect the child. . . . I used to give a speech to new teachers in which I began by enumerating all the adjectives used to describe our kids: *slow, poor, impoverished, deprived, oppressed.* We get so busy looking at children in terms of labels that we fail to look for the *potential* — and to demand that kids live up to that potential. I tell these teachers, 'Do not think that because a child cannot read a text, he cannot read *you.'* Children can tell right off those people who believe in them and those who patronize them. They can tell once they come into the room — as if there's a smell in the air — they can tell right away if this teacher means business or if this teacher is, as they say, *jive.* They rise to whatever expectations are set. They rise or fail to rise. And when they rise, they can sometimes rise to great heights."

And so it was in this room on that day that Michallene Hooper read a draft of a profile of her friend Jennifer:

> "Nothing is more important than my education," declared Jennifer Rene McKnight, ninth-grader of Markham Intermediate School, who thinks very highly of her education. She plans on getting a scholarship for college and becoming a worker in the medical field. . . . This tall, slim, dark-skinned fourteen-year-old was born and raised in Los Angeles and has always been for helping her fellow Los Angelenos and influencing them to do the same. . . . Once while she was [stranded in the rain] a boy of her age with an umbrella offered to walk her home. "And after that," explained Jennifer, "I have never doubted the abilities of my neighbors. There's no telling what these good people are capable of or are going to do."

And it was in this room that the class held what Yvonne called a Quaker reading of Maya Angelou's inaugural poem, "On the Pulse of Morning." Each student selected some lines that spoke to him or her and read them, in sequence, into a tape recorder, creating a class reading, a new rendering:

> Across the wall of the world,
> A River sings a beautiful song. It says
> Come, rest here by my side . . .
>
> So say the Asian, the Hispanic, the Jew
> The African, the Native American, the Sioux . . .
>
> I, the Rock, I, the River, I, the Tree
> I am yours — your passages have been paid.

And it was in this room that Evonne Santiago — the girl who, in reading *The House on Mango Street,* recalled her old house in New Jersey — it was Evonne who explained to the class what she thought Maya Angelou's poem meant:

> She tells us our faults so we can see what to do with our country, she's telling us how to make it a better country. . . .
>
> The rock means strength. And the river — you know how a river goes through the land and picks up different water, well, that's like different cultures. And the tree is America — that can grow big and strong. . . .
>
> She's asking all these people — the Asian, the Hispanic, the African American — she's asking them to come under the tree, to let their dream grow. And she writes it for the inauguration because the president, he has to lead the country, he has great influence. If we grow today, we will be strong tomorrow. . . .

And all day long in this room, in every class — just as she did every day   20
here in this room — Yvonne Divans Hutchinson demonstrated, encouraged, celebrated, and guided students through an active and critical reading process that undercut the common perception that reading simply involved the decoding of words, that print had single, basic meanings that
students had to decipher quietly and store away. She had students write in a
"Reading Journal" a dialogue between themselves and the author of whatever book they were currently reading, "agreeing, disagreeing, sympathiz-
ing, questioning — engaging the *ideas* in the pages." Before distributing an
essay on courage, she asked her students to talk about a movie or television
show in which people acted courageously, and from those examples try to
explain what courage meant — all this to raise to critical consciousness
their own definitions of courage. She had been involved in the development
of a new statewide proficiency exam — one that encourages students to
offer interpretations of texts — and she handed out a draft of the scoring
guide and urged her students to analyze it. And Mariah Legans, whose Cubist plea for tolerance decorated the wall behind Yvonne's desk, said that
"when they say *literal* they mean that you just write down what you got
from the reading, but when they say *thoughtful* they mean you put some interpretation in it." And Michallene Hooper, the author of the personality
profile, explained that when they ask for *implications,* they're referring to
those times "when you read something, and it won't just come right out and
say what it meant, but kind of suggests it." And from there the class began
to discuss what it meant to read critically.

And in this room, at the end of the day, Rahsaan Thorpe took a moment
to look at his paper that Yvonne had on yet another display, a response to a
quotation about the value of interracial friendships. It began:

> I recall from ages eight to twelve, I was in close relation to other races. I
> grew up in a house-apartment, and during my time living there many
> neighbors came and went. Until one Christmas Eve a family moved in next
> door to me. The next morning I looked outside, and there was a [Salva-
> doran] boy sitting alone playing. I saw him and decided to make conversa-
> tion, and ever since that day, we have been friends. . . .

And from there, Rahsaan and the others went out to 104 Street or to
Compton Avenue, some leaving for surrounding communities, some walking home, holding their words clean and tight.

Understanding the Text

1. In your own words, explain how Watts came to be a largely African American community. What, according to Rose, were the causes of economic decline in Watts?

2. What presuppositions do some teachers at Edwin Markham Intermediate
   School have about Watts students?

3. Describe Yvonne Divans Hutchinson's teaching techniques. How does she attempt to reach students who prefer the streets to school?

4. Describe Rose's tone and how it shapes a reader's response to the teacher and students at this middle school.

Exploring and Debating the Issues

1. In your journal, reflect on the encouragement — or lack of it — that you received as a child in school. How did your teachers' and parents' assumptions about your learning ability influence your academic success?

2. In this selection, Yvonne Hutchinson criticizes the practice, common among her colleagues, of labeling students according to background or ability. Write an essay in which you evaluate the validity of Hutchinson's criticism.

3. According to Rose, Hutchinson selects her literary texts to reflect her students' backgrounds. In an argumentative essay, support, challenge, or complicate the assumption that students best learn when they can personally identify with reading materials. To support your position, you may draw on your own educational experiences or those of friends.

4. Yvonne Hutchinson is trying to teach her students to read and think critically. In class, discuss what critical reading and thinking is. To what extent would a college-level definition differ from a definition for high school students?

SYLVIA S. FOX

Teacher Shortage

In 1996, the state of California began to implement a program to achieve class-size reductions in classrooms throughout the public school system. One problem: there weren't enough credentialed teachers to teach the newly reduced classes. In this article, originally published in *California Journal,* **Sylvia S. Fox** reports on the ways in which California educators are responding to the shortage, in part by making certain that uncredentialed teachers who are already in the classroom receive the guidance and support they need as they work to fulfill their credentialing requirements. Sylvia S. Fox makes her home in Sacramento, where she is a professor of journalism at California State University, Sacramento.

Their sixth-grade classrooms sit back to back at the far corner of David Lubin Elementary School in the Sacramento City Unified School District.

Both first-time teachers, Nicole Andrews and Karna Cataline were handed the keys — and the responsibility — for their very first classrooms in August. Although both are working with temporary permits, neither is fully credentialed.

Andrews, who has a master's degree in English, taught part time for four years at local colleges — finally realizing that the hiring freeze for full-time faculty in higher education wasn't going away. She had her thirty-day emergency teaching permit but hadn't even substituted in a classroom when she spotted a flyer about a teaching internship that would place her in a full-time, salaried teaching job with benefits in the Sacramento city school district. The catch: she had to participate in a two-year, on-the-job training program that would lead to a teaching credential.

Cataline is teaching with a first-year emergency permit, after working part time as an aide at the school for six years while she raised her two children. She was in the substitute teaching pool when the full-time position suddenly opened a week before classes began.

The California credentialing structure is undergoing a hurried over-haul — some critics say too hurried — in order to produce enough qualified teachers to support a burgeoning student population, replace retiring teachers, and fill slots created by class-size reduction. Recent legislation is aimed at expanding statewide recruiting efforts, as well as providing support for new teachers. But it will be several years and substantial funding before recruitment and training can catch up with need.

Largely due to the demands of class-size reduction, the number of teachers with emergency permits for kindergarten through sixth grade doubled to 12,300 in 1996–97. More than 10,000 emergency permits for K–6 have been issued so far this year, with the Commission on Teacher Credentialing predicting the final tally may top 14,000.

The total number of emergency permits for all grades has reached a record-breaking 21,000 — a figure that is unacceptable to former state senator Gary Hart, a former teacher and Senate Education Committee chairman who is now director of the Institute for Education Reform at California State University, Sacramento. "As long as you have 21,000 people who don't have the minimum qualifications," Hart said, "it must be a state of emergency."

Bob Salley, director of certification for the credentialing commission, predicts the number of emergency permits won't decrease until 1999–2000. "Not all districts are as far along with implementation and expansion for class-size reductions as others," Salley said. "This year and next, the number will go up for emergency permits." If all the programs in place for recruiting, training, retention and teacher support are going full-bore, he added, they should have substantial impact by 1998–99. He hopes to see a drop in emergency permits by the following year.

Linda Bond, the commission's governmental affairs director, said school districts want to place the most qualified teachers in the classroom first, then "backfill" with emergency permit holders. The latter are most often individuals who have a college degree and have passed the CBEST, the basic skills test required for all teachers, but are missing a subject area and teacher training — or may simply be teaching outside their subject areas.

Recruitment is the first wave of attack, she said, especially targeting al-   10
ready credentialed teachers who have been teaching in private schools or
have left the teaching profession. This group includes the "phantom teaching force" — those who earn a teaching credential and never use it. Out-of-
state teachers who are credentialed also are being recruited, and Assembly
Bill 1620, introduced this session by Assemblyman Jack Scott (Democrat,
Pasadena) and sponsored by the commission, would ease current credentialing restrictions for qualified out-of-state teachers.

Bond says the commission's goal is to provide teacher training on a
timely basis, either through the conventional method, whereby a college
graduate enters a university teacher preparation program — or through an
alternative program, such as the teaching internships, which allow professionals to change careers holding a full-time teaching job while receiving
structured-on-the-job training. "What we're seeing . . . is an increased focus
on alternative routes to teacher credentialing," said Paul Warren, director of
the educational unit at the Legislative Analyst's Office.

Nicole Andrews, on the job in her Sacramento classroom, says she
would never have made the switch to a very demanding "twelve hours a day
every day" teaching job in a public school without the internship. "I had
been in school for nine years," she said. "I needed to make a living."

While simple math says the numbers aren't even close to filling the current need, interest in teaching jobs is on the rise.

State Superintendent of Public Instruction Delaine Eastin said that following the announcement of class-size reduction, the number of applicants
scheduled to take the CBEST doubled. Jan Cross, coordinator of the Teacher
Preparation Program at CSU Sacramento, said phone inquiries have increased "exponentially" for the traditional teacher-training program. In a
recently formed partnership between CSUS and the University of California, Davis, six hundred inquiries were logged for sixty available slots — with
instruction aimed at teachers currently employed under emergency permits or those considering a career change.

Frank Meder, coordinator of the Sacramento city school district's in-   15
ternship program, said he is getting fifteen to twenty calls a day about its internship program through CSU Sacramento, although there are only fifty
slots available in the fall semester.

Michael McKibbin, who helps coordinate alternative certification for
the commission, said the past three years have shown massive growth in
the number of internships, from less than 5 percent to almost 25 percent of
all teachers coming up through an internship program.

The governor's proposed state budget earmarks another $1 million to
expand alternative certification in fifty-three university and district internship programs raising funding to $7.5 million annually. Designed to reduce
the number of teachers on emergency permits, the effort will push candidates through a rapid credentialing program that supporters say is the most
practical and pragmatic method — certainly the most cost-effective for
someone wanting to become a teacher.

Cataline says she would like to take advantage of the internship opportunity because required classes are arranged around a full-time teaching job, which is impossible under the traditional approach. Because she converted her thirty-day permit into a one-year emergency permit, she has no priority for a position for next year. In fact, districts prefer not to renew an emergency permit if they can get a credentialed teacher. She also faces a five-year time limit for her emergency permit because of recent legislation.

Scott says the state rushed into class-size reduction without fully realizing the consequences — and one of those has been a lack of credentialed teachers. "I don't have to be a mathematician to see we've increased the need [for credentialed teachers] by 50 percent," he said.

Although Scott, former president of Pasadena City College, is a strong   20
supporter of class-size reduction, he also cautions that "reform will do us very little value if the teachers aren't qualified." The commission estimates that two-thirds to three-fourths of all emergency permit holders never become fully certificated. McKibbin says lack of on-the-job support for new teachers is a critical issue because the least experienced teachers may also be put in some of the toughest teaching situations.

"They may never get help or get the worst classroom," McKibbin said. "Our data say they're going to drop out, and I can understand why they do."

He said internship programs provide necessary structure and support. Andrews talks to her teaching mentor at least two hours a week, has monthly contact with her teaching supervisor, and the principal drops in at least every other week to unofficially observe. She also takes twelve to fifteen university credits in teacher training each semester. She said the formal support has been "overwhelming." But she said the most useful assistance has been the intense peer support, created by a summer of working in the Phase I portion of teacher training, followed by evening classes the interns all take together twice a week and an ongoing phone network.

To create additional early support, Assembly Bill 351, authored by Scott and signed into law last year, establishes a preinternship credential aimed at reducing the number of teachers on emergency permits by moving them into preparation more quickly. If the pilot program is effective, the long-term goal is to replace emergency credentials except in areas of the state that are geographically remote or have other unique circumstances. Almost half of the interns in the Sacramento district program this year had worked on emergency permits.

McKibbin cites three critical elements for success: get the teacher qualified quickly in the subject matter, give new teachers "survival skills" — often as simple as learning how to be sure the same number of kids come back from the bathroom as leave — and provide ongoing peer support.

McKibbin said teacher training for emergency permit holders is critical   25
to the ultimate success, or failure, of the state's push for education reform. "We've got to get these people trained," he said. "We know who's going to get blamed [if they're not], and it's not going to be the politicians."

Virtually everyone involved in California education agrees that class-size reduction is the most innovative, dramatic, and downright exciting educational reform they've seen in years.

But the success of smaller classes ultimately will hinge on the ability to find enough qualified bodies to stand in front of an elementary class and deliver the right words that will raise reading and math scores statewide — the fundamental promise on which the 1996 implementation of class-size reduction is based.

Despite the obstacles, 94 percent of California districts decided to go with class-size reduction. "They did this with their shirttails hanging out, even though it was on short notice, in a big hurry, without adequate classrooms and with emergency permits," said Eastin.

She and others cautioned, however, that California's most troubled districts with the poorest student performance will have a more difficult time getting qualified people to work there. "If we have a shortage of teachers," says the Legislative Analyst's Warren, "the least attractive place to teach will feel it first."

Understanding the Text

1. What are the causes of the current shortage of qualified teachers in California public education, according to Fox?
2. What strategies for resolving the shortages are being implemented?
3. Why has it been difficult to keep new teachers in the classroom, according to this selection?
4. What do teachers need in order to succeed in the classroom?

Exploring and Debating the Issues

1. If your college or university has a teacher-training program, study its curriculum, and write an essay discussing whether you believe that it adequately prepares students to be successful public-school teachers. To develop your ideas, you might interview students who participate in the program or faculty who teach in it.
2. Many private-school teachers are not required to have teaching credentials, and yet a private-school education is in demand for those who can afford it. Write an essay arguing for or against the necessity of a teaching credential for public-school teachers.
3. Interview some of your fellow students who want to be teachers, and record their reasons why a teaching career attracts them. Alternately, interview students who have no interest in a teaching career. Use your findings as the basis of an essay in which you explain people's motivations for entering the teaching profession.
4. Some people have proposed that the solution to California's public-school problems, including its teacher shortage, is to privatize education. Conduct a debate in class over whether education should be handed over to private interests.

JAMES RICHARDSON

What Price Glory?

The California Master Plan for Higher Education pledges a tuition-free education to every California resident enrolled at a UC, CSU, or community college campus. So what's all that money everyone's forking out to attend a public college or university? It's a fee, and as everyone who has attended a California college or university in the last ten years knows, those fees have been rising steeply in the 1990s. In this article, originally published in *UCLA Magazine*, **James Richardson** (b. 1953) outlines the almost Orwellian process by which a tuition-free promise was transformed into an escalating system of educational fees. A graduate of UCLA, Richardson is a senior writer with the *Sacramento Bee*.

W hen I went to UCLA in the early 1970s, my father wrote a check for $212 each quarter for my student fees. I lived in an apartment that rented for $90 a month, which I split with a roommate. We survived on Ragu spaghetti sauce. Whether I would finish school in four years was not an issue.

I neither had to work during the school year, nor did my parents have to borrow money to pay my way. Summer jobs in a can factory back in Kansas provided me with all the extra cash I needed for the next school year. While my college education was not free, the cost was not particularly burdensome for a middle-class family living, as could be done in those days, on a sole breadwinner's wages.

For decades, however, Californians had enjoyed the promise of a *free* education from kindergarten through college. And it was a truly extraordinary promise. In the early 1940s, both of my parents went to UC Berkeley, then the nation's finest public university. They paid only books and board. Nothing like a UC education, in Berkeley, Los Angeles, and across the entire system as it expanded up and down the state, was offered anywhere else in the United States.

California's modern blueprint for its colleges and universities, the Master Plan for Higher Education, enacted in 1960 and still in force, pledges as a matter of public policy a tuition-free education to all who are qualified. But over the past three decades, California's commitment to its future has steadily eroded as "student fees" have first crept, then shot, upward. "A free education was absolutely one of the pillars of the Master Plan," observes Warren Fox, executive director of the California Postsecondary Education Commission, which regulates higher education in California and is the steward of the plan. "And we've lost it."

The University of California's nine campuses now charge "educational   5 fees" and "registration fees." The California State University system (CSU), with twenty-two campuses, charges a "university fee" and an "instructional-related activities fee." The state's 106 community colleges charge students an "academic unit fee." Call these costs what you will, the fact is the price of higher education in the Golden State is a lot higher than it used to be.

My generation was perhaps the last to benefit from anything resembling California's post–World War II promise. Undergraduate students in the University of California system today pay $4,166 a year in fees. The cost of room and board at UCLA is, on average, an additional $6,400 — and Berkeley is even pricier. Today's students work longer hours while in school, borrow more to meet rising costs (an average of $4,300 a year), and are forced by economic constraints to take longer to complete their undergraduate educations.

The cost of going to the University of California today manifests itself not only as a financial burden on students and their families, but also profoundly on society at large. The career choices made by students, particularly those who go to UC's professional schools and are faced with $10,000 a year in fees, are undoubtedly skewed by what they spend on their educations. This contradicts one of the public university's central purposes: to produce graduates who will take lower-paying public service jobs after they graduate to give something back to the community. UC graduates — California's best and brightest, who despite rising fees are still trained largely at public expense — now increasingly find it financially impossible to serve those most in need.

The steadily escalating fees at the University of California mirror a wider national trend. Over the past fifteen years, while household income rose 82 percent, college tuition climbed 234 percent nationally, according to the U.S. General Accounting Office. During the same period, state support for higher education fell across the nation by an average of 14 percentage points; universities have become increasingly dependent on tuition to balance the budget.

The annual budget for the University of California's nine campuses totals $11.1 billion and is enormously complicated. The state now provides less than 20 percent of the funding; the bulk comes from the federal government, through individual and corporate donations, from endowments and student fees. (UC also operates three national laboratories, which are entirely funded by the federal government to the tune of $2.3 billion a year — only slightly less than the cost of instruction at all the campuses.)

Still, the University of California is less expensive, if only by a bit, than most other top-tier public schools including the University of Michigan ($6,074 in tuition annually), the University of Virginia ($4,648) and the State University of New York ($4,656). Moreover, the price tag on a UC education is substantially lower than that of private universities. The annual tuition for an undergraduate education at Stanford University, for example, stands at $20,490 a year.

By these standards, an education at a UC campus remains a bargain. "I think our fees are quite reasonable," says former UC President Clark Kerr, widely viewed as the author of California's higher education master plan. "Those who benefit so much themselves" — meaning college graduates who will earn an average of 80 percent more over their lifetime than those without degrees — "should be able to pay it." Nevertheless, there are many

10

inside UC circles who believe that the problem with fees is not so much that they are the highest in the university's history but that they shot up so drastically in such a short period — more than 500 percent in the twenty-five years since my own college days.

Indeed, UCLA Chancellor Charles E. Young favors gradually increasing fees and student financial aid. Currently the UC system's fee structure returns to students fully one-third of all fees collected in the form of financial assistance. In 1993–94, the last academic year for which statistics are available, the university systemwide awarded an average of $7,105 to each of the 91,776 students who qualified for aid.

Young argues that fee increases and the corresponding growth of the financial aid pool have enabled the poor to have wider access to college than might otherwise be possible, and there is considerable statistical evidence proving that he is correct. Especially with affirmative action admissions considerations on the way out in the UC system, the ability to subsidize low-income students could prove essential to maintaining any semblance of diversity in the university's student body.

With their fees, middle- and upper-income students are, in effect, carrying the tuition load for lower-income students. The result has been steady enrollment increases in the 1990s for two groups: low-income students, who receive aid, and high-income students, for whom fees are not an issue. At the same time, however, enrollment has steadily shrunk among the middle class, defined as those with a yearly family income between $30,000 and $90,000. "The dilemma is what is happening to the middle class," confirms UC system budget director Larry Hershman. "More people are going to have to save and borrow."

High fees for higher education in California were not born of economic necessity but were an outgrowth of political expediency. In 1967 California had a new governor: Ronald Reagan. He sensed public disgust growing with student protesters' disrespect for the taxpayers who were giving them a free, first-rate education. By the end of the 1960s, there were more than 200 arrests at UCLA, UC Berkeley, and UC San Diego; in 1969 alone there were 584 arrests at San Francisco State College. Voters saw little reason to coddle students they viewed as spoiled children, and Reagan rode the electorate's collective resentment into the statehouse. 15

In his first year in office, Governor Reagan argued that the state should stop subsidizing protesters and start making students pay tuition for their education. His position was hugely popular with the populace. But Reagan was opposed by Assembly Speaker Jesse Unruh, who found unconscionable the idea of scuttling California's promise of a free education.

By virtue of their elective positions, both Reagan and Unruh were members of the UC Board of Regents, and they faced off at a heated regents meeting in the UCLA faculty center on Aug. 31, 1967. Some regents, particularly oilman Ed Pauley, pleaded with Reagan that day not to bring up the tuition issue. Pauley did not want to go back on California's promise, nor did he wish to see the governor embarrassed. But Reagan rebuffed him, replying, "I for one have no intention of discussing anything but tuition."

Arguments on both sides were heard, and the regents voted 14–7 against Reagan's tuition proposal. Then they broke for lunch. When they returned, Reagan was all smiles. During the break, a deal was brokered that has held firm to his day: the regents agreed to accept a "charge" on students so long as it was not called "tuition." The letter of the Master Plan's guarantee of tuition-free higher education was preserved, even as a mockery was made of its spirit.

By the early 1970s, the regents had imposed more than $600 in charges a year; fees mounted steadily through the 1970s and 1980s. Students and their parents grumbled, but the increases were relatively modest and predictable through the gubernatorial terms of Democrat Jerry Brown and Republican George Deukmejian.

But in the early 1990s, as the California economy slid into its worst   20
downturn since the Great Depression, the Democratic-controlled Legislature and Republican Governor Pete Wilson increasingly saw student fees as the way to keep the state's higher education systems afloat. The debate in Sacramento was not about whether to raise fees, but by how much. In 1980, UC student fees were $1,634 a year. Fifteen years later, they had nearly tripled. And other segments of public higher education in California were hit even harder: community college fees tripled in just ten years.

As fees climbed, enrollments plummeted. Estimates are that 200,000 students disappeared from California's college and university campuses in the early 1990s. The devastation suffered by the CSU system could be seen a few miles away from the state capitol as CSU Sacramento closed two of its four dorms.

Two years ago, with the economy recovering and Democrats exploiting student fees as a campaign issue, Governor Wilson proposed a "compact with higher education" to stabilize fee increases and forestall further budget cuts. His proposal called for an annual 4 percent real increase in state appropriations to higher education and steady 10 percent student fee increases.

So far, the state has done better than the compact provides. For the past two years, the Legislature has "bought out" the student fee increases by providing enough additional funding to replace revenue the fee hikes would have produced. The budget game is now played thusly: the UC Regents propose a student fee increase, the Legislature and governor come up with the extra money, the regents defer the increase. It appears to be working. With fees stabilized, enrollments have begun to recover. The entering UC class this fall was the largest since 1991.

The game will be played again this spring for the 1997–98 budget cycle. For the third year in a row, UC officials proposed a fee increase — 9.7 percent this time, which would cost the state an estimated $33 million to absorb. This time around, however, the university did not seek a total buyout of the proposed increase. Included in the $370 in added fees each student would have paid was a $40 "technology fee" intended to generate a $4 million down payment on the overhaul and modernization of UC's computer systems and teaching technologies. UC President Richard Atkinson said he wanted the new fee imposed on students systemwide, regardless of what the state did with the rest of the budget. He also anticipated increasing the technology fee each year into the foreseeable future.

Last fall, Atkinson argued that the proposed fee hikes were in keeping   25
with the compact made with higher education by the governor and that it was time for the university to uphold its end of the bargain. "There is no question the university has been faced with very tough problems these last few years," Atkinson said, "but I think we have served the state well. Now we must ensure that our programs remain of high quality."

In January, however, Governor Wilson proposed a full buyout of student fee increases — including the technology fee — and additional funds for one of Atkinson's highest priorities: increasing UC faculty pay. Currently UC professors are paid an average of $73,000 a year but still lag about 3 percent behind faculty at comparable institutions.

Wilson's proposal headed for the Legislature where, like all of his budget proposals, it faced an uncertain future. There was even some talk among lawmakers of a fee *decrease* during the opening gambit of the budget game.

But, as Jess Bravin, a Boalt Hall law student who is the student representative on the Board of Regents, points out, the UC-Wilson agreement is of recent origin and temporary duration. "We speak of the 'compact' like we're talking about the Mayflower Compact," says Bravin. "The most important compact is the one made between the state of California and California families in 1868, when UC was established. In 1992 or so we decided to pass on to families the cost of instruction. But this is a very significant violation of a much earlier and more important compact."

The ongoing debate over student fees only hints at the larger economic challenges facing the UC system, and all of higher education in California, in the years to come. A huge new generation of college students will descend on the universities and colleges in the next decade in what many are calling "Tidal Wave II." That the students are coming is certain: they are in the elementary and secondary schools now. But the inundation will come at a time when budget experts predict there will be no funds left for higher education because the prisons, welfare, Medi-Cal, and K–12 education will have sapped the entire state budget.

So far, the reaction of leaders of UC, CSU, and state policymakers alike   30
is to "study the problem." The studies vary in their specific projections, but not their overall conclusions. "California appears to be in a state of denial," says a report by the Santa Monica–based RAND Corporation. "Budgets are no longer considered from the perspective of what is required to support the needs of the state's higher education sector, but rather of how much of

the budget is left to be spent on it." RAND predicts that in 2010 nearly a million California students who are qualified to go to college under the prevailing Master Plan will be shut out either because there will be no space for them or they will be unable to afford the costs.

Patrick Callan, executive director of the California Higher Education Policy Center, a San Jose–based think tank, advises all those concerned about the future of higher education in California to wake up. "Everyone will have to make extraordinary efforts immediately, or we will lose higher education," he warns. "Ten years from now, we'll be talking about the crisis in higher education the same way we talk about our failing K–12 schools today."

Understanding the Text

1. How did the California Master Plan's promise of a free public higher education system come to be subverted, according to Richardson's history?
2. Why does Richardson call the state budget process for funding higher education a "game" (para. 24)?
3. Despite the recent steep increases in University of California fees, why do such people as Clark Kerr still refer to them as "quite reasonable" (para. 11)?
4. Why does Patrick Callen predict a crisis for the future of California higher education?

Exploring and Debating the Issues

1. Recently, higher education, both public and private, has been escalating in cost. In your journal, explore the effects of these cost increases on your life as a student. If you are facing financial difficulties, how are you attempting to resolve the problems? If you're not, what suggestions would you offer students who are?
2. Richardson writes that "middle- and upper-middle-income students are, in effect, carrying the tuition load for lower-income students" (para. 14). In class, debate the justification for this practice. To develop support for your position, you might investigate your school's scholarship offerings for lower-income students.
3. California's Master Plan promised access to higher education to all qualified high school graduates in the state. In class, discuss the impact of recent tuition increases and political initiatives, such as Proposition 209, on students' access to a college or university education. Use your class discussion as a basis for an essay in which you argue whether the Master Plan should be upheld or eliminated as public policy.
4. Richardson asserts that the predicted increase in college-age students will "come at a time when budget experts predict there will be no funds left for higher education because the prison, welfare, Medi-Cal, and K–12 education will have sapped the entire state budget" (para. 29). In class,

brainstorm ways of saving costs at your campus or redistributing state money to make it more available for higher education. Then select several of the more viable suggestions, and use them as the basis of an argument for changing the method of funding higher education in California.

5. Write a letter to your state legislators or to the governor in which you argue your view of fee increases in higher education. Be sure to consider how revenue should be generated if you argue that fees should be stabilized or cut.

SUSAN E. BROWN

The ZIP Code Route into UC

Is ZIP code really destiny? In this essay, **Susan E. Brown** (b. 1948) argues that it may well be, at least in relation to the California college or university you attend. Wealthier school districts can give their students an edge in the competition for spaces in the UC system, thus calling into question the Master Plan's promise of equal opportunity for all. A legal advocate for educational and other equity issues, Brown is currently in private practice in San Francisco. She was director of higher education for the Mexican American Legal Defense and Education Fund when she wrote this essay in1989 for the Pacific News Service.

California's system of higher education has been celebrated as the nation's model system, providing equal access to the American dream. But a look at who is admitted to the prestigious University of California campuses shows that ZIP codes may be as critical as grade point averages in determining who gets in and who stays out.

This is how the system works. The top 12.5 percent of the state's high school graduates are eligible for the University of California; the top 33.5 percent are eligible for the state universities; for everyone else there is open access to community colleges with the option, after two years, of transferring into a four-year institution.

California's goal has been a democratic one of making higher education available to one and all. The reality, however, reveals a system that favors the rich and the few. The list of the feeder high schools that send more than one hundred students each to UC reads like a social register. It includes Beverly Hills, Palos Verdes, Santa Monica, Rolling Hills, Palisades, and, in the San Fernando Valley, Granada Hills, Birmingham, and Taft. With the exception of San Francisco's Lowell and University High Schools, the UC feeders are in predominantly, if not exclusively, white, affluent enclaves. Not surprisingly, the mean family income for freshmen at UC Berkeley last fall was nearly sixty thousand dollars, well above the national average.

Both the California Master Plan and Education Code are structured in such a way that students not originally eligible for a state university may be able to transfer after two years at a community college. But to the extent that transfer from a community college to UC works at all, it works primarily for the select, the affluent — and principally the white — community college. The top ten community college feeder campuses to UC for fall 1986 were mainly in affluent residential communities: Santa Monica (252 transfers), Diablo Valley (241), Santa Barbara (227), Orange Coast (207), Cabrillo (151), El Camino (143), De Anza (139), San Diego Mesa (138), American River (132), and Saddleback (132).

By contrast, consider Fresno City College, which serves large numbers   5
of minority students from a predominantly agricultural region. Only one black and four Latinos (out of a total student body of thirteen thousand) transferred to UC in 1986. Imperial Valley Community College, serving a similar student body, sent only three Latinos to UC campuses out of a freshman class of 1,341 that year. At predominantly black Compton College, only two blacks transferred to a UC campus in 1986.

Statewide, the 106 community colleges in California sent a total of 189 blacks and 485 Latinos to the eight UC campuses, an average of six minority students from each college. Yet approximately 80 percent of underrepresented minorities who enter college in the state begin their studies in a community college.

While it is surely important to maintain high standards, the goal of a tax-based state educational system should be the development of talents and skills from all socioeconomic groups. Public education by its very nature must reflect the entire population that supports it. What California has, instead, is a perfectly correlated system of family income to educational benefits — that is, the wealthiest are rewarded with access to the University of California; middle-income students end up at the California State University; low-income students begin and end their higher education at community colleges.

One possible solution to the perpetuation of a hereditary elite is to expand eligibility to UC and CSU to the top 12.5 percent and top 33.5 percent of students at every high school. There is nothing in state law or the California Master Plan to prevent this more egalitarian approach. Without such a remedy, California will merely continue to favor students from those schools with honors courses, enriched curriculums, well-equipped science laboratories and optimal learning conditions.

Shouldn't a serious student at an inner-city school who graduates in the top 10 percent of his or her class have the same access to the benefits of California's postsecondary system as his or her counterpart in an exclusive private or magnet public school? If not, we should recognize that we are rewarding accidents of birth and that our current system of admissions to the University of California is, in truth, determined by ZIP code.

Understanding the Text

1. Summarize in your own words the evidence that Brown offers to demonstrate that "our current system of admissions to the University of California is, in truth, determined by ZIP code" (para. 9).

2. Which social classes do the three units of California higher education — the University of California, the California State University system, and the community colleges — each serve, according to Brown?

3. What does Brown mean by the term "hereditary elite" (para. 8)?

4. What solution to current problems in demographic enrollment patterns does Brown propose for California's higher education system?

Exploring and Debating the Issues

1. In class, discuss the evidence that Brown presents to support her argument. How effective do you find her use of statistics? Are there any factors affecting college admissions that she fails to mention?

2. Write a letter to Brown from Ruben Navarrette, Jr.'s perspective ("Well, I Guess They Need Their Minority," p. 150), advising her on how to achieve her goals.

3. Compared to students from impoverished areas, students from wealthier communities tend to have access to better public schools — and hence a better chance of meeting the eligibility requirements of the University of California system. Write an essay arguing for or against the proposition that different standards should be used in granting admission to students from underprivileged school districts.

4. Write an essay in which you support, refute, or complicate Brown's assumption that "the goal of a tax-based state educational system should be the development of talents and skills from all socioeconomic groups" (para. 7).

WARD CONNERLY

Race Preferences Lose in Court — Again

In the battle over affirmative action, no one has been more prominent on the front lines than **Ward Connerly**. A passionate, outspoken opponent of racial preferences, Connerly was a leading force in the UC Regents' 1994 decision to phase out affirmative action throughout the UC system. He then became a leader of the movement that led to the passing of Proposition 209 in 1996. In this op-ed piece, Connerly reflects on the Ninth U.S. Circuit Court of Appeals ruling that upheld Proposition 209 in 1997, a ruling that was followed a few months later by the U.S. Supreme Court's final upholding of the measure. A University of California regent and businessman, Connerly is also chair of the American Civil Rights Institute.

U pon hearing that a panel of the Ninth U.S. Circuit Court of Appeals had upheld Proposition 209, President Clinton said that the supporters of racial preferences would have to "regroup."

Indeed, regroup they must. But I hope they realize the damage they are doing to our society by trying to frustrate the will of the majority of Americans, who want to achieve a society of genuine equality for all and special privileges for none.

Anyone with a sense of history and an appreciation of the principles of American democracy must know that a system of policies that grants preferences to some citizens at the sacrifice of others cannot long endure. Such policies amount to discrimination, and the American people oppose discrimination.

Most of us know that, indeed, affirmative action and other attempts to "build diversity" have become a system of preferences. The people of California said on November 5, 1996, when they voted for Proposition 209, that they would not tolerate such policies.

Since then, the will of the majority has been obstructed by the decision   5
of one judge, a decision that can only be described as perverse. The ruling that Proposition 209 was unconstitutional because it supposedly discriminated against women and minorities has to be one of the most Orwellian decisions in the history of American jurisprudence.

It might be useful to remind ourselves of the clear and simple language that the people of California embedded in their Constitution last November:

> The state shall not discriminate against, nor grant preferential treatment to, any individual or group on the basis of race, sex, color, ethnicity or national origin in the operation of public employment, public education or public contracting.

On Tuesday, a three-judge panel of the Ninth Circuit reaffirmed the fundamental truth of Proposition 209 when it said that preferences based on race and gender are constitutionally suspect and can be abolished by a state without violating the rights of any individual. This decision puts a nail, if not a spike, in the coffin of race and gender preferences.

Now the people of California can get on with the business of making the dream of equal opportunity a reality, without the use of artificial preferences that are divisive and promote the ethnic polarization of our society. We must now focus on ways of providing access for all of our children to an education that prepares them for the rigors of a competitive society.

We must find ways of guaranteeing to minority and women contractors that they will have an equal opportunity to bid on public contracts. We must ensure that we do not return to the "good old boys" days in which women and people of certain colors and ethnic backgrounds were denied the right to enjoy employment for those reasons.

I have confidence that the people of California will not return to those   10
days. But the heavy lifting must now begin to provide that reassurance to others who are not as confident as I. For many, their fears are genuine and must be addressed in deeds and not just words.

The Ninth Circuit's decision also should focus the federal government's attention to the writing on the wall. The executive branch should bring itself into compliance with the spirit of Proposition 209 and with the growing body of case law being handed down by courts throughout the land.

The quest to achieve a society where all of our citizens receive equal treatment under the law has always been a struggle for America. On November 5, 1996, the people of California moved that cause forward in a major way. On April 8, 1997, the Ninth Circuit propelled it even further.

Understanding the Text

1. Why does Connerly write that opponents of Proposition 209 are doing damage "to our society by trying to frustrate the will of the majority of Americans" (para. 2)?

2. What are the differences in connotation between the phrases *affirmative action* and "race and gender preferences" (para. 8)? How do these phrases reflect the two sides of the affirmative action debate?

3. Proposition 209 applies only to California public institutions. What does Connerly believe its influence should be on the rest of the nation?

Exploring and Debating the Issues

1. Connerly recognizes that barriers to equal opportunity do exist in America. In class, brainstorm policies that might be implemented to overcome such barriers without resorting to racial or gender preferences.

2. In an essay, support, refute, or complicate Connerly's assertion that racial preferences amount to discrimination.

3. During the campaign for Proposition 209, Connerly was heavily criticized for being an African American who opposed affirmative action. Do you believe that such criticism is just?

4. Interview several students on campus, perhaps of one demographic or institutional group, on their views of affirmative action and Proposition 209. Use your results as the basis of a paper in which you discuss your campus's position on this controversial subject.

NATHAN GLAZER

Blacks Only?

Opponents of affirmative action often complain that the policy applies to so many groups — white women, the handicapped, Vietnam veterans, people of nontraditional sexual orientation, to name just a few — that virtually anyone could be included under its wing. Even if that charge is valid, it no longer applies to public hiring and education in California with the passage of Proposition 209. But as **Nathan Glazer** (b. 1923) points out in this selection reprinted from the *New Republic,* even opponents of affirmative action have been dismayed by Prop. 209's effects on the population that the policy was originally intended to benefit — African Americans. A professor of education and sociology at Harvard University, Glazer is the editor, coeditor, or author of numerous books, including *Beyond the Melting Pot* (1990) and *We Are All Multiculturalists Now* (1997).

Fewer people voted for Proposition 209, the amendment to the California Constitution that bans affirmative action, than said they would in pre-election polls. I suspect that, when faced with the voting machine, many voters experienced a twinge of terminal horror: they hesitated to take the fateful action that would sweep away procedures, offices, and agencies we had lived with for twenty-five years. Many of us who had thought or written in opposition to affirmative action experienced a similar reaction when it finally seemed something decisive would be done. Complexities that had not been obvious in the debate or in popular thinking suddenly emerged, like a genie from the bottle.

The last few months have seen an upsurge of new thinking on affirmative action, mostly by its opponents. Thoughtful articles, all stopping short of advocating the policy's total abandonment, have appeared in the *New Republic* (by James Q. Wilson and by Glenn Loury), the *New Yorker* (by Alan Wolfe), and even the *Weekly Standard* (David Frum) and the *National Review* (Dinesh D'Souza). All showed surprising flexibility. Among the defenders of affirmative action, there has been comparatively little new thinking. Their approach seems to be to stand pat and hope that they can count on enough liberal judges to maintain the status quo.

What gives pause to opponents now? It is the clear knowledge that the end of affirmative action, honestly implemented, means a radical reduction in the number of blacks attending selective colleges, universities, and professional schools. The consequences for other "protected" minorities and women would be less drastic. Hiring and promotion policies wouldn't change much, either: the Texaco case demonstrates that business can be kept well in line when it comes to jobs. And preferences for government contractors are already difficult to maintain in the face of clear Supreme Court decisions.

Higher education, though, is a different story. There, the end of affirmative action means facing the prospect that the number of African American students accepted into selective institutions would drop from 6 or 7 percent to around 2 percent. In other words, the predominant pathway to well-paying and influential jobs for blacks would all but disappear. This would be a disaster for race relations and for the prospect of a fuller integration of African Americans into the mainstream of American society.

The simple question then becomes: are we willing, in the name of the principle of color-blindness, to accept this result and to deal with its damaging consequences for race relations and for the ultimate goal of a decent multiracial society? Some try to duck this question by advocating that we end affirmative action but improve primary and secondary education for blacks so they can qualify for selective institutions. This sounds reasonable, but it is unfortunately no answer: we have been trying to improve education for decades, with some limited success. But we are nowhere near getting substantial representation of blacks in selective American institutions of higher education on the basis of color-blind admissions.

So what is to be done? Richard Kahlenberg's proposal to substitute economic hardship criteria for racial criteria won't maintain blacks at their current percentages, unless it is implemented transparently for that purpose. James Q. Wilson argues that for undergraduate institutions the objective of racial diversity is legitimate, and preferences for this purpose are as defensible as those for athletes or alumni children. He contends that racial diversity is not, however, a legitimate objective for law and medical schools. But why not? One could find more compelling reasons to preserve racial preferences for professional schools. Black doctors disproportionately serve black patients, black lawyers disproportionately serve black clients. The argument can go back and forth: don't blacks deserve the best doctors and the best lawyers? To which the answer is, don't blacks also have the right to gain access to doctors and lawyers who they think will be more understanding and empathetic?

We are all — even the defenders of affirmative action — opposed to quotas. We are all for a fuller incorporation of the black minority into American life. (Asians, apparently, can fend for themselves, and so, for the most part, can Latinos.) Can we restrict affirmative action only to African Americans? I suggested this in 1987, and this is what Frum and D'Souza propose. It seems politically impossible, even if we could argue that there is constitutional legitimacy for such a limitation. Can we find a way to reconcile some degree of selectivity or preference, limited to the one group that clearly has the most claim to it, with the language and ideals of the Fourteenth Amendment and the Civil Rights Act of 1964, and with the parallel language of California's Proposition 209, which is modeled on these precedents?

An approach that broke down the affirmative action package, by group and by kind of preference, could win solid majority support. But there is much work to be done. Up to now, only the opponents of affirmative action have been willing to outline the contours of a compromise. The defenders insist on holding on to the whole bag.

The intention of the Civil Rights Act was to prohibit discrimination against blacks. If we take its language and intention seriously and literally, it also prohibits discrimination in favor of blacks. Universities and professional schools want to maintain this kind of preference, for good reasons and bad, as we see from the fierce resistance in these institutions to Proposition 209. Can we grant preference to the group that initiated the civil rights revolution, while maintaining the color-blindness incorporated in the Civil Rights Act of 1964 and Proposition 209? Or do the two objectives fatally contradict each other?

It seemed a reasonable thing to ban all discrimination on the grounds   10
of race in 1964: we thought then that legal discrimination was the only problem. Now, after a quarter-century of experience, we have discovered that it goes deeper. Clear and seemingly intractable inequalities persist in the measured abilities and aptitudes of different groups. As a result, the way we justify our commitment to incorporating blacks into our institutions of higher education, our government, our businesses, becomes an exercise in hypocrisy. Can we find a way to free our thousands of decision-makers to make the choices on admission and employment and promotion that seem right and proper to them? Some of us think that allowing this would not, overall, harm the hope of a fuller integration. But we are now stuck between the absolutes of color-blindness and of quotas. Can we find the legal language, the political coalitions, to institute the more limited affirmative action that our society needs?

Understanding the Text

1. According to Glazer, how did many former critics of affirmative action adjust their position after the passage of Proposition 209?

2. Why does Glazer distinguish between affirmative action in admission policies in higher education and affirmative action in employment policies governing hiring and promotion in business?

3. What evidence does Glazer provide to support his argument that affirmative action should be restricted to African Americans?

4. What assumptions underlie Glazer's statement that "Clear and seemingly intractable inequalities persist in the measured abilities and aptitudes of different groups" (para. 10)?

5. Where in his selection does Glazer anticipate objections to his argument? What strategies does he use to counter those objections?

Exploring and Debating the Issues

1. In an essay, support, oppose, or modify Glazer's argument that affirmative action should be limited to African Americans.

2. Glazer assumes that some minority groups, such as Asian Americans or Hispanics, do not need affirmative action. In class, form teams and debate this assumption. To collect evidence for your team's position, you may want to conduct interviews with students on your campus of varying ethnic backgrounds.

3. Glazer refers to several authors who have revised their formerly fervent opposition to affirmative action. Visit your library, and read one of the authors Glazer mentions. Then write an essay in which you analyze whether the author you selected would support or oppose Glazer's argument.

4. Adopting Glazer's perspective on race relations in America, write a response to Ward Connerly's position in "Race Preferences Lose in Court — Again" (p. 144). As you draft your response, try to anticipate and answer Connerly's likely objections.

5. Write an argumentative essay in response to Glazer's query: are the objectives of the 1964 Civil Rights Act and Proposition 209 contradictory? To develop your ideas, you might visit your college library and research the background of both legal measures.

RUBEN NAVARRETTE, JR.

"Well, I Guess They Need Their Minority"

How would you feel if you were admitted to a prestigious university and none of your friends thought you deserved to get in? That is the dilemma that **Ruben Navarrette, Jr.** (b. 1968) describes in this excerpt from *A Darker Shade of Crimson: Odyssey of a Harvard Chicano* (1993). Reflecting on affirmative action college admissions policies and their effects on minority applicants, Navarrette declares his desire to be viewed as an individual whose grades and performance have gotten him where he wants to go. A writer and lecturer who now resides in the San Joaquin Valley, Navarrette is editor in chief of *Hispanic Student USA* and has contributed to *Hispanic* and *Change* magazines as well as to the *Los Angeles Times,* the *San Francisco Chronicle,* and the *Fresno Bee.*

Affirmative action tantrums, although often unfair, are understandable. We start with the presumption that all parents deem their offspring immensely qualified to attend any college they choose. Inevitably, there are some who are confronted by the unpleasant April reality that — after years of compassionate child rearing, private tutorials, family reading time, and expensive SAT prep courses — their child is simply not able to pull that off.

For them, minority students perform an invaluable service. Disappointed parents loyally reject the very real possibility that Johnny and Jessica were, in the sterile file room of some admissions office littered with empty coffee cups, simply outgunned by another more qualified, more interesting candidate of the same color. Instead, they trumpet to golf partners that their children are the victims of a chic, new kind of discrimination. Reverse discrimination. It seems to them particularly insidious because it affects those who are not accustomed to being hampered by the color of their skin.

So messy is the issue of affirmative action that it blurs the usual lines separating those who label themselves "liberal" or "conservative." Even those teachers who were usually supportive of Latino students, in this case, only compounded our discomfort.

One day a teacher, a self-professed liberal and voting Democrat with whom I had agreed on numerous political issues during the recent election, approached me in his European history class. He had heard through the gossip that permeated the teachers' lounge that I had been accepted to high-caliber schools. He intended to support my achievements. He chose entirely the wrong words. Instead of reminding me, as he could have, that I had earned one of the highest grades in his class and that I had consistently impressed him and my classmates with my work in it, he said only one thing.

"You know, I'm in favor of affirmative action. . . ."   5

As he returned to his desk, as proud of himself as if he had just sent a check to the American Civil Liberties Union, I realized that I had not mentioned affirmative action. It was he who had invoked the term and he who had instinctively, even if approvingly, linked the concept to my admission to these various colleges. . . . I knew that any congratulatory remarks to my white classmates would conspicuously lack any reference to affirmative action.

The teachers' lounge gossip persisted, and my ears burned. "Did you hear about Ruben Navarrette? Well, I guess they need their minority." At one point, a teacher of mine came to my defense. Fed up with innuendo from his colleagues — ironically people paid to build kids up and not tear them down — he lost his temper one morning and snapped back.

"Look, you wanna compare Ruben with your favorites . . . let's do it. Let's go to the registrar, get the transcripts and scores, and lay it all out. Then we'll see who's qualified!"

His colleagues relented and shifted their gossip back to local affairs and divorces and the like.

A man is embarrassed to admit the petty torments of a boy. Still, those   10
were lonely and hurtful days for me. Especially lonely and extra hurtful for one simple reason: those white students doing the accusing were my friends. We were close. We had grown up together, met each other's parents, confided in one another our schoolyard crushes on pretty girls. We trusted one another, in the kind of fragile trust that exists between children and adolescents. That trust was shattered in the spring of our senior year in high school by a wave of innuendo and slander. Children parroting adults. My friends' affirmative action tantrums left me with an acute sense of isolation, even betrayal. I was alone. Not knowing in whom to confide. To trust.

April became May, and the days were longer. I remember that at that crucial window in time, the one thing that I wanted was for someone, anyone, to put their hand on my shoulder, to hug me and tell me what I already knew: I was qualified, more than qualified, to be accepted by a school like Harvard. Each morning, as I reluctantly pulled my tired young body from its resting place, I hoped that this would be the day without innuendo, accusation, or insults disguised as compliments. I hoped that this would be the day that teachers, principals, and classmates would swallow their prejudice and own up to the truth: I had excelled according to their own standards of excellence and had done my modest part to bankrupt their sacred myth that Mexican Americans were somehow not as good as whites. But that day would not come for me. And even as I write this, I know that it has not come for hundreds of thousands of bright Latino students across the country.

There was a harsh irony to all this. If I found myself alone in those few months, it was because for many years before that I had painted myself into such a corner through my academic achievement. Since elementary school, I had done my homework, obeyed my teachers, strived for As instead of Bs, and through it all, distanced myself from my fellow Mexican American classmates. It was no accident, then, that as I sat in calculus class or physics or a variety of advanced placement courses, I was surrounded by white faces.

There were other Latinos, of course, but Latinos like me — smart, ambitious, with no trace of an accent. We were presumably immune to discrimination; low expectation was a foreign concept. We dated white girls. We considered ourselves acceptable to white America, and so we expected to be accepted by white America. Imagine our profound disillusionment after April's accusations.

Not so privileged were the others. Young men with dark skin, dark hair sprayed stiff and motionless, dark eyes. Hollow eyes devoid of hope. Knowing things that a valedictorian did not. I knew them, once. We played kickball during recess in a dusty elementary school. Five or six of us gathered routinely in the bathroom in sixth grade and gawked at pictures from forbidden magazines, played poker, talked about girls' developing anatomy, and gingerly toyed with tools of vice. There was intimacy. We felt at ease with one another. Each of us, Mexican. Each of us, headed down a different road.

In junior high school — a crucial point for students labeled "at risk" by educators — we lost one. One day, he dressed differently. Acted differently. He cut class, then classes, then the school day, then the school week. A thirteen-year-old was getting tougher, harder before my eyes. He cared about sex, alcohol, intimidation, money, and most of all being *cool*. We acknowledged each other with a wave, then a nod, then not at all. He gave up on education; education reciprocated. His vices became more serious. Later, it was juvenile hall and then county jail, maybe prison. I don't know.

The others remained in school, struggling to graduate. School was to be endured, not enjoyed. In our senior year, they leaned neatly against the wall of a high school corridor in between classes, single file, side by side. Dressed impeccably in clean white T-shirts, khaki pants, and patent leather shoes. Hard bodies, hard faces. Hollow eyes. The *pachucos*[1] of the 1940s, immortal-

15

[1]Mexican youths of the 1930s and 1940s who developed their own style and language living in American barrios. [Eds.]

ized in Luis Valdez's play *Zoot Suit*, had gracefully evolved into the *cholos*[2] of the 1980s. Hands in pockets, perhaps caressing a switchblade or even a gun. Certainly not a pencil. I didn't know. Because I didn't know them anymore. I walked their gauntlet on my way to some stuffy, high-browed class where I would study abstraction with people like me. Unlike me. I smiled to an old friend from kindergarten. We didn't talk. What would we talk about? What would my five acceptance letters mean to him? Nothing. Absolutely nothing.

Still, there was a respect between us, and perhaps mutual admiration. Maybe they liked that I was engaged daily in academic battle with the *gringos*, the sons and daughters of those who had treated our parents so badly. And, unnerving to some, in the competition for grades, I was winning. Taking the same tests, reading the same books, *Good with your hands. . . .* Hands full of acceptance letters to places that have rejected you.

In return, I admired my old friends' strength, their strong sense of self. They would not later write editorials in national newspapers with headlines like: "How Mexican Am I?" They knew. They also knew discrimination. They might have snickered at my disillusionment and said that, of course, white people think themselves superior. Of course. "Where have you been for seventeen years?" they might have said to me, shaking their heads mockingly that someone who knew so much could know so little.

The intimacy of our youth was gone. It had been sacrificed years before at the altar of academic success. We were no longer close. The American educational system's first and most thorough lesson is one of division. Remedial students. Honors students. Gifted students. *Better* students.

And so, when I was beseiged by the insults of white classmates, my old   20
friends were not there for me. Could not be there for me. I was in another world. What would they have done to defend me, anyway? They likely would not have been able to debate reflectively citing newspaper articles defending affirmative action.

I dreamed of a confrontation. An old friend would come to my rescue against the pack. He would enter the high-browed classroom for better students. He would approach the student body president and tell him that his homeboy had beaten him out not because of some improper system but because he was simply smarter than him. He would point the finger at the end of his muscular, brown arm at the terrified young white man turning paler each second and expose him as a child of privilege. He would mock the young man's contention that things should be "equal" in the admissions process by reminding him that the two of them lead lives that are anything but equal. He would invite him home to see the squalor and the neglect and the hardworking parents who had been told by guidance counselors to work in the canneries. And so they had, providing for their children an existence that compared more closely to those in Third World countries than it did to that of the privileged young man who trembled before him. He would argue finally that for Latinos, the ticket out of the American un-

[2]Gang members. [Eds.]

derclass was in the hands of ambitious and successful Latinos like his old friend, and how dare he or anyone else get in the way of that progress with their snide, childish, self-centered remarks.

In my splendid fantasy, the *cholo* would win the debate with the student body president because the victor knew something that the loser did not. He knew what it was like to be considered less intelligent, less capable, less, less, less by a system that was grooming others to succeed in his place. He knew what it was like to be Mexican American in public school. But the student body president, surrounded by friends, would not concede. My old friend would lose his temper and strike out in a more primitive, though more effective, way. Like our fathers had done at the same school three decades before, he would resort to knocking the shit out of his opponent before being hauled away to face punishment.

But reality was not so comforting. There was no rescue. The *cholos* stayed in their world. I was alone in mine. In that tiny school, as in life, they were separated from me (and from those whom the educational system expected more of than a life of dropping out, pregnancy, and crime) by a wall much higher, much more formidable than the one that they leaned on in between classes. This was my fight, and mine alone. At stake, I realized for the first time, was not only my own pride and self-image but also the dignity and progress of a whole race of people.

Should the reader tire of my complaining or see it as mere whining, I offer here a true story of an academic casualty in this battle for respect. As a college student and recruiter for Harvard, I spoke one day to a high school class in the San Joaquin Valley about the admissions process at Ivy League schools. A young man confronted me about what he considered to be the impropriety of race-conscious admissions. He spoke with passion and anger. Surprising to me at the time, he was Mexican American. He was angry because he claimed that, no matter what his accomplishments, he would never be taken seriously by his white classmates. We argued. We resolved nothing.

Three months later, I received a phone call from a friend in the admissions office. Had I heard? The same young man, an outstanding student, had been accepted into both our incoming class and that of Yale. He had decided, the caller continued, to reject both offers of admission and instead attend a small, less assuming college in New England. My friend was baffled. For the young man to stay in California was one thing. Yet to be willing to travel 3,000 miles but not to accept what were clearly more highly coveted spots in schools like Harvard or Yale seemed not to make much sense. For me, given the frustration, and perhaps embarrassment, that I saw in the young man's eyes during our heated exchange months earlier, I understood at once his desire to pick a less conspicuous apple from the tree.

"Tell me," I asked my friend. "If you're invited to a party, but don't feel that you deserve the invitation, would you go?"

"You don't mean . . ." the voice fell off to a whisper. "Shit!"

Ultimately, the young man in question was not spared, as he had hoped he would be, the ribbing of his high school classmates even though he had chosen to attend the small, less assuming college in New England at which he never felt comfortable and from which he eventually withdrew. A statistic in a government study, he and his nearly 1400 SATs now went on to attend a community college in Fresno. There, he was no longer subjected to ribbing by classmates and instructors, who finally considered him to be exactly where he was "qualified" to be. He became one of the hundreds of thousands of Mexican American students who attend community college in California, and not one of the just over one hundred such students who at any given time attend Harvard, apparently those who constitute a more controversial and threatening entity.

Understanding the Text

1. Why does Navarrette say that "minority students perform an invaluable service" (para. 2) for white parents disappointed in their children's college admissions?

2. When Navarrette was admitted to Harvard University, what reactions did he face from his teachers and fellow students (both white and Mexican American)?

3. Summarize in your own words Navarrette's attitude toward whites.

4. Why did the Mexican American student from the San Joaquin Valley refuse admission to Harvard and Yale?

5. Why does Navarrette say that Mexican American students who attend schools such as Harvard University are "controversial and threatening" (para. 28)?

Exploring and Debating the Issues

1. Write a letter to the San Joaquin Valley student whom Navarrette describes, advising him on how to respond to the ridicule he received from his peers. (Or write a letter to Navarrette in which you defend the San Joaquin Valley student's choices.) Share your letter with your classmates.

2. In your journal, reflect on how attending your college has shaped your sense of personal identity. Has your status as a college student affected your relationship with high school friends?

3. In the wake of Proposition 209, public colleges and universities are prohibited from using affirmative action in their admissions procedures, but private institutions throughout most of the rest of the nation still may do so. In class, form teams, and debate whether affirmative action in college admissions does more harm than good. In addition to Navarrette's selection, you may want to read or reread Ward Connerly's "Race Preferences Lose in Court — Again" (p. 144) and Nathan Glazer's "Blacks Only?" (p. 147).

4. Navarrette claims, "So messy is the issue of affirmative action that it blurs the usual lines separating those who label themselves 'liberal' or 'conservative'" (para. 3). Interview at least ten students and faculty on their political position and views of affirmative action, and use your findings as a basis for an essay in which you evaluate the validity of Navarrette's claim.

PETER SCHRAG

Language Barrier:
California's Bilingualism Mess

In 1998, California voters passed Proposition 227, a ballot initiative designed to end bilingual education in the state's public schools. In this article, which originally appeared in the *New Republic,* **Peter Schrag** (b. 1931) describes the buildup to the election, as well as the general background to the issue, noting that the "California debate could also have national implications for America's self-perception as a single nation with a single culture." Once again, it seems, whatever happens in America happens in California first. Schrag is the author of numerous books and articles. His latest book is *Paradise Lost: California's Experience, America's Future* (1998).

For the better part of a generation, bilingual education, variously defined and often misunderstood, has been fought over by true believers often more interested in ideology than pedagogy. But rarely has there been a more significant confrontation than the one shaping up over California's Proposition 227, the so-called English for the Children initiative. Prop. 227 wouldn't prohibit bilingual education for the state's 1.3 million students who are classified as "limited English proficient" and who make up roughly a quarter of the state's public school population. But it makes it so hard for parents to enroll children in bilingual classes that it would drastically reduce instruction in any language but English.

Like many other California ballot initiatives, Prop. 227, largely funded by a conservative Silicon Valley entrepreneur named Ron Unz, has already left ripples in state and national politics. Last fall, before California Republicans convened for their state convention, some of their leaders issued loud warnings that GOP support of the Unz measure would further alienate Hispanics, who were already disaffected by the GOP's support of recent ballot measures aimed against affirmative action and illegal immigration. But the warnings didn't keep the party's rank and file from endorsing it, nor did they stop U.S. House of Representatives Speaker Newt Gingrich from making antibilingualism a part of the GOP's national agenda.

In fact, the partisan political fallout may be limited because, as Unz correctly divined, most Hispanic parents want their children to learn English as rapidly as possible. Some Latino leaders have tried to describe Unz's measure as immigrant bashing, but their case is weak. Indeed, all the polls show that Prop. 227 has strong support even among Hispanics. If it passes, Prop. 227 is almost certain to spark similar efforts elsewhere, which will be seen by both sides as major events in defining the larger cultural parameters of American public education. Too bad the coming controversy probably won't do much to clarify the issue, much less help us get beyond the either/or debate over bilingual education that we've been mired in for twenty years.

In most places, bilingual education means that limited English proficient (LEP) students learn English as a second language while they learn other subjects (math, geography, science) at least partly in their native language so that, in theory, they can keep up with their English-speaking peers. But often the objectives of the classes are confused, the quality of instruction is poor, and the criteria used to determine who gets put into a bilingual class and when students are ready to "transition" into regular classes are murky. Is the purpose only to get students into regular classes as rapidly as possible, or is the purpose also some form of (Hispanic) "cultural preservation"? In addition, since bilingual education brings in state and federal dollars for every student enrolled in it, school districts that once had no incentive to pay attention to non–English-speaking kids now have a motive for stuffing them into bilingual education and keeping them there. Predictably, bilingual education has given rise to a powerful lobby of consultants and bureaucrats with a vested interest in maintaining and expanding the program.

Two years ago in Los Angeles, some two hundred Latino parents, many   5
of them minimum-wage garment workers, became so angry at the unwillingness of administrators at the Ninth Street Elementary School to teach their children in English that they boycotted the school. Some of those students had been in bilingual classes for six years and couldn't write a simple English sentence, which was not surprising since for some LEP students English instruction consisted largely of three hours on the playground and in the lunchroom "mixing" with English-speaking children. And since it's virtually impossible to find enough qualified teachers for the scores of languages that California's students bring to school, it's not unusual to find Korean or Hmong students being instructed in Spanish — and it's even more commonplace to find hundreds of classes taught by people who have only the barest command of their students' language. Even the bilingual lobby acknowledges that many so-called bilingual classes are educationally deficient.

Unz calls this "a failed system," and he's right. But his remedy is almost as rigid as the Kafkaesque system it would replace. In place of today's common presumption — that any foreign-born student who doesn't do well in English should be in a bilingual class even if she speaks English better than her native language — Prop. 227 makes a year in English immersion automatic for children who don't speak English well enough to attend a regular class. Bilingual education would be available only if parents, most of whom speak no English and are intimidated by official bureaucracy, appeared personally at their child's school each year and petitioned for a waiver to allow the child to be placed in a bilingual class. But since no waiver may be granted until the child has been failing in a regular class for at least thirty days, the waiver system is a prescription for academic defeat (and a powerful argument in the federal equal protection suit that will almost surely be filed if the measure passes).

To be sure, the nation's bilingual programs have been a morass of contradictory purposes, varying practices, and uncertain standards. The failure and dropout rates for Hispanic students, who constitute 70 percent of those defined as LEP, are also disproportionately high. But only about 30 percent of those students are in bilingual classes, and there's no evidence that the success rate for those who are not is any higher. And since the training and competence of the teachers, the techniques, the funding, the classroom setting, and the backgrounds of the children being taught all vary immensely, the picture is even more complex. What works with one group in one language may not work with another, and so systematic, up-or-down comparisons are virtually impossible. There is not even any good research on what percentage of those classified as LEP really belong in that category.

The most comprehensive recent review of what research there is, conducted by a panel appointed by the National Research Council and released last year, concluded that native-language instruction can be "helpful." But the NRC panel cautions against any across-the-board generalizations about any approach. And since there is very little good data on how LEP students learn math or science or history, the problems become even more complicated. Most obviously, in the words of Stanford Professor Kenji Hakuta, who chaired the NRC panel, "studies quickly have become politicized by advocacy groups selectively promoting research findings to support their positions. . . . Rather than choosing a one-size-fits-all program, the key issue should be identifying those components, backed by solid research findings, that will work in a specific community."

Prop. 227, which many California education groups condemn as interfering with local school control, will settle neither the political nor the pedagogical argument. Nor will it be the Armageddon of the culture wars that English-first militants would like it to be. But it will almost certainly intensify a debate that bears directly on the fortunes of a large minority of American students. Nearly 6 percent of the nation's public-school enrollment — some 3.2 million students — are classified as LEP, and their numbers are growing.

The California debate could also have national implications for America's self-perception as a single nation with a single culture. The prevailing American belief is that immigrant children have always been pushed into — and assimilated through — mainstream classes taught entirely in English. But during much of the nineteenth century, both public and parochial schools often taught in both English and German — or French, or Dutch, or whatever the dominant local immigrant language was. Those choices were based not on pedagogical theory but on ethnic politics. All that ended with the jingoism of World War I, when some states passed laws banning German speech, and mobs raided schools and burned German textbooks.

Nevertheless, in states like Texas and Florida, where business and political leaders understand their regions' interdependence with Latin America, and where Hispanic voters are much more influential than they have been in California, there is considerably more tolerance for, and interest in, bilingual assets. The first major bilingual program of the post–World War II period was established (in 1961) not for disadvantaged Mexican Americans or

Puerto Ricans but in response to pressure from Miami's middle-class Cuban refugees, who wanted their children to learn English and to preserve their language and culture.

That fragment of history underlines the major point of the NRC panel: there is no all-purpose approach, and schools and researchers should concentrate on finding what works for particular individuals and groups, issues that are often subject to bitter dispute in many other areas of American education. Indeed, it seems that one of the biggest problems with much bilingual education in U.S. schools is that it has sacrificed instruction in phonics and other basics to a whole-language ideology built around woolly notions of self-esteem.

Unfortunately, neither the ongoing debate over bilingual education nor the California initiative process lends itself to fine distinctions or even to the crude demarcations that the country draws in its debates over educational issues. It would be nice if this time there were a little more understanding of the nuances. But we have long been stuck in a binary argument that Prop. 227 will perpetuate rather than settle.

Understanding the Text

1. Why does Schrag claim that "often the objectives of the [bilingual education] classes are confused" (para. 4)?

2. Explain in your own words why Schrag considers as overly simplistic the accusation that Proposition 227 was motivated by immigrant-bashing racism.

3. What does Schrag mean when he labels bilingual education as practiced in California a "Kafkaesque" system (para. 6)?

4. How, in Schrag's view, had ideology clouded rational discussion of the advantages and disadvantages of bilingual education?

Exploring and Debating the Issues

1. Schrag laments that the discussion over bilingual education has become a simplistic "either/or debate" (para. 3). Write your own position statement on bilingual education, taking care to avoid the polarized positions that Schrag decries.

2. Interview several students at your college or university who were educated in bilingual classes to learn what their experiences were. Then write an essay in which you assess the value of such classes from the students' point of view.

3. Proponents of bilingual education cite the importance of "cultural preservation" (para. 4), as Schrag writes, while opponents wish to hasten the assimilation of non–English-speaking students. In an essay, argue your opinion on this issue.

4. Proposition 227 dictates educational practice: it legislates how teachers can and cannot instruct their students in their classrooms. Write an essay in

which you argue whether public-school teaching techniques should be determined at the ballot box. To develop your ideas, read or reread Peter Schrag's "California, Here We Come" (p. 222).

ROMESH RATNESAR

The Next Big Divide? Blacks and Hispanics Square Off over Bilingual Education

In California communities from East Palo Alto to Compton and Watts, once black-majority school districts have become Latino majority, and with the shift in population have come shifts in culture and power. In this *Time* piece, **Romesh Ratnesar** (b. 1975) reports on one of the "flash points" that have been sparked by such demographic changes, as the existing black power structures find themselves being challenged by Latino majorities over everything from bilingual education to the naming of an elementary school. Romesh Ratnesar writes for *Time* magazine.

H ere is the kind of scene that probably won't be discussed before the President's advisory board on race relations: in California's working-class town of East Palo Alto, a group of Hispanic parents went before the black-controlled school board last April to demand better bilingual education for their children. Before the meeting ended, police had to be called in to break up a fight between two participants: one a Latina and the other an African American woman who had told her to "go back to Mexico."

Until now, the racial issue in public education has been sorting out the competing claims of white versus African American students: Who should be bused where? Or how many dead white males should crowd the curriculum? But the newest racial flash point in schools in many parts of the United States pits Hispanic parents against African American ones. The disputes like East Palo Alto's arise in part from frustration over how to spend the dwindling pot of cash in low-income districts. But they also reflect a jostling for power, as blacks who labored hard to earn a place in central offices, on school boards, and in classrooms confront a Latino population eager to grab a share of these positions.

In East Palo Alto blacks made up 85 percent of the student population a decade ago; today almost 70 percent of the 5,000 students are Latino. But while the composition of the schools has changed, the composition of the people who run them has not. A black woman, Charlie Mae Knight, has served as superintendent for the past eleven years; the five-person school board has just one Hispanic member; and only one of the district's school principals is Latino. Says David Giles, a lawyer who represents East Palo Alto's Latino parents in their battles with the district: "African Americans struggled for years to gain control of institutions here. To now see this community of immigrants come here and ask for some of the resources is threatening to them."

And in many cities it has already led to bitter face-offs. In Dallas the school district's first Hispanic superintendent, Yvonne Gonzalez, resigned in September amid corruption charges brought by black employees; in response, Hispanic leaders demanded that the black associate superintendent who led the assault on Gonzalez step down too. In an episode in Washington early this year, Hispanic parents accused an African American principal of taping the mouths of two Latino students who had allegedly cursed their teacher and parading one of them through the school. The city's superintendent immediately pledged to hire more bilingual teachers and a full-time multicultural administrator. Hispanic-black tension also underlined [the 1996] ebonics controversy in Oakland, California. The black-majority school board's announcement that African American students spoke their own second language was made, in part, to garner a share of the federal bilingual funds that Oakland's blacks perceive as solely helping Latino students.

Invariably, the issue that drives Hispanic parents into local school politics is bilingual education. In East Palo Alto Latino parents filed a complaint with the state earlier this year demanding that the school district provide English-deficient kids with general instruction in Spanish along with daily English lessons. Says parent Sergio Sanchez: "[The administration] always says yes, yes; they promise to do things, but they never change. We need a new face in there." Many of the city's blacks, for their part, don't see the value — and resent the cost — of bilingual education. "If they want to learn Spanish, they should go to Mexico," says Lorraine Holmes, who has grandchildren in the system. Claims parent Evan Moss: "The school district is spending an awful lot of money on bilingual education when it could be used to educate all children."

Bilingualism isn't the only point of conflict. Hispanics in East Palo Alto are using their increasing clout to protest what they say is the schools' overall mediocre performance and the inefficiency of its bureaucracy, as well as alleged instances of cronyism and graft. Parents like Sanchez accuse Knight of stirring up racial resentments among blacks to deflect criticism about her administration. Knight dismisses her critics, saying, "Whenever whites are in charge of Latinos, they don't get the same kind of push that a black superintendent does. People . . . tend to distrust those who look more like them."

That distrust, which runs in two directions, seems to touch everything in the district. Not long ago, Latino residents decided to rename one of the elementary schools after the late activist Cesar Chavez, as a mark of cultural pride. But on the day of the dedication, supporters of the name change showed up at the school to find a group of blacks there too — protesting. They thought the Latinos wanted to honor Julio Cesar Chavez, the boxer, and they disapproved. Recalls Matias Varela, a Hispanic resident who heads the county's arts council: "It was a total misunderstanding between the two groups." Or perhaps it was the clearest sign that such conflicts might be eased if the two groups were to spend some time swapping stories about each other's political struggles.

Understanding the Text

1. In discussing a school-board meeting in East Palo Alto, Ratnesar observes, "Here is the kind of scene that probably won't be discussed before the President's advisory board on race relations" (para. 1). What are the implications of this observation?

2. What are the underlying social, cultural, and political tensions that have divided African Americans and Hispanics, according to Ratnesar?

3. How do the views of African American and Hispanic parents differ over the issue of bilingual education?

Exploring and Debating the Issues

1. Using Jack Miles's views ("Blacks vs. Browns," p. 241) on race relations as your critical perspective, analyze the economic bases of the conflict between African Americans and Hispanics over bilingual education.

2. In class, discuss the effect of Ratnesar's exclusive focus on black-Hispanic conflict while ignoring the larger racial context in California, which includes whites and Asians. Does this focus affect the validity of his discussion? How might his readership — a broad national audience — contribute to his choice of focus?

3. One of the causes for conflicts that Ratnesar describes is demographic change. In some communities, although an African American majority population has been transformed into a Hispanic majority community, the power structure remains in the hands of the former majority. In an essay, discuss whether you believe a city's school administration, and other authoritative bodies, must reflect proportionally the racial makeup of those whom they govern.

4. In a journal entry, consider whether the implementation of Proposition 227 will diffuse or exacerbate the racial tensions that Ratnesar describes. Compare your entry with those of your classmates.

CHITRA BANERJEE DIVAKARUNI

Yuba City School

Chitra Banerjee Divakaruni (b. 1956) is the author of six books of stories and poetry in English, but she can remember the days when her tongue felt "stiff and swollen" when having to speak English to her child's schoolteacher. Reflecting on the feelings of her son, whose native language is Punjabi but who attends a school where others speak English and Spanish, Divakaruni dramatizes the experiences of California's many South Asian immigrants, whose own bilingual needs have gone largely unnoticed in the controversy over bilingual education. A poet and short story writer whose works include *Leaving Yuba City* (1997), *The Mistress of Spices* (1997), and *Arranged Marriage* (1995), Divakaruni teaches creative writing at Foothill College.

From the black trunk I shake out
my one American skirt, blue serge
that smells of mothballs. Again today
Neeraj came crying from school. All week
the teacher has made him sit   5
in the last row, next to the fat boy
who drools and mumbles,
picks at the spotted milk-blue
skin of his face, but knows
to pinch, sudden-sharp,   10
when she is not looking.

The books are full of black curves,
dots like the eggs the boll-weevil lays
each monsoon in furniture-cracks
in Ludhiana. Far up in front   15
the teacher makes word-sounds
Neeraj does not know. They float
from her mouth-cave, he says,
in discs, each a different color.

Candy-pink for the girls   20
in their lace dresses, marching
shiny shoes. Silk-yellow
for the boys beside them,
crisp blond hair, hands raised
in all the right answers. Behind them   25
the Mexicans, whose older brothers,
he tells me, carry knives,
whose catcalls and whizzing rubber bands
clash, mid-air, with the teacher's
voice, its sharp purple edge.   30
For him, the words are
a muddy red, flying low and heavy,
and always the one he has learned to understand:
idiot, idiot, idiot.

I heat the iron over the stove. Outside   35
evening blurs the shivering
in the eucalyptus. Neeraj's shadow
disappears into the hole
he is hollowing all afternoon.
The earth, he knows, is round, and if   40
one can tunnel all the way through,
he will end up in Punjab,
in his grandfather's mango orchard,

his grandmother's songs lighting
on his head, the old words   45
glowing like summer fireflies.

In the playground, Neeraj says,
invisible hands snatch at his uncut hair,
unseen feet trip him from behind,
and when he turns, ghost laughter   50
all around his bleeding knees.
He bites down on his lip
to keep in the crying. They are
waiting for him to open his mouth,
so they can steal his voice.   55

I test the iron with little drops of water
that sizzle and die. Press down
on the wrinkled cloth. The room fills
with a smell like singed flesh.
Tomorrow in my blue skirt I will go   60
to see the teacher, my tongue
stiff and swollen
in my unwilling mouth, my few
English phrases. She will pluck them
from me, nail shut my lips. My son   65
will keep sitting in the last row
among the red words that drink his voice.

Understanding the Text

1. Why does Divakaruni's son Neeraj cry after school?
2. Read the poem aloud in class. How does reading it aloud affect your response to it?
3. Why does Divakaruni say that her tongue will be "stiff and swollen" (line 62) when she speaks with her son's teacher?
4. Catalogue all the images Divakaruni uses to describe language and speech.

Exploring and Debating the Issues

1. Divakaruni comes from the Punjab region of India. How do her son's difficulties in school, along with those of students from relatively small immigrant populations, complicate the debate over bilingual education in California? Consult Peter Schrag's "Language Barrier: California's Bilingualism Mess" (p. 156) and Romesh Ratnesar's "The Next Big Divide? Black and Hispanics Square Off over Bilingual Education" (p. 160) to develop support for your position.

2. If you are not a native English speaker, write a journal entry (it could be a poem) reflecting on your own experiences in school.

3. Most of the bilingual education debate focuses on students, but educators agree that much of the success of English language instruction depends on a student's home life. In class, brainstorm ways of helping immigrant parents who do not speak English to become more involved in their children's education.

4. Consider the poem aesthetically, and analyze its imagery and the way it achieves its effects. Alternately, rewrite the poem as a prose narrative. What differences do you observe between the poetic and the prose forms?

Researching the Issues

1. Visit your college library, and research the provisions of California's 1960 Master Plan for Higher Education. Then use your findings as the basis for an essay that argues whether the vision of the Master Plan still holds for California college students today.

2. Interview at least five students on your college campus about their goals and aspirations. Then use the results of your interviews to formulate an argument about whether higher education can help students achieve the California dream in the 1990s.

3. As a class project, form teams and arrange to offer tutoring services to needy students, whether on your own campus or, perhaps, at a local public school. Keep a journal or log of your tutoring experiences; use these entries as the basis of an essay in which you explain the educational needs of the students with whom you worked.

4. Rent a videotape of a film that features an educational setting, such as *To Sir with Love, Dead Poets' Society, Stand and Deliver,* or *Higher Learning.* Then write a critique of the film: How realistic is its depiction of educational issues such as the school environment, teacher-student relationships, the learning process, and student motivation?

5. Interview at least five students who have immigrated to America (whether legally or not) about their experiences in U.S. schools. Then use your findings as the basis of an essay in which you explain the obstacles facing nonnative students — and what strategies for success your interviewees devised.

6. Research the costs of other state university systems such as New York's and Michigan's and construct a table comparing them to the costs of the UC and CSU systems.

7. If you attend a public college or university, investigate the ways your school has responded to Proposition 209, as well as the effects the

---

CALIFORNIA ON THE NET

1. Visit your college or university's web site. Evaluate its usefulness to you as a student, to prospective students, and to the public.

2. The battle over bilingual education has been joined not only at the ballot box but also on the web. Conduct a research survey of web sites devoted to this controversy. What are the arguments for or against bilingual education, and what balance do you see in viewpoints expressed? For a pro–Proposition 227 site, you might visit English for the Children (http://www.onenation.org); for an opposing view, visit the No On Unz homepage (http.www.noonunz.org).

3. Because of the many court challenges to Proposition 209, implementation of the measure was not immediate. Until the U.S. Supreme Court upheld the initiative in 1997, its final legal outcome was unknown. Use a search engine to trace the ways in which 209 has been implemented by colleges and universities and people's responses to that implementation. For a pro-209 site, visit the University of California at San Diego's Students Against Discrimination and Preferences site (http://www-acs.ucsd.edu/~sadp); for an anti-209 site, check out Children Now's site (http://www.childrennow.org/election/Prop 209.html).

---

proposition has had on student enrollment. If you attend a private university, investigate the affirmative action policies of your campus. Use your findings to formulate a report in which you either defend the admissions procedures or recommend changes to them.

8. Investigate the controversy triggered in 1998 when the San Francisco Board of Education proposed using racial quotas for the authors on its list of approved texts for its schools.

9. Research the Oakland Board of Education's proposal to consider speakers of ebonics, or Black English Vernacular, as ESL students.

10. Investigate the debate about a "core curriculum" that raged at Stanford University, among other universities, in the early 1990s. Then study your own school's curriculum. To what extent do you see your school's curriculum as influenced by the intellectual debate that occurred earlier in the decade?

4 Developing the Dream
Issues in California Land Use

Inhabiting Paradise

Throughout much of American history, the shape of the land has largely determined the pattern of its settlement. Thus, the stony uplands of New England fostered an economy of small homesteads and river-driven mills, while the coastal plain of the Southeast allowed the creation of vast farms. Cities like Detroit and Chicago, which began as transportation centers, grew up along navigable rivers and lakes, while ranching became a way of life in arid states like Texas and Montana that were too dry for agriculture. The thick natural forests of Washington and Oregon led to economies based on timber production, and the flat, fertile prairies of the Midwest encouraged the cultivation of corn and wheat. While humans certainly forced the land to conform to their will, nonetheless that will was shaped, at least in part, by the land itself.

In California, this pattern of development has worked the other way around. Here, the shape of human desire has led to a vast transformation of the natural environment. Although Los Angeles lacks both water and a natural harbor, for example, it became the second-largest city in the nation by piping in water from the Owens Valley and by dredging out a harbor at San Pedro. Too arid for cultivation of any kind, the Imperial Valley became one of the most intensively farmed regions in America, thanks to a diversion of the Colorado River. Hillsides apparently too steep to build on have yielded to engineering feats that cantilever houses out over canyon walls, while seismically engineered skyscrapers cast their shadows on the San Andreas fault. Indeed, one of the few concessions to nature that we find in California's development patterns is the ubiquitous stucco construction of its single-family housing—a mark of that material's superiority to masonry in an earthquake-afflicted land.

But as a spate of recent earthquakes has demonstrated, there are limits to what human desire can accomplish. From Loma Prieta to Northridge, Landers to Coalinga, the earth has challenged, and overthrown, our best technologies. And as hillside dwellers from the Oakland Hills to Santa Barbara, Malibu, Laguna Beach, and San Diego have learned, natural ecologies that have evolved to burn will in fact burn, while what doesn't burn may well slide. Resilient though we are in the face of such disasters, Californians have had to face, time and again, the consequences of disregarding the natural shape of the land.

It has not always been this way, of course. Before the arrival of the Europeans, California's Indian population adapted its lifestyle to the land in which they dwelled, living in small hunter-gatherer groups that took what the land had to offer without modifying it significantly. Later, the Spanish developed a rancho culture that accepted the aridity of Southern California, scattering cattle and a sparse human population over thousands of square miles of land. But the story of California since the Mexican-American War has been one of transformation, of massive projects that have diverted rivers for water and irrigation, blasted transportation routes through solid rock, and filled in bays for housing tracts, as in the Bay Area's Foster City. In only a century and a half, California has been virtually transfigured.

The Price of Progress

The physical transformation of California has until recently taken place in the name of progress and growth, hitherto sacred words in a history of explosive expansion. This expansiveness, itself a major component of California's promise of endless opportunity, has not been without its cost, however. Was providing a growing San Francisco with a sure water supply, for example, worth damming the Tuolumne River and thereby flooding the Hetchy Hetchy Valley, a place second in beauty, John Muir believed, only to Yosemite? Should the farmers in the Owens Valley have been forced to pay the price for the diversion of their water southward so the San Fernando Valley might sprout with housing tracts, or should the Colorado River have been drained to irrigate the corporate farms of the Imperial Valley? As we experience the consequences of unchecked growth — pollution, overcrowding, and crime — we must ask: was it worth it, after all?

"Dam Hetchy-Hetchy!" John Muir exclaimed. "As well dam for watertanks the people's cathedrals and churches, for no holier temple has ever been consecrated by the heart of man." But the Hetchy Hetchy Valley was dammed, and we today can never know what it once looked like. So too can we never know what the Central Valley looked like before it was plowed under, or the San Fernando Valley, before it was filled with houses. For better or for worse, the California land has been transformed in the last century and a half, leaving us now with the decision of just how much further the transformation will continue.

The readings in this chapter tell the story of how California came to be so transfigured. A large part of it is the saga of water, a saga filled with dramatic color and infamous corruption, panoramic vision and abysmal blindness. Some readings confront you with the controversies surrounding growth itself: whether California can afford to continue to transform the land in pursuit of unending economic expansion. Are we better off for all the water projects and engineering feats that have made it possible for so many of us to live here, or has the price been too high, the dream having mortgaged our future to an unpayable environmental debt? Did the first Californians—Native Americans, who held the land as a sacred trust rather than as an opportunity for the creation of wealth—have the right idea after all?

But if so, then what? With thirty-three million people in the state, can we continue to occupy California *and* respect its natural environment? Can we find a sustainable balance between growth and preservation? Such are the questions that all Californians must now confront, as even the water developers concede that, with or without droughts, there are no new sources of available water. The land, in the end, is finite and cannot endure infinite demands. The California dream is boundless, but the California earth may be finally setting limits on our desire.

The Readings

Our readings in this chapter begin with Malcolm Margolin's poetic description of the Native American view of the land of California, a worldview in which humans see themselves in relation to natural creation rather than as masters of it. Then Arthur F. McEvoy provides a description of "California Indians as Capable Resource Managers," showing how the first Californians successfully made use of their environment without either depleting or transforming it. Gary Snyder follows with a report on the ways in which he and his neighbors in the foothills of the Sierra Nevada are striving today to manage their lands in an ecologically sustainable manner, while David Mas Masumoto's reflection on his own experience as an organic farmer in the Central Valley offers a possible vision for a less toxic future for California agriculture. Gerald W. Haslam's overview of the effects of irrigation on the Central Valley, the massive water projects that transformed the arid plains into an agricultural cornucopia, weighs the costs as well as the rewards of this transformation, thus questioning whether those who have followed the Indians have been quite so capable as resource managers. Margaret Leslie Davis then presents "Mulholland's Legacy," an assessment of the monumental aqueduct that made the expansion of Los Angeles suburbs possible, while Marc Reisner tells the sorry story of the Kesterson Reservoir in the San Joaquin Valley, one of the darker episodes in the history of California irrigation. Mike Davis's "Sunbelt Bolshevism" follows with a class-based interpretation of the slow-growth movement in Southern California, questioning the motives of middle-class conservationists, and Gary Soto concludes the chapter with a sad poetic reflection over the dispossession of the first Californians.

MALCOLM MARGOLIN

Among Kin

In the Western tradition, people tend to regard themselves as being separate from and superior to the natural world. But as **Malcolm Margolin** (b. 1940) writes in this essay, Native
Americans don't see things this way. For California's earliest human settlers, the natural
world appears as a vast interlocking web of animate and inanimate species, and human
beings are but a part of that web: relatives, not rulers. The difference between these two
worldviews can be measured by the changes five hundred years of European settlement
have wrought on a land occupied by Native Californians for thousands of years. Currently,
Margolin is publisher of Heyday Books and publisher and coeditor of *News from Native
California,* a quarterly magazine on California Indians. He has also written several books,
including *The Ohlone Way: Indian Life in the San Francisco–Monterey Bay Area* (1978)
and *East Bay Out: A Personal Guide to the East Bay Regional Parks* (1988), and has
coedited with Yolanda Montijo *California Indian Stories and Memories* (1995).

At the heart of the California Indian understanding of the environment is the sense that everything—plants, animals, mountains, rocks,
streams, everything—is alive. And everything is alive in much the same way
that people are alive: with intelligence, power, and history.

In such a world, people did not stand out as separate from the things
around them. When the people of the northern Sierra foothills were asked
the name for themselves, they responded, "Maidu." It was long assumed
that Maidu meant people, which it does. But, as linguist William Shipley has
pointed out, it means not only people, but perhaps something like *being.*
Animals, birds, fish—these too are "Maidu." In other words, when asked
who they were, these people did not say, "We are human," but with great
inclusiveness, and I think great wisdom, they said, "We are beings."

The dominant culture in this country today puffs itself out and makes a
big deal out of being human. "Man is the measure of all things," enthused
the Greek philosopher Protagoras, and in countless ways the dominant culture extols the human over "brute" creation.

Yet are we really so different from other beings, from bears for example?
Anthropologist Anna Gayton, who worked among the Yokuts and Western
Mono in the 1930s, gave the following wonderful anecdote, a story that suggests that bears not only shared the same landscape as humans, not only
shared many of the same foods, but on occasion, at least, they even shared
a joke:

> Palaha, who was a fine hunter, told of an experience. He set up a rude plat-
> form in an oak tree where he intended to hide just before dawn to drop
> acorns down as a bear lure, then shoot the animal as it fed. He went out as
> planned—it was barely light. As he came under the tree something hit him
> on the head; acorns were falling from the platform. Looking up, he saw a
> small bear standing on the framework and nuzzling at the hoard of bait
> which rolled off the sides. This Palaha thought excessively funny: that their

positions should be reversed, and that the bear was doing to him what he had intended doing to the bear. But beyond this was the sense that the bear thought it funny too, that somehow it was intentional on the animal's part to indulge in a humorous trick.

What did it feel like to grow old in a world in which the plants, animals, rocks, and mountains were seen as family members? A Wintu woman, Sadie Marsh, recalled hearing her grandfather pray to the World Maker, Olelbes— "He-Who Is Above." As part of the prayer he talks directly and intimately with the things around him—the deer and other animals whose "nature it is to be eaten," the rocks, trees, acorns, sugar pine, water, and wood. He talks to these other beings as one might talk to kin, sharing with them his sadness and regret, calling upon them to witness his approaching death and to mourn for him. As he addresses them, we hear the voice of a man who is about to depart from a world in which he is thoroughly at home:

> Oh Olelbes, look down on me.
> I wash my face in water, for you,
> Seeking to remain in health.
> I am advancing in old age; I am not capable of anything any more.
> You whose nature it is to be eaten,
> You dwell high in the west, on the mountains, high in the east, high in the north, high in the south;
> You, salmon, you go about in the water.
> Yet I cannot kill you and bring you home.
> Neither can I go east down the slope to fetch you, salmon.
> When a man is so advanced in age, he is not in full vigor.
> If you are rock, look at me; I am advancing in old age.
> If you are tree, look at me; I am advancing in old age.
> If you are water, look at me; I am advancing in old age.
> Acorns, I can never climb up to you again.
> You, water, I can never dip you up and fetch you home again.
> My legs are advancing in weakness.
> Sugar pine, you sit there; I can never climb you.
> In my northward arm, in my southward arm, I am advancing in weakness.
> You who are wood, you wood, I cannot carry you home on my shoulder.
> For I am falling back into my cradle.
> This is what my ancestors told me yesterday, they who have gone, long ago.
> May my children fare likewise!

The reference to "northward arm" and "southward arm" is provocative and informative. In English we would refer to the right arm and the left arm, and we might also describe a certain mountain as being to our right or left, in front of us or in back of us, depending upon which way we are facing at the moment. We use the body—the self—as the point of reference against which we describe the world. The Wintu would never do this, and indeed the Wintu language would not permit it. If a certain mountain was to the north, say, the arm nearest that mountain would be called the northward arm. If the person turned around, the arm that had previously been referred to as the northward arm would now be called the southward arm. In other words, the features of the world remained a constant reference, the sense of self was what changed—a self that continually accommodated and adjusted to a world in which the individual was not the center of all creation.

Understanding the Text

1. What does the Native American term *Maidu* mean?
2. Why does Margolin use stories and prayers to illustrate his position?
3. How, according to Margolin, do California Indians view themselves in relation to their environment?
4. How does the California Indian sense of people's place in the world differ from that of the dominant culture in America?

Exploring and Debating the Issues

1. The hunter Palaha "shared a joke" with the bear in the Yokut tale, yet he has set a trap so he can kill the animal. In your journal, discuss whether it makes a difference to feel a close relationship with the animals one hunts.
2. Writing as if you were Malcolm Margolin, write a letter to Central Valley farmers in which you condone or denounce their use of water. To develop your ideas, consult Gerald W. Haslam's "The Water Game" (p. 191) and Marc Reisner's "Things Fall Apart" (p. 198).
3. In class, read aloud the Wintu prayer that Margolin relates. Then discuss the effect of the oral recitation and the prayer's significance for land-use issues in California.
4. Write an essay in which you argue whether the Californian Indian worldview as described by Margolin complements or contradicts the California dream. To develop your ideas, consult James J. Rawls's "California: A Place, A People, A Dream" (p. 8).

ARTHUR F. McEVOY

California Indians as Capable Resource Managers

The California Indians sometimes are portrayed as acorn gatherers who passively enjoyed the bounty of the land. But as **Arthur F. McEvoy** (b. 1952) shows in this analysis of California Indian economies, they made shrewd calculations of the "carrying capacity" of their lands and proved themselves to be "capable resource managers" whose ability to sustain themselves for thousands of years without significantly altering the environment contrasts profoundly with current land-use practices in California. A professor at Northwestern University, Arthur F. McEvoy is the author of *The Fisherman's Problem: Ecology and the Law in California Fisheries, 1850–1980* (1986), in which this selection originally appeared.

Indian society in California was distinctive in its high density of population, its insularity, and the remarkable complexity of its hunting and gathering economy. While groups in the northwestern and southern coastal regions shared many ethnographic traits with tribes to the north and east of them, respectively, in general the mountains, desert, and ocean that isolated California from the rest of the world physically also insulated its aboriginal cultures from outside influence, enabling them to flourish in their own ways. At the heart of these people's adaptation to their peculiar environment, which contained an extremely variegated, if thinly spread, supply of edible plants and animals, was an economy based on painstaking, seasonal, and broadly diffused effort rather than on special skills or concentration on any particular resource. Aboriginal society in California was sedentary, technologically unsophisticated, relatively free from conflict either with nature or with neighbors, and, to a degree remarkable among North American Indians, free from privation.

The most critical resources were those the Indians processed and stored for use during the lean months of the winter and early spring (viz., acorns, large game, and fish). Because the addition of easily caught salmon did nothing to diminish their access to other staples, it is no surprise that the most populous tribes in central California were those along the Sacramento and San Joaquin Rivers. The Wintuan-speaking Patwin, Nomlaki, and Wintu groups living along the Sacramento from the delta to its headwaters together made up the largest coherent linguistic group in northern California and, according to Kroeber, were "[among] the most important in the development and diffusion of customs." At the southern limit of the salmon, a line between Monterey Bay and the bend in the San Joaquin River, the Plains Miwok, Yokuts, and Monache people of the San Joaquin Valley also took great quantities of the fish.

The Southern California Bight, between Point Conception and San Pedro Bay, and the islands offshore supported the only maritime cultures in aboriginal California, those of the Chumash and the Gabrielino. Here the coast faces to the south, protected from the prevailing winds that bring fog and high surf to more northerly areas. The rocks and cliffs that divide land from sea to the north and south here give way to sandy, gently sloping beaches. The water is calm and visibility high; the large, verdant Channel Islands loom just offshore. Their geographical situation, combined with the exceptional fertility of the Santa Barbara Channel, drew these people out onto the ocean. Here, too, adequate timber and natural petroleum seeps, not available either to the north or the south, provided planks and caulking for seaworthy canoes. These facilitated trade with the islands and fisheries for sea mammals and for many of the finfish that became commercially important after 1850. An arid hinterland inhibited food production away from the coast and further encouraged the maritime adaptation, which was unique to the area.

The ability to draw on the productivity of the Channel waters, as well as a fertile coastal strip and abundant shellfish resources, permitted human populations to bloom along this part of the coast. The Chumash aggregated into villages of as many as a thousand people each along their stretch of the coast. Wealth and concentrated numbers led in turn to a flowering of culture. The Spanish reckoned the Chumash superior to all other California tribes with which they had contact. With their neighbors, the Gabrielino, the Chumash share the recognition of modern anthropologists as "the wealthiest, most populous, and most powerful ethnic nationality in aboriginal southern California."

Like all hunter-gatherers, California Indians were intimately familiar   5 with the ecology of their food resources and actively manipulated their environment in order to enhance its stability and productivity. Fishery use was qualitatively different among the Yurok and other Lower Klamath culture area peoples and so merits individual treatment. Throughout the region, many groups used artificial fires, for example, with considerable skill to encourage the growth of plants upon which they and the birds and mammals they hunted depended for forage. According to Henry T. Lewis, there were probably few areas in California with any appreciable Indian population whose physical aspect was unaffected by it. In general, the nearly universal use of fire by preagricultural peoples to manipulate their environments by itself calls into question the widely assumed ecological passivity of such peoples.

The Indians seem to have harvested as much from their environment as it could predictably yield. Comparing Sherburne Cook's estimates of the population of central California tribes with his own indices of the productivity of acorns, game stocks, and fisheries in each of their territories, Martin A. Baumhoff found that a linear function of resource productivity accurately predicted the populations of groups in both fertile and barren areas. He concluded that each group's population was in equilibrium with the carrying capacity of its local environment. All groups traded food with each other, to some extent, and were apparently accustomed to supplying emergency rations to neighboring villages in temporary need. There was some, but not much, ability to secure a surplus beyond the community's needs in a moderately severe winter.

Carrying capacity is a function not only of the inherent productivity of a habitat but also of a people's strategies for production. It is a social measure as well as a strictly biological one. That hunting and gathering economies such as those in aboriginal California operated at relatively low population densities did not relieve them of their need to husband their resources if they were to sustain their ways of life. One way in which the California Indians did so was to spread their productive effort over a wide range of resources, each in its season. If a particular crop failed or if salmon or game were scarce in any season, there were usually other foods to fall back on. Central California Indians developed their fishing technology and devoted their time to fishing only to the point at which salmon provided a predictable share of their subsistence in conjunction with the other foodstuffs available to them. The overall fertility of the California environment meant that hunting and gathering could support large numbers of people; meanwhile, the Indians' broad subsistence base contributed to the great stability of their economies.

Although they also took more overt measures to limit their demand for food, one effect of this diffusion was to limit the Indians' use of fish or any other single resource to within prudent bounds. Avoiding the risk of crop failure was thus the standard by which the Indians limited their harvest and kept it safely below the long-term maximum yield that any particular resource could sustain. For southern coastal groups, this was the reason for limiting their shellfish collecting to a small part of their seasonal round. Despite their advanced fishing methods, they continued to rely chiefly on a diversified economy, with acorns the main staple. One study concluded that the maritime capability was itself a response to the overuse of the shellfish upon which the Chumash and Gabrielino relied more heavily and from an earlier time. It made their basically diffuse economies more efficient and more secure but did not supplant them. To have intensified their fishing or any other of their harvests, say, by developing an agricultural specialization, would have at once increased the Indians' exposure to risk and diverted labor away from other pursuits, thereby bringing an initial drop in overall productivity. The Indians, who were secure but who had stretched their economy to its limit, had no incentive to do this.

Of prime importance to the California Indians was the practical concern of maintaining the security of life as they knew it. A more specialized economy held no inherent attraction for them as long as their own methods continued to support them in good style, just as it does not for hunter-gatherers surviving in the late twentieth century. But their complex economic strategy did not emerge and did not endure simply as a matter of chance. They developed it, over time and no doubt at some cost, and maintained it deliberately. Because they used all the resources their habitats would yield safely to their productive system, California hunter-gatherers faced the fundamentally political problems of regulating the harvest and distributing natural resources no less than later Californians with different kinds of economies. For them, as for their successors, resource management was a function of social and political institutions.

Perhaps most basic among the social tools with which California Indians limited their demand for food was population control. The Indians' lack of technological sophistication does not fully explain their apparent ability

10

to live within their ecological means because they could always have tried to feed more people with the same economy. Yet, they did not. Malthusian "positive" checks on population—war, famine, and the like—do not seem to have been significant to the lives of aboriginal Californians. Infanticide, abortion, taboos on intercourse during lactation, meaningful social roles for celibates, and other deliberate controls on human fertility, however, do. The Pomo apparently resorted to a number of tactics, from contraception to geronticide, to protect their relatively dense population from exposure to the risk of famine. Scattered evidence survives of systematic removal of twins, defective infants, or infants of deceased mothers among other California groups, particularly those with fertile habitats and dense populations such as the Yurok and the coastal Chumash. Deliberate, socially sanctioned regulation of their numbers, in response to perceived conditions in individual families, in the community, and in the environment, was crucial to the Indians' ability to balance their demand for food with the capacity of their habitats to produce it.

More directly, California Indian communities limited access to their resources by assigning rights to them. Individual communities claimed exclusive use of all important food-producing resources and denied them to outsiders except under carefully controlled conditions. In general, the more concentrated or critical a resource, the more explicitly the Indians articulated rights to it. Individual "ownership" was far more common in the Klamath River area, where salmon was of overwhelming importance, than anywhere else in California. Northwestern coastal groups lay claim to specific stretches of beach adjoining their villages and defended them against trespass. In central and southern California, where staples were more varied and dispersed, native groups commonly vested their ownership in the community at large. Individuals and households might claim sole use of a particular oak tree or fishing spot for a season, but for the most part important hunting, fishing, and gathering locations belonged in common to the whole community. Well-defined rights to resources not only limited their use but permitted tribes to monitor the effect of their harvesting at specific sites over time and to adjust their use accordingly.

Although individuals sometimes held property of a sort, it was certainly not absolute and resembled a form of trusteeship rather than property in fee simple under Anglo-American common law. Individuals had no right to alienate resources that were crucial to their community's well-being. Nor was shared property left to suffer "the tragedy of the commons." Tribes and villages administered the harvest of communally owned resources according to carefully prescribed and closely supervised procedures, usually in a ceremonial or ritual context. The world-renewal religion of northwestern California was the most complex such ritual system. In central California, the Kuksu religion of the Patwin, Maidu, and Pomo also contained strong elements of world renewal. In both areas, secular and administrative functions entwined with spiritual ones. Shamans, whose social role was to mediate between the community and the spiritual forces that infused the natural world, organized the harvest of key resources, supervised their distribution, and appeased their spirits so as to ensure the continued prosperity and well-being of the group.

Central California communities could harvest neither acorns, fish, nor game until the local shaman performed the appropriate first-fruit rites, which might take several days. Acorn harvests were crucial to central and southern California Indian economies and were most carefully hedged about with ritual. Salmon also received the ceremonial protection of the Kuksu religion, although these rites were perfunctory as compared with those in the northwest. In southern California, civil authorities directed the harvest, storage, and distribution of acorns and presumably shellfish as well, although again not without the assistance of shamans who observed first-fruit rites for them. Individual tribes always invited their neighbors to attend their ceremonies and used the occasion to trade with them and exchange gifts. Trade and reciprocity, integrated within a ceremonial context, relieved competition for scarce resources and helped maintain good relations between neighboring groups.

The ritual organization of production and exchange articulated and reaffirmed to the Indians their interdependence with each other and with the natural world. According to Harold Driver, a belief in active, watchful, and potentially vengeful animal spirits was "probably universal" among North American Indians. The Indians had to use them carefully and propitiate them for their sacrifice if they were to rely on their continued abundance. Animism was the way in which the Indians, like most hunter-gatherers, expressed their awareness of the fact that their lives and those of their food resources were ecologically intertwined. It was the job of the shamans to mediate between the two camps: to interpret for their communities the will of the natural world and to ensure that the former used its resources in prudent ways. This is no more or less than what modern scientific resource agencies with their staffs of ecologists do, although they do so from the standpoint of a profoundly different world view.

There is no reason to suppose that the communion between Indian society and the world around it was perfect. As one Sacramento Valley native put it, "Everything in the world talks, just as we are now, the trees, the rocks, everything. But we cannot understand them, just as the white people do not understand Indians." There is also no reason to suppose that the balance they maintained among environment, production, and ideology at the time of contact with Westerners was not something that developed over a long period of time and with occasional mistakes. We have indirect evidence of some of the mistakes, but the history of the process is lost. It does seem clear, however, that the balance they eventually struck was an enduring and prosperous one. California Indians managed their fisheries and other resources by strategically gearing their productive effort to the ecological realities of the world as they understood them, so as at once to lead comfortable lives, to distribute wealth equitably, and to sustain their resources and their economies over the long run.

Understanding the Text

1. What does McEvoy mean by "the widely assumed ecological passivity" (para. 5) of the California Indians, and how does he debunk this belief?
2. What evidence does McEvoy present to demonstrate that "carrying capacity . . . is a social measure as well as a strictly biological one" (para. 7)?
3. In McEvoy's view, what role did California Indian rituals play in their resource management strategies?
4. How do traditional California Indian notions of property ownership and control differ from those of modern mainstream California culture?
5. Trace the differences among the California Indian economies by geographical region.

Exploring and Debating the Issues

1. Both McEvoy and Malcolm Margolin "(Among Kin," p. 170) discuss the California Indians' relationship with the land. Compare and contrast their selections, paying close attention to both content and tone.
2. Before the arrival of the Spanish, California Indians lived in a relatively close, naturally isolated environment in which they determined the population appropriate to the land's carrying capacity. In "The Welcome Mat Is Threadbare" (p. 73), Yeh Ling-Ling argues that "Until our national leaders recognize that our current level of immigration far exceeds this country's carrying capacity, no real remedies to America's problems will be found" (para. 11). Debate in class whether California is reaching the limit of its carrying capacity today.
3. The California Indians, McEvoy states, were "technologically unsophisticated" (para. 1). How does technology alter human relationships to the land, including its carrying capacity? To develop your ideas, read or reread Gary Snyder's "Cultivating Wildness" (below), David Mas Masumoto's "As If the Farmer Died" (p. 185), or Marc Reisner's "Things Fall Apart" (p. 198).
4. Select one California Indian group that McEvoy mentions, and research their culture and economy. To what extent does your research reveal that your group practiced capable resource management, as McEvoy argues?

GARY SNYDER

Cultivating Wildness

One of the best-known of the Beat generation poets, **Gary Snyder** (b. 1930) has long been a leading figure in American literary history and culture. But his credentials as an environmentalist are equally as impressive, and as Snyder shows here, his vision for a sustainable future in California land-use policy reveals a level of practical know-how that is anything but naive idealism. Through the management of his own land in the foothills of the Sierra Nevadas, Snyder accordingly offers a proposal for public-private land-use cooperation that could serve as a model for the rest of the nation. The author of numerous volumes of poetry and essays, Snyder's more recent works include *Right in the Trail* (1990), *No Nature: New and Selected Poems* (1992), *A Place in Space: New and Selected Prose* (1995), and *Mountains and Rivers without End* (1996).

J ets heading west on the Denver-to-Sacramento run start losing altitude east of Reno, and the engines cool as they cross the snowy Sierra crest. They glide low over the west-tending mountain slopes, passing above the canyon of the North Fork of the American River. If you look north out the window, you can see the Yuba River country, and if it's really clear you can see the old "diggings"—large areas of white gravel laid bare by nineteenth-century gold mining. On the edge of one of those is a little hill where my family and I live. It's on a forested stretch between the South Yuba canyon and 2,000 treeless acres of old mining gravel, all on a forty-mile ridge that runs from the High Sierra to the valley floor near Marysville, California.

From the air, you can look out over the northern quarter of the Greater Sierra ecosystem: a vast summer-dry hardwood-conifer forest, with drought-resistant shrubs and bushes in the canyons, clearcuts, and burns.

In ten minutes the jet is skimming over the levees of the Sacramento River and wheeling down the airstrip. It then takes two and a half hours to drive out of the valley and up to my place. The last three miles always seem to take the longest: we like to joke that it's still the bumpiest road we've found, go where we will.

Back in the mid-1960s I was studying in Japan. Once, while I was on a visit to California, some friends suggested that I join them in buying mountain land. In those days land and gas were both still cheap. We drove into the ridge and canyon country, out to the end of a road. We pushed through manzanita thickets and strolled in open stretches of healthy ponderosa pine. Using a handheld compass, I found a couple of the brass caps that mark corners. It was a new part of the Sierra for me. But I knew the assembly of plants—ponderosa pine, black oak, and associates—well enough to know what the rainfall and climate would be, and I knew that I liked their company. There was a wild meadow full of native bunchgrass. No regular creek, but a slope with sedges that promised subsurface water. I told my friends to count me in. I put down the money for a twenty-five acre share of the one hundred acres and then returned to Japan.

In 1969, back for good in California, we drove out to the land and made   5 a family decision to put our life there. At that time there were virtually no neighbors, and the roads were even worse than now. No power lines, no phones, and twenty-five miles—across a canyon—to town. But we had the will and some of the skills as well. I had grown up on a small farm in the Northwest and had spent time in the forests and mountains since childhood. I had worked at carpentry and been a Forest Service seasonal worker, so mountain life (at 3,000 feet) seemed doable. We weren't "in the wilderness" but rather in a zone of ecological recovery. In the hills beyond us, the Tahoe National Forest stretched for hundreds of square miles.

I had been a logger on an Indian reservation in the ponderosa pine forests of eastern Oregon, where many trees were more than two hundred feet tall and five feet through. Up north it was drier and a bit higher, so the understory was different, but it was the same adaptable cinnamon-colored pines. The trees down here topped out at about one hundred feet—getting toward being a mature stand but a long way from old growth. I talked with a ninety-year-old neighbor who had been born in the area. He told me that when he was young he had run cattle over my way and had logged here and there and that a big fire had gone through about 1920. I trimmed the stump on a black oak that had fallen and counted the rings: more than three hundred years. There were still lots of standing oaks that big around, so it was clear that the fires had not been total.

Besides the pine stands (mixed with incense cedar, madrone, a few Douglas firs) our place was a mosaic of postfire manzanita fields with small pines coming through; stable climax manzanita; an eight-acre stand of pure black oak; and some areas of blue oak, gray pine, and grasses. Also lots of the low ground-cover bush called kitkitdizze in the language of the Wintun, a nearby valley people. It was clear from the very old and scattered stumps that the land had been selectively logged once. A neighbor with an increment borer figured that some trees had been cut about 1940. The surrounding lands and the place I was making my home flowed together with unmarked boundaries—to the eye and to the creatures, it was all one.

We had our hands full the first ten years just getting up walls and roofs, bathhouse, small barn, washhouse. A lot of it was done the old way: we dropped all the trees to be used in the frame of the house with a two-man falling saw and peeled them with drawknives. Light was from kerosene lamps; we heated with wood and cooked with wood and propane. Wood-burning ranges, wood-burning sauna stoves, treadle-operated sewing machines, and propane-using Servel refrigerators from the 1950s were the targets of highly selective shopping runs. Many other young settlers found their place in northern California back in the early 1970s, so eventually there was a whole reinhabitory culture living this way in what we like to call Shasta Nation.

I set up my library and wrote poems and essays by lantern light, then went out periodically, lecturing and teaching around the country. I thought of my home as a well-concealed base camp from which I raided university treasuries. We named our place Kitkitdizze, after the aromatic little shrub.

The scattered neighbors and I started meeting once a month to talk   10
about local affairs. We were all nature lovers, and everyone wanted to cause as little impact as possible. Those with well-watered sites, with springs and meadows, put in small gardens and planted fruit trees. I tried fruit trees, a chicken flock, a kitchen garden, and beehives. The bees went first. They were totally destroyed in one night by a black bear. The kitchen garden did fairly well until the run of dry winters that started in the 1980s and may finally be over. And of course, no matter how you fence a garden, deer find a

way to get in. The chickens were constant targets of northern goshawks, red-tailed hawks, raccoons, feral dogs, and bobcats. A bobcat once killed twenty-five in one month. The fruit trees are still with us, especially the apples. They, of all the cultivars, have best made themselves at home. (The grosbeaks and finches seem to always beat us to the cherries.)

But in my heart I was never into gardening. I couldn't see myself as a logger again either. Except for cutting downed oak and pine for firewood, felling an occasional pole for framing, and clearing the low limbs and underbrush well back from the homestead to reduce fire hazard, I hadn't done much with the forest. I wanted to go lightly, to get a deep sense of it, and I thought it was enough to leave it wild and to let it be the wildlife habitat it was.

Living in a place like this is absolutely delicious. Coyote-howl fugues, owl exchanges in the treetops, the almost daily sighting of deer (and hearing the rattle of antlers at rutting season), the frisson of seeing a poky rattlesnake, tracking critters in the snowfall, seeing cougar twice, running onto humongous bear scats—sharing all this with the children—is more than worth the inconveniences.

My original land partners were increasingly busy elsewhere. It took a number of years, but we bought out our old partners and ended up with the whole one hundred acres. That was sobering. Now Kitkitdizze was entirely in our hands. We were cash-poor and land-rich, and who needed more second-growth pine and manzanita? We needed to rethink our relation to this place, with its busy—almost downtown—rush of plants and creatures. Should we leave it alone? Use it, but how? And what responsibility came with it all?

Now it is two grown sons, two stepdaughters, three cars, two trucks, four buildings, one pond, two well pumps, close to one hundred chickens, seventeen fruit trees, two cats, about ninety cords of firewood, and three chainsaws later. The kerosene lights have been replaced by a photovoltaic array powering a mixed AC/DC system. The phone company put in an underground line to our whole area at its own expense. My wife, Carole, and I are now using computers, which are the writer's equivalent of a nice little chainsaw. (Chainsaws and computers both increase macho productivity and nerdy stress.) My part-time teaching job at the University of California, Davis, provides me with an Internet account. We have finally entered the late twentieth century and are tapping into political and environmental information with a vengeance.

The whole Sierra is a mosaic of ownership—various national forests, 15 Bureau of Land Management (BLM) land, Sierra Pacific Industries land, state parks, and private holdings—but to the eye of a hawk it is one great sweep of rocks and woodland. We, along with most of our neighbors, were involved in the forestry controversies of the past decade, particularly in regard to the long-range plans for the Tahoe National Forest. We were part of a nationwide campaign to reform forest practices. The upshot was a real and positive upheaval on a national scale in the U.S. Forest Service and the promise of "ecosystem management" on our public lands—something that is not yet clearly defined.

We turned our focus next to nearby public lands managed by the BLM. It wasn't hard to see that they were a key middle-elevation part of a passageway for deer and other wildlife from high country to the valleys below, with our own holdings part of the same corridor. Soon we were catapulted into a whole new game: the BLM area manager for central California, Deane Swickard, became aware of our interest, drove up, and walked the woods with us, talked with us, consulted with the community, and then said, "Let's cooperate in the long-range planning for these lands. We can share information." We agreed to work with him and launched a biological inventory, first with older volunteers and soon with our own wild teenagers jumping in. We studied close to 3,000 forested acres. We crawled on hands and knees, belly-slid on snow, bushwhacked up and down canyons in order to find out just what was there, in what combinations, in what quantity, in what diversity.

Some of it was tallied and mapped (one local youth just back from college had learned GIS — Geographic Information System — and put the data into a borrowed Sun Sparc workstation), and the rest of our observations were put into bundles of notes. We had found some very large trees, located a California spotted owl pair, noted a little wetland with carnivorous sticky sundew, described a unique barren dome with plants found only in serpentine soils, identified large stands of vivid growing forest, and been struck by the tremendous buildup of fuel. The well-intended but ecologically ignorant fire-exclusion policies of the government agencies over the past century have made the forests of California an incredible tinderbox.

The droughty forests of California have been shaped for millennia by fire. A fire used to sweep through any given area, we are now told, roughly every twenty-five years and in doing so kept the undergrowth down and left the big trees standing. The native people also deliberately started fires, so that the California forests of two hundred years ago were structured of huge trees in parks that were fire-safe. Of course there were always some manzanita fields and recovering burns, but overall there was far less fuel. To "leave it be wild" in its present state would be risking a fire that might set the land back to first-phase brush again. The tens of thousands of homes and ranches mixed among the wooded foothills down the whole Sierra front could burn.

These studies and explorations resulted in the formation of the Yuba Watershed Institute, a nonprofit group made up of local people, which is sponsoring projects and research on forestry, biodiversity, and economic sustainability with an eye to the larger region. One of the main joint-management-plan conclusions was to try to reduce fuel load by every available means. We saw that a certain amount of smart selective logging would not be out of place, could help reduce fuel load, and might pay some of the cost of thinning and prescriptive burning. We named our lands, with the BLM's blessing, the Inimim Forest, from the Nisenan word for pine, in recognition of the first people here.

The work with fire, wildlife, and people extends through public lands and private parcels (with willing owners) alike. Realizing that our area plays   20 a critical biological role, we are trying to learn ground rules by which humans might live together with animals in an "inhabited wildlife corridor." A San Francisco State University project for netting and banding migrant songbirds during nesting season (information for a Western Hemisphere database) is located on some Kitkitdizze brushlands, rather than public land, simply because it's an excellent location. Our cooperative efforts here can be seen as part of the rapidly changing outlook on land management in the West, where public-private partnership is being talked about in a big way. Joint-management agreements between local communities, other local and committed interests, and neighboring blocks of public lands are a new and potent possibility in the project of responsibly "recovering the commons" region by region. The need for ecological literacy, the sense of the home watershed, and a better understanding of our stake in public lands are beginning to permeate the consciousness of the larger society.

Lessons learned in the landscape apply to our own lands too. So this is what my family and I are borrowing from the watershed work as our own three hundred-year Kitkitdizze Plan: we'll do much more understory thinning and then a series of prescribed burns. Some patches will be left untouched by fire, to provide a control. We'll plant a few sugar pines where they fit, burn the ground under some of the oaks to see what it does for the acorn crop, burn some bunchgrass patches to see if they produce better basketry materials (an idea from the native basket-weaving revival in California). We'll have a percentage of dead oak in the forest rather than take it all for firewood. In the time of our seventh-generation granddaughter there will be a large area of fire-safe pine stands that will provide the possibility of the sale of an occasional valuable, huge, clear, old-growth sawlog.

We assume something of the same will be true on surrounding land. The wildlife will still pass through. Visitors from the highly crowded lowlands will come to walk, study, and reflect. A few people will be resident on this land, getting some part of their income from forestry work. The rest will come from the information economy of three centuries hence. There might even be a civilization with a culture of cultivating wildness.

You can say that this is outrageously optimistic. It truly is. But the possibility of saving, restoring, and wisely (yes!) using the bounty of wild nature is still with us in North America. My home base, here at Kitkitdizze, is but one tiny node in an evolving net of bioregional workers.

Beyond all this studying and managing and calculating, there's another level of knowing nature. You can go about learning the names of things and doing inventories of trees, bushes, and flowers. But nature often just flits by and is not easily seen in a hard, clear light. Our actual experience of many birds and wildlife is chancy and quick. Wildlife is known as a call, a cough in the dark, a shadow in the shrubs. You can watch a cougar on a wildlife video for hours, but the real cougar shows herself only once or twice in a lifetime. One must be tuned to hints and nuances.

After twenty years of walking right past it on my way to chores in the   25
meadow, I actually paid attention to a certain gnarly canyon live oak one

day. Or maybe it was ready to show itself to me. I felt its oldness, suchness, inwardness, oakness, as if it were my own. Such intimacy makes you totally at home in life and in yourself. But the years spent working around that oak in that meadow and not really noticing it were not wasted. Knowing names and habits, cutting some brush here, getting firewood there, watching for when the fall mushrooms bulge out are skills that are of themselves delightful and essential. They also prepare one for suddenly meeting the oak.

Understanding the Text

1. In your own words, trace the evolution of Snyder's attitudes toward the land from the 1960s to the present.

2. Why does Snyder consider life at Kitkitdizze "absolutely delicious" (para. 12)?

3. What assumptions underlie Snyder's "optimistic" (para. 23) vision of a public-private management of the land?

4. Why have forest-service fire-suppression practices made wildnerness areas more vulnerable to fire, according to Snyder?

Exploring and Debating the Issues

1. In your journal, reflect on the effect that being in a natural or wild area had on you during a day trip or longer vacation.

2. In an essay, adopt the perspective Malcolm Margolin articulates in "Among Kin" (p. 170), and evaluate Snyder's attitudes toward and use of his land.

3. Snyder lives in a near-wilderness area. Discuss in class the extent to which his visions of living harmoniously with the land can be applied to urban or suburban life.

4. Write an essay in which you agree, disagree, or modify Snyder's contention that "the possibility of saving, restoring, and wisely . . . using the bounty of wild nature is still with us in North America" (para. 23).

5. Gary Snyder is best known as a poet. Read some of his poetry (in collections such as *The Back Country* and *Turtle Island*), and write an essay in which you discuss his poetic treatment of the environment.

DAVID MAS MASUMOTO

As If the Farmer Died

Today the Central Valley is better known for its gigantic agribusinesses than for individual farmers, but the breed has not entirely disappeared. One such farmer is **David Mas Masumoto** (b. 1954), a third-generation Japanese American who, while not tending his family's eighty acres of peach trees and grapevines in Del Rey, writes the stories and essays that are making him one of California's newest literary voices. In this selection from *Epitaph for a Peach: Four Seasons on My Family Farm* (1995), Masumoto reflects on his decision to abandon his war against the "weeds" that infest his fields, regarding them instead as "native grasses" that belong there. By foregoing the costly, and toxic, use of chemical pesticides, Masumoto thus offers a model for other Central Valley farmers. Winner of the 1986 James Clavell National Japanese American Literary Contest, Masumoto is also the author of *Silent Strength* (1985) and *Country Voices* (1987).

Allowing Nature to Take Over

I used to have armies of weeds on my farm. They launch their annual assault with the first warm weather of spring, parachuting seeds behind enemy lines and poking up in scattered clumps around the fields.

They work underground first, incognito to a passing farmer like me. By the end of winter, dulled by the holidays and cold fog, I have my guard down. The weeds take advantage of my carelessness.

The timing of their assault is crucial. They anticipate the subtle lengthening of each day. With exact calculation they germinate and push upward toward the sunlight, silently rooting themselves and establishing a foothold. The unsuspecting farmer rarely notices any change for days.

Then, with the first good spring rain, the invasion begins. With beachheads established, the first wave of sprouting creatures rises to boldly expose their green leaves. Some taunt the farmer and don't even try to camouflage themselves. Defiantly they thrust their new stalks as high as possible, leaves peeling open as the plant claims more vertical territory. Soon the concealed army of seeds explodes, and within a week what had been a secure, clear territory is claimed by weeds. They seem to be everywhere, no farm is spared the invasion.

Then I hear farmers launching their counterattack. Tractors roar from   5
their winter hibernation, gunbarrel-gray exhaust smoke shoots into the air, and cold engines churn. Oil and diesel flow through dormant lines as the machines awaken. Hungry for work, they will do well when let loose in the fields. The disks and cultivators sitting stationary throughout winter rains await the tractor hitch. The blades are brown with rust stains, bearings and gears cold and still since last fall. But I sense they too may be anxious to cleanse themselves in the earth and regain their sleek steel shimmer.

Even the farmers seem to wear peculiar smiles. Through the cold winter season, they were confined to maintenance, repairing equipment, fixing broken cement irrigation gates, replanting lost trees and vines. Their hibernation culminates with a desk assignment at the kitchen table, where they sit surrounded by piles of papers, laboring on taxes (farmers are required to file by March first). After restless hours of poring through shoe boxes of receipts and trying to make sense of instructions written by IRS sadists eager to punish all of us who are self-employed, farmers long for a simple task outside. We are anxious to walk our fields, to be productive, to work our land. A full winter's worth of pent-up energy is unleashed on the tiny population of weeds.

Within a day or two, the genocide is complete. Fields become "clean," void of all life except vines and trees. Farmers take no prisoners. I can sometimes count the number of weeds missed by their disks. "Can't let any go to seed," a neighbor rationalizes. Each seed becomes a symbol of evil destruction and an admission of failure.

Farmers also enlist science to create a legion of new weapons against the weeds. They spray preemergent herbicides, killing latent seed pods before they germinate. Others use contact or systemic killers, burning the delicate early growth of weeds and injecting the plants with toxins that reach down to the roots. As spring weeds flourish between rows, a strip of barren earth beneath each vine or tree magically materializes from a spray applied a month or two before. At times I wonder what else is killed in order to secure the area.

A weed might be defined as any undesirable plant. On my farm, I used to call anything that wasn't a peach tree or a grapevine a weed. I too considered a field clean if it contained nothing but dirt, barren of anything green except what I had planted. All my neighbors did likewise. We'd compete to see whose field would be the cleanest. But our fields weren't clean. They were sterile.

We pay a high price for sterility, not only in herbicide bills and hours of disking but also in hidden costs like groundwater contamination. Some farmers can no longer use a certain herbicide because the California Department of Agriculture tested and discovered trace residues contaminating the water tables beneath their farms. It had been widely used because it kills effectively and is relatively cheap; for about $10 per acre it would sterilize an entire field.

But signatures of a clean field can stay with the farm for years. Behind my house, I planted some landscape pines, hardy, cheap, grow-anywhere black pines — that kept dying. They died a slow death, the needle tips burning before turning completely brown, the top limbs succumbing first, the degeneration marching down toward the heartwood like a deadly cancer. Uncertain of the cause of death, I gave up trying to grow the pines after the third cremation. Staring at the barren area I at last discovered the reason: nothing grew on that strip of earth. The preemergent herbicide I once used remains effective and has left a long-term brand on the land.

But I now have very few weeds on my farm. I removed them in a single day using a very simple method. I didn't even break into a sweat. I simply redefined what I call a weed.

It began with an uncomfortable feeling, like a muse whispering in my ear, which led to an observation about barren landscapes. It doesn't make sense to try and grow juicy grapes and luscious peaches in sterile ground. The terms *juicy* and *luscious* connote land that's alive, green most of the year with plants that celebrate the coming of spring.

A turning point came when a friend started calling his weeds by a new name. He referred to them as "natural grasses." I liked that term. It didn't sound as evil as "weeds," it had a soft and gentle tone about it. So I came to think of my weeds as part of the natural system at work on my land, part of allowing nature to take over my farm.

And nature did take over. Once I let my guard down and allowed a gen-   15
eration of seeds to germinate, they exploded everywhere. For years I had deceived myself into thinking I had destroyed every weed seed. I was wrong, they were just waiting for an opportunity.

The first weed of spring is the pineapple weed, covering the vine berms. But it quickly wilts with the first heat of May. Chickweed hugs every tree, growing into a lush mat before dying with the first eighty-degree days. This grass may be allelopathic, producing toxins that kill competing weeds. Because few other plants grow through the mat, the yellowed and dry chickweed works like a protective mulch guarding the tree trunks.

By the middle of spring, the grasses flourish and a sea of weeds fills all but the sandiest and weakest earth. I try to keep my vine and orchard berms clear, a lesson gleaned from an earlier confrontation with a weed named mare's tail. This tall and slender creature can grow straight up into a vine leaf canopy and out the top. Mare's tail doesn't hurt vines, but at harvest the workers must battle the pollen and fight through a wall of stalks and leaves to reach the precious grapes. So I try and keep my new natural grasses away from the vine berms and tree trunks.

As nature takes over my farm, everything grows voraciously. New insect life swarms in my fields. Aphids coat sow thistle like pulsating black paint. Normally aphids aren't a problem for grapevines and peach trees, they would rather suck on sow thistle. But they are denied that meal because of the thousands of lady beetles that invade my fields for spring feasting. I wonder what other invisible life thrives in the natural grasses, what pathogens and parasites join my farm. I can't measure their presence but I feel secure, and the grapes and peaches still look fine.

I walk my fields and feel life and energy. In the evening a chorus of voices calls out, legions of insects venturing out to feed. On family bike rides we have to keep our mouths closed or bugs will fly in.

I often think, There's something going on out here, and smile to myself.   20

I was a fool to try to control weeds. I fooled myself by keeping fields sterile without knowing the long-term prices I was paying. Allowing nature to take over proved easier than I imagined. Most grasses will naturally die back without my intervention, and I've learned to recognize those few that I should not ignore. Most natural grasses are not as bad as farmers fear.

In the eyes of some farmers, my farm looks like a disaster, with weeds gone wild. Even my father grows uncomfortable. He farmed most of his life during an era of control, and to him the farm certainly now appears completely chaotic. He keeps a few rows next to his house weed-free as if to maintain a buffer between him and a lifetime of nightmares from fighting weeds.

I still have bad dreams about some obnoxious grasses like Bermuda, but my nightmares ended once I stopped thinking of them as weeds.

Lizard Dance

While weeding, I feel something tickle my calf. Without stopping my shovel, I brush the back of my leg. It happens again and I assume the clumps of johnsongrass I dug out are rolling off their pile, the thick stalks and stems attacking their killer in a vain attempt at revenge. Finally, I shake my right leg, and the thing bolts upward.

Immediately I throw down my shovel and stamp my feet. The adrena-   25
line shoots into my system and my heart races. I initiate my lizard dance, shaking my leg, pounding my feet, patting my pants as the poor creature runs wild up my leg. The faster I spin and whirl, the more confused the lizard becomes and the more frantically he scrambles up and down the dark caverns of my pant leg.

In the middle of my dance, I begin laughing, recalling the familiar feel of a lizard running up my pants, through my shirt, and down my sleeves. My body dances uncontrollably to the feel of its tiny feet and little claws grabbing my skin. I try to slow down, knowing the lizard will too if we both relax.

But as the creature scampers up higher and higher my imagination runs wild. Vulnerable body parts flash in my mind.

If other workers were around, they would laugh, watching me tug at my belt, frantically trying to drop my pants. With luck, I won't open a crevice in my shorts, inviting the lizard into another dark hiding place. Instead he'll be attracted to daylight, leap out of my crotch, and tumble to the ground, dazed for a moment before scampering into the safety of weeds and undergrowth.

I enjoy the return of lizards to my farm. They were plentiful in my youth, soaking up the rays of the sun, eating bugs and insects, living happily in the patches of grasses and weeds. Then we disked and plowed their homes and sprayed to kill most of their food. The lizards left.

I didn't plan on raising lizards, but they're part of a natural farm land-   30
scape. Besides, their presence reminds me of my childhood. I can't return to those days but I can try and foster new life on the farm, along with laughter and the lizard dance.

Farming with Chaos

Chaos defines my farm. I allow natural grasses to go wild. I see new six-legged creatures migrating into my fields, which now look like green pastures. I watch with paranoid panic, wanting to believe all will be fine while terrified I may lose the crop and even the farm. I need a lesson on managing chaos.

The small town of Del Rey is two and a half miles from my farm. When Japanese immigrants first settled there in the early 1900s, one of the first structures erected was a community hall, a place for meetings, gatherings, dinners, and festivals, a refuge from the tough life in the fields. The grounds around the hall were never truly landscaped. The sparse collection of trees and shrubs was lost in droughts and freezes, taken out for a basketball court, or neglected during World War II, when all Japanese were forced to evacuate the West Coast, leaving the trees without a caretaker. But there are still a few trees and bushes at the old hall, sporadically cared for during community gatherings. At one of these meetings I was taught my first lesson on chaos.

Two old-timers were pruning one of the Japanese black pines. They were retired farmers and gardeners, a common dual profession for struggling farmers who found that they could supplement their income by tending other people's gardens. The two old men worked in silence as they clipped away, pulling off needles and shaping the tree. The pine was not an eighty-year-old bonsai masterpiece. It was probably something left over from one of their gardening jobs, an extra pine donated to the hall perhaps fifteen years ago and gradually shaped and pruned.

I asked if I could help. They both nodded without looking up and kept working. I waited for some direction but they kept probing the bottom of each limb, stopping at a small outgrowth and quickly snapping it off. Their fingers gently raked the branches, tugging and separating unwanted growth. Their glassy old eyes wandered across the needles, stopping and guiding clippers, then moving on, scanning and studying the tree.

"How do you know what to cut?" I asked. One glanced up and smiled softly. His entire face seemed to mold around the grin as if all the wrinkles worked in unison to accommodate the gesture. A smile was familiar to that face.

I repeated my question and he whispered something in Japanese I could not hear or understand. They both returned to their clipping and snipping. The next time, just as he cut a small branch, I pointed and asked, "Why did you cut that one?"

He looked up as if wakened from a trance and blinked. "*Saa* . . . I don't know." He returned to his work.

I was relegated to watching their movements, trying to guess why they cut or passed on a branch, why some needles were pulled and thinned and others weren't. Their hands massaged the pine, their eyes wandering up and down a scaffold as fingers stroked and probed the interior of the tree. I tried with my hands but was quickly entangled in decisions. When do you leave a new branch and for how long? What was the rule when pruning? What are the criteria for cutting? I was overlooking something very basic, something I couldn't see in front of me.

The pine was only maintained once or twice a year. It had a wild quality about it, unlike the meticulously tended backyard Japanese garden variety. It was a living chaos, a reflection of the natural ebbs and flows of erratic irrigations, unprotected frosts and heat waves, and inconsistent care from an aging ethnic farm community. Yet out of this uncontrolled growth, these two old-timers were sculpting a beautiful tree, simple and innocent.

I never did grasp the art of pruning that pine tree. Later, during a summer heat wave, when the farmers were all out desperately trying to get water to thirsty grapes and trees, one of the hall's pine trees died. (I also learned that both old men had acute hearing problems and probably hadn't heard any of my questions.) But as I try to farm more naturally, I keep thinking of those two farmers and their dancing hands. They had no secret pruning method. Perhaps there is no secret to farming and managing chaos—you blend tradition and science with some common sense and trust you'll have a crop. In fact, most good farmers I know are like those two old men, tending to their trees and vines as best they can, comfortable with their work, and confident that the final product will be fine. Whether they know it or not, seasoned farmers are already experts at chaos.

40

As If the Farmer Died

This year I've abandoned my old farmwork schedules, which were often set by the calendar. I have no set mowing program or irrigation timeline. I devote more hours to monitoring my fields, and I curb my impulse to find quick fixes. Not only can I identify the pests that are munching on my fruits, I also recognize when they don't seem to be doing any more damage than usual. I'm learning to live with them, realizing that I've probably always had these pests but never scrutinized the farm so closely. I monitor the weeds as they creep up to new heights and discover some I have never seen before. I watch for new lush growth and wonder if the compost I added last fall is working. Each day I accumulate impressions more than lessons, as I develop the instincts of those two old farmers.

I used to farm with a strategy of un-chaos. I was looking for regularity, less variability, ignoring the uniqueness of each farm year. But now my farm resembles the old pine at the Del Rey Hall; wildness is tolerated, even promoted. The farm becomes a test of the unconventional, a continuous experiment, a journey of adaptation and living with change. I've even had to change my ways of counting. It's no longer important how *many* pests I have, what matters is the ratio between good bugs and bad bugs. I try to rely less and less on controlling nature. Instead I am learning to live with its chaos.

Understanding the Text

1. Explain in your own words what Masumoto means by the farming strategy of "un-chaos" (para. 42).
2. According to Masumoto, what are the different connotations of the words "weeds" and "natural grasses" (para. 14), and how do they affect our attitudes toward the land?
3. Why does Masumoto call this essay "As If the Farmer Died"?
4. What is the tone of Masumoto's essay? How does it affect our response to the farmers who have not adopted his "chaotic" (para. 22) farming method?

Exploring and Debating the Issues

1. In your journal, reflect on any gardening practices that you or your family may engage in. Have you shared the desire for a "clean" (para. 7) garden, or do you prefer a "chaotic" (para. 22) garden environment?
2. Compare and contrast Masumoto's and Gary Snyder's ("Cultivating Wildness," p. 178) attitudes toward their land. How are their visions similar and different? How might their uses of their land affect their visions?
3. Masumoto is a fruit-tree farmer. In class, debate the proposition that, if Masumoto's farm is invaded by Mediterranean fruit flies, he should be required to spray his trees with malathion.
4. When discussing the pruning techniques of the two Japanese farmers at the community center, Masumoto is deliberately general in his description of their secret to wise plant nurturing. In class, discuss Masumoto's purpose in relating this anecdote.
5. In an essay, argue for or against the proposition that Masumoto's chaotic farming method should be applied to large-scale farming as well as to his small family farm.

GERALD W. HASLAM

The Water Game

Though now one of the most productive agricultural regions in the world, the Central Valley was not always a promising place to grow crops. In this overview of the development of Central Valley agriculture, **Gerald W. Haslam** (b. 1937) explores both the rewards and the costs of the vast irrigation projects that transformed the Valley from an arid savannah to an agricultural cornucopia. A native of the Central Valley and a professor of English at Sonoma State University, Haslam has written and edited numerous collections of short stories and essays focused on the Valley, including *California Heartland: Writing from the Great Central Valley* (1978), *That Constant Coyote: California Stories* (1990), *Condor Dreams and Other Fictions* (1994), *The Other California: The Great Central Valley in Life and Letters* (1990), from which this selection is taken, and *The Great Tejon Club Jubilee* (1996).

John Phoenix is acknowledged to have been one of the West's first great humorists. Phoenix was actually the *nom de plume* of a mischievous and talented graduate of West Point, George Horatio Derby. A topographical engineer for the United States Army, Derby wrote hilarious sketches even while on military assignments. In 1849, however, when he was dispatched to survey the Great Central Valley's farming potential, the wag turned grim.

The area north of Fresno—now the richest agricultural county in America—he reported, was "Exceedingly barren, and singularly destitute of resources, except for a narrow strip on the borders of the stream; it was without timber and grass, and can never, in my estimation, be brought into requisition for agricultural purposes." Near present-day Bakersfield in Kern County (the nation's second-most productive), he found "the most miserable country that I ever beheld."

That same parched vale is now the most abundant agricultural cornucopia in the history of the world. Last year it produced over fifteen billion dollars in agriculture. How was that transformation possible? Distinguished historian W. H. Hutchinson says there were three principal reasons: "Water, water, and *more* water."

The control and manipulation of water in the arid West have been the key to everything from economics to politics here. Without water projects, there would be few Idaho potatoes; without water projects, little Arizona cotton, no Utah alfalfa. There would also be no Phoenix, no Las Vegas, and no Los Angeles—not as we know them, anyway. There would be no Reno or El Paso or Albuquerque, either, because they too have grown in desiccated areas.

The American West is, in the main, arid to semiarid land. But the natural beauty and value of arid lands has rarely been apparent to people whose ancestors migrated from green Europe, so enormous amounts of money have been spent and rapacious bureaucracies created in an effort to "make the desert bloom." Nonetheless, only a tiny portion of the land has so far been "developed," but that has bloomed abundantly.   5

Unfortunately, these efforts have also produced the seeds of their own doom: problems such as soil salinization, compaction, and subsidence; the leaching and concentrating of natural toxins from previously dry earth; the overuse of agricultural chemicals, which in turn concentrate in the environment; and the devastation of once-huge aquifers in order to flood-irrigate crops better suited to other climates in other places. These developments now seem to have placed Westerners on a path trod by Assyrians, Mesopotamians, and Aztecs, desert peoples who also once challenged nature—and failed.

In the past year, ten photographers have embarked on a project to dramatize this long-ignored environmental crisis. "We've been managing water as an abstract legal right or a commodity," points out Robert Dawson, the Californian who initiated the endeavor, "rather than the most basic physical source of life. We believe that water is misused nationwide. We're focusing on the arid West because development here stands in high relief against the vast, open landscape. It's here that the impact of technology, government, and human ambition is most visible." Many major water-policy decisions remain to be made, and only an informed public can do that.

Nowhere are the gains and losses associated with water manipulation more obvious than in Dawson's home region, the Great Central Valley of California, the physical and economic core of our richest state. All significant cities here, the state's heartland, grew near watercourses; it is an oasis civilization.

But it isn't the existence of cities that makes this area vital. It is the fact that 25 percent of all table food produced in the United States is grown in this single valley.

The climate here seems close to perfect for farming: following a short, 10 splendid spring, an extended summer develops. Sun prevails and the horizon seems to expand. Thanks to water pumped or imported, the list of crops grown in this natural hothouse is continually expanding as new varieties are planted: exotic herbs and condiments this year, kiwi fruit and frost-free berries the next. Meanwhile, native plants are rare and native animals — pronghorns, grizzlies, and condors — stand stuffed in local museums.

Here, too, a largely Hispanic workforce toils on great farms owned by corporations because this remains a place where poor of any background can at least try to escape the cycle of poverty, one generation laboring that another might take advantage of the region's rich promise. But it isn't an easy climb; there has tended to be a direct link between centralized irrigation systems and centralized political and economic power, and that in turn has created a paternalistic, class-ridden society with nonwhites on the bottom.

Modern agribusiness is competitive, and Valley farmers and ranchers have been notable, inventing such agricultural devices as special adaptations of the clamshell dredge, peach defuzzers, olive pitters, wind machines to fight frost, hydraulic platforms for pruning, pneumatic tree-shakers for bringing down the fruit and nuts — a technological nascence of amazing creativity. But none of them would mean much without imported or pumped water.

Many farmers date their entry into Valley agriculture to the period just after World War I when the unregulated pumping of ground water allowed fields to burgeon. Eventually farmers were pumping more and more from wells that had to be drilled deeper and deeper into unreplenishable aquifers. When the Central Valley Project and the California State Water Project — the two largest and most complex irrigation systems on earth — were completed, it seemed that at last the tapping of irreplaceable ground water in the Valley could cease.

Today, more than twelve hundred dams have been built and thousands of miles of canals cross this one-time desert. Even that hasn't stopped subsurface pumping; it has actually expanded since those huge stores of surface water became available. Pumping now exceeds replenishment by more than a half-*trillion* gallons annually, while ecosystems hundreds of miles to the north are threatened by the diversion of their rivers and creeks.

Writer Wallace Stegner has suggested that this area's—and by analogy,   15
the West's—agriculture may have "to shrink back to something like the old, original scale, and maybe less than the original scale because there isn't the ground water there anymore. It's actually more desert than it was when people first began to move in." Hutchinson adds, "We have to stop pretending we're frontiersmen dealing with unlimited water. There's too damn many of *us* and too damned little of *it.*"

Giant agribusinesses in the Valley can buy that water for less than ten dollars per acre foot, while northern California householders have paid well over one thousand dollars for the same acre foot—with the difference subsidized by taxpayers. It seems to critics that such water is too cheap to use wisely and that both hubris and ignorance are manifest in the illusion that moisture unused by humans is somehow squandered, the natural world be damned—and dammed. Ironically, most people—including most Westerners—seem to prefer not to be aware of all this, lest salads and beef suddenly become more expensive.

Irrigation is big business, and both the vast water projects in California were justified, in part at least, as measures that would save existing family farms and perhaps increase the number of acres cultivated by small farmers. In fact, both have led to more and more acres coming under cultivation by huge corporations—Chevron U.S.A., Prudential Insurance Company, Shell Oil Company, Southern Pacific Railroad, J. G. Boswell Company, Getty Oil, among others.

How has the quest for water changed the West? Last year, driving in the southwest corner of Central Valley, I decided to investigate Buena Vista Lake, where I'd fished when I was a boy. I crossed the California Aqueduct, then drove west and finally stopped the car. An immense agricultural panorama opened before me, cultivated fields of various hues extending in all directions.

All its tributary streams have been diverted and its bed is now dry so, ironically, Buena Vista Lake must be irrigated. As I gazed at this scene, a red-tailed hawk wheeled overhead, riding a thermal. Far to the east a yellow tractor shimmered through heat waves like a crawdad creeping across the old lake's floor. I saw no dwellings, few trees.

That hawk swung far over a green field where tiny fingers of water from   20
elsewhere glistened through rows and where a lone brown man, an irrigator, leaned on a shovel.

Welcome to the real West, where agribusiness executives in corporate boardrooms, not cowboys or Indians or even irrigators, are the principal players.

Understanding the Text

1. What does Haslam mean when he says that water projects "have placed Westerners on a path trod by Assyrians, Mesopotamians, and Aztecs" (para. 6)?

2. What gains and losses does Haslam find in the history of Central Valley irrigation?

3. How has irrigation shaped the social class system of the Central Valley, according to Haslam?

4. What does Haslam learn when he returns to his boyhood recreation area, Buena Vista Lake?

Exploring and Debating the Issues

1. In class, brainstorm the pros and cons of heavy irrigation in the Central Valley. Then form teams, and debate Wallace Stegner's proposition that farming "shrink back to something like the old, original scale" (para. 15) in this region. Be sure to offer solutions to the groundwater problem if you oppose Stegner; if you support him, suggest alternative means of livelihood for displaced farmers.

2. Haslam notes that agribusiness customers in the Central Valley pay ten dollars for an acre foot of water while urban consumers can pay as much as a thousand dollars for the same amount. Write an essay arguing for or against taxpayer subsidization of agricultural production through this differential price structure for water.

3. In your journal, describe how you would plan the future of the Central Valley if you had the power to dictate water policy there. Share your entry with your classmates.

4. Write an essay in which you analyze the role water has played in making the California dream possible. To develop your ideas, read or reread James J. Rawls's "California: A Place, A People, A Dream" (p. 8), Joan Didion's "Notes from a Native Daughter" (p. 51), and Margaret Leslie Davis's "Mulholland's Prophecy" (below).

5. Haslam criticizes large agribusiness in his essay. Write an argument in support of or in opposition to his position. To develop your ideas, you may wish to consult Joan Didion's "Notes from a Native Daughter" (p. 51) or Marc Reisner's "Things Fall Apart" (p. 198).

MARGARET LESLIE DAVIS

Mulholland's Prophecy

The San Fernando Valley was once an arid and empty expanse of economically unattractive land. William Mulholland changed all that by engineering the aqueduct that made the Valley bloom — and enriched the landowners who pushed for the project in the first place. But as **Margaret Leslie Davis** (b. 1960) observes in this excerpt from her book *Rivers in the Desert: William Mulholland and the Inventing of Los Angeles* (1993), Mulholland's legacy has been ambiguous, both enriching the Los Angeles area and threatening it with a growth rate it can no longer afford. A Los Angeles attorney, Davis is also a staff writer for the *Los Angeles Daily Journal,* a legal publication, and author of *Lovers, Doctors, and the Law* (1988). She is currently working on a biography of Beverly Hills oil tycoon Edward Doheny.

What is the legacy of William Mulholland? Critics argue that Los Angeles would have been better off had the population and prosperity envisioned by Mulholland never been promoted. There is some support for this view. Today, Mulholland's tree-lined home at St. Andrew's Place is in the center of a rundown urban expanse, a stone's throw from the site of looting and arson in Korea Town during the 1992 civil disturbance in Los Angeles. The Mulholland Orchard in the San Fernando Valley no longer exists; in its place is a K-mart discount department store. Because of smog, the magnificent vistas from the twisting Mulholland Highway can be seen only on a few clear days each year.

But there is another side to the legacy. The cup is overflowing in America's second city as never before. Tides of immigrants from other parts of the world have forever altered its social landscape. Foreign investment is soaring, and Los Angeles County, previously not considered an industrial stronghold, now leads the nation in manufacturing exports. The city is a leader in architectural innovation, education, and the arts. The phrase "melting pot" has now been revised by city leaders who speak of a "giant salad bowl," of trade, capital, labor, and cultures. Futurists place Los Angeles at the epicenter of the Pacific Rim — a key zone for international trade in the next century.

Mulholland's ingenuous masterpiece, the Los Angeles Aqueduct, did indeed make possible the waves of immigration that brought the burdens and costs of a city growing too fast for its planners, but the resultant diverse population will prove an advantage in the global village of the future.

Without Mulholland's aqueduct, Los Angeles would have been limited in growth, to probably not more than 250,000 people. The aqueduct made possible a metropolis where natural conditions forbid it. The annexation of the San Fernando Valley, a direct result of the aqueduct, instantly made Los Angeles the largest city in the world in terms of geographic size, and from that moment forward, as Mulholland predicted in his celebratory toast in 1913, the citizens of Los Angeles were to be a people "doomed to success."

Mulholland's malapropism was prophetic — eight decades later, the   5
sprawling giant has grown to a region over a hundred miles in diameter sustaining a population of 14.5 million, and the city of Los Angeles is expected to match the population of America's largest city, New York, near the year 2010. But the promised success now decays under the burden of urban sprawl, violence, unbreathable air, and rationed water.

The Los Angeles populace enters 1993 facing a seventh year of drought and a further decline in their quality of life. Even in wet years the region is dry, receiving on average one-third the amount of rain as New York and half that of Chicago.

In May 1990, Los Angeles instituted mandatory water rationing, requiring households to cut water use by 10 percent. In spite of rationing, and even with the possibility of a new aqueduct, it is unlikely the region's critical water problems can be solved. As the twenty-first century approaches, the same problems that challenged William Mulholland confront the city again.

Present sources of water are not adequate and will be further reduced as Arizona and Nevada exercise their legal rights to Colorado River water in coming years. In addition, the problem of drought years has never been adequately addressed. Los Angeles faces long- and short-term problems of confounding complexity.

The city of Los Angeles, one researcher commented, "would do well to relinquish its tropical self-image and come to terms with its arid climate." Enforced conservation is likely to become the only solution. Even when the drought ends, Los Angeles will have to endure restrictions on lawn-watering and car-washing and will have to forego the luxury of abundant swimming pools, lush landscaping, and other water extravagances. Conservation devices in addition to the low-flow faucets, toilets, and shower heads already required will be mandatory. Water bills will increase, and penalties for overuse will stiffen. A massive education program is needed to teach consumers to adapt themselves to a desert environment.

The populace, baffled by the complexity of water issues and misled by public leaders enamored of ever-expanding development, is prone to insist no water shortage exists. The history and fable of Los Angeles's water campaigns has left the public suspicious, uncertain of the truth and leery of scare tactics. What is needed is another visionary Mulholland to genially deliver the bad news and rally support for a creative solution, for there are no more rivers to bring to the desert.

10

Understanding the Text

1. What, in Davis's view, is the legacy of William Mulholland and the Los Angeles Aqueduct?

2. Why does Davis consider prophetic William Mulholland's comment that Los Angeles was "doomed to success" (para. 4)?

3. Why does Davis say that "enforced conservation" is the only likely solution to Los Angeles's water problems (para. 9)?

4. Why are southern Californians inclined to deny the existence of water problems?

Exploring and Debating the Issues

1. In what ways has the Los Angeles Aqueduct enabled southern Californians to adopt a "tropical self-image" (para. 9)? To develop your ideas, consult James J. Rawls's "California: A Place, A People, A Dream" (p. 8).

2. Write a letter in which you attempt to persuade Los Angeles residents that they need to adopt the water conservation measures that Davis suggests. To develop your argument, you may want to read or reread Gerald W. Haslam's "The Water Game" (p. 191), Marc Reisner's "Things Fall Apart" (below), or Charlie Stoddard's "An Age of Limits and Definitions" (p. 46).

3. In class, form teams and debate the proposition that "Los Angeles would have been better off had the population and prosperity envisioned by Mulholland never been promoted" (para. 1).

4. Write an essay in which you argue whether the cost of water conservation measures should be borne primarily by homeowners or farmers. To develop your position, consult Gerald W. Haslam's "The Water Game" (p. 191).

MARC REISNER

Things Fall Apart

The story **Marc Reisner** tells in this selection is a nightmare that began with good intentions. The vast irrigation projects of the San Joaquin Valley needed a place where all that water could drain; the migrating fowl that fly over the Valley needed a place to rest and feed. So the creation of the Kesterson Reservoir seemed to be a good solution to both problems — until the birds began to die of selenium poisoning from the irrigation runoff. A former staff writer for the Natural Resources Defense Council, Reisner tells this tale and others like it in *Cadillac Desert* (1986), an environmentalist history of western water policy. A resident of San Francisco, he is also the author of *Overtapped Oasis: Reform or Revolution for Western Water* (1990) and *Game Wars: The Undercover Pursuit of Wildlife Poachers* (1991).

In the Colorado Basin, the effects of wastefully irrigating saline lands are not, for the most part, being felt by those doing the irrigating. Thanks mainly to the taxpayers, the farmers who are contributing the lion's share of the salts to the river have had drainage facilities built which flush the problem down to someone else. In the San Joaquin Valley, it is a different story. The San Joaquin's problem is unique — an ingenious revenge by nature, in the minds of some, on a valley whose transformation into the richest agricultural region in the world was wrought at awesome cost to rivers, fish, and wildlife. Several times in the relatively recent geologic past — within the last couple of million years — the valley was a great inland sea, thick with diatomaceous life and tiny suspended sediments which settled near the middle of the gently sloping valley floor. Compressed and compacted, the stuff formed an almost impervious layer of clay that now underlies close to two million acres of fabulously productive irrigated land. In the middle of the valley, the clay membrane is quite shallow, sometimes just a few feet beneath the surface soil. When irrigation water percolates down, it collects on the clay like bathwater in a tub. In hydrologists' argot, it has become "perched" water. Since the perched water does not have a chance to mingle with the relatively pure aquifer beneath the clay, it may become highly saline, as in Iraq. The more the farmers irrigate, the higher it rises. In places, it has reached the surface, killing everything around. There are already thousands of acres near the southern end of the valley that look as if they had been dusted with snow; not even weeds can grow there. An identical fate will ultimately befall more than a million acres in the valley unless something is done.

For years, the planners in the state and federal water bureaucracies have talked about the need for a "master drain" to carry the perched water out of the San Joaquin Valley. It is more accurate to say that their *reports* have talked about it, while the officials, whose main concern was building more dams to satisfy the demands of the irrigators, ignored the need for drainage because neither they nor (they guessed) the public and the farmers could face the cost. "In the early and mid-1970s," says van Schilfgaarde,[1] "the state's position was that no drainage problem exists. The early reports all said that the State Water Project makes no sense without a drain because it would add inevitably to the perched water problem. But the public doesn't read reports, so no one mentioned them. Then, a few years ago, when the problem began threatening to become critical, there was suddenly an awful drainage problem that threatened the future of agriculture in California."

Today, three decades after the first reports spoke of the need for a huge, valleywide drainage system, no such system exists. A modest-sized spur, called the San Luis Drain, is being completed as a part of the Westlands Water District, which, by introducing a prodigious amount of new surface water into a relatively small area, threatened to waterlog the lands downslope. But the water carried off by the San Luis Drain has nowhere to go until a master drain is built. For the time being, it is being dumped into a manmade swamp called Kesterson Reservoir, near the town of Los Banos, which slowly fills and evaporates according to the intensity of the valley heat and the irrigation cycle. From the air, the reservoir, when it is full, is an attractive sight to migrating waterfowl, which descend on it by the tens of thousands as their ancestors once descended by the many millions on the valley's primordial marshes and shallow lakes. The presence of all of those coots, geese, and ducks at Kesterson Reservoir gave the Bureau an idea about how to solve one of the most daunting problems associated with the master drain: its enormous cost. By the time the San Luis Drain, a modest portion of the proposed master drain, is completed, its price tag will be more than $500 million. In 1984, Interior Secretary William Clark made an offhand projection that solving the drainage problem valleywide could end

---

[1]Jan van Schilfgaarde, director of the U.S. Department of Agriculture's Salinity Control Laboratory in Riverside, California. [Eds.]

up costing $4 to $5 billion. That comes to about $5,000 an acre to rescue the affected lands, which is more than most of the land itself is worth. The farmers, a number of whom are corporations or millionaires, are understandably loath to pay the bill. If one wrote off a third of the cost as a wildlife and recreational benefit, however, it would be easier to swallow. That is exactly what the Bureau and California's Department of Water Resources, in a 1979 interagency study entitled "Agricultural Drainage and Salt Management in the San Joaquin Valley," proposed to do in the case of the master drain, which, in that report, was projected to cost $1.26 billion in 1979 dollars. Ascribing annual benefits of $92 million to the master drain, the Bureau and the state's Department of Water Resources elected to write off about a third of that total, or $31.7 million, as a nonreimbursable benefit, payable by the taxpayers, for the creation of artificial marshes. If one were to divide the number of ducks which might reasonably be expected to use those manmade wetlands into $31.7 million, they would become very expensive ducks indeed. When the Bureau's dams went up, regulating the rivers and allowing the marshlands to be dried up—about 93 percent of the Central Valley's original wetlands are gone—it virtually ignored the economic value of the millions of ducks it was about to displace. Now, suddenly, they have become almost priceless.

Due to a distressing twist of fate, however, the Bureau of California may consider themselves lucky if they succeed in writing off *any* part of the master drain to wildlife benefits. Sometime in 1982, hunters and biologists around Kesterson Reservoir began to observe that many overwintering birds seemed lethargic and sick—so ravaged by some strange malady that they could not even float on the water, and often drowned. At first, duck hunters and conservationists put forth an explanation that the farm lobby had always pooh-poohed—that pesticides and other chemical wastes in the sumpwater were making the birds die. By 1984, however, biologists were quite certain that the main cause of the ducks' awful fate was selenium, a rare mineral, toxic in small doses, that occurs in high concentrations in southern Coast Range soils—exactly those soils which, washing down from the mountains over aeons, formed the Westlands Water District. The *San Francisco Chronicle*, which has carried on a long, bitter battle against water exports to the valley and southern California, has played the story for all it is worth. But none of its news stories and editorials had quite the impact of a poignant front-page photograph of a gorgeous dying male pintail duck at Kesterson Reservoir, a duck about to sink like a doomed boat to the bottom of the poisoned manmade marsh its presence is to subsidize.

Since there can be only one ultimate destination for the wastewater   5
carried by the master drain—San Francisco Bay—the spectacle at Kesterson has infuriated many of the five million people who reside in the Bay Area. They may pollute the bay badly enough themselves, even if they do not admit it; but to have a bunch of farmers grown wealthy on "their" water, and subsidized by their taxes, sending it back to the bay full of toxic wastes, selenium, boron, and salt—that is intolerable. The farmers, the Bureau,

and the Department of Water Resources might reject such reasoning as simplistic and emotional. But the fact is that the people of the Bay Area appear to have the political clout to prevent the drain from ever reaching there, and they seem determined to use it. It matters little that the salts in the wastewater (the selenium and boron and pesticides are another matter) would hardly affect the salinity of a great bay into which the ocean rushes every day. What matters is that the San Joaquin Valley farmers asked for water and got it, asked for subsidies and got them, and now want to use the bay as a toilet. To their urban brethren by the ocean, living a world apart, all of this smacks of a system gone mad.

Understanding the Text

1. What are the geological conditions that led to the appearance of perched water in the San Joaquin Valley?
2. Why is a drainage system so vital to the San Joaquin Valley?
3. What miscalculations were made by the California Department of Water Resources in the creation of the Kesterson Reservoir?
4. What were the reasons for the death of wildlife at Kesterson Reservoir?

Exploring and Debating the Issues

1. Assuming the role of a farmer, write a letter to Reisner in which you respond to his comment, "What matters is that the San Joaquin Valley farmers asked for water and got it, asked for subsidies and got them, and now want to use the bay as a toilet" (para. 5).
2. In class, form two teams that represent San Joaquin Valley farmers and San Francisco Bay environmentalists, and debate the construction of a master drain from the Valley to the Bay.
3. Reisner points out that irrigating land can also destroy it with salt pollution. Write an essay arguing whether the development of Central Valley agriculture—a major part of the California economy—is worth the price.
4. In class, discuss the tone of Reisner's selection. What assumptions about the various groups he discusses—farmers, state bureaucrats, biologists, urbanites—are revealed through his tone?
5. Write an essay in which you argue whether the cost of protecting wildlife from such human-caused disasters as the Kesterson Reservoir should be borne by all state citizens.

MIKE DAVIS

Sunbelt Bolshevism

Despite the California dream's vision of unlimited horizons, the environmental consequences of unchecked economic development are coming home to roost, and many Californians are joining the ranks of the slow-growth movement. But in this excerpt from *City
of Quartz* (1992), **Mike Davis** (b. 1946) contends that not all the motives of slow-growth
advocates are environmentally grounded. Land values—what one can charge per home or
lot—are what many slow-growth proponents are out to preserve, Davis argues, not the
land itself. A former meatcutter and long-distance truck driver from Fontana, Davis now
teaches urban theory at the Southern California Institute of Architecture. He is also the author of *Prisoners of the American Dream: Politics and Economy in the History of the U.S.
Working Class* (1986) and *Ecology of Fear* (1998) and coeditor of *Fire in the Hearth: The
Radical Politics of Place in America* (1990).

> The slow-growth movement is not a fad, it is a major revolution.
> —*Los Angeles Council member Marvin Braude*

The Frankenstein of West Hills[1] is a familiar kind of terror to suburban
politicians in the Los Angeles area. Many of them live in fear of being
ground to bits by the incessant conflict of microscopically parochial interests. It is, I suppose, another example of how southern California stands
simplistic social theory on its head. Elsewhere affluent homeowners are
imagined to be the contented bulwark of the status quo. But south of the
Tehachapis they act like *sans culottes*,[2] wielding the parish pump as a
guillotine. Indeed it was precisely Valley homeowners like the West Hills
group who were the shock troops of Howard Jarvis's tax revolt in 1978: an
epochal event that helped end the New Deal era and pave the way for
Reaganomics.

Now, more than a decade later, angry homeowners are engaged in a
more diffuse, but no less significant struggle over the politics of growth.
With roots in literally hundreds of homeowners' associations, a so-called
slow-growth movement has emerged out of the Brownian motion of local
land use grievances (like the Canoga Park redesignation) to challenge the
most powerful economic interest in California today: the land development
industry. Like Proposition 13 earlier, the new revolt seemed to erupt out of
the crabgrass with little prior warning.

The first rumble was in January 1985 when a coalition of homeowners
won a court order stopping the City of Los Angeles from allowing highrise
development flagrantly in excess of its own General Plan. Their precedent

---

[1]An upscale suburban community that changed its name to distinguish itself from
Canoga Park, a working-class neighborhood of which it was once part. [Eds.]
[2]Radical republican during the French Revolution; revolutionary. [Eds.]

planted the seed for the success of Proposition U in November of 1986. Heralded by the *Times* as the "first major challenge to Los Angeles's growth ethic in a hundred years," Proposition U reduced developable commercial density in the city by half and imposed a ten-point growth management plan.[3] A year later, Council member Pat Russell, the key strategist of Mayor Bradley's "pro-growth" majority on the Council, was dramatically upset by a dark-horse slow-growth advocate.

In the meantime homeowner-backed slow-growth insurgencies dominated the 1987 and 1988 local elections in scores of Los Angeles suburbs and outlying cities.[4] In spite of the absence of a countywide growth-control initiative, these local skirmishes yielded an impressive balance sheet of new building restrictions and development moratoria. Already superheated real estate markets reacted with hysteria. Anticipating that the slow-growth movement would further constrict the limited supply of developable land, hordes of house-hungry buyers rushed into the market: a self-fulfilling prophecy that led to Tokyo-type escalations in median home values in Los Angeles and Orange Counties during 1987.

Land inflation only fanned the flames of growth protest throughout the   5
suburbanizing, "pro-growth" frontiers of southern California. In the Reaganite fastnesses of southern Orange County (where only semiliberal Irvine breaks the mold) the traditional conservative consensus was splintered by a bitter struggle between latifundian developers and wealthy homeowners. The initially commanding lead of the "Sensible Growth Initiative," with its stringent "quality of life" standards for new development, was barely surmounted in the June 1988 election by the unprecedented scare campaign (stressing higher taxes and job flight) mounted by Donald Bren and his fellow *haciendados*. Chastened by the close call in Orange County, developers in neighboring Riverside County, home of two of the fastest-growing suburban fringes in the country (Moreno Valley and Elsinore-Temecula), spared no expense in vilifying their own fledgling slow-growth movement. Measure B (November 1988), which would have restricted future development in the county's unincorporated areas, was beaten three to two after pro-growth forces outspent slow-growth fifty-five to one. A similar developer-financed, pro-growth blitzkrieg edged out popular growth-control initiatives in San Diego County.

Having portrayed the slow-growth movement as virtually invincible in 1986, the press now claimed that the 1988 developers' counteroffensive had left the movement in shambles.[5] In fact, the struggle, which had begun

---

[3] *Times,* 12 October 1986.

[4] According to the California Association of Realtors, seventy-six growth-control ballot measures were put to the vote throughout the state in 1986 to 1988. Nearly half originated in Los Angeles, Orange, or San Diego Counties, and 70 percent were successful. (*Times,* 31 July 1988; and my compilation of Southern California growth measures.)

[5] See the premature obituary: "Decisive Defeats Leave State's Slow-Growth Movement in Disarray," *Times,* 10 November 1988.

as largely unreported guerrilla skirmishes, was changing from a war of ma-
neuver—with dramatic results at the polls—to an increasingly complex
war of position, involving the courts, the state legislature, and various regu-
latory bodies, as well as local government. And, whatever the immediate
balance of forces, there is no question that growth controversies continue
to polarize and reshape the southern California political landscape. But
what interpretation do we give to that vague cipher known as "slow
growth"? And where on a traditional spectrum of political and social forces
can we locate a "movement" composed of strange molecules like the West
Hills homeowners?

To some analysts the southern California slow-growth rebellion of the
late 1980s merely seemed a recapitulation of the experience of affluent Bay
Area counties in the previous decade. Beginning with Petaluma's famous
1973 experiment in growth management, more than two dozen cities, along
with the designer counties of Marin and Napa, had imposed some kind of
moratorium or cap on residential development. The Bay Area has achieved
a degree of growth limitation unequaled in any other metropolitan region
in the country—evoking envy as well as criticism for the resulting "suburban squeeze," land inflation, and chronic job/housing disjunctions. From
this perspective, southern California has only been catching up with the
Bay Area precedent of how to protect and regulate the good life.

But, without denying important overlaps, crucial differences distinguish the Bay Area and Southland versions of growth protest. In the first
place, the slow-growth movement in the south has been overwhelmingly a
movement of *homeowners,* with some environmentalists serving as organic
intellectuals and apologists. Although the movement invokes the populist
rhetoric of "community control" and "neighborhood power," tenants, with
few exceptions, play no role nor are their interests usually addressed (except in opposition). The singularity of the "People's Republic of Santa
Monica" aside, there is no counterpart to the inclusive parochialism, say, of
the recent Agnos coalition in San Francisco, which, while dominated by
wealthy homeowners, included a significant representation of renters and
urban have-nots.

Second, land-use politics in southern California have tended to generate sharper contradictions and entrenched opposition than in the north. As
David Dowall and other students of the Bay Area experience have discovered, large developers in Petaluma-type milieux have often monopolized
lucrative positions within growth-controlled local residential markets.[6] Although such accommodations can be found on a case-by-case basis in the
south, growth issues are more commonly perceived as a zero-sum game,
sowing virulent economic conflict and electoral upheaval. And the stakes
are often immense, as homeowners have sought to slow down or stop

[6]David Dowall, *The Suburban Squeeze: Land Conversion and Regulation in the San
Francisco Bay Area* (Berkeley: U of California P, 1984), 139–42.

billion-dollar, multiphase projects. Indeed the assault on the development process—and, by implication, upon the rights of corporate land ownership and laissez-faire urbanization—has been sufficiently subversive at times to warrant George Will's warning of "Sunbelt Bolshevism."[7]

Finally, an important ideological difference. Growth-control politics in   10
the Bay Area have been incubated in a specific regional tradition of patrician conservationism represented by the Sierra Club, the Bay Conservation and Development Commission, and California Tomorrow. "Responsible environmentalism" constitutes a hegemonic discourse in which all sides, developers and their community opponents, must formulate their arguments. The taproot of slow growth in the south, however, is an exceptionalistic local history of middle-class interest formation around home ownership. Environmentalism is a congenial discourse to the extent that it is congruent with a vision of eternally rising property values in secure bastions of white privilege. The master discourse here—exemplified by the West Hills secessionists—is homestead exclusivism, whether the immediate issue is apartment construction, commercial encroachment, school busing, crime, taxes, or simply community designation.[8]

Slow growth, in other words, is about homeowner control of land use and much more. Seen in the context of the suburban sociology of southern California, it is merely the latest incarnation of a middle-class political subjectivity that fitfully constitutes and reconstitutes itself every few years around the defense of household equity and residential privilege. These diverse "movements" have been notoriously volatile, but their cumulative impact upon the shaping of the sociospatial structure of the Los Angeles region has been enormous.

Understanding the Text

1. What assumptions about suburbanites does Davis make in his selection, and how do they shape his argument?

2. What does Davis mean by the title "Sunbelt Bolshevism" (para. 9)?

3. What are the motives, according to Davis, of proponents of slow growth?

4. How, in Davis's view, do the slow-growth movements in southern and northern California differ?

[7]George Will, "'Slow Growth' Is the Liberalism of the Privileged," *Times*, 30 August 1987.

[8]Of course, both ideological positions—environmentalist noblesse oblige and crabgrass xenophobia—end up defending substantially the same conservative interests. As George Will explains: "The 'slow-growth' movement here and elsewhere represents the growing desire of the possessing classes for 'conserving government,' for laws to protect the value of the positional goods in a choice location. Conserving government is the liberalism of the privileged; it is activist government protecting the well-positioned from inundation by change and competition." Ibid.

Exploring and Debating the Issues

1. Davis implies that the "elitist" motives of slow-growth advocates compromise the environmental benefits of restricting development. Write an essay in which you support or refute Davis's position.

2. Davis blames the slow-growth movement for the inflation of home prices in the late 1980s in southern California. In class, brainstorm possible alternative causes for this inflation. Use the class discussion as a basis for an essay in which you support, refute, or complicate Davis's assumption.

3. In class, list on the board the many metaphors and analogies Davis uses throughout this selection. Then analyze the language: What are its connotations? Does this language contribute to the persuasiveness of Davis's argument?

4. Write an essay in which you argue whether the slow-growth movement assists or hinders state residents' ability to attain the California dream. To develop your ideas, you may wish to consult James J. Rawls's "California: A Place, A People, A Dream" (p. 8) or Charlie Stoddard's "An Age of Limits and Definitions" (p. 46).

5. Visit your college library and investigate California's real estate boom of the late 1990s. To what extent does it illustrate Davis's slow-growth hypothesis? What other national and international economic factors might have influenced real estate values during this period? To develop your ideas, consult John Cassidy ("The Comeback," p. 274) or Michael J. Mandel ("Silicon Valley: Taking Its Place in the Pantheon," p. 285).

GARY SOTO

The First

Gary Soto (b. 1952) has emerged as one of California's leading voices in contemporary poetry and short-story writing. Having grown up in Fresno, Soto offers a Central Valley view of California literature, one that he often injects with his Latino background and heritage. In this poem, Soto sadly reflects on the first Californians, the Native Americans whose world was swept away by the European conquest, never, this poem concludes, to return. The author of numerous collections of poetry and short stories, Soto's recent works include *Baseball in April and Other Short Stories* (1990), *Chato's Kitchen* (1995), *New and Selected Poems* (1995), and *Buried Onions* (1997).

After the river
Gloved its fingers
With leaves
And the autumn sunlight
Spoked the earth   5

Into two parts,
The villagers undid
Their houses,
Thatch by thatch,
And unplucked   10
The stick fences
That held grief
And leaned from the wind
That swung their way.
What the sun raised—   15
Squash and pumpkin,
Maize collared
In a white fungus—
They left, for the earth
Was not as it was   20
Remembered, the iguana
Being stretched
Into belts
The beaver curling
Into handbags;   25
Their lakes bruised
Gray with smoke
That unraveled from cities.
Clearing a path
Through the forest,   30
A path that closed
Behind them
As the day opened
A smudge of its blue,
They were the first   35
To leave, unnoticed,
Without words,
For it no longer
Mattered to say
The world was once blue.   40

Understanding the Text

1. In a prose paragraph, summarize the sequence of events that Soto poetically describes.
2. Why does Soto refer to "the iguana/Being stretched/Into belts" and "The beaver curling/Into handbags" (ll. 21–25)?
3. What is the effect of the short-line structure of this poem?

Exploring and Debating the Issues

1. Write a poem of your own about the effects that human beings have had on California's natural environment. Share your poem with your class.

2. Compare Soto's description of Indians being dispossessed of their land with the chant, quoted in Malcolm Margolin's "Among Kin" (p. 170), describing an old man's preparation for death in a world "in which he feels completely at home."

3. The people whom Soto calls "the first" (l. 35) are not all gone; California Indians continue to live in modern society, seeking to preserve what is left of their sacred territories. Conduct a research project to determine how particular California Indians, such as the Chumash, are involved in current land-use issues.

4. Soto concludes his poem by saying "it no longer/Mattered to say/The world was once blue" (ll. 38–40). In an essay, agree, disagree, or expand on this statement. To develop your ideas, you can consult any of the readings in this chapter.

Researching the Issues

1. Rent a videotape of the movie *Chinatown,* and write a critique of the film's accuracy in presenting California's water politics. Support your critique with additional library research on the history of California water development.

2. Using your college library, research the effect on Mono Lake and its wildlife of water diversions to southern California. Then write a report comparing the condition of the lake in the early 1980s to its current status following agreements to reduce the amount of water that is diverted from its tributaries.

3. Research a local land-use controversy (such as a proposed housing development in an environmentally sensitive area or landfill near a residential zone). As part of your research, interview both opponents and proponents, and use your results to formulate an argument in support of or against the proposal you choose.

4. Mike Davis claims that the southern California slow-growth movement differs substantially from northern California's. Conduct a library research program to find out whether this is true, and report your conclusions.

5. Marc Reisner's report on the history of the Kesterson Reservoir was published in 1986. Research the current status of the reservoir, and report on the changes, if any, that have occurred since Reisner's book appeared.

CALIFORNIA ON THE NET

1. Visit Santa Clara University's web site devoted to Native Americans in California (http://www.scu.edu/SCU/Programs/Diversity/natopics/html). Explore the many links this site offers, and write a research report on California Indians' views about the environment.

2. Californians' views of the natural world are conditioned, of course, by the state's vulnerability to natural disasters. The constant threat of earthquakes has become an explicit feature of land-use policy in California, prompting the state to issue maps of geologically hazardous areas. Visit the California Department of Conservation web site (http://www.conserv.ca.gov), and select the link to these maps. Write an essay in which you argue how developers, homeowners, and municipalities should use these maps in their planning.

3. Because there are no new sources of water for California, conservation will have to be part of future water planning in the state. Form a research team, and investigate the state's plans for water conservation. To assist your research, visit web sites of the California Urban Water Conservation Council (http://www.cuwcc.com) and the California Department of Water Resources (http://www.dwr.water.ca.gov).

6. One of the most publicized of recent land-use controversies involves the protection of endangered spotted owls in granting logging rights on public lands. Research this controversy (which includes northern California logging communities as well as those in Washington and Oregon), and write an argument for or against restrictions on logging in spotted owl habitats.

7. As a number of selections in this chapter demonstrate, current California agricultural practices are resulting in massive land and water pollution. Alternative farming methods (such as organic farming and dripwater, rather than trench, irrigation programs) could ameliorate some of the environmental problems inherent in current methods of agriculture in California. Research some of the alternatives to conventional farming technology in California, and write an argument supporting or opposing measures such as tax breaks and subsidies to encourage alternative farming methods.

8. In recent years, several ballot initiatives have been devoted to conservation and wildlife issues, including two regarding the California mountain lion. Visit your school's library, and explore the politics surrounding such initiatives.

9. The sustainability movement is a multifaceted approach to environmentally sensitive resource management. Investigate the origins of the movement and its current proposals.

5 Governing California
Democracy, Demography, and the Politics of the Dream

Rule by Initiative

13. 187. 209. 227. Sometimes California's politics seem to be written in numbers. If you don't recognize them, the numbers listed here refer to some of the divisive, and nationally influential, ballot initiatives that have convulsed California's political landscape over the past twenty years. Indeed, in some ways, the fact that Californians so often resort to ballot initiatives, rather than turn to their elected officials, to resolve their political differences is just as significant as the particular content of those initiatives themselves.

To refresh your memory, Proposition 13 was the ballot initiative passed in 1978 that slashed existing property tax bills and profoundly affected the ability of state and local governments to raise revenues. Proposition 187, passed in 1994 and still mired in the courts, would deny most social services, including education, to illegal immigrants, while Proposition 209, passed in 1996, effectively ended public affirmative action programs in the state, especially in hiring and education. And Proposition 227, passed in 1998, will, if upheld in the courts, effectively end bilingual education in California's schools.

In this chapter you will find readings that address specific political controversies and the initiative process itself. For here, as in so many other areas of American life, California stands as a beacon to the rest of the nation. When Californians slashed property taxes in 1978 through a direct ballot, states throughout the country followed suit. When California passed Prop. 187, the U.S. Congress followed by creating new restrictions on social services for *legal* immigrants in the Welfare Reform Act of 1997. And while the full effect of Propositions 209 and 227 are still to be felt around the country, few doubt that they will have an impact. Even when Californians vote down a ballot initiative, as they did in 1998 with Proposition 226 — an initiative that would have restricted the political activities of labor unions — there is a national reverberation. Proposition 226 was itself initially proposed and funded by non-Californians who openly declared that they intended to use California as a springboard for similar initiatives around America.

Looked at one way, ballot initiatives represent direct democracy in action. When voters become frustrated with the inaction of their elected representatives, they can take direct control through the initiative process. But looked at another way, ballot initiatives bypass the normal processes of representative democracy and can threaten to undermine those processes, as legislators decide to avoid the more controversial issues at hand and let the initiative process take over. Thus, the most controversial matters, like affirmative action and immigration policy, end up in the public arena where unelected individuals or groups can propose their own solutions without any need for compromise. Ultimately, the most divisive ballot initiatives end up in the courts, where judges, not voters or their elected representatives, make the final decisions.

Beyond the Ballot Box

But politics is not simply a matter of elections. The word *politics* itself is derived from the Greek word for the most important social unit of the ancient Greek world: the city state. For the ancient Greeks, one's place in the *polis,* or "city state," was the most important factor that determined one's identity. To be a citizen in the polis meant to interact in a cooperative way with other citizens: this is the original meaning of *politics.* In this sense, *everything* we do in society is political.

This is an especially important lesson for Californians today, who live in a state where rapid demographic change has led to a diversified social environment. To be politically successful, in the ancient Greek sense, we all must learn how to interact cooperatively with others whose cultural, racial, and religious backgrounds are, more likely than not, different than our own. Thus, although politics as the struggle of one set of interests against another is indeed a part of the modern political process, we may also see politics as the science of getting along together.

For this reason we have included readings in this chapter that highlight the racial and cultural issues now dominating California's current political climate. We include these readings not simply to provide grist for debates over who is right or wrong in any given political controversy (though such debates may indeed be a part of your classroom experience) but, rather, to stimulate the kind of thinking that converts political controversy into political consensus.

To put this another way, our emphasis in this chapter is on particular political issues and the shape of the political process itself — not on particular political parties. Whether you are a Democrat, a Republican, a Green, a Libertarian, or, as more and more voters identify themselves, an Independent is not the point as you consider these issues. All that matters is that you are Californians. In a state whose citizens are becoming increasingly polarized because of highly emotional political issues, and whose politically partisan representatives sometimes seem to be as paralyzed as they are polarized, it would be no small thing if you, along with your classmates, could find a way to resurrect the Greek sense of politics. If somebody doesn't do this soon, we can expect only more ballot initiatives and more instances of judges deciding our most pressing issues for us.

The Readings

We begin this chapter with an excerpt from Matthew A. Cahn and H. Eric Schockman's political science textbook on California government and the cultural demography that drives the democratic process in the state. Next, Peter Schrag explores the tendency that Californians have to settle their most controversial differences through ballot initiatives, and then Jean Ross analyzes the effects of what may be California's most significant initiative, the tax-slashing Proposition 13. Steve Scott follows with a report on the rise of the Latino vote in California as demographic change begins to translate into political change, and Jack Miles's provocative essay on "Blacks vs. Browns" suggests that the racial divisions that so often divide Californians are by no means always written in black and white. Next, Al Martinez presents a plea for all races in California to please just get along together. Richard Steven Street then shows how the previously marginalized Latino residents of Kettleman City organized to fight the construction of a toxic waste incinerator in their community, and Anna Deavere Smith, adapting the words of California Congresswoman Maxine Waters, concludes the chapter with a reflection on the causes, and aftermath, of the Los Angeles riots.

MATTHEW A. CAHN and H. ERIC SCHOCKMAN

Political Culture in California

If any single word could sum up California's political landscape, *diverse* would be it, for as **Matthew A. Cahn** (b. 1961) and **H. Eric Schockman** (b. 1949) show in this selection from *California: An Owner's Manual* (1997), California is more culturally, ethnically, economically, and geographically diverse than any other state in the union. Providing a quantitative as well as qualitative overview of California's political diversity, this text provides an empirical foundation for the readings that follow it in this chapter. A professor of political science at California State University, Northridge where he is director of the Center for Southern California Studies, Cahn has published *Environmental Deceptions: The Tension Between Liberalism and Environmental Policy in the United States* (1995), *Thinking About the Environment* (with Rory O'Brian, 1997), and *Public Policy: The Essential Readings* (with Stella Theadoulou, 1995). Schockman is associate dean for student affairs at the University of Southern California, where he also teaches courses in the Department of General Studies and Political Science. His publications include *Community in Crisis: The Korean American Community after the Los Angeles Civil Unrest* (1994) and *Rethinking L.A.* (with Michael J. Dear and Greg Hise, 1995).

West of the West

As the most populous state, California has emerged as a leader of national politics, economics, and culture. . . . [The state] has always been considered somewhat different from the rest of the nation. It is, as

Theodore Roosevelt pointed out, "west of the West." Yet California has emerged as a dominant trendsetter, establishing models and approaches that are emulated throughout the nation. By 1995, California's population grew to more than thirty-two million people — 12.3 percent of the total U.S. population.[1] There are many reasons for this. The most common, though, is that people like living on the edge.

People, Diversity, and Culture

Neither a melting pot nor a salad bowl, California is a mosaic of cultures and communities. From the first civilizations among Native American communities, through the period of the Spanish Conquest and the cultural imperialism of the Missions, to the period of Mexican settlement, and ultimately, the mass white migration of the 1870s and 1880s, California has evolved into an often uneasy jigsaw of competing interests. California's complex network of urban, suburban, and rural areas makes up the nation's most diverse population, representing hundreds of distinct cultures and communities. The cataclysmic demographic changes in the state speak for themselves. In 1940, whites comprised 89.5 percent of California's population, Latinos 6 percent, Asians 1.9 percent, African Americans 1.8 percent, and Native Americans 0.2 percent. By 1995, whites made up only 52.8 percent, while Latinos grew to 31 percent of the state population, Asians and Pacific Islanders collectively to 9.3 percent, African Americans to 5.9 percent, and Native Americans to 0.7 percent.[2] (See Table 1 for 1990 statistics.)

However, these numbers tell only one part of the story. Births among these communities allow us a glimpse of California's evolving ethnic character. Latinos represent 44.8 percent of new babies born in the state, whites 36.9 percent, African Americans 7.5 percent, Filipinos 2.6 percent, Chinese 1.9 percent, Vietnamese 1.3 percent, Koreans 0.7 percent, Asian Indians 0.6 percent, Japanese 0.5 percent, Native Americans 0.5 percent, Pacific Islanders 0.5 percent, and Cambodians 0.4 percent.[3] In all, California's population represents more than thirty distinct ancestries, as Table 2 illustrates.[4] At the same time, immigration brings over two hundred thousand people a year into the state, increasingly from Latin American countries, Asia, and Eastern Europe. By 2040, California's population is expected to be 50 percent Latino, 32 percent white, 12 percent Asian, and 6 percent African American.[5]

[1]California Department of Finance, Population Research Unit, *California Statistical Abstract Report* 95 E-1.

[2]Ibid., *Report* 88, p. 4; 93, p. 1.

[3]California Department of Health Services, *Vital Statistics,* 1994.

[4]U.S. Bureau of the Census, *1990 U.S. Census* (Washington, DC: U.S. Government Printing Office, 1990).

[5]Population Research Unit, *Report* 88, p. 4; 93, p. 1.

Table 1. Demographic Characteristics of the United States and
of California, 1990

	Population	White	Black	Latino	Asian	American Indian
United States	248,710,000	80.3%	12.1%	9.0%	2.9%	0.7%
California	29,668,000	69.9	7.4	25.8	9.8	0.8

Source: *The 1992 Information Please Almanac* (Boston: Houghton, 1991); California Department of Finance, State Census Data Center, *Current Population Survey* (March 1994).

Table 2. California Population by National Ancestry, 1990

Ancestry	Population	Percent of State Population
Mexican	6,070,637	21.4%
German	3,676,049	12.9
English	2,370,828	8.3
Irish	1,951,628	6.9
Italian	1,079,022	3.8
Filipino	731,685	2.6
Chinese	704,805	2.5
French	580,485	2.0
Scotch-Irish	399,870	1.4
Scottish	393,809	1.4
Polish	378,077	1.3
Swedish	370,470	1.3
Salvadoran	338,769	1.2
Dutch	335,739	1.2
Russian	327,675	1.2
Japanese	312,989	1.1
Vietnamese	280,233	1.0
Portuguese	275,492	1.0
Norwegian	263,646	0.9
Korean	259,941	0.9
Danish	163,964	0.6
Asian Indian	159,973	0.6
Guatemalan	159,177	0.6
French Canadian	132,643	0.5
Puerto Rican	131,998	0.5

(continued)

Table 2. California Population by National Ancestry, 1990 (continued)

Ancestry	Population	Percent of State Population
Arab	123,933	0.4
Welsh	119,081	0.4
Pacific Islander	110,599	0.4
Hungarian	104,722	0.4
Greek	102,178	0.4

Source: U.S. Bureau of the Census, 1990 U.S. Census (Washington, DC: U.S. Government Printing Office, 1990). All groups over one hundred thousand.

California's diversity reaches well beyond ethnic differences. Geography is playing an increasingly important role in cultural definition. In 1990, 92.6 percent of Californians lived in urban areas, up from 80.7 percent in 1950, 52.3 percent in 1900, 20.7 percent in 1860, and only 7.4 percent in 1850.[6] California has been the most urbanized state in the nation since 1980. This urbanization, however, is split between classically urban cities, such as Los Angeles, and growing suburban areas, such as Orange and Ventura Counties. The residents of suburban areas remain suspicious of urban cores, while residents of urban areas see suburban growth as the abandonment of cities by the upper middle class. Add to this the rural Californians in the central Valley and northern portion of the state, and a second filter of California's cultural mosaic comes into focus.

What we really have are three Californias. Urbanites are concerned with rebuilding aging city infrastructure, as well as improving social and economic conditions, including minimizing crime, improving urban schools, bringing jobs back into urban cores, and improving public transit. Suburbanites are fundamentally concerned with keeping urban problems out of their neighborhoods, though increasingly the suburbs are facing similar challenges. Rural residents are concerned with maintaining their rural economies, be that agriculture or timber products, and with battling encroaching urbanization. The interaction of these three Californias creates a heady mix of politics that is exacerbated by the racial undercurrent: since urban cores are increasingly black, Latino, and Asian, and suburban and rural areas are generally white, racial tensions accent the claims of different geographic interests.

Income represents a third filter to California's diversity. As Table 3 demonstrates, uneven income distribution across the state and across

[6]Population Research Unit, *Report* 86, p. 3 n4.

Table 3. Median Family Income and Population by County

County	Median Income	Rank	Population
Alameda	$49,625	5	1,362,900
Alpine	34,444	33	1,230
Amador	34,655	31	33,850
Butte	30,516	46	204,300
Calaveras	34,015	35	38,700
Colusa	21,251	57	18,000
Contra Costa	55,888	2	883,400
Del Norte	31,056	43	29,250
El Dorado	43,376	11	148,600
Fresno	32,602	40	764,800
Glenn	25,648	56	27,100
Humboldt	34,468	32	128,900
Imperial	19,872	58	141,500
Inyo	35,441	28	18,900
Kern	35,915	27	627,700
Kings	29,999	47	116,300
Lake	27,848	52	57,500
Lassen	36,050	26	29,800
Los Angeles	36,541	23	9,244,600
Madera	30,861	44	109,500
Marin	60,689	1	245,500
Mariposa	31,244	42	16,550
Mendicino	30,751	45	86,200
Merced	29,123	49	202,800
Modoc	29,570	48	10,700
Mono	36,578	22	11,250
Monterey	32,754	38	371,000
Napa	41,342	13	120,600
Nevada	35,206	29	89,500
Orange	46,730	7	2,641,400
Placer	44,157	9	210,000
Plumas	33,239	36	21,500
Riverside	36,082	25	1,393,500
Sacramento	43,502	10	1,149,200
San Benito	36,106	24	43,050
San Bernadino	39,039	17	1,618,200
San Diego	39,115	16	2,720,900

(continued)

Table 3. Median Family Income and Population by County (continued)

County	Median Income	Rank	Population
San Francisco	37,196	20	759,300
San Joaquin	38,120	18	530,700
San Luis Obispo	37,009	21	236,000
San Mateo	52,981	4	695,100
Santa Barbara	37,740	19	396,900
Santa Clara	54,672	3	1,607,700
Santa Cruz	39,376	15	242,600
Shasta	33,137	37	166,100
Sierra	34,416	34	3,360
Siskiyou	28,499	50	46,500
Solano	47,457	6	377,600
Sonoma	43,279	12	432,200
Stanislaus	34,929	30	420,000
Sutter	32,170	41	74,900
Tehama	27,314	54	55,700
Trinity	27,933	51	13,950
Tulare	27,274	55	355,200
Tuolumne	32,744	39	53,300
Ventura	44,764	8	720,500
Yolo	40,211	14	153,700
Yuba	27,484	53	64,100
State median	$40,706		Total: 32,344,000

Source: California Franchise Tax Board, 1995; California Department of Finance, Population Research Unit, *California Statistical Abstract Report* 95 E-1, 95 E-2.

ethnic lines adds further tension to California's cultural mosaic. While the median household income statewide is $40,706, median incomes across counties vary markedly. For example, Marin County (just north of San Francisco) enjoys a median household income of $60,689, the highest in the state, while in the farming areas of Imperial County the median household income is $19,872. The median household income in California's urban counties is far lower than in the largely suburban counties, while the rural counties' median income is lower yet. For example, Los Angeles County (one of the most urban) has a median household income of $36,541, while neighboring Ventura County (largely suburban) has a median household income of $44,764. At the same time, the rural counties in the northernmost portion of the state have somewhat lower incomes: Trinity County has a median household income of $27,933; Siskiyou County is at $28,499; Modoc

County is at $29,570.[7] Looking at income across ethnic lines reveals that while 9.7 percent of white families live below the poverty line, 16.8 percent of Asian families live below the poverty line, as do 29.1 percent of black families and 31.6 percent of Latino families.[8] Thus, personal economic security has become a contentious issue throughout the state.

Beyond the three filters discussed above, there are several communities of interest that face unique problems and present distinct pressures on politics and policy. The issues reflected in these communities include religion, gender equality, sexual identity, age, and employee rights. Religion continues to play a major role in California. Urban Jews and Catholics, for example, continue to vote overwhelmingly Democratic. In several areas the "religious right" has targeted local school boards in an effort to influence curricula. Gender politics has remained a dominant influence throughout the state as organizations such as NOW (National Organization of Women) and CARAL (California Abortion Rights Action League) fight for women's issues, from equal rights to abortion rights. Gays and lesbians have organized to pursue equal rights and to combat homophobia and violence. Much of the passion in the recent fight over gays in the military and the current battle over same-sex marriages has been supplied by California's powerful gay communities in Los Angeles and the Bay Area.

In the past twenty years, age has emerged as a defining characteristic in defining communities of interest. Seniors have organized in interest groups such as AARP (American Association of Retired Persons) to balance the strong influence of the "baby boomer" generation. Boomers (those Americans born in the boom of births following World War II, between 1945 and 1964) are now the generation in power in most economic, political, and social institutions. And, like all previous generations who have attained positions of influence, boomers have pursued political and economic agendas that maximize their generational interest.

Unlike previous generations, however, boomers have developed extraordinarily high levels of power. This is a result of two phenomena. First, having enjoyed the highest standard of living of any American generation, boomers have attained unprecedented economic wealth. Second, the sheer number of boomers relative to the general population has given them a distorted sense of self-importance. Partly in response to the boomer generation, and partly in response to the issues that have always affected older citizens, seniors have become politicized and efficiently organized. AARP, for example, has emerged as one of the strongest interest groups in the state and nationwide, providing policy balance to the boomers.

The most recent generation of Americans to come of age is only now 10 beginning to develop a cohesive political identity. The so-called Generation

---

[7]California Franchise Tax Board, 1995.
[8]California Department of Finance, State Census Data Center, *Current Population Survey*, March 1994.

X can expect to earn less than their parents while facing significantly higher costs for housing and durable goods. In short, Generation X will absorb most of the costs while enjoying few of the benefits of America's postwar economic boom and the stifling debt-based growth of the 1980s. As a generation, Xers are angry and cynical. Simultaneously, however, Xers are uniquely prepared for the political and economic shifts expected over the next twenty-five years. Unlike their predecessors, Xers anticipate a shifting political and economic environment and are developing the skills necessary to cope with it. Xers are generally more concerned with deficit spending and the growing national debt than either boomers or seniors, and Xers are generally less committed to any single political party. Xers are only now beginning to flex their political muscle. Within the next decade, Xers will become dominant players in policy making.

There are, of course, a variety of other communities of interest existing within California. Organized labor continues to be a major influence in policy debates. And, while union representation continues to drop in the private sector, public-sector unions such as SEIU (Service Employees International Union) are gaining membership and influence. Environmentalists as a community are gaining influence as well, presenting challenges to traditional power centers in timber, agriculture, and industry throughout the state. These communities of interest are increasingly adding demands to the policy discourse. In response to this ever-increasing diversity in ethnic, social, and economic interests, the state has developed a unique equilibrium-based politics with an ever-shifting center of balance.

Political Culture

Each of the communities previously discussed contributes to California's complex political culture. The multitude of political and demographic subcultures in California has led to an amazingly fluid, and often conflicted, political culture. California is not merely heterogeneous; it is full of cross-cutting schisms and overlapping memberships in communities of interest. Each of these communities shares some common experience and values, giving rise to the various political subcultures.

Culture can be understood as a set of experiences and symbols that frame community cognitions. Language, history, rituals, and values all give focus to the way one sees the world. Political culture, therefore, can be understood as the set of experiences and symbols that focus political cognitions. California's diverse population represents a complex web of political subcultures, giving the state a mosaic of cultural influences and political pressures rather than a single culture. The result of these competing influences is an extremely passionate pluralistic process. Ultimately, though, it is California's diversity that may give the state its greatest strength. While diversity has created conflictual politics, its passion has also created innovation in public policy.

California's Emerging Importance

Over the past century, California has evolved from a sparsely populated frontier state to the most populous state in the nation and has emerged as a dominant player in national politics. California's importance is a result of its population size, as well as its economic power, cultural influence, and perhaps most important, its diversity. Based on GNP alone, California would rank as the eighth-largest economy on the planet. The resulting spending power has made California enormously important in national politics. California's manufacturing base has long been critical to the nation's military, and its lead in aerospace and technology has positioned the state for continued growth throughout the next century. In addition, California's entertainment industries — film, music, television — have served to export a cultural self-image that, while artificial, has served to foster the evolution of popular culture throughout the nation.

Understanding the Text

1. Summarize in your own words what the authors mean by "three Californias" (para. 5).

2. Why do Cahn and Schockman say that "personal economic security has become a contentious issue throughout the state" (para. 6)?

3. What are some of the political "communities of interest" (para. 7) that Cahn and Schockman identify, and what effect have they had on state politics?

4. What reasons do the authors give for California's emerging importance in U.S. culture and politics?

Exploring and Debating the Issues

1. Cahn and Schockman claim that there is an "uneven income distribution across the state and across ethnic lines" (para. 6). Study Table 3 to determine the extent to which the data support this contention. For additional information, particularly on ethnicities, you might want to visit your library and consult census figures.

2. Cahn and Schockman refer to three filters that influence California politics: race, geography, and income. Rank these according to what you consider their relative importance, and give reasons for your ranking.

3. While political discussion in California often focuses on racial issues, Cahn and Schockman point out that religion, gender, and sexual orientation are also potent forces in the state's politics. Choose one of these "communities of interest" (para. 7), and research the role it has played in recent California elections.

4. The authors presume that Generation X has a certain profile and political identity. In an essay, support, refute, or modify their depiction of Generation X's political habits and beliefs.

PETER SCHRAG

California, Here We Come

In recent years, Californians have come to settle, perhaps tentatively, many of their most divisive political differences through direct ballot initiatives — such as Propositions 187, 209, and 227. But as **Peter Schrag** (b. 1931) suggests in this article, which originally appeared in the March 1998 *Atlantic Monthly,* there is a potential price to pay when elected representatives step aside and let the electorate take the constitution into its own hands — one of them being an eventual disillusionment among the voters themselves. The former editorial page editor at the *Sacramento Bee* and author of numerous books and articles, Schrag has also written *Paradise Lost: California's Experience, America's Future* (1998).

This June marks the twentieth anniversary of the passage of Proposition 13, the California voter initiative that has in many respects had a political and social impact on this era — not just in California but across much of the nation — almost as profound and lasting as that of the New Deal on the 1930s, 1940s, and 1950s.

The effect on California — which had been well above the national average in what it spent to educate its children, to provide free or nearly free higher education to every person who wanted it, for highway construction, and for a range of social services for children and the needy — was traumatic. Cutting local property taxes by more than 50 percent and capping the tax rate at 1 percent, Proposition 13 and the various initiatives that followed in its wake forced California to a level of spending far below the national average for such things as K–12 schooling, public-library services, the arts, and transportation. The respected journal *Education Week* said last year of California schools, "a once world-class system is now third-rate." Even with a booming economy, California remains in the bottom third among the states, and far below the other major industrial states, in what it budgets per pupil.

Just as important, the march of ballot initiatives, the attack on legislative discretion, and the related acts of "direct democracy" that Proposition 13 helped to set in motion — involving taxes and spending, affirmative action, immigration, school policy, environmental protection, three-strikes criminal sentences, term limits, campaign reform, insurance rates, and virtually every other public issue — continue with unabated force, in California and beyond. In November of 1996 voters in twenty-three states were polled on a total of ninety initiatives, the most in more than eighty years (a decade ago there were forty-one), on everything from hunting rights to gambling to logging regulations to sugar production to the legalization of medical marijuana use (which was approved in Arizona and California).

This June, as if to honor the anniversary of Proposition 13, Californians will again confront a large array of sometimes nearly incomprehensible ballot measures, among them yet another one on term limits and one that would all but end bilingual education. Each proposed reform further restricts the power of the legislature and local elected officials to set priorities, respond to new situations, and write budgets accordingly. When half of the state's tax-limited general fund must, under the terms of one initiative, be spent on the schools; when a sizable chunk must, under the mandate of the state's three-strikes measure, be spent on prisons; and when lesser amounts must, under the terms of still other initiatives that have been approved in the past decade, be spent on the repayment of bonds for parkland and transportation projects, the amount left over for everything else shrinks with Malthusian inevitability — as does the state government's capacity to cope with changed circumstances. When cities and counties are prohibited from raising property tax rates beyond Proposition 13's 1 percent, and when it is difficult to raise other revenues without a vote of the electorate (in many instances a two-thirds vote) or of the affected property owners, local control is drastically reduced.

Just as inevitably, public policy is increasingly distorted by the shifting of costs from the general fund to the Byzantine system of fees, assessments, and exactions that local governments have devised in their attempts to get around tax limits and other restrictions. This reinforces the larger shift from a communitarian to a fee ethic — in the support of parks and playgrounds, in the construction of new schools, and in financing a range of other services that used to be funded entirely from general taxes. As one California letter writer complained to a newspaper, why should citizens contribute to "the methodical pillaging and plundering of the taxpayer, forcing those who have no kids to pay through the nose for someone else's"?

Direct democracy is an attractive political ideal, as close to our own experience as the New England town meeting. It has never worked, however, in large, diverse political communities, and the belief that electronics, direct mail, and televised slogans can replace personal engagement has so far looked far more like fantasy than like anything derived from hard political experience. In the case of the initiative, the new populism — unlike the reform movement that wrote the initiative into the constitutions of nineteen states around the turn of the century — seems to want greater engagement in government less than it wants an autopilot system to check government institutions with little active involvement by the citizenry beyond occasional trips to the polls to vote on yet more initiatives.

California sparked the antigovernment, antitax mood that has gripped the nation for most of the past two decades, and it remains the most extreme illustration of that mood, a cautionary tale for those enamored of plebiscitary democracy. But is now hardly unique. Virulent antiinstitutionalism, particularly with respect to government, has become a prevailing theme in our national political discourse. A decade after Ronald Reagan left office, his facile dismissal of government as "the problem," not the solution, remains a talk-show staple, a posture that serves to exonerate both civic laziness and political ignorance. And this attitude, which has become banal toward representative government, now also encompasses the related institutions of constitutional democracy: the courts, the schools, the press. Voting and serious newspaper readership are declining together. The communitarian civic ideal that they represent is giving way to "markets," a fee-for-service ethic, and the fragmented, unmediated, unedited exchange of information, gossip, and personal invective.

The media — new and old alike — may ensure against the power of Big Brother to dominate communications, but they also proliferate shared ignorance at an unprecedented rate: what used to be limited to gossip over the back fence is now spread in milliseconds to a million listeners during the evening commute, and to thousands over the Internet. And at the fringes are the militias and the "patriots," collecting weapons and supplies, training in the hills, and hunkering down against the black helicopters and the coming invasion of United Nations troops. That kind of ignorance and extremism, the new media, and the surrounding paranoia about government have all become commonplace in the past decade. Oliver Stone's *JFK* and the videos promoted by Jerry Falwell about the alleged murder of Vincent Foster work the same territory.

Tracy Westen, the president of the foundation-funded Center for Governmental Studies, in Los Angeles, has constructed a "digital scenario" for the election of 2004 — a not altogether wild fantasy about thirty-five California voter initiatives on various subjects, all of which have been circulated for "signatures" online, along with a spectrum of arguments pro and con, available at the click of a voice-activated mouse, from every conceivable source. In combination with a number of new elective offices, including drug commissioner and gay-rights commissioner, those measures contribute to a total of two hundred ballot decisions for each voter to make.

Among Westen's futuristic initiatives is one urging Congress to approve   10
an amendment to Article V of the U.S. Constitution such that the language guaranteeing every state a "Republican form of government" is modified to permit the states to replace representative democracy with direct democracy. Westen points out that most of the technology for this politopia — individually targeted campaign ads, interactive "discussions" with candidates, electronic voting — already exists. Since "state legislatures seem to be fighting more and doing less . . . and leaving the real legislation to the people," the scenario continues, "it seems the trend toward 'democracy by initiative' is inevitable." A few years ago the Canadian fringe Democratech Party wanted to submit all government decisions to the public through electronic referenda. An official Democratech statement said,

> Representative government assumes that the people need to elect someone to represent them in a faraway legislative assembly. But with modern, instantaneous communications, the people can directly make their own decisions, relegating politicians to the scrap heap of history.

Three years ago the *Economist* mused about the possible benefits of replacing representative democracy with Swiss-style direct democracy, in which the voters "trudge to the polls four times a year" to decide all manner of plebiscitary questions. This process would prevent lobbyists and other special interests from buying the outcome, because "when the lobbyist faces an entire electorate ... bribery and vote-buying are virtually impossible. Nobody has enough money to bribe everybody."

California shows that the process of bedazzling voters with sound bites, slogans, and nuanced bias works as effectively in the initiative process as it does in electoral politics. Offers that sound like something for nothing (a 50 percent property-tax cut, or a guaranteed level of education funding, or a state lottery offering a payoff for schools as well as for the lucky winners) may not be bribes, but they are the nearest thing to them. And when they work at the ballot box, their effects may last far longer than those of conventional legislation.

The larger danger, of course, is precisely the nondeliberative quality of the California-style initiative, particularly in a society that doesn't have the luxury of slow alpine trudges during which to reflect on what it's about to do. Nothing is built into the process — no meaningful hearings, no formal debates, no need for bicameral concurrence, no conference committees, no professional staff, no informed voice, no executive veto — to present the downside, to outline the broader implications, to ask the cost, to speak for minorities, to engineer compromises, to urge caution, to invoke the lessons of the past, or, once an initiative is approved by the voters, to repair its flaws except by yet another ballot measure (unless the text of the initiative itself provides for legislative amendment). Indeed, if the past decade of initiatives in California demonstrates anything, it is that the majoritarianism essential to the ethos of direct democracy almost inevitably reinforces an attitude of indifference if not hostility toward minority rights. All these dangers would be exacerbated, of course, by electronic or other forms of absentee balloting, whereby voters would no longer be required to go to the local school or church or social hall and encounter their fellow citizens participating in the same civic ritual — and thus be reminded that they are, after all, part of a larger community.

To say all that, probably, is merely to say awkwardly what the Framers of the Constitution said better in Philadelphia, what Hamilton, Madison, and Jay said in *The Federalist,* and what scores of delegates said in 1787 and 1788 at the various state conventions leading up to ratification, even before the Terror of the French Revolution: unchecked majorities are a danger to liberty almost as great as oligarchs and absolute monarchs. ...

Twenty-four states have some form of initiative in their constitutions, most of them dating from the Progressive Era. Recently there have been moves in a number of other states — including Rhode Island and Texas — to write the initiative process into their constitutions.   15

The pressure does not come from Hispanics or other newly active political groups, who tend to vigorously oppose these constitutional changes as openings to yet more measures like California's Proposition 187 — which, until it was blocked by a federal court, sought to deny schooling and other public services to illegal immigrants. Rather, the impetus is from Ross Perot's United We Stand America and other organizations that are overwhelmingly white and middle-class. And in the states that already have the ballot initiative, there is increasing pressure to use it, sometimes generated by the dynamics of political reform itself. In California, political officeholders, from the governor down, have become initiative sponsors as a means of increasing name recognition and raising or stretching political campaign funds. And as initiatives circumscribe the power and discretion of legislatures, often the best way of responding to new circumstances — and sometimes the only way — is through yet another initiative. The result, for better or worse, is an ongoing cycle of initiative reform, frustration, and further reform.

Yet despite all the unintended consequences and the inflexibility of the initiative and other devices of direct democracy, they seem to have one thing in common, whether they are used by liberal environmentalists or by tax-cutting conservatives: they are the instruments of established voter-taxpayer groups, particularly the white middle class, against urban politicians and political organizations that represent the interests and demands of minorities, immigrants, and other marginal groups. At the turn of the century the Yankee establishment in Boston and other cities sought to create political institutions and devices to dilute the power of the upstart Irish. In its impulse and spirit the current pressure for plebiscitary solutions driven by the general electorate, in which the white middle class can still dominate, is not all that different.

The celebratory history of direct democracy centers on its inclusiveness, but in our politically more sophisticated (and no doubt more cynical) age there is a need to understand that defense of the initiative may be less disinterested than it seems. The groups that embrace and cheer it are not just "the people" fighting "the interests" or "the politicians," much less battling "Satan" and "Mammon," as the editor of the *Sacrameto Bee* put it in the heyday of the Progressives. They are often established political interest groups trying by extraordinary means to further a cause or repulse the advances of other groups. More important, each initiative reduces the power and accountability of legislatures — and thus the general ability to govern, meaning the ability to shape predictable outcomes. And whereas the initiative may well further the Jeffersonian objective of tying government down, and thus preventing mischief, it also vastly reduces the chances that great leaders, and the visionary statecraft with which they are sometimes associated, will arise. In the battle over the initiative the Framers would be the first to recognize that our politics, rather than being too conservative, are in the Burkean[1] sense not nearly conservative enough.

---

[1]Edmund Burke (1729–1797): English politician and orator. [Eds.]

Understanding the Text

1. Why does Schrag label Proposition 13's effect on California "traumatic" (para. 2)?

2. What evidence does Schrag give that Proposition 13 set off a state and national ballot initiative trend that continues today "with unabated force" (para. 3)?

3. What are the dangers, according to Schrag, of conducting the state's legislative processes through the ballot box?

4. What assumptions underlie Schrag's belief that the initiative process leads to political ignorance?

5. Explain in your own words what is meant by the "digital scenario" (para. 9) for future elections.

Exploring and Debating the Issues

1. Agree, disagree, or expand on Schrag's contention that the ballot initiative process is basically an instrument of "established voter-taxpayer groups, particularly the white middle class, against urban politicians and political organizations that represent the interests and demands of minorities, immigrants, and other marginal groups" (para. 17). To develop your ideas, consult Steve Scott, "Reality Votes" (p. 234), Al Martinez, "Can We All Get Along?" (p. 256), or Matthew A. Cahn and H. Eric Schockman, "Political Culture in California" (p. 213).

2. Ballot initiatives are an instance of direct democracy, while state legislatures exemplify representative democracy. Write an essay in which you analyze the advantages and disadvantages of direct and representative democracy, focusing your discussion on specific political issues that concern today's voters.

3. Schrag assumes that the initiative process leads to less voter participation in the political process. Research voter participation rates in California statewide elections to determine what, if any, correlations exist between voter participation and the numbers and nature of ballot initiatives.

4. Survey students on your campus to determine their voter participation rates. What percentage of students vote, and what reasons do they give for their voting behavior? Use your results in an essay in which you assess Schrag's prediction that future voters will become increasingly apathetic.

JEAN ROSS

What Has Proposition 13
Meant for California?

One of the most influential ballot measures in California history, Proposition 13 slashed property taxes and launched a national antitax crusade when it was passed in 1978. But as **Jean Ross** (b. 1957) reveals in this article that originally appeared in *California Voter,* a publication of the League of Women Voters of California, Prop. 13 also rewrote the way state and local government works in California. Unable to control their own revenues due to Proposition 13 limitations, hard-pressed municipal and county governments must look to Sacramento to fund many of the services that they are required to provide – but the money is not always forthcoming. The executive director of the California Budget Project, Ross has written numerous policy reports on California state government.

Proposition 13 and its linear descendants frame the financial relationship between California's state and local governments. The twentieth anniversary of the passage of Proposition 13 presents an opportunity to reflect on the measure's impact on how government delivers and finances the services it provides. Ironically, perhaps the greatest legacy of Proposition 13 and its offspring, Proposition 62, is a dramatic transfer of responsibility from local government to the state. The irony lies in the fact that voters have acted to transfer power from the government bodies they say they trust most to the body that enjoys considerably less favor — the state legislature.

Just how did this shift come about? First, Proposition 13 slashed local government's property tax revenues by 53 percent. The magnitude of the reduction forced the state to assume a larger share of responsibility for financing services delivered by local governments, most notably education. Second, Proposition 13 restricted local governments' ability to replace lost revenues by requiring two-thirds of the voters to approve any measure raising taxes for a specific purpose (a "special" tax). Finally, Proposition 13 shifted responsibility for allocating the remaining property tax dollars from local government to state lawmakers. State lawmakers utilized this authority first in the early 1980s to bail out cities and counties by assuming a greater share of the responsibility for financing schools and again in the early 1990s to shift property tax revenues away from counties, special districts, and cities back toward public education in order to reduce the state's share of school funding.

The sponsors of Proposition 13 successfully came back to the voters in 1986 with Proposition 62 and again in 1996 with Proposition 218. Both measures further limited local governments' ability to raise revenues to finance public services. Proposition 62, a statutory rather than constitutional change, required local governments to submit any tax increase to the voters and was later found unconstitutional. In the wake of the court decision, Proposition 218 was placed before the voters, which changed the state constitution to require voter approval of any tax increase, to limit the use of special assessments that are often used to support services ranging from street lights to irrigation, and to restrict the use of fees.

The inability of local governments to control the revenue side of their budgets led to increased state involvement as population growth and demographic shifts increased demands for local services. Until the passage of Proposition 218, cities enjoyed considerable ability to raise revenues to

---

WHO DOES WHAT: A GUIDE TO CALIFORNIA'S LOCAL GOVERNMENTS

Cities
- Public safety including police and fire protection, nuisance abatement, street lighting, and emergency medical services.
- Transportation including street maintenance, public transit, parking, airports, ports, and harbors.
- Community development including planning, community services, business promotion, and redevelopment.
- Health including solid waste.
- Culture and leisure including parks, libraries, recreation, golf courses, stadiums, and auditoriums.
- Public utilities including water and electricity.
- General government including city councils, city attorneys, accounting, and similar functions.

Counties
- Public assistance including welfare, social services, general relief, children's services, and adult services.
- Public protection including courts, sheriffs, jails, fire protection, flood control, soil and water conservation.
- Health and sanitation including public health, medical care, mental health, drug and alcohol services, and sanitation costs.
- Public ways and facilities including roads, transportation terminals, public transportation, and parking.
- Education including school administration, library services, and agricultural education.
- Culture and leisure including parks, libraries, recreation, golf courses, and auditoriums.
- General government including boards of supervisors, finance, property management, legal counsel, and administration.
- Counties provide city services within unincorporated areas of the county.

Special Districts
- Provide either special-purpose or community services within defined geographic areas. There are over 4,800 special districts formed for 54 purposes. The most common types of districts include community service districts, maintenance districts, water districts, and lighting districts.

VOTER INITIATIVES AND THE RELATIONSHIP BETWEEN THE STATE AND LOCAL GOVERNMENTS

Proposition 13 (June 1978)

- Limited property tax rates to 1 percent.
- Allowed reassessment of property to market value only on change of ownership.
- Transferred responsibility for allocating property tax revenues to the state legislature.
- Required two-thirds voter approval of local taxes designated for a specific purpose.
- Required measures raising state taxes to be approved by a two-thirds vote of each house of the legislature.

Proposition 4 (November 1979)

- Imposed expenditure limits on all levels of California government.
- Required the state to reimburse local government for mandated costs or expenditures imposed after January 1, 1975.

Proposition 62 (November 1986)

- Required approval of new local general-purpose taxes by a two-thirds vote of the governing body of a local agency and a majority of the voters. Largely invalidated by the courts.

Proposition 98 (November 1988)

- Established a minimum funding guarantee for K–12 education and community colleges. The guarantee applies to the sum of funding schools receive from state and local sources.

Proposition 111 (June 1990)

- Increased the state gas tax to pay for transportation infrastructure.
- Revised the formula used to calculate state and local government expenditure limits.

Proposition 218 (November 1996)

- Required new general-purpose local taxes to be approved by a majority of the voters and special-purpose taxes to be approved by a two-thirds vote of the voters.
- Prohibited school districts from imposing a general-purpose local tax.
- Limited the use of benefit assessments and imposed protest and notice provisions on governments' attempting to impose benefit assessments.
- Restricted the use of property-related fees by local government and imposed new notice and protest provisions.
- Allowed voters to repeal any existing local tax, fee, or assessment by a majority vote.

replace lost property taxes by virtue of their independent status vested in the state constitution. Counties lacked this independence and had much more limited revenue-raising authority granted by the legislature on a tax-by-tax basis.

Counties, the hardest hit by Proposition 13 and related changes, now   5 receive 64 percent of their annual budgets as transfers from the state and federal governments. The nature of many of the services administered by California's counties is largely responsible for the intermeshing of state and county finances. Counties administer health and social service programs as agents of the state, are mandated by the state to provide cash assistance and medical care to the indigent, and administer courts and jails within the confines of laws and procedures established by state law. Cities, on the other hand, are responsible for services that, in general, have minimal if any state involvement.

Shared responsibility for many programs existed even prior to the passage of Proposition 13. Historically, state and federal dollars have paid a substantial fraction of the cost for many locally delivered services. In fact, analysis identifies the structure of the so-called sharing ratios that determine the relative contribution of state and local financial responsibilities as one of the primary factors precipitating the taxpayer revolt. Under the pre–Proposition 13 system, for example, a county's share of costs for the MediCal and Supplemental Security Income/State Supplement Programs (ssi/ssp, a program that provides cash assistance to needy elderly and disabled individuals) was tied to local property values. As property values skyrocketed during the 1970s, so did costs incurred by counties. State costs, on the other hand, declined, resulting in a large state surplus and rapidly escalating local property tax bills.

After the passage of Proposition 13, the fate of local services became more closely tied to the actions of state lawmakers. Over the course of the 1980s and early 1990s, lawmakers repeatedly shifted the balance of responsibility for financing a number of services. The frequent policy changes, the number and complexity of the formulas used to allocate responsibility, and the inherent conflict between one level of government establishing the standards with another responsible for the actual delivery of services resulted in widespread confusion and increasing tension between state officials, local program administrators, and those concerned with the quality of available services.

A 1991 effort known as "realignment" attempted to establish some degree of certainty and defined areas of responsibility for one set of programs with joint state and county participation. Realignment increased counties' programmatic and financial responsibility for a number of mental health and social service programs. In addition, counties received revenues from a half-cent sales tax rate and an increment of vehicle license fee revenues distributed according to a formula designed to reflect local demand for services. While the recession of the early 1990s reduced revenues relative to prior program funding, realignment is considered a success by nearly universal agreement.

The larger challenge of clarifying the relationship between the state and local government, like most in public policy, is more complex. Many observers argue that a sweeping restructuring of the relationship between the state and, in particular, counties, will increase voters' satisfaction with public services. While on the surface such an effort appears appealing, issues involved with actually implementing its delivery under a state-prescribed mandate raise a number of important considerations. If relieved of this mandate, some counties might not choose to provide care, leading to a spread of communicable disease and the migration of individuals in need of health care to nearby counties who opted to continue to provide services. This, in turn, would increase neighboring counties' costs, and increase the pressure on these counties to limit the availability of services. One potential consequence of this type of realignment of responsibility is a race to the bottom. One alternate path to clarifying financial and programmatic responsibility — a state financed and administered health system for the poor — could displace local infrastructure, such as public hospitals and community clinics, and impose a top-down system on a diverse set of local circumstances and communities.

A happy medium ties back to limits imposed on the ability of local government to respond to local priorities and state and federal requirement by Proposition 13 and its offspring. Under the current constitutional confines, local officials are responsible for financing public services required by the state and federal governments and desired by local voters. They must do so, however, with one hand tied behind their backs — the hand that allows local government to determine the amount of revenues available to support public services. 10

Needed reforms include a return to majoritarian democracy with the elimination of supermajority vote requirements. Currently, local governments are hampered by supermajority vote requirements for earmarked local taxes and bond approvals by restrictions imposed by initiatives. These initiatives were passed with the support of less than two-thirds of the voters, yet now require a two-thirds vote for future taxing. Another important change would guarantee local governments their share of property tax revenues. Finally, there's reform of the property tax system itself. Proposition 13's cap on property tax rates and reassessment on change of ownership provisions give a competitive advantage to long-time property owners. While there may be a policy justification for extending this type of advantage to homeowners, there is little economic or policy rationale for providing disparate treatment to commercial property owners based solely on the length of ownership. A system whereby commercial property tax bills reflect the value of investments would eliminate the so-called fiscalization of land-use decisions whereby local governments favor large retail and auto malls, which generate sales tax revenue, over manufacturing or residential development.

The path to reform requires greater public awareness of what government does and how public services are financed. Public opinion research reveals a significant gap between the reality and perceptions of public budget practices. While clarifying the responsibilities of different levels of government will make the task of public education easier, it isn't the answer in and of itself. Without structural change, California's local governments will be ill equipped to meet the challenges of a rapidly changing economy and increasingly diverse population.

Understanding the Text

1. In your own words, summarize how Proposition 13 has transformed the relationship between state and local governments in California.

2. What dangers does Ross see in the elimination of state mandates for county services?

3. What ways of ameliorating the effects of Proposition 13 does Ross propose?

4. Why does Ross call for a greater public awareness of the state and local budgeting process?

Exploring and Debating the Issues

1. Because of Proposition 13, a person who owns a home that has been sold (and therefore reassessed to market value) since 1978 can pay substantially higher property taxes than a neighbor who owns a house that was purchased before 1978 and has never been reassessed. While the U.S. Supreme Court has ruled this difference in tax payments to be constitutional, many claim it to be an unfair system of taxation. Write an op-ed piece arguing for or against the argument that Proposition 13 should be repealed in light of this inequity.

2. Research the effects of Proposition 13 or Proposition 218 on your own community's abilities to raise revenues and to provide public services.

3. Debate in class the desirability of a supermajority, or two-thirds vote, requirement for all tax proposals. Develop support for your team's position by researching recent bond measures to raise funds for such services as education, libraries, or public parks.

4. While Proposition 13 is popular among those who benefited from it — primarily homeowners who purchased their homes before 1978 or in the early 1980s — it is often criticized by those who do not reap its benefits. Conduct a survey to determine the attitudes that members of your community have about this proposition. Be sure to ask your informants what they presume Proposition 13 mandates and what effect they believe it has on state and local governments.

STEVE SCOTT

Reality Votes

In the last two decades California has undergone a demographic transformation that will soon take its Latino population from minority to majority group status. Until recently, this growth was not reflected electorally, but as **Steve Scott** (b. 1957) reports in this article for *California Journal,* that is now changing. With more and more Latino citizens and voters participating in the political process, the California political landscape is coming to include a new generation of powerful Latino leaders who are helping to determine the shape of things to come in California's future. As a senior editor at the *California Journal,* Scott covers politics, higher education, and social issues.

The swearing-in of a new city council in the southeast Los Angeles County city of Lynwood is hardly the sort of event likely to attract one of the L.A. media's patented ground and air attacks, especially since there wasn't a celebrity in sight. So it was no surprise when only two television cameras, one from Spanish-language network Telemundo, were on hand to record the formal changing of the political guard in the Lynwood City Council chambers. In fact, the real surprise was that there were even two.

If some of those on hand are to be believed, this early December induction ceremony was a window into the political future of California, or at least of its more visible urban centers. For on that day, the city known only three short decades ago as "Lily White Lynwood" got its first Latino council majority and its first Latino mayor. Even more striking than the ethnicity of the new regime was that of the old guard — not "lily whites" who had long since deserted the municipality for more distant suburbs, but African Americans, including the first black ever elected to the Lynwood City Council. Although the campaign had been largely waged over issues of economics and government ethics, the racial significance of the transition was not lost on anyone in the room.

"They put on a good show . . . but you don't have to go too far past the superficial statements to find the great problems between the two," said Sergio Bendixen, the Telemundo reporter on hand to document the events.

There is little doubt that California is on the leading edge of a national redefinition of racial diversity, one which acknowledges that race is no longer merely a "black and white issue." It isn't simply the much-discussed population trend, which will carry California into "majority minority" status by the early part of the next century. These new populations are rapidly and visibly assimilating into mainstream society. "There is not one census tract in California that does not have a Latino household in it," said Harry Pachon, director of the Tomas Rivera Center at Scripps College in Claremont. "You're not talking about a segregated society. It's an integrated society."

The social and cultural implications of this integration are apparent to anyone strolling through Horton Plaza mall in San Diego or twisting their 5 radio dial in downtown Los Angeles. But this transformation has been far less visible in the ephemeral world of electoral politics. New immigrants are, by definition, noncitizens and thus nonvoters. Even those who have attained citizenship have opted out of participating in elections, some because of bad memories about politics in their homelands, others because they were still too consumed with trying to build their lives in the United States.

No mas.

The past two years have been witness to a new burst of political involvement among groups previously viewed as political afterthoughts. According to exit polls conducted by the *Los Angeles Times* after the 1996 elections, Latinos constituted 10 percent of the state's electorate, as opposed to 7 percent in the 1992 election. Much of this increase was attributable to a surge in new citizen registrants, who voted in higher percentages than ever in the state. This past year's mayoral primary in the city of Los Angeles saw Latino participation surpass that of African Americans, traditionally a higher-propensity voting bloc. Latinos' proportion of the off-year electorate also matched that of another high-propensity voting group — white Jewish liberals who inhabit the city's Westside and portions of the San Fernando Valley.

"A tremendous number of them are first-time voters, either through naturalization or through coming of age," said Pachon, whose institute conducted extensive research on racial attitudes and voting trends in Southern California. "It's an electorate that's being supplied by new streams of voters that are not present among non-Hispanic voters."

The transformation is still a long way from dramatically affecting statewide outcomes. Anglo voters still comprised nearly three-fourths of the electorate in 1996 and were roughly two-thirds of the voting universe in the L.A. municipal elections. But there was more than enough happening on the margins to hint of what's to come, and it wasn't just in Lynwood:

- Latino membership in the state Assembly grew from nine to fourteen. All five of the newcomers — four Democrats and one Republican — were elected in districts previously represented by whites.

- Japanese American Democrat Mike Honda beat out three Democratic rivals to win a safe San Jose Assembly district that was 50 percent Latino and 23 percent Asian. Honda's campaign slogan: *Si Se Puede* ("Yes, you can").

- Latina Democrat Loretta Sanchez narrowly upset GOP icon Robert Dornan in an Orange County congressional race that turned on the votes of newly naturalized citizens voting in their first election. Although the result has been the subject of a year-long voter fraud investigation, four years earlier, a Latino couldn't even win the Democratic nomination to face Dornan.

- Higher than expected Latino turnout boosted the margins of victory for both Los Angeles Mayor Richard Riordan and a crucial school construction bond for Los Angeles Unified School District.

- Latinos now occupy both the chairmanship of the state Democratic Party (Art Torres) and the speakership of the state Assembly (Cruz Bustamante).

Of course, Latino political leaders have been trying for decades to moti-   10
vate the so-called sleeping giant of potential Hispanic voters, without success. So why the sudden interest in politics? Democrats and demographic researchers say a good deal of the credit goes to one man: Governor Pete Wilson.

Wilson all but merged his 1994 reelection campaign with the effort to pass Proposition 187, an initiative aimed at cutting off all but emergency services to illegal immigrants. While Wilson insisted he had no quarrel with legal immigrants, the tenor of his campaign advertising left many Latino and Asian immigrants feeling under attack, regardless of citizenship or socioeconomic status. The alienation from Wilson and his party deepened two years later. The governor embraced Proposition 209, another racially charged initiative that sought to ban affirmative action, and a new Republican Congress, warmed to Wilson's issue, approved legislation restricting public services to all noncitizens, legal or illegal. A rush to naturalization ensued, and when all those newly naturalized citizens went to register to vote, they had one clear enemy in their minds. "The initiatives won, the Republicans lost," said Tony Quinn, a Republican analyst and political consultant.

"Pete Wilson will be known in the future as the 'father' of Latino California," said Gregory Rodriguez, research fellow at Pepperdine University's Institute for Public Policy. "He's done what thousands of activists could never have done. He gave us a massive civics lesson, and . . . made people decide where they want to be. He pushed people off the fence."

Though few Republicans are willing to publicly blame Wilson for turning many Latinos against their party, most concede the GOP's image among Latino and Asian immigrant groups has been tarnished by the two initiative fights, especially among middle-class Latino citizens, who had been trending the GOP's way. Stuart Spencer, a GOP guru and former political advisor to President Ronald Reagan, was sufficiently exercised about his party's trend that he wrote its leaders a three-page memo warning of a descent into "permanent minority status" if more wasn't done to reach out to Latinos and Asians.

"Our party has a sad and politically self-defeating history of alienating immigrants and new voters," wrote Spencer, in a memo endorsing Latino Reuben Barrales, GOP candidate for state treasurer.

Many other Republican activists and party professionals say they've   15
been tarred with a bad rap by skilled Democratic spin doctors who, they say, played "the race card." GOP political consultant Wayne Johnson admits

his party may have been "eating [its] seed corn" in 1994 and 1996 by focusing solely on the existing voter pool, rather than looking at how that pool might be changing. But he also insists Republicans were offended and caught off-guard by the charge that the initiatives were racially motivated, and were not able to effectively counterattack.

"To charge someone with racism is the ultimate smear," said Johnson. "It is a genuinely cheap shot, and the Democrats love to hurl it."

Drawing in new voters, however, is only part of the calculus that has produced the recent spate of Latino political victories. New confidence, maturity, and organizational skill are also evident in the efforts of Latino leaders in the Legislature to increase their numbers in Sacramento and Washington.

While Latino candidates in urban enclaves such as East Los Angeles continue to fit the liberal, pro-labor mold, more pragmatic candidates are emerging elsewhere in the state. Freshman Assemblyman Dennis Cardoza (Democrat, Ceres), for instance, carried impeccable credentials with the important agricultural community in his district. Fellow Assembly freshman Tony Cardenas (Democrat, San Fernando) was able to play up his ties to the district, having lived in the region longer than either of his two main primary opponents, both of whom were white. Many candidates backed by Latino Caucus chair Senator Richard Polanco (Democrat, Los Angeles) have also benefited from the help of veteran Democratic political consultant Richard Ross.

This "crossover appeal" of the candidates has been matched with legislative priorities which mix a pragmatic emphasis on crime and education with strategic attempts to counter Wilson's perceived hard line on immigration. During this past year's budget fight, Speaker Cruz Bustamante (Democrat, Fresno) inserted the issue of immigration directly into the budget debate, holding out for a state-only program to protect legal immigrants from losing food stamps. Eventually, he was forced to accept a compromise, but the mere fact he'd brought the subject up — to the obvious irritation of Senate President pro Tempore Bill Lockyer (Democrat, Hayward) indicated the degree to which Latino leaders are asserting their independence.

"I'm a Latino and I'm proud of that, but I'm also an American and I'm 20
proud of that, too," said Assemblyman Antonio Villaraigosa (Democrat, Los Angeles), who serves as Bustamante's majority leader. "This 'Latino' agenda is really an American agenda."

The "agenda" has found support among most non-Hispanic Democrats, but that doesn't mean there is contentment under the Democratic "rainbow." "Politics is a zero-sum game," said Rodriguez. "The more Latinos are elected, the fewer of someone else will be elected." Latino political prominence is ruffling feathers on L.A.'s Westside and in the parts of San Fernando Valley, traditionally the strongholds of the region's politically influential Jewish community and the last reliably Democratic pocket of white voters. Cardenas's 1996 victory came in a district that had been represented by one-time Democratic Assembly leader Richard Katz. Jewish and

Latino community leaders have squared off over the reconstruction of the earthquake-damaged County-USC hospital and building priorities for the Metropolitan Transportation Authority. Valley Assemblyman Robert Hertzberg (Democrat, Van Nuys), who has ties to both communities, says the tensions are simply a "natural progression."

Perhaps a more visible sign of the new assertiveness of Polanco and other Latino leaders has been their forays into communities — such as Lynwood — which are led by African Americans but which have sizeable, even majority, Latino populations. In 1996, Polanco, Bustamante, and other Latino leaders made strategic contributions in several legislative races dominated by black candidates, frequently squaring off against contenders with connections to more traditional black leaders such as Representative Maxine Waters (Democrat, Los Angeles). Political scientist Bruce Cain of the Institute of Governmental Studies at the University of California, Berkeley, says these episodes may become even more frequent — and more productive — after the next redistricting. "In past [reapportionments] in Los Angeles, the trick has always been to make accommodations to Latinos by shoving African Americans [in districts] to the west," said Cain. "Nineteen-ninety-two was the last time they'll be able to do that."

While acknowledging that Latino leaders have become better at playing the game, African American political leaders insist observers should not make too much of the political tensions between the two groups. Assemblyman Kevin Murray (Democrat, Los Angeles), chair of the Legislative Black Caucus, notes that none of the Latino gains in the Legislature came at the expense of African Americans. While black political influence has suffered in the short term, Murray blames it on the adjustment to life after term limits. "You're not really concerned about power if you have Willie Brown," said Murray. "We had a very good run, and we didn't anticipate [term limits]." As for the suggestion that African Americans could be redistricted out of power, Murray believes that, even if the districts change, their leadership will remain the same because the voter pool will remain the same.

"Once Latinos reach the socioeconomic status when they become high propensity voters, they move out of the inner city," said Murray. "Everybody keeps predicting these battles between blacks and Latinos for mostly black seats. The reality is it is not going to happen."

So what is going to happen? Well, one thing on which everyone agrees 25 is that the rate of participation among Latinos is going to continue to climb. Quinn predicts Latinos's percentage of the electorate will grow about 1 to 2 percent a year until it peaks at about 35 percent sometime in the next century. Democrats are considerably more bullish. Ross paints a scenario which he believes could produce as many as 300,000 additional Democratic votes in 1998 alone, between the coming-of-age of young Latino voters and the continued enfranchisement of newly naturalized citizens.

As working class nonvoters become working class voters, the prospect for tension between Democratic constituencies also continues to grow. The man in the best position to bridge this gap is Bustamante. But while he has gone out of his way to be cordial to political leaders of other ethnicities, Bustamante has been unable to fully consolidate his speakership, leaving the field open to wannabes, some of whom are intent on influencing the coming redistricting. As the battle for power of the urban core is joined, Democratic leaders also are confronted with the challenge of holding together the fragile gains seen in 1992 and 1996 among working class and suburban white voters. It was the desertion of these voters in the wake of 1978's Proposition 13 that produced the "Reagan Revolution."

"The notion that Ronald Reagan somehow created the 'Reagan Democrats' is absurd," said Ross. "We made the Reagan Democrats when we raised the property taxes of our mothers and fathers."

Ironically, Rodriguez believes the Democrats' best hope to meet this array of political challenges lay in another minority community that showed signs of coming of age in 1996 — Asian Americans. Asians' percentage of the 1996 electorate in California doubled over that in 1992, from 3 percent to 6 percent. While Asian contributors gained considerable — often unwelcome — attention in the aftermath of the election, the fact that they participated as dramatically as they did shows a new attentiveness to politics. Perhaps most important for Democrats, Asian candidates — such as Honda and Sacramento Representative Robert Matsui (Democrat, Sacramento) have that all-important "crossover" appeal.

"Asian Americans are the most integrated residentially of all groups," said Rodriguez. "They play a very special role. They're nonwhite, but they're not threatening to whites."

Asian candidates may also be one of the keys to helping Republicans rebound from the effects of the last few years. Like Democrats, Republicans are at a crossroads, divided between those who want to press ahead on the immigration and affirmative action fronts and those who want to downplay such "wedge" issues in favor of a return to basics. "A lot of things Republicans talk about with respect to lower taxes, et cetera are appealing [to middle-class Latinos]," said Quinn.

"[In our polling], 30 to 35 percent of Latinos say they'd vote for Republicans in the future," said Pachon. "This is not a lock for the Democratic Party, and it's not a complete shutout for the Republicans."

Before the GOP can win back its share of minority voters on the merits, however, they have the larger task of rebuilding trust among alienated immigrant constituencies. Although Johnson believes his U.S. Senate client, Matt Fong, has the potential to be a bridge builder, he laments that "we [Republicans] do not have leadership in which they can have confidence."

Many believe the key to the future lies in the 1998 statewide elections, especially the coming contest over bilingual education. The initiative to all but eliminate multiple-language instruction in state schools will likely be on the June ballot and already both parties are scrambling to react. Republican Party leaders tried to keep the GOP from going public with its support at the party's autumn state convention, only to have the rank and file vote to endorse it anyway. The GOP's membership looked positively prescient when a subsequent *Los Angeles Times* poll showed the measure with broader support among Latinos than among the general population. Bustamante's Assembly leadership team, which had summarily blocked a reform bill that had passed the Senate, are now scrambling to put forth a more modest reform.

Rodriguez said the *Times* poll was a deserved comeuppance for a leadership sometimes guilty of what he referred to as "linear orthodoxy," and is a sign of political maturity among Latino voters. "That means we've grown up . . . that we don't need lawyers to do our speaking for us," said Rodriguez. For Republicans to take advantage, however, all depends on how the campaign is ultimately conducted.

"It was not the content of [Propositions 187 and 209], but rather it was   35 the way they were played out," said Quinn. "As long as that doesn't happen [with bilingual education], it [Latino backlash] is a transient thing. As long as Republicans support [the initiative] for the right reasons."

And as both parties have learned over the course of the last few years, sometimes doing something for the "right reason" can make all the difference.

Understanding the Text

1. What does Scott mean when he says that "California is on the leading edge of a national redefinition of racial diversity" (para. 4)?

2. Why, in Gregory Rodriguez's words, will Governor Pete Wilson "be known in the future as the 'father' of Latino California" (para. 12)?

3. In Scott's view, why do some Latino politicians have electoral "crossover appeal" (para. 19)?

4. What role, according to the article, will Asian American voters play in future California politics?

Exploring and Debating the Issues

1. Investigate the demographics of your home town or legislative district. Have there been any population changes recently, and if so, how have they affected local politics?

2. Conduct an informal campus survey of students of different ethnicities to determine their political party affiliations. Use your results in an essay in which you test Scott's predictions of future demographic trends in California politics.

3. Write an essay in which you agree, disagree, or modify the charge that, although Propositions 187 and 209 passed, the California Republican Party lost as a result.

4. In this article, Scott presumes that voters cast their ballots with their race in mind. Write an essay in which you support, challenge, or complicate this presumption; you may base your argument on your own experience as a voter or on the experiences of friends or relatives.

JACK MILES

Blacks vs. Browns

National news reports on the L.A. riots focused on the reactions of black Angelenos in the aftermath of the first Rodney King beating trial. But as **Jack Miles** (b. 1942) points out in this essay originally written for the October 1992 *Atlantic Monthly,* such reports ignored another dimension of the unrest: the impact of Latin American immigration on the black underclass. In this provocative essay, Miles explores the changes that immigration has wrought on the social texture of Los Angeles, focusing on the evolving relationship between "black" and "brown" L.A. An editor and reviewer who has served as president of the National Book Critics Circle, Miles is the author of the best-selling *God: A Biography* (1995).

During the 1980s, according to census figures released last May 11 [1992], the United States admitted 8.6 million immigrants. In the context of U.S. immigration history this is a staggering number — more than in any decade since 1900 to 1910. Worldwide, half the decade's emigrants had made the United States their destination. Of them, 11 percent — more than three-quarters of a million — further specified their choice as Los Angeles. By the end of the decade 40 percent of all Angelenos were foreign-born; 49.9 percent spoke a language other than English at home; 35.3 percent spoke Spanish. This is the city where, two weeks before those figures were released, the most violent urban riot in American history broke out: fifty-one people were killed, and property worth $750 million or more was lost.

Though the occasion for the riot was the acquittal of four white policemen on charges of assaulting a black traffic offender, Latinos as well as African Americans rioted. Why? What was Rodney King to Latinos? Did a race riot, once begun, degenerate — or progress — into a bread riot? Was it a vast crime spree, as devoid of political content as the looting that followed the 1977 blackout in New York City? Of those arrested afterward — of whom more than half were Latino — 40 percent already had criminal records. Was the riot a defeat of the police? If it was a hybrid of all these, was it, finally, an aberration from which, by hard work, America's second-largest city could recover? Or was it the annunciation of a new and permanent state of affairs?

I work at the *Los Angeles Times,* writing a column for that newspaper's book supplement and unsigned editorials three or four times a week for its editorial page. On the day after the first night of the riot, one of my colleagues said to me, as we left to hunt for a still-open restaurant, "When the barbarians sacked Rome in 410, the Romans thought it was the end of civilization. You smile — but what followed was the Dark Ages." Think of what follows here as the voice of a worried Roman — in front of a television set, watching the Goths at their sack.

Meeting Latino Los Angeles

I came to Los Angeles in 1978, to work as an editor in the branch office of the University of California Press at UCLA. The first home I owned here was a house trailer in Malibu. In 1981 a Santa Ana — one of the notorious local windstorms — ripped off the carport attached to the trailer and did some further damage to the roof. My wife and I had some insurance, but not enough. To help me complete my do-it-yourself repairs, I hired two Mexican boys from the pool of laborers who gathered daily near a shopping center just off the Pacific Coast Highway. One of the two, Ricky Rodriguez (not his real name), just fifteen years old when we met him, would become almost literally a member of our family.

One Sunday afternoon, after Ricky had been working with me part-time for several weeks, a Coast Highway landslide cut Malibu in half, and we invited Ricky to stay overnight. The buses weren't running. His alternatives, both illegal, were sleeping on the beach and sleeping in some neglected patch of brush along the road. He accepted the invitation and on the morrow brought my wife and me a breakfast in bed consisting of fried eggs and peanut butter sandwiches. In the sudden, unforeseen intimacy of the moment, a kind of conversation began different from any we had yet had. We began to learn something about his family.

Ricky, his mother, two sisters, and a brother were living in City Terrace Park, a neighborhood in East Los Angeles, as the permanent houseguests of another sister, her husband, and their two small children: nine people in a two-bedroom cottage. Ricky's brother-in-law, at the time the only American citizen in the family, was a cook whose generous employer had bought him this cottage. (Later, Juan José — called Juanjo for short — would open his own burrito shop.) Ricky invited me to visit his family, and I did so. I had never been in the barrio before.

Ricky continued working for us over several months. Relations remained friendly, and he eventually asked if we would adopt him, purely for legal reasons: to make him a citizen. His mother and I visited a sympathetic Chicano immigration lawyer, but Mexico's laws protecting its children made the move legally complicated. I did agree, however, to tutor Ricky through his remaining two years of high school — and here we return to the riot as an event in a mecca for immigrants.

As a taxpayer, I was surprised — not that I wasn't happy for our young friend — to discover that his status as an illegal immigrant was no bar to his attending high school at state expense. He did have to show a birth certificate; but, interestingly, his mother, a short, stout, indomitably cheerful woman who had crossed the border as a single mother with four children, of whom the youngest was a toddler at the time, had brought birth certificates with her. She had had education on her mind from the start, and a Guadalajara certificate was certificate enough for Wilson High School, which received money from the state on a per capita basis and would have lost money had illegal immigrants been denied admission.

Another surprise came in Ricky's senior year, when he asked if I would accompany him to the Department of Motor Vehicles and permit him to take a driving test in my car. (My presence and signature may have been required in some other capacity as well; I can no longer quite remember.) I knew by then that illegal immigrants commonly drove the streets and freeways of Los Angeles without any kind of driver's license. Ricky wanted a license mainly because it provided an identification card and a degree of cover for someone seeking work. He took and passed the test in the Lincoln Heights DMV office not far from downtown Los Angeles.

But here again I was surprised that no proof of legal residency was re-   10
quested for the receipt of a California driver's license. On the Coast Highway, I had witnessed hair-raising "sweeps" by Immigration and Naturalization Service agents on the very corner where I had hired Ricky. Such chases farther south, at an INS checkpoint on Interstate 5, north of San Diego, led with grim frequency to traffic deaths. Why did the INS not simply come to the DMV office in Lincoln Heights and arrest applicants? As we waited in line to deliver Ricky's completed written test, we overheard the clerk administering the same test orally — in Spanish — to a short older man with a coppery Amerindian face. He would have fallen one answer short of the passing grade had she not given him a broad hint.

The DMV office had as foreign a feel to it as the *correo*[1] in Mexico City. One heard almost no English at all. Ricky took his test not long after Election Day that year. The contrast between the two populations — the one in the polling station, the other at the DMV — was overwhelming. The DMV office seemed to be a part of the American administration of some foreign — or indigenous but subject — population. . . .

Blacks vs. Latinos

About a month after the riot a friend sent me a copy of an unsigned editorial from a Mexican American newspaper, *La Prensa San Diego,* dated May 15. What other Latinos had begun to insinuate, *La Prensa* angrily spelled out: Blacks were not victims. Latinos were victims. Blacks were perpetrators.

> Though confronted with catastrophic destruction of the Latino businesses, which were 60 percent of the businesses destroyed, major looting by Blacks and by the Central Americans living in the immediate area, and a substantial number of Hispanics being killed, shot and/or injured, every major television station was riveted to the concept that the unfolding events could only be understood if viewed in the context of the Black and White experiences. They missed the crucial point: the riots were not carried out against Blacks or Whites, they were carried out against the Latino and Asian communities by the Blacks!

---

[1]Post office. [Eds.]

What occurred was a major racial confrontation by the Black community, which now sees its numbers and influence waning.

Faced with nearly a million and a half Latinos taking over the inner city, Blacks revolted, rioted, and looted. Whatever measure of power and influence they had pried loose from the White power structure, they now see as being in danger of being transferred to the Latino community. Not only are they losing influence, public offices, and control of the major civil rights mechanisms, they now see themselves being replaced in the pecking order by the Asian community, in this case the Koreans.

The editorial ended by declaring "the established Mexican American communities" to be "the bridge between Black, White, Asian, and Latinos." It said, "They will have to bring an end to class, color, and ethnic warfare. To succeed, they will have to do what the Blacks failed to do; incorporate all into the human race and exclude no one."

There was, to put it mildly, little in that editorial to suggest that desperately poor, fifteenth-generation African Americans might be within their rights to resent sudden, strong, officially tolerated competition from first-generation Latin Americans and Asian Americans. But *La Prensa*'s anger clearly arose not just from the riot, perhaps not mainly from the riot, but from frustration at television's inability to see Latin Americans as a part of the main action at all.

I don't think that any clear pattern of blacks attacking Latino businesses or Latinos attacking black businesses can be established. Koreans do plainly seem to have been singled out for attack — by some Latinos as well as by many blacks. But state officials believe that at least 30 percent of the approximately four thousand businesses destroyed were Latino-owned. Both *"Somos Hermanos"* and "Black Owned Business" were frail armor even when those labels were honestly applied. As the police reestablished control, thousands of arrests were made; more than half of the arrestees were Latinos, but the older, second-generation, law-abiding Mexican American community resented the lack of differentiation in the label "Latino." This community insisted with some feeling that in the communities it regarded as truly and more or less exclusively its own there had been no rioting. By implication this was the beginning of an anti-immigrant stance within the community.

What counts for more, however, than any incipient struggle between older and newer Latino immigrants is the emerging struggle between Latinos and blacks. *La Prensa* is right to stress the raw size of the Latino population. The terms of engagement, if we take our cue from the rappers, would seem to be black versus white or black versus Asian. But the Korean population of Los Angeles County is just 150,000, a tiny fraction of the Latino population of 3.3 million. Of the 60,560 people in Koreatown itself, only 26.5 percent are Asian; more than 50 percent are Latino. Blacks are the most oppressed minority, but it matters enormously that whites are no longer a majority. And within the urban geography of Los Angeles, African Americans seem to me to be competing more directly with Latin Americans than with any other group.

15

I find paradoxical confirmation for this view in the fact that some of the most responsible leaders in both groups want to head it off. A month after the riot my wife and I received the June newsletter of the Southern California Interfaith Taskforce on Central America, a group to which we have contributed a little money over the past several years. SCITCA, originally a lobby for the victims of state-sponsored violence in (principally) El Salvador and Guatemala, has more recently expanded its agenda to include the fate of Central Americans now settled in Los Angeles. It has effectively lobbied, for example, for a relaxation of the municipal regulation of street vendors.

In the wake of the riot SCITCA was worried about anti-immigrant backlash. Joe Hicks, of the Southern Christian Leadership Conference, and Frank Acosta, of the Coalition for Humane Immigrant Rights of Los Angeles, wrote in the newsletter,

> In the aftermath of the recent civil unrest, . . . immigrants and refugees in particular have been targeted for blame, violence, and civil rights abuses. . . . Fears of overcrowding, the burden on local communities, competition for scarce jobs, drainage on public resources through the education and social welfare systems are all commonly held apprehensions about the impact of immigrants in our communities. Similar fears were voiced during the migration of African Americans from the South to the northern cities earlier this century. In the past few years, however, a growing number of social scientists, economists, and researchers have concluded that the social and economic impact of immigration is overwhelmingly positive. By and large, it is the prospect of freedom and economic opportunity, not welfare, that draws immigrants to the state.

Hicks and Acosta were astute to recognize that the movement of millions of blacks from the rural South to the urban North was a migration as enormous as any from abroad, but the fate of those black immigrants and the cities that received them rather subverts the lesson the two writers want to draw. And alongside the recent pro-immigration literature that the two cite is a small but growing body of even more recent literature suggesting that whether we will it or not, America's older black poor and newer brown poor are on a collision course.

A married couple, both white, both psychiatric social workers in the Los Angeles Unified School District, recently told us of several monolingual school social workers who had been let go to make room for bilingual workers. With so many Spanish-speakers in the district, the rationale for requiring social workers to have a knowledge of Spanish is clear. Our friends have, in fact, been diligently studying the language to protect their own positions. And yet it struck them as tragically shortsighted that most of the dismissed social workers were black.

A member of our church administers a subsidized day care center in northwest Pasadena, once a black neighborhood, now, like South Central Los Angeles, an extremely overcrowded black and Latino neighborhood. Black welfare mothers, our friend reports, are increasingly turned away

20

from the center because on the neediest-first principle they no longer qualify. Latino mothers, often with more children than the blacks and with no income even from welfare, are needier and claim a growing share of the available places. Are the Latino mothers illegal? Are they just ill-equipped to apply for welfare? The kindly day care people don't ask.

Hicks and Acosta exhort: "The poor communities of Los Angeles cannot get caught up fighting over the peanuts that have been given to them by the economic, political, and educational institutions of America." But even if these communities make common political cause, do they have any choice about economic competition? The General Accounting Office reports that janitorial firms serving downtown Los Angeles have almost entirely replaced their unionized black workforce with nonunionized immigrants.

If you live here, you don't need the General Accounting Office to bring you the news. The almost total absence of black gardeners, busboys, chambermaids, nannies, janitors, and construction workers in a city with a notoriously large pool of unemployed, unskilled black people leaps to the eye. According to the U.S. Census, 8.6 percent of South Central Los Angeles residents sixteen years old and older were unemployed in 1990, but an additional 41.8 percent were listed as "not in the labor force." If the Latinos were not around to do that work, nonblack employers would be forced to hire blacks — but they'd rather not. They trust Latinos. They fear or disdain blacks. The result is unofficial but widespread preferential hiring of Latinos — the largest affirmative action program in the nation, and one paid for, in effect, by blacks.

Pierre Venant, a French photographer of international reputation, made the acquaintance of Father Greg Boyle, a Jesuit who until recently worked in a part of the barrio so badly wracked by gang violence that funerals are held almost weekly. Out of a desire to help Father Boyle, Venant began teaching photography in the barrio and photographing gang members and their sometimes exceedingly elaborate, mural-sized, almost liturgical graffiti. I asked him once whether he had ever considered teaching in the black ghetto. He answered no, that there was something so nihilistic, so utterly alienated, in the black youths he had met that he doubted he could make a connection with them. He was apologetic but plain: it was just easier with the Mexicans. "Maybe it is the Catholicism," he said, "or something in the Latin personality." . . .

The Comfort Factor

My wife and I sold the trailer in 1986 and bought a small house in an unincorporated chunk of Los Angeles County, adjacent to Pasadena on the east. Of twenty households on our block, one is Asian (Chinese), two African American, and one Latino (he is Puerto Rican, she is Mexican). None of the houses on the block is large enough to accommodate live-in help, but several of us do employ gardeners. All the gardeners are Latino, and when a slight brown man walks down a driveway, he is understood to be there for good reason. Were a tall black man to do the same, there is not one of us who would not immediately be on the *qui vive*.[2] My sadness about the American estrangement just mentioned doesn't make me act any differently at such a moment.

Black men complain that they cannot shop without being shadowed by   25
a suspicious shopkeeper. The same in effect goes for the black teenagers who show up unannounced on our block. These are kids who skip out of the junior high school in the next block, picnic on our lawns, steal from our garages and back yards, and occasionally vandalize parked cars. The retirees living on the block watch the kids especially closely. One retiree once managed to videotape an attempted garage break-in. The school's officials — not always sympathetic (until recently the principal was a black woman) — identified the culprits from the tape.

We, who live peacefully with the black families on our block, are afraid of these black kids. I contrast our attitude toward them with the attitude taken in neighboring Sierra Madre, almost completely white and Republican, toward a group of as many as twenty Latino men who gather each morning except Sunday in a park near the fire department. They are day laborers, the poorest of the poor, awaiting work. In principle (and especially toward the demoralizing end of a day when no one has hired them), they ought to be desperate, but they are in the main clean, quiet, mannerly, polite to the residents, and agreeably fraternal with one another. This very conservative, old-fashioned community tolerates their presence calmly.

Whether or not Latinos are completely trustworthy (I have already mentioned the bloody barrio gang wars), I think that they do enjoy the trust of Anglos and Asians in Los Angeles. In the yard, in the house, with the baby, in the hotel room or the hotel corridor, in the parking garage, in a hundred locations, work, however menial, creates a vulnerability and thereby a brief intimacy between server and served. In all these places the average white or Asian Angeleno prefers to have — and usually does have — a Latino rather than an African American doing the work. Whence at least some of the disorientation and diffuse anxiety at the television footage of rioting Latinos: Had that young man dashing out of the liquor store been in your back yard earlier in the week? Was that woman trundling a shopping cart of looted groceries out of the supermarket your neighbor's live-out? ("Live-out" is Angeleno for a domestic servant who works for you five or six days a week, all day, but doesn't sleep over.)

I do not discount, as I mention this "comfort factor," that inexperienced Latino noncitizens may be much easier to exploit than experienced black citizens. Ricky was hired at less than the minimum wage to do drywall plastering on Santa Monica condominiums that sold for more than $1 million each. The contractor trained him on the job. Ricky learns quickly,

[2]On the alert. [Eds.]

and his by-then confident bilingualism was a major plus for his employer. He was promised a "real" job after this unofficial apprenticeship ended, but no such job ever materialized. His brother Victor, who owns a car, worked briefly for a messenger service. He was required to use his own car. No mileage, insurance, or fuel costs were paid by his employer. He was paid by the mile only when actually delivering a package but was required to keep himself available for an assignment even when none was forthcoming. The Latinos I know think that Asians are particularly likely to cheat and brutalize their Latino employees in ways like these.

And I do not mean, either, to sanctify Latinos at the expense of blacks. Victor called me as I was writing this article to report that Miguel, "Mike," the youngest brother in the family, was about to get out of jail. Ricky is also in jail as I write, and one of his earlier criminal ventures began with my wife. Near the end of Ricky's senior year his mother told me that he was dejected because he couldn't afford to attend the prom: no car and no money to rent a tux. I said I would rent the tux for him. My wife, who had just bought a used Honda and hadn't yet sold her 1969 Volkswagen, agreed to lend him the VW for the occasion. He had a good time at the prom but didn't return the car for two days. Graduation came a few weeks later. (The commencement speaker was State Senator Art Torres, whose remarks were all about Latino progress, but when the awards were given out, the few Asians in the student body won them all.) By custom, on the day after graduation local high school seniors head for Magic Mountain, an amusement park. Ricky asked to borrow the car again. We were already planning to sell it to him and let him pay us in installments from his first job. He was prematurely developing a proprietory attitude toward it. My wife had a premonition. I overrode it. He stole the car and skipped town.

The odd consequence of this episode was an intensification of my relationship with Ricky's family, especially his mother. The police, once they knew the car had been "borrowed for keeps," wouldn't list it as stolen. But if I couldn't call it stolen, I couldn't get it off my insurance policy. I had to gamble that if Ricky's ties to us were breakable, his ties to his family were not. It worked. Ricky eventually returned the car, and afterward even paid us $250 for it — less than it was worth but, given his resources, a meaningful gesture.

By that time we had a new baby in the house, and we lost touch with the Rodríguez family — until a few years later, when Victor called to invite us to his wedding. Ricky, who had been working as a house painter near Sacramento, was back in Los Angeles, nattily dressed and doing well, it seemed, as a salesman in a car dealership. Victor spoke of him with a kind of relief. But some months after the wedding Ricky and Victor's sister Elena called to ask, on behalf of their mother, if I would stand bail. Ricky had been stopped on a traffic charge, and a computer check showed that he was wanted for parole violation in the north. I declined, but later, on a trip to Sacramento, I visited him in the minimum-security jail where he was serving his sentence. I learned then that during his first northern period he had become a father. The child, a boy, was being raised by its mother and her parents, Anglos with whom Ricky claimed to be on friendly terms, though clearly all contact had been lost. After his release from jail Ricky moved in with Victor, Victor's wife, and their new baby, but within weeks he had been arrested again, this time on a drug charge. When Victor called about Mike, he said that Ricky, too, would be out in a month or two.

Sometimes, as I have reflected on our checkered ten-year friendship with the Rodríguez family, I have wondered whether Latinos do not have a better local reputation, and blacks a worse one, than each deserves. But how much difference does reputation ultimately make? True, walking the streets of downtown Los Angeles, I do not expect to be panhandled or shaken down (the two grow increasingly similar) by Latinos; I do fear that from blacks. True, I am wary of black men and generally nonchalant with Latinos. I think my attitudes are typical. And yet, all that aside, if there were no Latinos — and no other immigrants — around to do all the work that is to be done in Los Angeles, would blacks not be hired to do it? I think they would be. Wages might have to be raised. Friction might be acute for a while. But in the end the work would go looking for available workers.

Labor's View: The Rodney King Riot as a Bread Riot

I am not alone in thinking so. In July of last year the Black Leadership Forum, a coalition headed by Coretta Scott King and Walter E. Fauntroy and including Jack Otero, the president of the Labor Council for Latin American Advancement, wrote to Senator Orrin Hatch urging him not to repeal the sanctions imposed on employers of illegal aliens under the Immigration Reform and Control Act of 1986. "We are concerned, Senator Hatch," the group wrote,

> that your proposed remedy to the employer sanctions-based discrimination, namely, the elimination of employer sanctions, will cause another problem — the revival of the pre-1986 discrimination against black and brown U.S. and documented workers, in favor of cheap labor — the undocumented workers. This would undoubtedly exacerbate an already severe economic crisis in communities where there are large numbers of new immigrants.

Labor leaders like Otero and another cosigner, William Lucy, of the Coalition of Black Trade Unionists, are notoriously critical of free trade, especially to the negotiation of a free-trade agreement between the United States and Mexico. Their opposition to lax enforcement of immigration law, which creates a free trade in labor, is only consistent. What difference is there between exporting jobs and importing workers?

The politics of labor and immigration makes strange bedfellows. On   35 most issues the Southern California Interfaith Taskforce on Central America is an extremely liberal group, but on employer sanctions it sides with Senator Hatch. In effect, SCITCA would rather see wages go down and its Central

American clients have work of some kind than see wages stay high and penniless refugees be left with nothing. La Placita, the Mission Church of Our Lady Queen of Angels, near downtown Los Angeles, became for a time a sanctuary for illegal hiring.

Latino immigrants at the bottom of the labor market often claim to be doing work that "Americans" refuse to do. Are they thinking of black Americans? It may not matter. Commenting to a *New York Times* reporter on the extremely low employment rate for sixteen- to nineteen-year-olds in New York City in early 1992 — 12.6 percent — Vernon M. Briggs, a labor economist at Cornell University, said, "To an immigrant willing to work two or three jobs at once, five dollars an hour may not look bad. But to a kid from Brooklyn or the Bronx, it is a turnoff." To some of their parents these kids seem to be prima donnas, but in fact the influx of immigrants willing to work long hours for low wages has depressed wages and increased competition beyond anything that the parents ever faced. And the attitudinal difference between unskilled Americans of any race and their immigrant competition shrinks as the immigrants gain a clearer view of what faces them in the United States.

During his buoyant junior year at Wilson High School, Ricky carried a pocket dictionary. One day he told me that he had come upon an entry that had shaken him to his roots: *happy-go-lucky.* "That's my problem," he said. "I'm happy-go-lucky." Ricky's merry, open-faced manner was one of his greatest assets, but I think I know what he meant. I had often marveled that a boy up against so much could remain so high-spirited. I now think that he simply hadn't yet realized how much he was up against. Tension grew between him and Victor after his first release from jail. Victor wanted Ricky to take a job, any job, just to be working: dishwasher, gardener's helper, anything. Ricky drew the line at that kind of work. He was able to do rough carpentry, dry-wall work, simple plumbing. Besides his building skills, he was completely bilingual and could even write surprisingly coherent and error-free English. "I am an educated man," he said to me in a choked voice. Both words counted. Ricky was arrested again on a drug charge, but he has never been addicted. He was dealing, and he was dealing because as he had grown more American, he had grown impatient. "Ricky wanted money. That's what got him into trouble," Victor says. Jorge G. Castañeda put it differently in an op-ed piece in the *Times:*

> In Mexico and El Salvador, with the exception of the role played by the church in the latter country a few years ago, poverty and inequality did not outrage its victims, nor did it lead them to violence.... But the same deprivation, with the same inequities, in a radically different context, produces different effects. Poverty and injustice were not supposed to be the same: The United States was the land of social mobility, well-paid work and unlimited opportunities. Not any more. A Latin American migrant's future is often the same as his current reality: $4.50 an hour for unskilled labor for the rest of his or her life, maybe with a raise to $6 or $7 an hour, eventually.

But the young Mexicans or Salvadorans who do housework in Beverly Hills, garden in Bel-Air, or park Jags and BMWs for restaurants on Melrose had no idea this is what awaited them when they left Usulutan or Guanajuato. And the ideological bombardment they are now subjected to no longer helps them accept matters as they are. On the contrary, it incites rejection, indignation, and class hatred. Any spark can light the fire.

So, yes, Latinos compete with blacks for work at the bottom, but they also match them in rejecting $4.50 an hour as chump change. And then what? Then, among other things, readiness for a bread riot (a cake riot, if you will) in which the disappointed, by the thousands, steal what they once thought they could earn.

The question of how immigrant groups may fit into the American economy without dislodging or otherwise adversely affecting native groups is itself contained in the larger question of how an American economy carrying all these groups within it can compete against other national economies. In an article given wide distribution by the Federation for American Immigration Reform, Vernon Briggs claims that immigration accounts for 30 to 35 percent of the annual growth of the American labor force, a proportion virtually unknown elsewhere in the industrialized world. In 1989, Briggs writes, "the total number of immigrants from all sources admitted for permanent residence was 1,090,924—the highest figure for any single year since 1914 (and this figure did not include any estimate of the additional illegal immigrant flow or of the number of nonimmigrants permitted to work in the United States on a temporary basis during that year)."

The immigration story becomes the riot story by becoming a part of the 40 labor story. And by an irony that I find particularly cruel, unskilled Latino immigration may be doing to American blacks at the end of the twentieth century what the European immigration that brought my own ancestors here did to them at the end of the nineteenth. Briggs writes,

> When the industrialization process began in earnest during the later decades of the nineteenth century, the newly introduced technology of mechanization required mainly unskilled workers to fill manufacturing jobs in the nation's expanding urban labor markets. The same can be said of the other employment growth sectors of mining, construction, and transportation. Pools of citizen workers existed who could have been incorporated to meet those needs — most notably the recently freed blacks of the former slave economies of the rural South. But mass immigration from Asia and Europe became the chosen alternative.

The chosen alternative: those are the words that should disturb our sleep. People do not blow into our country like the weather. We let them in, and we have reasons for doing so. Or we should. In my city, on my own block, in my own house, I have seen the immigrant Latino alternative being chosen over the native black one.

But this is only the beginning of the problem. I am talking about a mistake that is now, as it were, complete. Blacks in Los Angeles having been largely closed out of the unskilled labor market, the earlier-arriving Latinos are now competing with the later-arriving Latinos. This is the embarrassing fact that *La Prensa* seemed so little able to face and that has led lately to a Latino Unity Forum. Briggs makes disturbing reading on the consequences of increasing the pool of unskilled applicants while the pool of jobs shrinks:

> No technologically advanced industrial nation that has 27 million illiterate and another 20 to 40 million marginally literate adults need fear a shortage of unskilled workers in its foreseeable future. Indeed, immigration — especially that of illegal immigrants, recent amnesty recipients, and refugees — is a major contributor to the growth of adult illiteracy in the United States. To this degree, immigration, by adding to the surplus of illiterate adult job seekers, is serving to diminish the limited opportunities for poorly prepared citizens to find jobs or to improve their employability by on-the-job training. It is not surprising, therefore, that the underground economy is thriving in many urban centers. Moreover the nature of the overall immigration and refugee flow is also contributing to the need for localities to expand funding for remedial education and training and language programs in many urban communities. Too often these funding choices cause scarce public funds to be diverted from being used to upgrade the human resource capabilities of the citizen labor force.

Briggs's analysis seems to me to make a mockery of the brave talk of a Los Angeles "recovery." What does it mean for the city to recover in an American society that is adding at least 700,000 immigrants a year to its population? The official "Rebuild L.A." coalition, headed by Peter Ueberroth, the former director of the 1984 Los Angeles Olympics and the former commissioner of baseball, will be hard enough pressed to cope just with the city's share of those new workers. Assimilating so many new workers while re-assimilating the thousands left jobless by the riot may well be more than the economy could handle even in a boom period, and southern California is still deep in recession. The recession may mean that fewer Americans will move to the state, but if San Diego County statistics for 1990–91 are any indication, foreign immigration may not be similarly slowed. In that period net domestic in-migration was just 427, a steep plunge in comparison with the increases of earlier years, but foreign immigration held steady at 19,442.

And competition for goods other than employment is more acute during a recession than at any other time. The Center for Immigration Studies estimates that direct public-assistance and education costs at all levels of government for immigrants and refugees entering the United States in calendar year 1990 totaled $2.2 billion. Immigrants and refugees made up 1.3 percent of the caseload of Medi-Cal, California's state-paid health care, in 1980; the California Department of Finance estimates that they will make up 13 percent by the turn of the century. The administrative office of the Los Angeles County Board of Supervisors reported in the spring of last year that federal costs for the citizen children of ineligible alien parents, including Medicaid and Aid to Families with Dependent Children, had risen from approximately $57.7 million in 1988–89 to $140.5 million in 1990–91 and could reach $533 million by the year 2000. If the burden of that welfare grows too great, another tax revolt could take place, and another safety valve could be removed from places like South Central Los Angeles.

Few Californians are aware, I think, of how many public school seats are filled by illegal immigrants. But as awareness grows, the already eroded support for public education at all levels may erode further. Nonimmigrant whites are still the majority in the state, and older whites — whose children may be grown — still turn out to vote more reliably than any other group. True, only some of the Asians burning up the track at the University of California are immigrants, but more are the children of immigrants. When whites in Berkeley's freshman class dropped to 30 percent, there was talk of a cooling of white support for the costly nine-campus system. As for the larger, more teaching-oriented California State University, it has never charged noncitizens legally resident in California a higher tuition; but a recent decision by Alameda County Superior Court Judge Ken Kawaichi now requires that illegal aliens receive the same generous treatment.

By July 1, when a budget impasse for fiscal 1992–93 forced California to begin paying many of its bills with scrip instead of money, some of the bitterest infighting had touched the third and nationally least known of the state's higher-education systems, the gigantic California Community Colleges system, with its 1.5 million enrollment. Would the heaviest community college cuts come in short-term vocational education, hurting blacks disproportionately? Or would continuing education take the hit, hurting older white women returning to the workforce? Little noticed in public comment on the budget battle was the fact that immigrants constituted 10 percent of 1990–91 community college enrollment. California was providing all-but-free higher education, in other words, to 150,000 immigrant undergraduates. For comparison, Harvard and Radcliffe together enroll fewer than 7,000 undergraduates. The community college system has to be regarded as a de facto incentive for immigration — a GI bill for people who were never GIs, as I once heard it described. If and when free higher education for immigrants, especially illegal immigrants, comes under attack, however, free elementary and high school education for them will almost inevitably come into question as well. And the social dislocation lurking in the latter question is almost incalculable.

In March [1991], *Science* published a research report by Georges Vernez and David Ronfeldt on Mexican immigration. The evidence in the report shows that recent immigrants are those who feel the greatest economic impact from still more recent immigrants. And because Mexican immigrants tend to be young and to have large families, they consume more in public services, especially educational ones, than they pay for. The researchers say that both the absolute size of the Mexican immigrant population and its relative concentration in Los Angeles and several other western cities are growing.

Vernez and Ronfeldt also argue that "heavy immigration into California...lets many low-wage industries continue expanding while their counterparts nationwide were contracting in the face of foreign competition." Their data show that in California "manufacturing grew five times the national average whereas wages grew 12 percent more slowly in the state, and 15 percent more slowly in Los Angeles." The implications for labor are clear: either manufacturing is exported to take advantage of cheap foreign labor, or cheap foreign labor is imported in numbers large enough to depress wages here. Open borders create a free trade in labor, and America's southern border, though not open by law, has been open enough in practice to move the Los Angeles labor market sharply away from the American mean.

Do we like it this way?

The short answer might be yes if we want more riots, no if we don't.

In his book *Los Angeles: Capital of the Third World,* David Rieff charges   50
that white Los Angeles has grown addicted to the ministrations of a Latino "servitor class," and there is something to his charge. In 1985 my wife and I paid $65 a week to a licensed, well-educated, decidedly middle-class Peruvian couple who cared beautifully for several infants and toddlers in a home they owned. Our newborn daughter was typically with them from 7:30 A.M. to 6:00 P.M., five days a week. My younger sister, who lives in Skokie, a suburb of Chicago, found this at the time an incredible bargain, and so it has seemed to New Yorkers and Washingtonians as well. Thus I no doubt fit Rieff's definition of white Angeleno indulgence myself.

The larger beneficiaries of cheap labor, however, seem to me to be the larger employers. Ricky's sisters Dolores and Graciela worked in a sweatshop assembling those little gadgets — two plastic eyelets joined by a length of cord — that tennis players use to keep their eyeglasses on. There were huge spools of the cord and barrels of the eyelets in the private home (of an Italian married to a Costa Rican) where they worked. And the profits from that little operation were surely peanuts compared with those made on the luxury condos where Ricky did his drywall work.

Obviously, Los Angeles should want to maintain a manufacturing base, large and small. But if the price is systematically depressed wages, and if the price of that depression is further riots, then the price is too high. . . .

The Judgments of the Lord

The same colleague who remembered the sack of Rome as we left the *Times* building, its windows still boarded up, the streets not yet patrolled by the National Guard, had earlier lent me his videotaped copy of the PBS Civil War series. Midway through the writing of this article I concluded my viewing of the series and heard an actor reading Abraham Lincoln's Second Inaugural Address. There is a strange, deep similarity between the logic of angry blacks who called the Rodney King riot understandable and inevitable — and, indeed, barely stopped short of calling it justifiable — and the logic of the man who wrote,

Fondly do we hope, fervently do we pray, that this mighty scourge of war may speedily pass away. Yet, if God wills that it continue until all the wealth piled up by the bondsman's two hundred and fifty years of unrequited toil shall be sunk, and until every drop of blood drawn with the lash shall be paid by another drawn with the sword, as was said three thousand years ago, so still it must be said, "The judgments of the Lord are true and righteous altogether."

My deepest, least argued or arguable hunch is that everything in America begins with that old and still unpaid debt. An America in which it was finally paid, in which blacks were no longer afraid and no one was any longer afraid of blacks — what could such a country not attempt? But if, to quote an ex-slave, all God's dangers ain't the white man, all God's dangers ain't the black man either. The earth, as the century ends, has many wretched, and we are living in their house.

Understanding the Text

1. What does Miles mean when he says he feels like a "worried Roman — in front of a television set, watching the Goths at their sack" (para. 3)?

2. What role does Ricky Rodríguez play in shaping Miles's attitude toward immigration?

3. Summarize in your own words Miles's attitudes toward other ethnicities.

4. What assumptions does Miles make about the effect of Latino immigration on the labor force in Los Angeles?

5. What relationship does Miles see between immigration and the Los Angeles riots?

Exploring and Debating the Issues

1. In class, discuss Miles's tone in this essay. What attitudes toward immigrants does it reveal? How does the tone affect the reader's response?

2. In your journal, respond to the following comment by Miles: "I have wondered whether Latinos do not have a better local reputation, and blacks a worse one, than each deserves. But how much difference does reputation ultimately make?" (para. 32).

3. In an essay, recommend ways to fit immigrant groups into the American economy and political system without displacing groups already here. To develop your argument, you may want to consult Yeh Ling-Ling, "The Welcome Mat Is Threadbare" (p. 73), and Rubén Martínez, "Refine Immigration Policy to Reflect History and the Moment We Live In" (p. 76).

4. To what extent do the economic and political conditions that Miles describes reflect the changes in the electorate outlined by Steve Scott in "Reality Votes" (p. 234)?

AL MARTINEZ

Can We All Get Along?

Watching children play on an L.A. school playground, **Al Martinez** (b. 1929) sees the possibility of a harmonious future for California's racially diverse population. After all, California history is punctuated by wave after wave of immigrants, many of whom faced
problems joining the status quo. But when the children leave the playground, Martinez
wonders, will they be able to sustain the spirit of the playground in a society riven by racial
conflict? A long-time columnist for such California newspapers as the *Oakland Tribune* and
the *Los Angeles Times,* Martinez is the author of such books as *Ashes in the Rain* (1989),
Dancing Under the Moon (1992), and *City of Angles: A Drive-by Portrait of Los Angeles*
(1996).

I was walking by an elementary school in the San Fernando Valley when I
stopped to watch a group of children at play. As I stood staring through
the mesh fence that surrounded the schoolyard, it occurred to me how
lovely their world must be. No rage fueled their competitive spirits, no jeal-
ousies fired their energies. Gender wasn't a question in their games, nor
were race or cultural history. A clean wind blew through their lives as they
ran from and toward each other, and at the end of their play they fell in a
heap of unrestricted laughter, their happiness isolated for a moment in a
world fenced off from hatred.

Then they went home.

What they faced at home, what they heard there, what was infused into
their souls there, were elements of the internal structure that will make
them what they will be once memories of the schoolyard fade and the world
beyond the fence becomes the world they will occupy for the remainder of
their lives. Will the joyful entanglements of their play emerge later as an
easy respect for one another, or will forces yet to be applied alter their perceptions and cause a retreat from the closeness they knew at play?

The children I watched that day represented all the major races and
cultures intermixing in California as we move toward a new millennium:
blacks, whites, Asians, and Hispanics, a microcosm of what the future holds
in a state that has not always welcomed diversity with parades and banners.
Hatreds rooted in economics and cultural beliefs have tarnished the gleam
in the Golden State since, and prior to, its inception.

The Chinese, at first welcomed in the 1840s because of their energy and   5
their willingness to work for low pay in the gold mines and on the railroads,
became the objects of hate-engendered legislation for those very traits. As
their numbers grew and their ambitions thrived, the state responded with
an ugliness difficult to forgive. The Chinese were taxed by race, barred from
testifying in court against whites, excluded from certain jobs, and prohibited from marrying Caucasians. They were beaten, robbed, and murdered,
their bodies left to rot in the cultural debris of our past.

256

A similar fate awaited the influx of Latinos at the turn of the century. Welcomed at first as cheap farm labor, they were deported by the thousands during the Great Depression, welcomed back in the state's brief Bracero program, then ousted again by INS agents responding to "Operation Wetback" and, later, to the termination of the Bracero program. Then in 1994, Proposition 187, supposedly aimed at illegal immigrants, created a new burst of xenophobia directed toward not the Danes or the British but those from south of the border whose millions still hunger for a better life beyond the Golden Door.

Two years later, Proposition 209 took aim at affirmative action and further widened the gap.

History reveals that laws, however crudely applied, can never stem the flow of immigrants yearning for betterment. A human instinct to improve has populated the world and will someday populate the stars. California is the proof of immigration's mighty force. Despite measures to keep foreigners out, a quarter of California's population, eight million, are foreign born, mostly from Latin America (51 percent) and Asia (33 percent). More than eighty languages are spoken in the state. By the year 2010, according to one estimate, the white population will be California's new minority.

One issue therefore becomes clear: we'd better take a lesson from those kids in the schoolyard and start getting along. Diversity is the word on which our future spins. Diversity of culture, diversity of color, diversity of language, diversity of religions, and diversity of dreams. Existing in a single political climate, elements of the differences between us can either lead to wars bloodier than any we've ever seen or to a rainbowed paradise more glorious than any we've ever imagined.

In multiculturalism exist the seeds of both. Former Governor Jerry   10
Brown, now an Oakland radio talk show host and candidate for mayor, senses danger in the emerging identity of minority groups if they don't expand beyond their clusters. He sees the clustering as a reaction to the state and the nation's racist history.

"What we have," he said to me, "is an identity perspective, a crisis. Each minority group feels it has to represent itself for protection against the outside world. It becomes a bundle of attitudes within itself, as opposed to citizens concerned with the total good. They are people looking at the world from the point of view of their own ethnic identity."

Brown sees a revival of civic life as a way of assuring that diversity will create the kind of California most of us want. "That's why I've come to Oakland," he said. "We're equally balanced among whites, blacks, Asians and Hispanics, and we're talking to each other. Oakland is an early warning portrait of California. There's no reason why it shouldn't succeed as a multicultural state. It will have to. If not, Bosnia."

Brown's point is well taken. A people suppressed is a people enraged because hatred hurts and not forever will the oppressed tolerate its pain. In my house growing up in East Oakland lived a stepfather of German descent whose very soul seethed with a multitude of antipathies. He entered my life before I ever set foot in a school, and I learned from him how terrible hatred can be. He spewed it on blacks, Jews, Asians, and Latinos, saving a special vitriol for me. I was a "spic" in his eyes, and he used physical force to establish his dominance over me. When, as he lay dying, I asked why he had hated me so, he only shook his head. There is no logical explanation for racial or ethnic hatred, no justification for its existence. We are molded by our progenitors, even those who assume the role by marriage and not blood, despite early realizations of how wrong that can be. I used the word *nigger* once in a rage when, during teenage, I found myself becoming my stepfather's son. The moment burns in memory with the heat of magnesium and no amount of later apologies, or subsequent years of fighting racism, will ever damp its fire. There is no atonement for the pain deliberately caused others. I never forgave my stepfather. Why should a young black boy at whom my ugly epithet was thoughtlessly hurled ever forgive me?

Lessons abound from personal experiences. To know how much hatred hurts is, in a perfect world, to later empathize with those who hurt. Only in recent history has awareness of cruelty and social upheaval caused us to re-evaluate our attitudes. The Jewish holocaust of World War II took us to the very brink of the abyss of horror from which we emerged stunned by what we had seen and heard and wondering how it could have happened and if it could happen again.

America's great social crusades of the 1960s, much of them centered in California, proved that racial and gender equality were no longer simply catchphrases. They had emerged as battle cries that belonged to those who stormed the barricades of the past to raise the flags of the future. Subsequent racial riots punctuated a black demand for cultural equality, women marched and sued to establish their place in the context of the American dream, and gay liberation became a new and powerful cry among a minority that finally emerged from the closet and found a voice of its own.

These are today's diverse, what the writer Ambrose Bierce once called "the great unusual." He lived in a different time when diversity did seem unusual, when racial levels dominated our social and political structures, before Jackie Robinson, before the courage of the children at Little Rock, Arkansas, before Martin Luther King Jr., before history caught up with hatred and forever altered the nature of our society. Today we struggle in the transition between now and then, "then" being that year 2010 when two-thirds of California's workforce will be today's minorities and three-fourths of our retirees will be Caucasians.

In a speech in Los Angeles, state Senator John Vasconcellos (Democrat, San Jose), citing those figures, emphasized a significant truth, that it's in the best interest of our future old age to provide a skilled workforce to sustain "the great economic engine we call California." Without it, without offering education, health benefits, and jobs to everyone, the engine will falter. "We Californians have the opportunity, the necessity, the responsibility to realize our great challenge," he said, "the promise of a multicultural democracy in the global economy."

A U.S. Census Bureau study points out that today, as in our past, the new immigrants to America demonstrate the same willingness to work as did their forebearers. Once it was building railroads and working the mines until those immigrants established footholds in an often hostile environment. Today, for the time being, it's cleaning tables and pulling weeds for minimum pay until the same energy that powered our ancestors elevates their social heirs into better jobs.

Meanwhile, the Census Bureau points out, unemployment among our current immigrants is just under 5 percent nationally, compared to about 4 percent among the native-born population. The difference is minimal. The same quest that fires our spirit fires theirs. Work, not the public dole, is the ladder that will get them to where they want to be.

Despite what occasionally seems to be a declaration of war on the state's immigrants, Californians are generally cautiously optimistic about the future . . . if you're white and make over $60,000 a year. A *Los Angeles Times* poll taken in October revealed that 46 percent of those asked believe that we're headed in the right direction. Forty percent thought otherwise. Not a ringing declaration of faith in the future exactly, but considering that just five years ago only 12 percent expressed an optimistic view and 82 percent felt we were sliding downhill toward hell, it was a vast improvement.

What bothers those who calculate California's future, however, is that the state's minority population still isn't sure we're going in the right direction, and therein may lie the ultimate answer to our destiny. Breaking the *Times* poll down, only 28 percent of the blacks and 38 percent of the Latinos questioned felt optimistic about the state's future. Similarly, analyzing it along economic lines, the majority of those who expressed optimism (58 percent) earned over $60,000 a year, compared to only 33 percent of those making under $20,000 a year. People living on the edge find it difficult beating the drums for tomorrow, and the edge is occupied mostly by blacks and Hispanics.

Where are we now?

Vasconcellos speculates that, "We could be at a place where diversity leads to strength. There's a lot of healthy prospects," he added, "if we're not blinded by old prejudices."

I heard this repeated many times over recently at a ceremony of the Los Angeles County Commission on Human Relations. Those who stood to receive annual awards for somehow bettering the human condition almost unanimously foresaw a future for California much brighter than they might have envisioned only a few years ago. They saw the state's millions reaching the top of a mountain built of old hatreds and, having achieved that most difficult of all climbs, moving on to other peaks, each of which would represent not simply a rejection of the past but an improvement for the future.

The question that awaits to be answered — "Can't we all just get along" — was asked by police-beating victim Rodney King at the height of the 1992 riots in South-Central Los Angeles, the worst social uprising in U.S.

history. The riots, in fact, began after a jury in Simi Valley acquitted four Los Angeles policemen in the videotaped beating that showed King, who is black, on the ground being pummeled by the white cops. It was later, pressed to comment on the riots, that King, an unlikely philosopher, asked the one question that remains a central factor in looking toward California's future: can we get along? I think we can because I think we must. There is growing evidence that the surge of history is on the side of those who march together away from an often violent and dismal past. There is hope.

The gloomy German philosopher Oswald Spengler, who wrote *Decline of the West*, encapsulated cultural diversity when he observed, "In the destinies of the several cultures that follow upon one another, grow up with one another, touch, overshadow, and suppress one another, is compressed the whole content of human history." What he didn't mention was the possibility of a diverse culture existing beyond suppression but still touching and still growing. That could be an element of human progress yet to be written as California edges hesitantly into a new millennium and a new epic of social realization.

Understanding the Text

1. What is the lesson that Martinez believes we can learn from elementary-school children?

2. Why does former governor Jerry Brown believe that Oakland "is an early warning portrait of California" (para. 12)?

3. How, as Martinez explains, do Californians' visions of the state's future differ according to their social class and ethnic identity?

4. What evidence does Martinez give for his optimistic belief that California can overcome its racial divisions and build a cooperatively diverse society?

5. Why does State Senator John Vasconcellos argue that it is in the interests of today's white majority to offer "education, health benefits, and jobs to everyone" (para. 17)?

Exploring and Debating the Issues

1. Divide the class into groups, and conduct an intensive study of campus life, exploring different areas including enrollments, housing, curriculum, and clubs and other student organizations. Does your campus reflect the ethnic diversity that Martinez describes? Are your campus's ethnic groups "getting along"? Explain why or why not.

2. Martinez claims that the state's minority populations tend to believe that California is not heading in the right direction. Conduct your own poll on campus to test whether this claim applies to a college or university population.

3. Jerry Brown believes that California is in danger of becoming another Bosnia — that is, divided into hostile ethnically divided camps. In an essay, argue for or against Brown's belief.

4. Martinez alludes to the history of Latino immigration to California. Research in greater depth the immigration patterns of Mexicans or of any other immigrant group to this state.

RICHARD STEVEN STREET

Battling Toxic Racism

The popular image of an environmental activist is that of a white, middle-class suburbanite, but as the saga of Kettleman City reveals, this image is both false and misleading. For the tale of Kettleman City, as told here by **Richard Steven Street**, is a gripping story of how a community of Central Valley Latinos, in alliance with environmental activists from around the state, successfully blocked the construction of a toxic waste incinerator near their homes. In so doing, they demonstrated that environmentalism knows no racial or social boundaries. An award-winning photographer and essayist, Richard Steven Street is the author of *A Kern County Diary* (1983) and *Breadbasket of the World: California's Great Wheat-Growing Era 1860–1890* (1984), as well as the coauthor, with Samuel Orozco, of *Organizing for Our Lives* (1992), from which this selection is taken.

E very day hundreds of semitrailers rumble in and out of Kettleman City, an isolated farming town just off Interstate 5, midway between Los Angeles and Sacramento. Many of those trucks are packed full of fruit and vegetables, the bounty of the San Joaquin Valley on its way to people around the world. However, other trucks contain a different cargo — a deadly cargo. These trucks deliver toxic waste bound for burial three miles outside of Kettleman City at the largest landfill west of Louisiana.

The residents of Kettleman City detest this dangerous traffic. Nevertheless, Chemical Waste Management, the owner of the landfill, is targeting the town for the site of a new toxic waste incinerator. The residents are calling it "a landfill in the sky" and have banded together to stop Chem Waste from building any more toxic facilities in their town. "Do you think we'd have this toxic mess here if we were a community of rich white people?" asks Mary Lou Mares, a lettuce cutter who has lived in Kettleman City for fifteen years. "Our rights have never been taken seriously."

Led by poor farm workers, hundreds of citizens of Kettleman City have formed *El Pueblo para El Aire y Agua Limpio* (People for Clean Air and Water), a multiethnic coalition whose aim is to stop the proposed incinerator. Many people are comparing the David-and-Goliath struggle of *El Pueblo* to the United Farm Workers (UFW) organizing campaigns of the

1960s. Similar to the UFW campaigns, the anti-incinerator coalition in Kettleman City must confront multimillion-dollar corporations, law enforcement, and hostile government agencies.

El Pueblo's most effective tactic to date has been a lawsuit filed on their behalf by California Rural Legal Assistance, a poverty law program that has been operating in rural California since 1965. This lawsuit is the first in the nation to charge that "environmental racism" played a role in a corporation's decision to build a toxic waste facility in a low-income community. The lawsuit accuses Chem Waste of targeting Kettleman City because it is largely a community of poor, monolingual, Spanish-speaking Mexican field hands. Kettleman's thirteen hundred residents are 95 percent Latino. The suit also discloses a nationwide pattern of building toxic facilities in low-income communities. All of Chem Waste's incinerator facilities are located in communities that are more than 75 percent poor people of color — communities such as Sauget, Illinois, Port Arthur, Texas, and the south side of Chicago.

When Chem Waste built its toxic landfill in Kettleman City in 1979, the corporation did not have to obtain approval from the local community because Kettleman City is unincorporated. There is no mayor, city council, planning commission, or newspaper. All Chem Waste had to do was buy an existing oil disposal company and apply for permits with the state and federal governments. Within a year it was not only operating a full-scale toxic landfill in Kettleman City, but it was using Interstate 5 as a kind of toxic runway for fleets of top loaders heaped with contaminated solids, tankers full of toxic liquids, and flatbeds stacked high with fifty-five-gallon drums of cyanide, benzene, asbestos, cleaning solvents, heavy metals, and hundreds of other chemicals.

"We noticed all the trucks rolling through and assumed they were going to some kind of construction project," explains Adela Aguilera, a teacher's aide and mother of three. "We didn't know what was going on." Strange, oily-garlic odors drifting into town with the evening winds first signaled that something nasty was brewing out in the Kettleman hills. Unexplained, nagging health problems ranging from nosebleeds to fainting spells led a small group of citizens to uncover the frightening truth — a truth that no government official had bothered to tell the largely Latino population who were being affected by it. With more than 200,000 tons of poisons rolling in every year, Kettleman City had been transformed overnight, with no public notice, from a rural backwater into the toxic capital of the western United States.

In 1988, Chem Waste applied for permits from Kings County to build an incinerator near the existing landfill. The corporation held its public hearings on the incinerator in Hanford, thirty-five miles from Kettleman City and the proposed site. Residents of Kettleman City were not told about the hearings. "We found out through Greenpeace," explains Ramon Mares. "They asked us if we knew that an incinerator was going to be built. We said no. We didn't know anything. Greenpeace began to educate us so we could fight it."

Although they were unfamiliar with the concept of environmental social justice, several Kettleman City residents had read about the community coalitions blocking hazardous dumping or incinerators in Emelle, Alabama, and in East Los Angeles. With the help of Greenpeace, residents learned the basics of grassroots activism — phone trees, meetings, and door-to-door organizing. "We began to understand our rights," recalls Bertha Martinez, who has lived in Kettleman for twenty-four years. "We saw we weren't alone."

After forming *El Pueblo,* Kettleman City's residents launched a campaign that has become a model for community organizations across the nation. They have created a unique coalition that cuts across racial and economic boundaries, pulling together Latino farm managers, migrant farm workers, and Anglo residents who own larger farms in the area. By linking up with civil rights organizations and environmental activists, *El Pueblo* publicized its cause, lobbied, marched, and gained the attention of activists and politicians nationwide.

"Chem Waste never imagined we'd fight," says Espy Maya, a mother of   10
four who is a leader in *El Pueblo.* "The company just thought we were a bunch of dumb little hicks and illegals, so hard up for work that we'd be tickled to death to get some menial jobs burning their poisons or burying them at their dump."

Some of the group's most surprising allies turned out to be former opponents. Downwind from the proposed incinerator, farmers like Jose Maya and Dick Newton, who usually had little patience for environmental causes supported by Greenpeace or the Sierra Club, found their interests to be in alignment. "If just one head of lettuce is contaminated, I'll lose the entire crop, and I'll be ruined," explains Maya, who grows 3,000 acres of lettuce, tomatoes, and cantaloupes. "All the farmers in this area will be ruined." As for Chem Waste's claims that its incinerator would be 99.99 effective in burning 100,000 tons of toxic material a year, *El Pueblo* notes that even if they accepted that, which they don't, the incinerator would still put ten tons of deadly ash into the air annually. "Chem Waste says that's acceptable," protests farmer Dick Newton, a resident of the town of Stratford. "What right does it have to force me to breathe highly toxic dust?"

El Pueblo has hammered away at local authorities who have denied the mostly Spanish-speaking members their rights. In addition to charging Chem Waste with discriminatory siting of the incinerator, *El Pueblo*'s suit also charged the Kings County Board of Supervisors with running a discriminatory public participation process. "The Kings County Board of Supervisors likes to hold public hearings in Hanford, thirty-five miles away from Kettleman City because they know that field hands can't get off work and make the long drive to attend the daytime meetings," says Espy Maya. "And when they did attend in the evenings, the farm workers couldn't understand anything because the meetings were always conducted in English, and the critical documents, some 3,000 pages of them, were never translated into Spanish."

El Pueblo protested these undemocratic hearings in a mass rally last fall when more than 1,000 people packed into Kettleman City. The

Reverend Jesse Jackson and Congresswoman Maxine Waters led the community in a march on Chem Waste and shut down the landfill for a day. Officials from Kings County claimed that Greenpeace and other "outside agitators" orchestrated the march, manipulating residents for their radical goals.

This accusation infuriates Apolonia Jacobo, a farm worker and member of *El Pueblo.* "Chem Waste is the outsider. Nobody from Chem Waste lives in Kettleman City. Their lawyers and representatives all drive in from Fresno and Hanford. The only reason why supervisors bow to them is money. Chem Waste's taxes pay for about 8 percent of the Kings County budget."

In December 1991, Kettleman residents scored a major victory in court. 15
State Superior Court Judge Jeffrey Gunther ruled that Chem Waste and Kings County had failed to provide adequate information on the air pollution effects of the toxic burner. The judge also ordered county officials to prepare and translate an extended summary of the environmental impact report into Spanish so that Kettleman residents could study it. In 1992 bids by Chem Waste to begin construction have twice been rejected by the judge. Construction on the incinerator is already years behind schedule. Now it may never be built. The people celebrated their victory with a mariachi party. "We Mexican people have made a difference," says Mary Lou Mares. "We have changed. Five years ago you would never have seen us challenging a big company like Chem Waste. Now we're not afraid. We know how to fight. We're in this for the long haul."

The campaign organized by *El Pueblo* to stop the toxic incinerator signals an important change in the nation's controversy over hazardous waste disposal. The group's actions have garnered coverage in numerous national magazines and newspapers, as well as on national television news programs.

In other countries, such as India and Brazil, poor people have long spearheaded movements to stop harmful development and environmental destruction. Now, in the United States, the contribution of poor people to environmental social justice, once seen by the public as the exclusive province of white middle-class activists, is no longer invisible. Mares explains, "We're in a country where we can be heard if we speak up. Many of us still believe that we can't talk, that we have to stay quiet, that we can't beat the government. But we can win. If we speak as a group, we can be heard."

Understanding the Text

1. In your own words, define the term "environmental racism" (para. 4).
2. In the view of Kettleman City activists, how did the political process obstruct rather than invite their participation in the controversy over toxic waste disposal in their community?

3. How did Chem Waste's proposal to build a toxic waste incinerator in Kettleman City unite a number of traditionally divided, and sometimes hostile, interests?

Exploring and Debating the Issues

1. This essay was originally published in 1992. Conduct a research project to learn what has happened since Chem Waste first planned to build a toxic waste incinerator in Kettleman City.

2. Read or reread Cesar Chavez's "The Organizer's Tale" (p. 345), and write an essay in which you evaluate the analogy between Kettleman City's "David-and-Goliath struggle" (para. 3) against Chem Waste and Chavez's founding of the United Farm Workers Union.

3. While the residents of Kettleman City oppose the location of a toxic waste incinerator in their community, America annually produces vast quantities of such waste that requires disposal. In class, form teams and debate whether Kettleman City is an appropriate location for this purpose.

4. Read or reread Steve Scott's "Reality Votes" (p. 234), and write an essay discussing the extent to which Street's essay illustrates the growing Latino political clout in California that Scott describes.

5. Read or reread Gary Snyder's "Cultivating Wildness" (p. 178), and then analyze whether the experience of Kettleman City verifies, negates, or complicates Snyder's vision of a public policy that meets the needs of both the environment and economic development.

ANNA DEAVERE SMITH

The Unheard
Maxine Waters, Congresswoman, 35th District

In April 1992, Los Angeles erupted in the wake of the first verdicts delivered in the Rodney King beating trial. As a part of the city's response to the rioting that seemed to tear L.A. apart, **Anna Deavere Smith** (b. 1950) was commissioned to create a performance piece devoted to the uprising. The result was *Twilight: Los Angeles, 1992,* a series of monologues in which Smith adopts the role of a number of the women and men who were, in one way or another, associated with the riots, using the words of the participants themselves. In this selection, Smith speaks as U.S. Congressional Representative Maxine Waters, from California's Thirty-fifth District, where much of the rioting took place. Here, in a monologue adapted from an actual speech delivered to the congregation of the First African Methodist Episcopal Church, Waters castigates the powers that be for ignoring the underlying causes of the riots, demanding redress of the conditions that caused a city to explode. Smith is a performance artist whose many pieces are building an epic series entitled *On the Road: A Search for American Character.*

(This interview is from a speech that she gave at the First African Methodist Episcopal Church, just after Daryl Gates had resigned and soon after the upheaval. FAME is a center for political activity in L.A. Many movie stars go there. On any Sunday you are sure to see Arsenio Hall and others. Barbra Streisand contributed money to the church after the unrest. It is a very colorful church, with an enormous mural and a huge choir with very exciting music. People line up to go in to the services the way they line up for the theater or a concert.

Maxine Waters is a very elegant, confident congresswoman, with a big smile, a fierce bite, and a lot of guts. Her area is in South-Central. She is a brilliant orator. Her speech is punctuated by organ music and applause. Sometimes the audience goes absolutely wild.)

F irst
African
Methodist Episcopal Church.
You all here got it going on.
I didn't know this is what you did at twelve o'clock on Sunday.   5
Methodist,
Baptist,
Church of God and Christ all rolled into one.
There was an insurrection in this city before
and if I remember correctly   10
it was sparked by police brutality.
We had a Kerner Commission report.
It talked about what was wrong with our society.
It talked about institutionalized racism.
It talked about a lack of services,   15
lack of government responsive to the people.
Today, as we stand here in 1992,
if you go back and read the report
it seems as though we are talking about what that report cited
some twenty years ago still exists today.   20
Mr. President,
THEY'RE HUNGRY IN THE BRONX TONIGHT,
THEY'RE HUNGRY IN ATLANTA TONIGHT,
THEY'RE HUNGRY IN ST. LOUIS TONIGHT.
Mr. President,   25
our children's lives are at stake.
We want to deal with the young men who have been dropped off of
America's agenda.
Just hangin' out,
chillin',   30
nothin' to do,

nowhere to go.
They don't show up on anybody's statistics.
They're not in school,
they have never been employed,   35
they don't really live anywhere.
They move from grandmama
to mama to girlfriend.
They're on general relief and
they're sleepin' under bridges.   40
Mr. President,
Mr. Governor,
and anybody else who wants to listen:
Everybody in the street was not a thug
or a hood.   45
For politicians who think
everybody in the street
who committed a petty crime,
stealing some Pampers
for the baby,   50
a new pair of shoes . . .
We know you're not supposed to steal,
but the times are such,
the environment is such,
that good people reacted in strange ways. They are not all crooks and   55
criminals.
If they are,
Mr. President,
what about your violations?
Oh yes.   60
We're angry,
and yes,
this Rodney King incident.
The verdict.
Oh, it was more than a slap in the face.   65
It kind of reached in and grabbed you right here in the heart
and it pulled at you
and it hurts so bad.
They want me to march out into Watts,
as the black so-called leadership did in the sixties,   70
and say, "Cool it, baby,
cool it."
I am sorry.
I know how to talk to my people.
I know how to tell them not to put their lives at risk.   75
I know how to say don't put other people's lives at risk.
But, journalists,

don't you dare dictate to me
about what I'm supposed to say.
It's not nice to display anger.   80
I am angry.
It is all right to be angry.
It is unfortunate what people do when they are frustrated and angry.
The fact of the matter is,
whether we like it or not,   85
riot
is the voice of the unheard.

Understanding the Text

1. What is Waters's attitude toward the rioters' actions?

2. What does Waters see as politicians' and officials' understanding of inner-city conditions and communities?

3. Why does Waters refuse to say "cool it" (ll. 71–72) to her constituency?

Exploring and Debating the Issues

1. In class, read aloud this selection, which comes from a speech Waters delivered to the First African Methodist Episcopal Church in Los Angeles. How does the oral rendition compare to reading the selection silently? Then rewrite the speech in a prose paragraph. How does that format affect your response to its message?

2. Waters refers to the Kerner Commission report. Research that report and explain why Waters considers it significant.

3. Waters refers to the "voice of the unheard" (line 87) in this selection. Read or reread Richard Steven Street's "Battling Toxic Racism" (p. 261), and write an essay in which you propose how the inner-city "unheard" might make their presence felt politically, as did the residents of Kettleman City.

4. In an essay, analyze how this selection complicates Al Martinez's vision for future racial harmony ("Can We All Get Along?," p. 256).

Researching the Issues

1. Research the structure of California's state government: the relationship between the state legislature, senate, and governor. Then write an essay in which you compare this structure with that of the federal government.

2. For several years now, the California budget has been overdue, sometimes by several months, because of political fighting among different factions in the legislature and governor's office. Proposals have been made

---

CALIFORNIA ON THE NET

1. Visit the California Home Page (http://www.ca.gov/s), and evaluate its effectiveness in making government accessible to the public.

2. The California Voter Foundation maintains a nonpartisan web site that provides information about upcoming elections. Visit their site at http://www.calvoter.org/cvf/home/html, and study the ballot measures slated for the next state election. Keeping in mind Peter Schrag's warnings ("California, Here We Come," p. 222) about direct democracy, evaluate the measures and argue whether they belong on the ballot.

3. Investigate the demographics of the county in which you live: how have they changed in the last year or so? For up-to-date demographic statistics, visit the California Department of Finance's web site (http://www.ca.gov/html/Demograp/E-1press.htm). Compare your findings with your classmates' results.

---

for a state constitutional amendment requiring passage of the budget by 30 June of each year, with sanctions for failure to do so. Research the causes of the budgetary delays, and write an argument that supports, opposes, or modifies this proposal.

3. In 1988, Californians passed Proposition 103, which established the elective office of State Insurance Commissioner and granted the state the power to regulate insurance rates. Since passage, the insurance industry has fought the measure in numerous ways. Research the history of this proposition, and write a report on the current status of its implementation.

4. Conduct an investigation into the post-riot history of the Rebuild L.A. task force, using newspaper sources and, if you live in the Los Angeles area, interviewing local businesspeople and politicians. Then write a report in which you evaluate the group's relative success or failure in achieving its economic and political goals.

5. Read the whole of Anna Deavere Smith's *Twilight: Los Angeles, 1992.* Then write an analytic essay in which you explain the psychological impact of the civil unrest on the community as Smith presents it.

6. Since the 1960s, California — and especially San Francisco — has been the center of gay politics in the United States. Research the history of the gay political movement in California, and write an essay in which you outline the ways gay activists used the political system to further their causes. You might begin your research by consulting the late Randy Shilts's *The Mayor of Castro Street: the Life and Times of Harvey Milk* (1982).

7. While the U.S. Supreme Court has ruled the state's term limits for legislators, as established by Proposition 140, is constitutional, the controversy

over term limits continues. Research the goals behind the term-limit movement, and then write an essay in which you argue whether those goals have been met.

8. Visit a town or city council meeting. Try to interview councilmembers or citizens before or after the session on how well they believe community concerns are addressed in this forum. Write an essay in which you evaluate the session: to what extent do you believe it served community needs and interests?

6 Of Work and Wealth
The Economics of the Dream

Plastics

In a cinematic interchange that became one of the defining moments of California's youth culture in the 1960s, a middle-aged man sidles up to a young college graduate, played by Dustin Hoffman, whose parents are hosting an elaborate graduation party for him. "I have just one word to say to you," the man whispers to the graduate, intending to give him a hot tip for the future: "plastics."

Audiences groaned, for the advice was meant to be ironic. It summed up what the movie, *The Graduate,* was saying about the sterile, materialistic values of California's middle- and upper-middle class in the 1960s: that life had become "plastic," meaningless, nothing more than a sterile pursuit of money.

Over thirty years later, the moment is still ironic — only the irony has been reversed. For as it turns out, the man gave some pretty good advice. It would have been even better if he had said "celluloid" or, better yet, "silicon" because both the film and the computer industries offer some of the best economic opportunities for today's college graduates.

It may seem odd to find a chapter on business in your composition reader, especially if you, like many who graduated from college in the 1960s, are also repelled by materialism. On the other hand, things have changed in the last thirty years, especially for the middle class. Economic restructuring, especially in the wake of the collapse of California's once-vaunted defense and aerospace industries, alongside gigantic increases in the cost of housing and transportation, have made it a great deal more difficult to achieve and maintain a middle-class lifestyle. And if you want your college degree to lead to a secure middle-class future, it won't do any harm to start thinking about the shape of California's economy.

The Times They Are a'Changing

For the times have indeed changed since the 1960s. The students who then sneered at the "plastic" world of their middle-class parents could also take for granted an economy that offered plenty of jobs, as well as housing costs that were about a tenth of what they are today. So considering both the promises and the drawbacks of California's economy isn't such a bad idea.

Something else has changed since the 1960s. It was once assumed that if you got a job with a large corporation, you'd stay employed with that corporation until your retirement. Sure, you had to conform to the rules, but at least you had job security. California's economic restructuring, much like that of the rest of the country, has changed all that. Few employees can expect to work for the same company for all of their working lives. Most workers, in fact, can expect to change not only their jobs but also their careers several times over the course of their lives. In such a world, one must be nimble, ever on the lookout for new opportunities and ever able to retrain yourself for those opportunities. Indeed, you yourself may be returning to college for precisely that reason, trading in one career for another that you hope will offer you a better way of life.

The purpose of this chapter, then, is to encourage you to think about the fluid and ever-changing economic landscape of the state. We cannot predict which careers will be most promising in California in the future, and the industries that we have included in these readings are hardly inclusive of the state's entire economy today. But by thinking now of the sort of world you will be entering or reentering, you should be better able to negotiate its twists and turns and understand its impact on the state.

The Engines of California's Prosperity

Today no single industry, or even any small group of industries, completely dominates California's economy. Indeed, the big mistake made in the 1980s was to allow the defense and aerospace industries to become too dominant, because when they collapsed, the economy collapsed with them for about five painful years. Today it is the diversity of California's economy that is leading the state not only into recovery but back to prosperity. Agriculture, biotechnology, oil production, international trade (especially with the Pacific Rim nations), tourism, financial services, clothing manufacturing and design, as well as a myriad of entrepreneurial enterprises, are just some of the areas in which the current economy excels.

But the two industries that cast the broadest shadows across the economic landscape today are the entertainment industry, generally headquartered in Southern California, and the computer industry, most famously headquartered in the Santa Clara Valley area (Silicon Valley) but now spreading from San Diego up the coast to Santa Barbara. And given Hollywood's growing penchant for computer-assisted special effects, not to mention animation spectaculars, these two industries often closely intertwine. At the same time, they have drawn the most cultural attention, capturing the imaginations of those who work in them and those who consume their products. For this reason, most of the readings in this chapter focus on the entertainment and the computer industries, though they are not the only games in town.

When thinking of the California economy, it is worth knowing that it is the eighth-largest economy in the world. This somewhat startling fact was often overlooked during the bleak years of the recession, as many commentators wrote off California as a hopeless economic basket case. The late 1990s are demonstrating that announcements of California's demise were much exaggerated, as the state now stands to outpace the nation in job growth.

The Perils of Prosperity

But as California returns to prosperity, it is important to note the underside of economic growth. One prominent feature of California's return to economic health, for example, has been the uneven nature of the recovery. These are boom times, for instance, in the Bay Area and Orange County, and even once-beleaguered L.A. County is coming back. But rural California is lagging behind, and inner-city populations everywhere in the state are being left out of the new prosperity. The gap between rich and poor, the haves and the have-nots, is growing larger and larger in the state, and if this gap is not addressed somehow, the price of uneven economic growth might be social catastrophe — as was demonstrated earlier in the decade in the L.A. riots.

Along with the potential social costs of California's economic recovery are the environmental costs. Economic growth leads to population growth and the need for more and more development: more housing, more highways, more schools, more water, more everything — except for more unspoiled land and unpolluted air and water. Already those living in the most populous and prosperous parts of the state are feeling the effects of uncontrolled economic development, from grid-locked traffic to air pollution to overcrowding and crime. The big question for California's future, then, is whether such growth can be conducted in a sustainable manner that balances economics against environmental quality.

Critical thinking about California's economy means more than seeking the best career opportunities. As inheritors of the state's future, you also have to think about ways to build a socially equitable and environmentally sustainable economy. There are no easy ways of doing this, of course, and few attempts are being made today to achieve such goals. But if you want the California dream to be there for you and your children, you would do well to start thinking about the matter now.

The Readings

John Cassidy gets the ball rolling here with an analysis of the dramatic economic comeback that has taken California from the depths of recession back to the forefront of American prosperity in the last few years. Michael J. Mandel follows with a report on one of the main forces behind the new California gold rush: the dizzying rise of Silicon Valley as the world center of high-tech development. Chris Hayhurst and Judith Stacey follow with analyses of the environmental and social price that California has had to pay for Silicon Valley success, focusing, respectively, on the toxic waste that technology generates and the gender inequality at the heart of the information industry. Lary May provides an historical background for the rise of the film industry, that other major player in the California comeback, while our excerpt from F. Scott Fitzgerald's *The Last Tycoon* offers an insider's view of the way in which the power elite in Hollywood determines just what makes it to the silver screen and what doesn't. James J. Flink next surveys the leading role California played in the mass motorization of America, followed by James D. Houston, who goes "In Search of Oildorado" and so leads us to an analysis of the oil industry's place in California's economy. The late Cesar Chavez follows with the story of the founding of the United Farm Workers Union, giving voice to the agricultural workforce that has yet to share in California's prosperity, while Luis Omar Salinas concludes the chapter with a poetic meditation on forty years of picking crops in the Central Valley.

JOHN CASSIDY

The Comeback

Just when everyone was writing off California as a lost cause, it roared back to take the lead once more in the American economy. **John Cassidy** (b. 1963) explores some of the reasons for California's dramatic rebound, highlighting the roles that the high-tech sector and the entertainment industry have played in the comeback but also noting some of the many less glamorous businesses that have also contributed to the California resurgence. Indeed, as one economist has noted, even in the depths of recession, California was never so badly off as it was said to be. So one might say that when things in California are bad, they're pretty bad, but when they're good, they're real good. Cassidy is a staff writer specializing in economics and finance at the *New Yorker,* where this article appeared in the February 23/March 2, 1998 issue.

W hen Henry Segerstrom looks out a window of his family's ranch in Costa Mesa, forty miles south of Los Angeles, he sees not the lima-bean farm he worked on as a boy in the 1930s but the San Diego Freeway, a ten-lane tapestry of concrete that extends from the San Fernando Valley to Irvine. A century ago, Segerstrom's grandfather, an immigrant from Sweden, leased twenty acres of Southern California scrubland, which he gradually built into a two-thousand-acre farm. His family cultivated the land until the forties, when they began to develop it. In 1967, the Segerstroms opened the area's first enclosed shopping mall, South Coast Plaza, and it has become one of the most popular attractions in Orange County. Segerstrom, who is seventy-four, is an extremely wealthy man. On a bright morning recently, he raised himself to his six-foot-one-inch height, grabbed a long wooden stick, and pointed at a map that showed how the San Diego and Santa Ana Freeways converge a few miles to the south. "These two roads have been the backbone of growth in this community," he declared.

Growth, a key word in the Californian lexicon, seemed to be in danger of disappearing during the early nineties, when the state was hit by a lengthy recession. Now growth is back, and so is the optimistic outlook that is embodied in developers like Segerstrom. "I am bullish on Orange County. I am bullish on California," he said, slowly and firmly. "California is probably the most creative place in the world today." It is easy to mock such statements as self-serving, but they reflect an attitude that has built the world's seventh-largest economy, in a state that was principally agrarian when Segerstrom was a child. Other parts of the country have also prospered in the past few years, but California has created jobs at a greater rate than the national average, and there are now about eight hundred thousand more people working in the state than worked there before the recession started. Some parts of the state, particularly the richer parts, are enjoying an old-fashioned boom.

Orange County is one such area. During the early nineties, it was racked by layoffs and falling real-estate prices as the defense contractors that had helped to finance the region's economic development were themselves poleaxed by Pentagon cutbacks. In 1994, the county suffered the ignominy of filing for bankruptcy after its treasurer, Robert Citron, made a series of disastrous investments. Three and a half years later, the near-bankruptcy has been largely forgotten. Property prices are up sharply, and the county's unemployment rate has fallen to 2.5 percent — one of the lowest rates in the nation.

Certainly recession and the financial humiliation haven't had much lasting impact on South Coast Plaza. A decade ago, Segerstrom decided to take his shopping center upmarket and invited Tiffany & Co., Versace, Barneys, Chanel, Hermès, and Tourneau, among other retailers, to open up alongside Macy's and Robinsons-May. "We wanted to recognize the growing affluence of Southern California, which we felt was not being effectively served by Beverly Hills," Segerstrom explained, using his stick to draw an imaginary horizontal line on the map from Los Angeles International Airport through Pasadena and into the San Gabriel Mountains. "Anybody above that line we thought would stick with Beverly Hills. Anybody south of it was ours." Most stores that accepted Segerstrom's invitation prospered, and development around South Coast Plaza now includes a Cesar Pelli–designed office building, a sculpture garden by Isamu Noguchi, and the Orange County Performing Arts Center. Segerstrom put up a bar chart and showed me how South Coast Plaza's annual sales had grown from a hundred fifty million dollars in 1977 to nine hundred fifty million dollars last year. The chart levelled off in the early nineties — "a blip," Segerstrom called it — but rose again after 1994. "We are approaching the magical point of a billion dollars a year in sales," he said.

The equation linking California and economic growth has been called into question before — notably when the Los Angeles land boom burst, at the   5 end of the 1920s — but never more intensely than during the early years of this decade. As riots followed recession, and earthquake followed riots, the apocalyptic aspect of the California character — an aspect stressed by writers like Cain and West — eclipsed the sunny optimism that is the state's official ideology. Hundreds of thousands of residents voted with U-Haul vans and moved to Oregon, Nevada, and New Mexico. Even the California business community, a circle in which boosterism is a watch-word, temporarily lost the script. "People here never thought anything like that could happen. They just couldn't believe it," I was told by Eli Broad, chairman of SunAmerica, a California-based financial company. In November of 1993, one of the state's most prominent economists — Larry Kimbell, who was then the head of the Business Forecasting Project at UCLA — said to a reporter, "If you want a job this century, leave California."

Since then, the California economy has created 1.3 million new jobs. The rebound has transformed the mood of the state's business and political leaders. California still has serious problems — rising economic inequality, crumbling schools, a dysfunctional political system, a massive influx of unskilled immigrants from Latin America and Asia — but at least it will be able to respond to them within the context of a growing economy. This is a far less ominous prospect than the one that the state appeared to be faced with a few years ago: managing the grievances of an increasingly heterogeneous and embittered populace in an environment where economic growth was a thing of the past.

To find out how this transformation came about, I traveled to Silicon Valley and met one of the few economists who never lost faith in California: Stephen Levy, the director of the privately funded Center for Continuing Study of the California Economy. Levy and his partner, Bob Arnold, spoke to me over lunch at an Italian restaurant on University Avenue, in Palo Alto. "We allowed the media to misreport the real nature of the state's economy, and that cost us unknown billions in outside investment," Levy told me. "It was really obvious, when you looked at the numbers closely, that the new economic base was in place to insure California's future."

Levy built his career on numbers. Every year, he produces a three-hundred-page report that contains figures on everything from the number of people working in the Los Angeles furniture industry (39,800) to the amount of venture capital invested in California firms last year (almost three and a half billion dollars). Over the next seven years, he says, "California will outpace the nation in jobs, income, household, and population growth."

This prediction is based on the state's having enjoyed what Levy calls "a very nontraditional rebound." In most business cycles, the industries that lead the economy into recession eventually lead it to recovery, but that wasn't the case in California. Aerospace, construction, and retail sales — the three sectors where employment fell most sharply during the recession—subsequently stabilized, but didn't regain many jobs. (Raytheon, a defense company, recently announced fifty-two hundred more layoffs across California.) The recovery was led by high technology, tourism and entertainment, professional services, and foreign trade.

One in eight Americans lives in California, but, if the calculations Levy   10 cites are correct, about one in five of the nation's high-technology jobs is located there. Some of these jobs are at well-established firms, such as Intel, Hewlett-Packard, and Sun Microsystems, but many are at smaller, fast-growing companies, such as PeopleSoft, Bay Networks, and Qualcomm. If, as many analysts suspect, the big industries of the future are biotechnology and Internet-related commerce, California appears well placed to exploit their growth. Orange County and San Diego County are already world leaders in medical-instrument manufacturing, while Los Angeles and the Bay Area have more multimedia firms than the rest of the country combined.

Silicon Valley itself is, to be sure, thriving. One morning recently, I drove from San Francisco to Santa Clara, a forty-mile journey that took two hours because of the traffic. When I arrived at the annual meeting of Joint Venture: Silicon Valley Network, a public-private-sector partnership set up to improve the quality of life in the area, a speaker was talking about the generosity of computer-industry folk. ("Eighty-three percent of Silicon Valley families give to charity, compared with 69 percent nationally," she assured the audience.) I picked up a copy of Joint Venture's "1998 Index of Silicon Valley," which told me that the new Klondike has a territory of fifteen hundred square miles (a bit less than Long Island), a population of 2.3 million, and a payroll of 1.2 million workers. Almost one in four Silicon Valley residents is foreign-born, one in three has a bachelor's degree or more, and the average household income in Santa Clara County, the heart of the Valley, is $101,000. The "Index" went on in this vein for thirty pages — about ten new firms are incorporated every day, an estimated fifty-three thousand new jobs were created in 1997, traffic delays have doubled in two years — and I felt exhausted just reading it. Becky Morgan, a former state senator, who is the president of Joint Venture, evidently felt the same way. "We can't grow at this rate forever," she told me after the meeting had ended. "A slowdown would be healthy as long as job growth doesn't turn negative."

A couple of days later, I drove through Oakland and Livermore to the vast emptiness of the Central Valley. About two hours from San Francisco, I stopped at Gustine, a settlement that is little more than some grocery stores, a drainage ditch, and a few hundred wooden houses. On the edge of town I took note of a new development — South Port, consisting of dozens of newly built houses on streets with Anglican names, like Canterbury Court. Its sales manager, a friendly fellow named Kendall Mitchell, said the properties were selling well, mostly to refugees from the Bay Area who don't mind the commute. "You can get two houses for the price of one here," he said as he showed me around a model house called the Saratoga, which proved to be a three-bedroom affair with a cathedral ceiling, a two-car garage, and a sizable back yard. "I can get you in here inside a week for $107,770," Mitchell continued. "That's with the stone fireplace included."

Most reference books say that agriculture is still California's biggest industry, but Stephen Levy says that it has been overtaken by tourism and entertainment, a swath of the economy which, according to his figures, employed more than half a million people last year. Joel Kotkin, a Los Angeles–based writer, refers to the burgeoning entertainment sector as California's "cultural-industrial complex," and he believes that it will play a role in the state's future similar to the one that was played in its past by the military-industrial complex. "It's not just film," he told me recently. "It's television, music, video games, multimedia, theme parks, restaurants. They are all linked."

The Los Angeles Economic Development Council recently released figures showing that two hundred and sixty-two thousand people were employed last year in the business of motion pictures and television — an increase of 83 percent since 1990. These numbers — and they don't include the legions of lawyers, accountants, agents, managers, cooks, beauticians, therapists, call girls, personal trainers, and so on who service the Hollywood workforce — were front-page news in the *Los Angeles Times.* Hollywood, it announced, "is rapidly moving from supporting player to star of the region's economy."

This shift is increasingly visible in the physical and social geography of   15
Los Angeles. Once confined largely to the corridor of land from Culver City to Burbank, the entertainment industry is now spreading out. Santa Monica, for example, which was once a sleepy seaside town, is now home to several well-established "industry" companies, including M-G-M/United Artists, Cinergi, and MTV, as well as a number of newer outfits, such as Santa Monica Pictures, Todd-AO Studio West, and Activision. Real estate prices have risen sharply, and some local residents now refer to the area as Brentwood South. Venice, Los Feliz, Culver City, and even the decrepit heart of Hollywood itself are being revitalized and gentrified by entertainment-industry money. If the DreamWorks studio ever gets built on the thousand-acre site of Howard Hughes's old helicopter plant in Playa Del Rey, the film colony will have extended its laager almost to Los Angeles Airport.

West Hollywood, which I started visiting in the mid-1980s, has also been transformed. Back then, parts of Sunset Strip were considered dangerous and seedy; now, the Strip is packed every night, as hordes of young and not so young revellers make their way from Bar Marmont to Skybar to Barfly. Even Ben Frank's, the all-night diner at Sunset and Alta Loma, has been made over; it is currently called Mel's Drive-In, and on Sunday at lunchtime it looks like a casting call for *Melrose Place.* "Everybody I know, their jobs have gotten better. Things are going well," Cynthia Desir, a self-described "real Westside girl," told me from her booth at Mel's. Desir's mother was killed in the Northridge earthquake in 1994, which soured her on Los Angeles for a while, but now she lives in Hollywood, works for Naked Lunch, a restaurant company, and is writing a script. ("Everybody in

L.A. is writing a script," she said. "You have to or they don't renew your lease.")

Joel Kotkin lives a few minutes from Mel's, and he turned out to be a fast-talking forty-five-year-old New Yorker who moved west twenty-seven years ago. "The development of California is one of the great stories, and I wanted to be the one who wrote it — or some of it, anyway," he said. Like Levy, Kotkin believes that the media have grossly underplayed the West Coast revival, and he appears determined to correct the imbalance himself. "California's hold on the science- and culture-based industries of the future remains remarkably strong and without parallel either domestically or globally," he wrote in a 1996 report, "California: A Twenty-First Century Prospectus." "In contrast to classic mass-production industries, these economic endeavors can not be easily duplicated by shifting production to lower-cost environments."

The latter point is key. Every so often somebody writes about "the next Hollywood" or "the next Silicon Valley," but they invariably fail to explain why Hollywood and Silicon Valley have remained at the leading edge of their respective industries for so long, despite the fact that both are congested, polluted, and expensive. Kotkin's answer, which he gleaned from recent academic literature on economic geography, is that both these places have evolved into self-sustaining "regional networks."

The basic ideas behind this concept go back to the Victorian economist Alfred Marshall, but they were resurrected by Michael Piore, an economist at MIT, and Charles Sabel, a professor at Columbia, in their 1984 book, *The Second Industrial Divide.* Piore and Sabel studied the craft industries of central Italy, where they found large numbers of small firms producing high-fashion versions of traditional goods, such as shoes, suits, bags, furniture, and ceramic tiles. The key to the area's success, they concluded, was that it was geographically dense but economically decentralized. Local firms competed against each other for sales but cooperated in things like employee training, marketing, and learning about the latest fashions. This system, which Piore and Sabel dubbed "flexible specialization," allowed the area to adapt quickly and produce high-quality goods for which customers were willing to pay a premium.

Economists have identified regional networks in places as diverse as Baden-Württemberg (machine tools), Georgia (carpets), and nineteenth-century Lancashire (where, according to Marshall, the textile industry was "in the air"). A few years ago, Annalee Saxenian, a professor at Berkeley, published an influential book entitled *Regional Advantage,* in which she identified Silicon Valley as another important regional network and argued that its success was due to a distinctive business culture, which she labeled a "network-based industrial system." When I spoke to Saxenian recently, she said that while she hadn't studied the film industry closely, she agreed with Kotkin that there are important resemblances between Hollywood and Silicon Valley. "You have these very fluid labor markets and these

20

communities of highly skilled people who recombine repeatedly. They come together for one project — in this case a new film, in Silicon Valley it would be a new firm — and then they move on," she said. "The system allows for a lot of flexibility and adaptiveness."

The parallels don't stop there. Both Silicon Valley and Hollywood have their own languages, a permissive attitude toward risk-taking, and a highly effective grapevine. Computer-industry executives don't like spending five hundred thousand dollars for a three-bedroom house in Mountain View any more than film-studio executives like handing over a million dollars for a similar house in Brentwood, but neither can afford to be anywhere else. "Information about new markets and new technology flows very quickly," Saxenian said. "This sustains the importance of geographic proximity, despite the fact that, theoretically, the technology allows you to be anywhere."

The implications of such academic work for California's future are profound. Ever since Cecil B. De Mille rented an L-shaped barn at the corner of Selma and Vine, the film industry, with its itinerant workforce and fly-by-night business practices, has been widely dismissed as a world unto itself. If Saxenian and Kotkin are correct, however, Hollywood actually prefigured a time in which Fordist mass production was replaced, at least partly, by the decentralized creation of individually designed goods, like films and video games. Most countries — let alone states — don't have a single important regional network within their borders. California has two, and they are both in industries where the potential for future growth appears to be unlimited.

Of course, the vast majority of Californians don't work in Hollywood or Silicon Valley. A few years ago, David Friedman, a Los Angles business consultant, persuaded AT&T and the City of Los Angeles to sponsor a research project that would examine those parts of the Southern California economy which weren't in the newspaper headlines. It was a project that Friedman had long wanted to undertake. When he was a graduate student at MIT, he carried out a similar exercise in Japan and turned it into a prize-winning book, *The Misunderstood Miracle*. After returning to the United States, Friedman became a corporate lawyer, but he always wanted to return to economics. So, having obtained the necessary financing, he and a group of researchers started going through Los Angeles business listings and trade directories, calling small firms, and asking them about their businesses. "We would say, 'We don't want any money from you, but could you please tell us what you do?'" he recalled when I visited him recently in his office downtown. "They would hesitate and say, 'You want to talk to *us*?' "

Friedman quickly learned that the Southern California economy was almost as diverse as its population. In East Los Angeles, he discovered a bicycle-maker, an oil-pipeline manufacturer, and the world's largest producer of tortilla chips. Downtown, he found hundreds of fashion businesses, many of them turning out their designs in local apparel factories. Out in the San Gabriel Valley, he came across a few hundred Asian firms that were making computers, and computer parts, for the Chinese market.

"You literally could find no data on these jobs," Friedman told me. "Nobody had ever been to speak to these people. This stuff might as well exist in Bolivia for all the attention it gets around here." The research team concluded that Los Angeles County was still one of the biggest manufacturing centers in the country and that up to half of the people employed in the region were working for firms of a hundred people or less. Of eighteen thousand five hundred companies surveyed, most were under fifteen years old, and many had been founded by immigrants. "The California élite is wildly unprepared for the type of economy that is generating the state's growth," Friedman said.

A few days after speaking to Friedman, I went for a two-hour drive with   25
José Legaspi, a Mexican American who has built more than a dozen supermarkets and shopping centers in Latino areas of Los Angeles. Legaspi, who is forty-five, arrived in Boyle Heights thirty-one years ago, and he still lives in East Los Angeles. I met him at his office in Montebello, an affluent Hispanic district about twenty minutes east of downtown; we drove west through Pico Rivera and Huntington Park into South Central, where the riots began in 1992, then took the Harbor Freeway north and circled back through the Eastside. "For a long time, the big retailers were not interested in the Hispanic market, but that is changing now," Legaspi told me as we passed along Pacific Avenue, a bustling thoroughfare in Huntington Park which has replaced downtown as the principal Latino shopping area. "When you have any big and powerful economic market, businesspeople have to figure out how to tap into it. Money has a wonderful way of changing behavior."

To somebody familiar with central Detroit, the South Side of Chicago, or East New York, the striking thing about the poor areas of Los Angeles is how many factories and shops they contain. Areas like Toy Town, Commerce, and Vernon look the way Long Island City must have looked fifty years ago, full of dust and trucks and grime. Some of the factories in these areas are no doubt sweatshops, but by no means all of them are, and, perversely, even the sweatshops demonstrate that capitalism has not abandoned these neighborhoods, as it has abandoned poor areas in other cities. The commercial districts that were burned down during the 1992 looting have been largely reconstructed, mainly owing to the efforts of Rebuild L.A., a public-private partnership that was set up after the riots. The major problem facing Legaspi these days, he told me, was not finding companies or banks willing to invest in minority areas but finding enough space there for them to develop. "There is very little land available. I am looking for a site to build a multiplex cinema, but I can't find one," he said.

I asked Legaspi about a recent report from the Rand Corporation, a public-policy research group, that cast doubt on whether many recent immigrants are likely to move into the middle class. "Most Hispanics have a middle-class mentality. Their income may not be middle-class, but their mentality is," he replied. "They have a very strong drive for self-improvement, for their children to be educated, for home ownership, and against state handouts." Legaspi could point to his own experience as an example of how immigrants can move up in California society. After graduating from Loyola University, in Los Angeles, he started representing tenants in real estate transactions, then moved into developing properties himself. Today he does business as far afield as Oakland and Mexico City; his daughter goes to private school in Pasadena; and his two sons both attend élite state universities. Legaspi admitted that he is not a typical case, but he maintained that he isn't an isolated example, either. "I graduated with nine hundred students at Roosevelt High School, in East L.A., and a lot of them are businesspeople and professionals," he told me.

Gregory Rodriguez, a research fellow at Pepperdine University, has provided some evidence that supports Legaspi's argument. Unlike many researchers, who gather data on individuals, Rodriguez looked at household-income figures, which seems reasonable. (Many immigrants live in households with more than one worker.) He concluded that about one in three foreign-born Latino households in Southern California is middle-class — defined either as a household that earns more than thirty-five thousand dollars a year or as a family that owns its own home. Rodriguez also found that Hispanic immigrants are making progress over time. Among those who arrived in the previous ten years, only about 9 percent owned their own homes; among those who arrived in the sixties, more than 50 percent were owner-occupiers.

The challenge facing California is to insure that this sort of progress continues. "The economic opportunities are great, but we could still blow it," Stephen Levy told me. "California's future depends on how Californian businesses and residents come to terms with government." Levy's argument is simple: the well-paying industries of the future will require highly skilled workers, and these can be either grown at home or imported. The first option requires resurrecting California's public-education system, which was once the envy of the nation; the second involves providing public facilities and cultural amenities, so that skilled people from elsewhere will want to move to the state. Either way means spending more public money — something that has proved extremely difficult since 1978, when California voters voted to sharply reduce their property taxes by passing Proposition 13.

The pessimistic view of California is cogently presented in a forthcoming book, *Paradise Lost,* by Peter Schrag, a former editorial-page editor of the *Sacramento Bee.* Schrag explains how much of California's current prosperity is based on the universities, colleges, and roads that were built in the two decades after the Second World War by three progressive governors: Earl Warren, Goodwin Knight, and (especially) Pat Brown. Since the passage of Proposition 13, California has been forced to curtail its capital investments in everything except prisons. (Since 1984, the state has opened twenty-one of them, bringing its portfolio to thirty-three.) In the national rankings of state-education spending per pupil, California has slipped to forty-third. In 1994, the National Assessment of Education Progress found that only 18 percent of Californian fourth-graders could read proficiently, placing the state just ahead of Louisiana. Two years later, a similar study of math proficiency found California ranking alongside South Carolina and Alabama.

"In the end, the story of California's public sector over the past generation is a chronicle of a place that has been living on and drawing down its accumulated social capital," Schrag writes. Given that the state's dominant voting bloc is older whites, while the most intensive users of public services are young members of minority groups, he sees no obvious way out of the current fiscal impasse. Nor is he alone in his skepticism. Stephen Carroll, an economist at Rand, told me, "There are a lot of very nasty trends in place. None of them is immutable, but it is going to take a very significant change in attitudes and in the nature of political leadership." Carroll co-wrote a recent report that predicted a six-billion-dollar shortfall in California's higher-education budget by 2015.

The gloomy argument can't be discounted, but there are some indications that California may be starting to move beyond Proposition 13, one of them being the recent approval of bond issues to finance school-building in a number of localities. Many Californians seem willing to pay somewhat higher taxes if they know exactly how the money is to be spent. Meanwhile, fast-growing areas such as Riverside–San Bernardino have shown that it is possible to construct schools and provide public services by imposing user fees on residents. As time passes, these trends seem likely to strengthen. The Howard Jarvis Taxpayers Association, which was formed by the campaigners for Proposition 13, still has tens of thousands of members, but they tend to be of retirement age. Meanwhile, the Hispanic voting bloc, which has a strong interest in public spending, finally seems to be stirring, as was demonstrated by the 1996 defeat of the Republican congressman Bob Dornan, in Orange County.

Perhaps the most encouraging sign of all is that California's economy seems capable — so far, at least — of powering on regardless of the state's political problems. "Look at Orange County," David Friedman told me. "They virtually stopped the government. A year and a half later, not only does nobody care but the county is voted the best place to live in America." (The survey was carded out by *Places Rated Almanac*.) Soon after I spoke to Friedman, the force of his argument was brought home to me when the Ford Motor Company said that it was moving the headquarters of its struggling Lincoln Mercury division from Detroit to Irvine. The announcement marked the first time that a major American auto company had decided to shift one of its major divisions out of Michigan, and it shocked car-industry veterans. "We want to get connected to the Californian attitude," Robert Rewey, Ford's vice-president of sales and marketing, told the *Los Angeles Times*. "We have to throw away our previous assumptions."

A willingness to jettison assumptions and try different things isn't just a cultural quirk; it is California's greatest economic asset. As long as the state maintains its openness — openness to new ideas, openness to new investments, and openness to new people — its prospects are good. If Californians can combine this flexibility with a rediscovered willingness to invest in public services, infrastructure, and education, then historians might someday study the state in the way that they used to study Japan, Sweden, and, indeed, California itself: as a model economy.

Understanding the Text

1. What does economist Stephen Levy mean by California's "nontraditional rebound" (para. 9)?

2. What are "self-sustaining 'regional networks'" (para. 18), and why does writer Joel Kotkin consider Hollywood and Silicon Valley to be such regions?

3. What surprises did business consultant David Friedman discover in his study of the Southern California economy?

4. According to this selection, what must California do to ensure future economic prosperity?

5. Why does Cassidy say that "a willingness to jettison assumptions . . . is California's greatest economic asset" (para. 34)?

Exploring and Debating the Issues

1. Write an essay in which you agree, disagree, or modify Cassidy's concluding judgment that California might exemplify "a model economy" (para. 34).

2. Cassidy's upbeat assessment of the California recovery briefly alludes to ongoing economic and political problems, including "rising economic inequality, crumbling schools, a dysfunctional political system, a massive influx of unskilled immigrants from Latin America and Asia" (para. 6). Write an essay in which you assess the future impact of one of these problems on the state's economic recovery.

3. In your journal, reflect on whether you and your family have participated in the economic rebound Cassidy describes. If so, was your participation due to any of the reasons Cassidy mentions? If not, what were the obstacles?

4. Compare Cassidy's discussion of economic growth with that of James J. Rawls in "California: A People, A Place, A Dream" (p. 8), focusing particular attention on their comments on the consequences of economic prosperity.

5. This selection originally appeared in the *New Yorker*, a national magazine aimed at upper-income readers. Write an essay analyzing how this venue may have affected the tone and content of Cassidy's article.

MICHAEL J. MANDEL

Silicon Valley: Taking Its Place in the Pantheon

With a market value of some $450 billion, it's little wonder that the business world gets excited when thinking about the Santa Clara region's golden beltway of high-tech industries, better known to the world as Silicon Valley. In this admiring portrait sketched originally for *Business Week,* **Michael J. Mandel** (b. 1957) presents some of the facts and figures behind the high-tech preeminence of the Valley, comparing it to such other industry-leading centers as Detroit, Wall Street, and Hollywood. He predicts that its starring role in the pantheon of modern business will not come to a close anytime soon. Mandel, the economics editor at *Business Week,* won the 1998 Loeb Award for writing. He currently resides in Millburn, New Jersey, and his latest book is *High Risk Society* (1996).

In the economic history of twentieth-century America, few places have achieved larger-than-life, almost legendary status. Wall Street, Detroit, and Hollywood — these names are synonymous with financial might, manufacturing prowess, and glamour. At times, they have dominated the rest of the economy, ruling over their industries and captivating the national imagination.

Now, Silicon Valley has joined the pantheon of mythic places — the first addition in more than fifty years. The information revolution is driving economic expansion, with computers and semiconductors accounting for some 45 percent of industrial growth since 1993. And Silicon Valley is the apotheosis of this revolution. Tech companies based in and around the Valley now have a market value of some $450 billion — a number approaching the market capitalization of the entire French stock market. As a group, these companies have trailblazed the business behavior and culture that define the Information Economy. (For a roster of the Valley's largest public companies, see http://www.businessweek.com.) In the United States, the only locale with near-comparable economic heft is Wall Street. Like high-tech companies in the Valley, New York–based financial-services companies have an aggregate market value of about $400 billion. By comparison, the auto companies and suppliers of Detroit — erstwhile epicenter of the manufacturing economy — are worth barely $100 billion.

Mind Game

That puts Silicon Valley front and center. What's more, if the economics of mythic places holds true in this fifty-mile corridor of startups and technological creativity, it won't lose its starring role in the Information Economy. True, the cost of living and doing business are far higher than in other places. But that matters less than issues such as the deep pool of top-notch people and suppliers, the chance for individuals to get rich — often, quick — and the readiness to latch onto change. These qualities simply cannot be duplicated elsewhere. Just as Hollywood and Wall Street draw the starstruck and money-minded elite, Silicon Valley attracts the best and brightest minds in technology.

Indeed, Silicon Valley is gaining a bigger share of brainpower across a wide array of industries. Semiconductor jobs in the Valley are up by 29 percent since 1993, according to Collaborative Economics Inc., a Palo Alto–based consulting firm, outpacing a 20 percent semiconductor gain nationwide. Software jobs are up an astounding 70 percent since 1993, double the national average, despite the costs and congestion of the area. "We were worried that all of California's brains would go to Idaho or Santa Fe," says Larry J. Kimbell, director of the UCLA Business Forecasting Project. "But the opposite is happening."

Moreover, Silicon Valley has shown time and again that it can reinvent   5
itself — a quality that will be key to its survival. Consider this: Wall Street and Hollywood have dominated the securities and movie industries since the 1920s by adapting to changing conditions. In contrast, U.S. auto makers, which date to the same period, became ossified and inflexible. While a substantial share of auto jobs remain in Detroit and its suburbs, the area is no longer a font of cutting-edge thinking. Foreign auto companies locate their new factories in Tennessee or South Carolina, not Detroit, while foreign technology companies are flocking to Silicon Valley.

How long can its dominance continue? Indefinitely — since it is both the engine and the model for the rest of the economy. The Valley's industrial landscape is America's dreamscape: tight links among companies and top-notch universities, unlimited access to venture capital, a roiling influx of brilliant engineers from around the world, and a diverse mix of high-tech companies, both large and small. What's more, the Valley is self-replenishing. The proceeds from one company's success are plowed back into the next generation of startups. "The wealth that has been created there stays there," says Mitchell L. Moss, an urban economist at New York University's Wagner School of Public Service.

A historic pattern also bodes well for the Valley. Mythic places, it seems, are not subject to the same cost constraints as other locales. Wall Street and Hollywood continue to thrive even though New York and Los Angeles have long been among the most expensive areas in the country.

By these standards, the congestion and high costs in Silicon Valley, as aggravating as they may be, are not out of line. Hourly manufacturing earnings are about 25 percent higher in Silicon Valley than elsewhere, but that's down from the 29 percent wage differential in 1992. Home prices this year are up sharply. Still, the gap with the rest of the country is no wider than it was in the early 1990s.

Perhaps a bigger problem is finding space in the Valley, which has long favored sprawling one- or two-story structures. Increasingly, companies cope by building up rather than out. Adobe Systems Inc. chose to build a new eighteen-story headquarters in San Jose. "You don't need to have spread-out facilities," says Douglas Henton, president of Collaborative Economics.

Can anything topple Silicon Valley? Its biggest strength today could be its most vulnerable point down the road — technological innovation. Here, Detroit offers an object lesson. The early auto-industry pioneers were intensely creative, with steam-powered and even electric-powered cars vying with gasoline models. Auto makers had little money for large manufacturing operations, so they relied on parts and components bought from outside vendors. Indeed, Detroit's initial competitive advantage over other areas came from its unmatched pool of skilled craftsmen, machine shops, and other suppliers. "In its early days, Detroit looked a lot like Silicon Valley," says Susan Helper of the National Bureau of Economic Research.

Out of Gas

But the astounding success of the big auto companies in the 1920s helped destroy the industry's flexibility. As car sales tripled from 1921 to 1929, Ford Motor Company and General Motors Corporation started making most of their own parts, eliminating the supplier network that had nurtured the industry. Henry Ford went so far as to process his own iron ore, and he rejected using aluminum because he couldn't control aluminum makers. Bendix, which invented fuel injection for fighter planes during World War II, couldn't get U.S. auto makers to use the new technology for years. No longer open to ideas from the outside, Detroit grew vulnerable to foreign competition. Ironically, the same strategies that had increased profits and control in the past had the effect of hermetically sealing the industry from within.

If you heed the paranoid rants on the Internet about the dangers of Intel Corp.'s high-tech hegemony, you may fret that Silicon Valley is headed down the same path. Hasn't Intel extended its influence from microprocessors to motherboards, whole PCs, networking devices, and supercomputers? Isn't Intel, even now, trying to take control of the graphics-chips market with its purchase of Chips & Technologies Inc.? Could Intel, in short, trigger a cascade of events that sends Silicon Valley sliding down the same slippery slope as Detroit?

Most Intel-watchers say the giant is too shrewd to fall into such a trap. It is more likely that Silicon Valley as a whole will follow Hollywood's model. From 1946 to 1956, Tinseltown's movie industry saw attendance drop by half as television became popular. New York, home to the TV networks, was the source of most early programming. But Hollywood struck back. In 1954, Warner Brothers made the first deal to produce films for television. By 1957, virtually all the dramas on TV were coming from Hollywood. Meanwhile, it kept its original franchise. Today, almost all of the highest-grossing pictures globally still come out of Hollywood.

Wall Street has also been forced to reinvent itself. In the late 1980s, the focus of global financial power seemed to shift to Tokyo and London, with

U.S. brokerages seeking out the biggest pools of capital. Fleeing New York's high costs, many Wall Street firms moved back-office operations out of Manhattan. Still, these companies have prospered by generating wave upon wave of financial innovation. "The search for new ways to make money is what New York specializes in," says NYU's Moss.

Like Hollywood and Wall Street, Silicon Valley embraces reinvention.   15
Most recently, it bounced back from defense cutbacks in the late 1980s and early 1990s that cost 40,000 jobs. By comparison, Boston's Route 128 is a cautionary tale: the minicomputer companies that made the region a major technological force in the 1980s — including such giants as Digital Equipment, Wang Laboratories, and Prime Computer — all failed to adjust to changes in the marketplace, especially the personal-computer revolution.

Not Silicon Valley. The diversity of its companies and workforce creates a more complex and robust economic mix than ever existed in Detroit or along Route 128. This try-anything milieu is what enabled Netscape Communications Corporation to hurl Microsoft Corporation a curveball in 1995 in the form of its popular Navigator Web browser. Sun Microsystems Inc. has pulled off a similar coup with its Internet Java software. In the same fashion, custom-chip companies such as LSI Logic still run circles around Intel when it comes to specialty chips. "Silicon Valley's distinct advantage is to create new markets," says Annalee Saxenian, a regional economist at the University of California at Berkeley and an expert on Silicon Valley.

The Valley — and the rest of the United States — must remain vigilant. Left uncontained, giants such as Intel and Microsoft could yet despoil the Valley's virtuous cycle if they become so successful that they either buy up or squeeze out too many small competitors. Such an outcome, while unlikely, would eventually foul the fertility of the region. Alternatively, a deep recession, combined with a big drop in the stock market, could kill off a lot of small companies and dry up the influx of capital.

And then there are earthquakes, floods, famines, and fire. But as long as innovation, diversity, reinvention, and sheer technological élan continue to suffuse Silicon Valley, the hippest companies will find a way there — and the tech elite will follow. Such is the power of mythic places — and right now, Silicon Valley is creating legends of its own.

Understanding the Text

1. What does Mandel mean by calling Silicon Valley one of the "mythic places" (para. 2)?

2. How will Silicon Valley's ability to reinvent itself enable it to remain on the top of the economic hierarchy, according to Mandel?

3. Summarize in your own words Mandel's extended comparison between Silicon Valley and Detroit.

4. What vulnerabilities does Mandel see in the Silicon Valley success story, and what evidence does he offer for the region's ability to overcome them?

Exploring and Debating the Issues

1. Write an essay in which you critique Mandel's analogy between Silicon Valley and Hollywood. To develop your ideas, consult Lary May's "The New Frontier: 'Hollywood,' 1914–1920" (p. 301).

2. Read or reread Chris Hayhurst's "Toxic Technology: Electronics and the Silicon Valley" (below), and write a response to Mandel from Hayhurst's perspective.

3. Analyze the tone and diction of this selection, which originally appeared in *Business Week*. How might the readership of this magazine affect Mandel's writing?

4. This selection was first published in 1997. Research the current economic status of Silicon Valley, and then write an assessment of Mandel's predictions.

CHRIS HAYHURST

Toxic Technology: Electronics and the Silicon Valley

Every silver lining has a cloud, and Silicon Valley is no exception. For as **Chris Hayhurst** (b. 1972) reports here, technological production is also toxic, making the Santa Clara region the home not only to the world's most valuable concentration of high-tech industry but also to twenty-nine Superfund cleanup sites. And because the technology gold rush that has enriched so many Californians is not likely to slow down anytime soon, toxic waste will probably get worse before it gets any better. Hayhurst, a resident of Santa Fe, New Mexico, is a contributor to *E* magazine and is the author of the forthcoming *Wild New Mexico: A Guide to the State's Roadless Recreation Areas.*

California's Santa Clara Valley, stretching from the southern reaches of San Francisco to San Jose, was once an agricultural paradise known as the "Valley of the Heart's Delight." Over the past twenty-five years, however, the region has been transformed from a grower's haven to a toxic wasteland. The culprit? High-tech — the electronics and semiconductor industry. Better known today as the Silicon Valley, Santa Clara County is home to twenty-nine heavily contaminated Superfund sites slated for federal cleanup efforts by the Environmental Protection Agency (EPA).

Over one hundred different contaminants have been detected in Valley groundwater — the most common include trichloroethylene (TCE), a carcinogen, and 1,1,1-trichloroethane (TCA), which impairs the immune system and causes central nervous system depression.

The electronics industry revolves around one minuscule yet important component: the semiconductor chip. If you were to dissect a computer and lay out all the organs, the brain would be an eight-inch long, fingernail-width silicon wafer intricately etched with millions of transistors. The most complex and expensive part of the computer, this chip also requires the most chemicals for production. Consider the junk-food diet chip manufacturing entails. On average, the production of one eight-inch wafer requires 3,787 gallons of waste water, twenty-seven pounds of chemicals, twenty-nine cubic feet of hazardous gases, and nine pounds of hazardous waste. These chemicals and gases include glycol ethers, which have been identified as "serious reproductive toxins" by the EPA; and arsine, one cylinder of which if leaked could be lethal to an entire semiconductor production staff. When 220 billion chips per year are taken into account, the electronic frontier looks like a dangerous place indeed.

The Valley's high-tech headache began in 1982 when a neighborhood action group in Santa Clara County discovered that the Fairchild Semiconductor Corporation had contaminated San Jose drinking water with a slew of toxic chemicals. Further investigation found birth-defect rates in the region to be three times higher than normal, leading outraged community members to combine forces with the Santa Clara Center for Occupational Safety and Health (SCCOSH) to form the Silicon Valley Toxics Coalition (SVTC). Seeking to keep communities and workplaces free from toxic contamination, by 1984 the Coalition convinced the EPA to add nineteen Valley sites to its Superfund list.

Semiconductor companies now have financial incentives to watch where they dump their sludge. As Ted Smith, executive director of SVTC, puts it, "If you screw up the groundwater, it's going to cost you a lot of money." Most companies have detoxified their operations enough to comply with government regulations, substituting environmentally friendly soap and water and citrus juices for some of the nastiest chemical solvents, and eliminating most ozone-depleting chlorofluorocarbons (CFCs) from the production process.

According to Smith, pollution has been reduced per unit of production, but the units are on the rise. "It's worse in the sense that there's a lot more high-tech manufacturing. That creates more stress on the environment as it requires more raw materials and generates more waste products."

In all likelihood the stress will continue to build: electronics is the world's largest and most rapidly expanding industry (nearly 140 new semiconductor manufacturing plants will be built worldwide before the turn of the century). And, says Smith, it's not realistic to think high-tech's growth can be quelled. Nor is that SVTC's goal. "We don't go out there shouting, 'No nukes.' It's more important to get inside the industry to establish environmental ethics within each company."

In November 1996, the EPA and the Clinton administration granted Arizona-based Intel, the world's largest semiconductor manufacturer, the right to change production processes without continually applying to the government for new permits designed to control toxic emissions. This gave Intel a competitive advantage over the rest of the semiconductor industry, where the latest, fastest technology is constantly evolving and the winner breaks the market first. "Intel and Microsoft try to get consumers to buy new gadgets every fourteen months," says Smith. "I don't see how that can continue."

Although environmentalists are critical of such giant steps toward deregulation, many of those in the semiconductor business are making an effort to move in the right direction. SEMATECH, a nonprofit consortium of eleven semiconductor manufacturers (including IBM and Motorola) based in Austin, Texas, has a $200 million annual budget, half of which is paid for by taxpayers through the U.S. Department of Defense. Ten percent of that ($10 million) has been earmarked for research on environmentally friendly technology. Miller Bonner, a spokesperson for SEMATECH, says that member companies are working to address environmental issues in the semiconductor industry. Says Bonner, "Finding the means of reducing the use of hazardous or dangerous chemicals is in our best interest."

Understanding the Text

1. Summarize the environmental hazards of microchip production, as described by Hayhurst.
2. What advantages was Intel granted that might affect future toxic-waste production?
3. What have been the local and national governmental responses to high-tech pollution, according to this selection? What differences are there?

Exploring and Debating the Issues

1. Do you agree or disagree with the U.S. government's granting Intel the right to change production processes without requiring new permits to control toxic emissions?
2. In an essay, explore the advice the residents of Kettleman City might give to Santa Clara County residents worried about high-tech pollution. How might economic self-interest influence the Santa Clarans' response to that advice?
3. In class, debate whether future economic growth in Silicon Valley is worth the cost of further toxic pollution.
4. Read or reread James J. Rawls's "California: A People, A Place, A Dream" (p. 8), and write an essay arguing whether the toxic pollution Hayhurst describes calls into question the California dream.

JUDITH STACEY

Land of Dreams and Disasters: Postindustrial Living in the Silicon Valley

When many people think of high-tech hotshots, they usually imagine nerdy young men wearing pen shields in their pockets. But when **Judith Stacey** (b. 1943) looks at the information industry, she sees men — and that's the problem. For with all the ballyhooing of the information superhighway and its expressways to prosperity, most of those on the road belong to the traditional power structure, leaving women and minorities on the sidelines. In this selection, which first appeared in her book *Brave New Families: Stories of Domestic Upheaval in Late Twentieth-Century America* (1998), Stacey explores the high-tech hierarchy and its implications for the future of the American family in the postindustrial era. Stacey is also the author of *In the Name of the Family: Rethinking Family Values in the Postmodern Age* (1996).

> When I moved here, there were orchards all around, and now there are integrated-circuit manufacturing plants all around. . . . that's been the thrill, because I've been part of it, and it's the most exciting time in the history of the world, I think. And the center of it is here in Silicon Valley.
>
> — *Female engineer at Hewlett-Packacrd, quoted in* San Jose Mercury News, *19 February 1985*

> You know what San Jose reminds me of? It's kind of a cow town in my estimation; it cracks me up that there's all this big stuff going on, this big industry, and Silicon Valley and everything. I mean, when I was a kid and my grandparents lived in Santa Cruz and we drove through San Jose, this was like a dust spot. You know, you got dust on your windshield when you drove through this valley. My uncle was an apricot and almond orchard man around here, and there wasn't anything in San Jose. San Jose was a town south of Oakland, south of the city; it was this little spot over there, and you passed it when you went to Santa Cruz or went down South.
>
> — *"Jan," interviewed August 1984*

A s the seedbed and international headquarters of the electronics industry, the Silicon Valley has been in the vanguard of postindustrial social transformations. Few could have been more astonished by this development than working people who inhabited the region before its technological makeover. In the 1950s, those who occupied Santa Clara County, a sprawling, fertile plain along the southern shore line of San Francisco Bay, inhabited a sparsely populated agribusiness area, one of the world's major prune and apricot suppliers, then known locally with pride, as "the garden of heart's delight." Most likely they worked on farms or in the canneries and food-processing plants that supplied the county's scant eight thousand manufacturing jobs. In 1955 they might have garnered a small share of benefits from the county's peak orchard production year without ever suspecting that local fruit groves were about to disappear even more precipitously than the modern families that tended or admired them.[1]

Residents in the 1950s could not have known that the northern portion of their county was about to become the "Silicon Valley." During the next three decades, the developing electronics industry would convert the garden of heart's delight into a world-renowned high-tech center, regarded alternatively as the solution to American economic malaise or as the prophecy of its decline, a "valley of toxic fright."[2] With ample defense contract funding, Stanford University, located in Palo Alto along the northwest county border, spawned the prolific seeds of scientific industry in this hitherto bucolic valley. Between 1950 and 1980 silicon replaced noncitrus fruit as the region's principal product, the local population grew by more than 400 percent — from nearly 300,000 to more than 1.29 million people — and the region's economy, ecology, and social structure were unrecognizably transformed.[3]

During the 1960s and 1970s, while many urban industrial areas in the United States began to decline, Santa Clara County enjoyed spectacular economic growth. Between 1960 and 1975 county employment grew by 156 percent, three times the national rate, as local manufacturing jobs increased to 130,000 and auxiliary employment in construction and services expanded apace.[4] The electronics industry provided jobs for almost one of every three county workers, and it generated most of the construction and

[1]One of the best sources for data on the occupational transformation of Santa Clara County and a superb ethnographic study of the electronics industry is John Frederick Keller, "The Production Worker in Electronics: Industrialization and Labor Development in California's Santa Clara Valley," diss., U of Michigan, 1981. See also R. Gordon and Linda M. Kimball, "High Technology, Employment and the Challenges to Education" (Silicon Valley Research Group, Santa Cruz: U of California, 1985); Dennis Hayes, *Behind the Silicon Curtain: The Seductions of Work in a Lonely Era* (Boston: South End, 1989); Anna Lee Saxenian, "Silicon Chips and Spatial Structure: The Industrial Basis of Urbanization in Santa Clara County, California," thesis, U of California, Berkeley, 1980; Lenny Siegel and Herb Markoff, *The High Cost of High Tech: The Dark Side of the Chip* (New York: Harper, 1985); Michael S. Malone, *The Big Score* (Garden City, NY: Doubleday, 1985). For a more congratulatory portrait of the Valley, see Everett M. Rogers and Judith K. Larsen, *Silicon Valley Fever: Growth of a High-Technology Culture* (New York: Basic, 1984).

[2]Michael Eisenscher, "Chasing the High Tech Rainbow: Reality and Fantasy in the Valley of the Silicon Giants" (paper presented at the Marxist Scholarship Conference, U of California, Berkeley, 1987).

[3]US Bureau of the Census, *Census of Population: 1950, 1980*. Official estimates projected that in 1990 the county population would be 1,518,000. United Way of Santa Clara County, "A Community Challenged: A Public Report of Human Needs in Santa Clara County," 3.

[4]Keller, "Production Worker in Electronics," iv; Robert Howard, "Second Class in Silicon Valley," *Working Papers*, Sept.–Oct. 1981, 22.

service needs that employed the majority of the rest.[5] In those heady days, the media and even some scholars portrayed the Silicon Valley as a true-life American fairy tale, and few were the voices raised, or heard, in dissent. The mecca of the new technological entrepreneurs, its worshippers proclaimed, was a sunny land where factories resembled college campuses, where skilled, safe, and challenging work was replacing the monotonous, degrading, dangerous labors of the now-declining industries, and where American technical know-how and entrepreneurial spirit once again would rescue the flagging U.S. economy and better the lives of all.[6]

An unusually high proportion (25 percent) of the electronics industry did consist of the most highly educated and highly paid salaried employees in any U.S. industry — engineers and professionals employed in research and design. Along with those heralded health clubs and fitness tracks, they were offered exceptional challenges and economic opportunities. As in "traditional" industries, however, the vast majority of these most privileged employees were white men (89 percent males, 89 percent non-Hispanic whites). During those start-up years in the 1950s and 1960s the industry also employed white men in most of its production jobs where they too enjoyed unusual opportunities. Even those with very limited schooling could advance into technical ranks, particularly those whom the military had first trained in mechanics before depositing them conveniently in nearby bases.[7]

But as the electronics industry matured, it feminized (and minoritized) its workforce, turning increasingly to female, ethnic minority, and recent migrant workers to fill production positions that offered far fewer advancement opportunities. By the late 1970s the industry's occupational structure was crudely stratified by gender as well as by race and ethnicity. White men were at the top, white women and ethnic minorities at the bottom. Almost half the employees were assembly workers and operatives; three-fourths of these were women, and 40 percent were minorities. Two groups of workers made up the middle: the moderately well-paid technicians and craft workers, also primarily Anglo males but into whose ranks women and Asians were making some inroads, and the clerical workforce composed over-

5

---

[5]Employment Development Department, "Future of Silicon Valley" (San Francisco: State of California, 1987), 2.

[6]See, for example, Rogers and Larsen, *Silicon Valley Fever*, and Moira Johnston, "High Tech, High Risk, and High Life in Silicon Valley," *National Geographic* 162.4 (October 1982): 459–76. Hayes discusses additional examples of this celebratory literature in *Behind the Silicon Curtain*, chapter 1. According to Siegel and Markoff, *High Cost of High Tech* (5), as recently as 1984 delegations of economic development officials headed by the king of Sweden and the presidents of Austria and France visited the Silicon Valley.

[7]For data on the occupational structure of the electronics industry, see Keller, "The Production Worker in Electronics"; Gordon and Kimball, "High Technology, Employment"; Marcie Axelrad, *Profile of the Electronics Workforce in the Santa Clara Valley* (San Jose, CA: Project on Health and Safety in Electronics, 1979); Siegel and Borock, "Background Report on Silicon Valley" (prepared for US Commission on Civil Rights [Mountain View, CA: Pacific Studies Center, 1982]).

whelmingly of Anglo women. These middle-income jobs were declining, however; in Silicon Valley, as elsewhere in postindustrial America, growth of new jobs is at the top and the bottom.[8] The preferred labor pool for the bottom continued to grow here during the 1980s as the proportion of non-white county residents increased dramatically.[9]

The popular media image of egalitarian and innovative work relations symbolized by engineers in blue jeans working at computers in open cubicles masks the startlingly unequal, far-from-innovative working conditions with which the industry's production workers contend. Electronics remains the only nonunionized major industry in the United States, and its production workers earn lower wages and endure greater risks and hardships than do their counterparts in most "traditional" industries. In 1981, for example, electronics workers earned an average wage only 57 percent of that paid to auto and steel workers, despite the mandatory wage concessions extracted from the latter.[10] Ironically, the "clean rooms" in which many electronics workers toil are filled with highly toxic solvents. Almost half of the occupational illness cases reported among semiconductor workers involve systemic poisoning from toxic materials, and the rate of occupational illness in electronics production in California is three times as great as in other manufacturing occupations.[11] Many electronics firms operate around the clock and require production workers to accept night and weekend shifts as well as long and highly irregular schedules. Yet they offer workers no job security and subject them to frequent, sudden layoffs and forced vacations.

In 1974 the first major slump in the electronics industry signaled its inherent volatility. Dependent on defense contracts and highly turbulent global market conditions, the industry's boom-bust cycle and the high

[8]Gordon and Kimball, "High Technology, Employment," 34–35. For data on the declining middle in the Silicon Valley, see the Association of Bay Area Governments, cited in Karen J. Hossfeld, "Divisions of Labor, Divisions of Lives; Immigrant Women Workers in Silicon Valley," diss., U of California, Santa Cruz, 1988, 39–40. See also sources cited in note 7.

[9]Official estimates suggest that between 1980 and 1990 the white population declined from 71 percent to 62 percent, while the nonwhite population rose to 38 percent. The Hispanic population grew from 17.5 percent to 20.6 percent, while the influx of Southeast Asian refugees rose from 8 to 14 percent of the total. United Way of Santa Clara County, "A Community Challenged" (pamphlet prepared by United Way of Santa Clara County, CA, Oct. 1989), 3–4.

[10]Eisenscher, "Chasing the High Tech Rainbow." According to Gordon and Kimball, "High Technology, Employment," 32, in 1984 the average starting hourly wage for unskilled electronics workers was between $3.50 and $5.50; that same year the average hourly wage for all production workers in electronics was $8.89 compared with $13.28 in petroleum and coal, $13.09 in steel, and $12.64 in the auto industry. Keller, "Production Workers in Electronics," argues persuasively that the largely unorganized character of the county workforce was a significant factor in its attractiveness to electronics corporate developers and that union-prevention policies have been an important priority of the industry.

[11]Eisenscher, "Chasing the High Tech Rainbow"; Hayes, *Behind the Silicon Curtain*, 65.

failure rate of firms promised recurrent unemployment. Corporate strategists began to ship many production jobs to cheaper labor areas in the United States and abroad and to replace "permanent" workers with a flexible fleet of what soon became the highest concentration of "temporary" workers in the nation — workers, that is, who lack all employee benefits.[12]

By ... 1984, "Silicon Valley fever" had begun to subside as most county residents directly or indirectly suffered ill effects of the electronics industry's previously concealed "downside." Increasing numbers of residents were out of work, and the entry-level work available promised few prospects for a family wage. Local unemployment rates rose in the 1980s, escalating sharply during the industry's severe prolonged slump in 1984 and 1985. Even after that recession had bottomed out, untrained, entry-level workers found that their best employment prospects were not in the electronics industry but as hotel housekeepers and security guards.[13]

Employed and unemployed alike suffered from the industry's destruction of their once-bucolic environment. As cancer rates and birth defects in the county rose alarmingly, outraged residents discovered that their water supplies had been contaminated by more than one hundred industrial chemicals that were known or suspected to be carcinogens, mutagens, or teratogens.[14] Air pollution and nightmarish traffic, predictable products of the region's decades of untrammeled, unplanned development, destroyed the celebrated quality of life that had once enticed so many to the fabled region. And yet the cost of living rose as sharply as the quality of life declined. This was not an anomaly; rather, as urban analyst Annalee Saxenian has demonstrated, it is a case of chickens fed by the industry's stratified employment policies now come home to roost. The skewed salaries that the industry paid its sizable professional and managerial elite raised local housing costs to among the highest in the nation, beyond the reach of its underpaid, often underemployed production workers.[15] The local media began to treat its audiences to the embarrassing spectacle of mounting

[12]Gordon and Kimball, "High Technology, Employment," 58. Also see David Beers, "Temps: High-Tech's Ace in the Hole," *San Bernardino Sun*, 28 May 1985, and David Beers, "Tomorrowland," *Image, San Francisco Examiner Magazine*, 18 Jan. 1987.

[13]Employment Development Department, "Annual Planning Information, San Jose Metropolitan Statistical Area 1987 to 1988" (San Francisco: State of California, Sept. 1987), 1.

[14]Eisenscher, "Chasing the High Tech Rainbow"; Malone, *Big Score*, 411–23. Carcinogens increase cancer rates, mutagens increase genetic defects, and teratogens increase birth defects.

[15]Saxenian, "Silicon Chips and Spatial Structure." Between 1970 and 1975 national housing costs rose 68 percent, while in the Silicon Valley they rose 92 percent. Rising housing costs outpaced earnings; between 1970 and 1976 family income rose 42.5 percent, but home costs rose 150 percent. See Alan Bernstein et al., "Silicon Valley: Paradise or Paradox?" (pamphlet prepared by Pacific Studies Center, Mountain View, CA, Oct. 1987), 43. As an example, Malone notes that four-bedroom homes bought new in 1965 for $15,000 were sold in 1980 for $200,000. Malone, *Big Score*, 335.

homelessness in the land of affluence. Most of the new homeless, moreover, were family units.[16]

Local and national media became more consistently preoccupied with   10
the escalating narcotics problems of the postindustrial era, and here too the
Silicon Valley gave cause for grave alarm. Illegal drug use in the county seat
cost its residents $500 million annually, and the region gained an unenviable reputation as the state capital for the use of PCP, a potent animal tranquilizer that induces behavior so violent that local police identify it as "the
single highest cause of officer injury in this department."[17] The federal Drug
Enforcement Agency identified Silicon Valley as "one of the biggest cocaine
users in the United States."[18] Drug dealing offered an irresistible occupational alternative to mounting legions of unemployed youth. Indeed the
electronics industry offered many workers on-the-job training in drug dependency, as foremen and coworkers distributed drugs to sustain workers
through the monotony and stress of lengthy shifts and speedups. More than
35 percent of the electronics employees surveyed by the *San Jose Mercury
News* in 1985 acknowledged using illicit drugs on the job.[19] In 1988 the
county Board of Supervisors and the San Jose City Council approved higher
bail and longer jail sentences for dealers as they passed a resolution introduced by a coalition of local church groups stating that "drugs represent a
severe health epidemic which is destroying the lives of our families and the
future of our community."[20]

Such regional maladies may have failed to shake the faith of some high-tech devotees, like the female engineer at Hewlett-Packard quoted at the
beginning of this essay, but in the 1980s more people declared themselves
eager to leave than to enter the South Bay futureland. Population growth in
Santa Clara County slowed considerably after 1980, falling below California

[16]While it is not possible to compile an accurate count of the homeless, the Santa
Clara County Office of Human Relations estimated that there were at least 13,495 homeless individuals residing in the county in 1985, 18,956 homeless in 1986, and 19,600 in
1989. United Way of Santa Clara County, "A Community Challenged," 17.

[17]Ray Tessler, "Churches' Holy War on Drugs," *San Francisco Chronicle*, 19 May 1988;
Hayes, *Behind the Silicon Curtain*, 22.

[18]Malone, *The Big Score*, 398. Also see Malone for accounts of drug use in the electronics industry.

[19]See Pete Carey and Alan Gathright, "By Work Obsessed: The Silicon Valley Ethics,"
San Jose Mercury News, 17–23 Feb. 1985. According to the *Mercury* survey, 35.3 percent of
electronics employees reported using narcotics while at work, while 43.6 percent reported
alcohol consumption; the comparable figures for employees in nonhigh-tech jobs was
23.5 percent for narcotics and 30.8 percent for alcohol. For personal testimony on the extensive use of drugs on electronics production lines, see Malone, *Big Score*, 5–6, 403–11.

[20]Tessler, "Churches' Holy War on Drugs." In 1989, when the total Santa Clara
County population numbered approximately 1.5 million people (of all ages), the County
Bureau of Drug Abuse Services estimated that approximately 112,000 were drug users. Of
these, 52,640 were daily users and 14,213 were using heroin. United Way, "A Community
Challenged," 18.

rates. As the decade neared its close, a Bay area poll found the once-glorified Silicon Valley to be the least popular county in the region. Almost half the county residents queried claimed they would prefer to live somewhere else.[21] It was a twist of cruel irony, therefore, when in 1989 Hewlett-Packard — the area's preeminent high-tech firm, credited by many with creating the Silicon Valley — cited the region's spiraling cost of living as the basis for its decision to move 10 percent of its computer manufacturing operations to a less-populated California valley.[22]

While the changing character of work in the Silicon Valley commanded global attention, most outside observers overlooked concurrent gender and family changes that preoccupied many residents. In earlier, self-congratulatory days, before the national political climate made feminism seem a derogatory term, local public officials liked to describe San Jose, the county seat, as a feminist capital. The city elected a feminist mayor and hosted the statewide National Organization for Women convention in 1974. Santa Clara soon became one of the few counties in the nation that could boast of having elected a female majority to its Board of Supervisors. In 1981 high levels of feminist activism made San Jose the site of the nation's first successful strike for a comparable-worth standard of pay for city employees. And, according to sociologist Karen Hossfeld, young working-class women who vehemently rejected a feminist identity took for granted women's rights to political and economic equality and to control their own sexuality.[23]

It should come as no surprise, therefore, that during these postindustrializing decades the Silicon Valley has also been the site of a significant degree of family turbulence. Much of the data on local family changes represent an exaggeration of the national trends described in the last chapter. For ex-

[21]Between 1980 and 1986, the region grew at a rate of 8 percent compared with 14 percent for the state; 85 percent of the region's growth was due to natural increase. See Employment Development Department, "Annual Planning Information," 1. The Bay area regional "popularity" poll is reported in Carl Nolte, "The North Bay Is Where Most Folks Want to Live," *San Francisco Chronicle*, 22 Feb. 1989: A6.

[22]John Schneidawind, "New Flight from Silicon Valley's High Costs," *San Francisco Chronicle*, 11 May 1989: 1.

[23]Janet Flammang, "Filling the Party Vacuum: Women at the Grassroots Level in Local Politics," *Political Women: Current Roles in State and Local Government* (Beverly Hills: Sage, 1984), 87–113, "Female Officials in the Feminist Capital: The Case of Santa Clara County," *Western Political Quarterly* 38.1 (1985): 94–118, and "Women Made a Difference: Comparable Worth in San Jose," *The Women's Movements of the United States and Western Europe*, ed. Ira Katznelson and Carole Mueller (Philadelphia: Temple University P, 1987), 290–309; Linda Blum, *Between Feminism and Labor: The Significance of the Comparable Worth Movement* (Berkeley: U of California P, 1992). Ironically, the San Jose comparable-worth strike was called when the feminist mayor and the city council — on which women held the majority of seats — failed to meet the city employees' demand to proceed on a proposed job study prerequisite to evaluating pay equity. For attitudes of Silicon Valley working-class women toward feminism, see Hossfeld, "Divisions of Labor," 356–63.

ample, while the national divorce rate was doubling after 1960, in Santa Clara County it nearly tripled. By 1977 more county residents filed divorce papers than registered marriages. By 1980 the divorce rate in the county seat ranked ninth among U.S. metropolitan areas, higher than Los Angeles or San Francisco. Likewise the percentage of "nonfamily households" grew faster in the Silicon Valley than in the nation, and abortion rates were one and one-half times the national figures. And although the percentage of single-parent households was not quite as high as it was in the nation as a whole, the rate of increase was more rapid.[24] The high marriage casualty rate among workaholic engineers was dubbed "the silicon syndrome."[25] County social workers and residents with whom I spoke in the mid-1980s shared an alarmist view of the fate of family life in their locale summarized in the opening lines of a feature article in a local university magazine: "There is an endangered species in Silicon Valley, one so precious that when it disappears Silicon Valley will die with it. This endangered species is the family. And sometimes it seems as if every institution in this valley — political, corporate, and social — is hellbent on driving it into extinction."[26]

These concurrent changes in occupational, gender, and family patterns make the Silicon Valley a propitious site for exploring the ways in which "ordinary" working people have been remaking their families in the wake of postindustrial and feminist challenges. The Silicon Valley is by no means a typical or "representative" U.S. location, but precisely because national postindustrial work and family transformations were more condensed, rapid, and exaggerated there than elsewhere, they should be easier to perceive. Yet most popular and scholarly literature about white working-class people portrays them as the most traditional, as the last bastion, that is, of the modern family. Relatively privileged members of the white working class are widely regarded as the bulwark of the Reagan revolution and the constituency least sympathetic to feminism and family reforms.[27] Those

---

[24]For data on divorce rates and household composition for Santa Clara County in comparison with California and the United States as a whole, see US Bureau of the Census, *Census of Population* for 1960, 1970, and 1980. During the 1970s the county recorded 660 abortions for every 1,000 live births, compared with a statewide average of 489.5 and a ratio of less than 400 for the nation. See US Bureau of the Census, *Statistical Abstract of the United States, 1981*. Also see Malone, *Big Score*, 395.

[25]Jean Hollands, *Silicon Syndrome: Survival Handbook for Couples* (Palo Alto, CA: Coastlight, 1983).

[26]Malone, "Family in Crisis."

[27]For literature describing working-class families as favoring "traditional" gender arrangements, see Mirra Komarovsky with Jane H. Philips, *Blue-Collar Marriage* (New York: Random, 1962); Lillian Rubin, *Worlds of Pain: Life in a Working Class Family* (New York: Basic, 1976); Susan Householder Van Horn, *Women, Work and Fertility* (New York: New York UP, 1988); Theodore Caplow et al., *Middletown Families* (Toronto: Bantam, 1983); and Robert Coles and June Hallowell Coles, *Women of Crisis: Lives of Struggle and Hope* (New York: Delacorte/S. Lawrence, 1978). In *Fear of Falling* (New York: Pantheon, 1989), Barbara Ehrenreich argues that the media constructed this stereotype of the blue-collar working class after they briefly "discovered" this class in 1969.

whose hold on the accoutrements of the American Dream is so recent and tenuous, it is thought, have the strongest incentives to defend it. Curiously, however, few scholars have published book-length, in-depth studies of such families in recent years.[28]

Conventional images of progressive, middle-class families embracing   15
egalitarian changes in gender and work patterns that "traditional" — that is to say, "modern" — working-class families resentfully resist fail to recognize the complexity, fluidity, and unresolved character of contemporary gender, class, and family arrangements. Only ethnographic research, I have come to believe, can capture this complexity sufficiently to dispel distortions in the popular clichés. . . . Indeed, working people . . . have served as the unrecognized pioneers of the postmodern family revolution.

Understanding the Text

1. According to Stacey, what is the employment hierarchy in Silicon Valley?
2. What, in Stacey's view, have been the social and economic downsides of Silicon Valley prosperity?
3. Why is the family, in Stacey's words, "an endangered species" (para. 13) in Silicon Valley?
4. Define in your own words what Stacey means when she refers to a "post-industrial" (para. 14) world.

Exploring and Debating the Issues

1. Compare the tone and content of Stacey's selection with that of Michael J. Mandel ("Silicon Valley: Taking Its Place in the Pantheon," p. 285). Which article do you find more persuasive, and why?
2. This selection was originally published in 1990, during a downturn in Silicon Valley's fortunes. How do you think the prevailing economic climate might have affected Stacey's essay?

[28]Joseph T. Howell's *Hard Living on Clay Street: Portraits of Blue Collar Families* (Garden City, NY: Anchor, 1973), the last ethnographic book about blue-collar white families in the United States that I know of, now is seventeen years old. Rubin's *Worlds of Pain*, a widely used interview study of working-class families, appeared in 1976. A recent invaluable ethnography of blue-collar men, however, makes a crucial contribution to an analysis of contemporary working-class family life. In *America's Working Man* (Chicago: U of Chicago P, 1984), David Halle recognizes the inadequacy of conventional formulations of working-class families and the methods employed by studies of these which fail to address the fluidity and ambiguity of family class positions, particularly in a period when more women are in the paid labor force than not. For these reasons, Halle scrupulously restricts his book title to designate its actual subject, working-class men. Unfortunately, he often fails to honor his own critique because he identifies working-class homes, neighborhoods, and so on, on the basis of husbands' occupations alone.

3. To what extent does Stacey's description of Silicon Valley support, challenge, or qualify James J. Rawls's vision of the California dream (see "California: A People, A Place, A Dream," p. 8)?

4. Stacey describes several media depictions of Silicon Valley. Visit your college library, and research current media portrayals of the region in popular magazines such as *Time* and *Newsweek*. Write an essay in which you analyze these images. Do they resemble the ones Stacey describes? How can you explain your findings?

LARY MAY

The New Frontier: "Hollywood," 1914–1920

When we think of the movies, we think of Hollywood. Indeed, the very word is shorthand for the entire film industry. But why did movieland come to Hollywood in the first place? After all, New York was the theater capital of America in the early days of the film industry, and yet in a few short years Broadway was overshadowed by Sunset Boulevard, and the world has never looked back. In this selection, **Lary May** (b. 1944) explains how it happened and why it happened, pointing not only to the fabled climate that made Hollywood a convenient site for year-round moviemaking but also to the men, most of them Eastern European Jewish immigrants, who built Hollywood around their own special vision of New World opportunity and freedom. The author of *Screening Out the Past: The Birth of Mass Culture and the Motion Picture Industry* (1983), from which this selection is taken, May is also the editor of *Recasting America: Culture and Politics in the Age of Cold War* (1989).

> All their lives they had slaved at some kind of dull, heavy labor, behind desks and counters, in the fields and at tedious machines of all sorts, saving their pennies and dreaming of the leisure that would be theirs when they had enough. Finally, the day came ... where else should they go, but to California, the land of sunshine and oranges.
>
> — *Nathanael West,* The Day of the Locust *(1939)*[1]

No matter how exaggerated his account may have been, Nathanael West caught the spirit of a modern vision, unique to America. Fans in the sumptuous movie house did not merely sit in an oasis of luxury in a barren land. Rather, it was possible to take much of the celluloid experience home with them. Yet they needed experts to show them how. In response to that need, the motion picture industry began to build a film capital on the West Coast. Other countries also centralized studios; but in America the production site was surrounded by a community where the stars really lived the

---

[1]Nathanael West, *The Day of the Locust,* New York, 1939, pp. 130–31.

happy endings, in full view of the nation. Here moviedom became much more than something seen on the screen or touched in the theater. At a time when the birth of a modern family and consumption ideals might have remained just a cinematic fantasy, Hollywood showed how it could be achieved in real life. Out in California, stars participated in an exciting existence, free from the former confinements of work and Victorianism. With this leisure utopia before the viewer's eyes, they might learn how to regenerate the frontier in new ways for the twentieth century.

To grasp the significance of this West Coast creation, we have to first confront earlier explanations of why the movie industry came to Southern California. A generation of film scholars have offered two basic reasons.[2] One was that the climate was ideal for filmmaking. In this region, Mediterranean balmy weather made it possible to film outdoors all year round, without the hindrance of snow or rain. Moreover, the area included deserts, mountains, and seashore, all near by. The second argument claims that, to escape Edison's trust, independents moved to the far end of the continent where they could flee quickly into Mexico if confronted with court subpoenas or demands for their pirated cameras.

Yet on examination, neither of these factors can explain the move. Filmmakers had survived Eastern weather for over twenty years, going to Florida, the Caribbean, or other winter filming locations including California, if sunny weather was required. In 1913, there were twenty film companies in New York, Philadelphia, and Chicago, and only four on the West Coast. Two of these were in California, but only one was in Los Angeles. On top of that, if proximity to Mexico had been a decisive factor in the patent war, independents would have gone to San Diego, two hundred miles closer to the border. But none did. There was also a violent and bloody revolution in Mexico at the time, which would have discouraged eager filmmakers. In fact, the first permanent studios in Los Angeles were established by solid members of the trust. More recent scholars offer an alternative to these views by pointing out that economic factors pushed the industry westward.[3] Though this is certainly part of the reason, it still does not explain why it took so long for moviemakers to see their interests in moving from east to west. No, something else was happening in Los Angeles besides escaping winters, trusts, and high costs.

To fathom this problem, we must realize that Hollywood emerged relatively late — over twenty years after Edison invented the camera, and over a decade and a half after the movies acquired a mass market. In retrospect, it

[2] For one among many see Arthur Knight, *The Liveliest Art*, New York, 1957, pp. 51–54.

[3] Anon., *How to Write a Photoplay*, New York, 1912, listed the addresses of all studios; "A History of Production in the East and West," *Directors Annual*, 1934, pp. 25–32, 325, in AMPASL. For example, *MPW*, January 1911, had notes from Los Angeles describing production on the West Coast, but it also had "notes" from Chicago; Boston; Jacksonville, Florida; Manhattan; Brooklyn; and San Juan, Puerto Rico. On the newer economic interpretation, see Robert Sklar, *Movie Made America*, New York, 1975, pp. 67–69.

is also clear that the West Coast production site would become more than merely a place to make films. Fan magazines, newspapers, and movies themselves would spotlight the comings and goings of movie stars — a lifestyle that was dramatically different from that of the nineteenth or even early twentieth century. Shortly before there was a Hollywood, this imagery had just begun to be projected on the nation's screens, catering to the tastes of the newly found middle-class audience adjusting to the corporate order and a new morality. The new code generated the promise that if immigrants, as well as those rebelling from Victorianism, had money and white skin, the consumer ideal would be available to them. Another related phenomenon was the audience's demand to see this cultural mixing made real. It was not enough to see it on the screen or to touch it in the movie house. Stars had to make the happy ending an extension of their own lives, for fans had to see that their idols could make it a reality. Was it not possible, then, that profits could be enhanced by creating a modern utopia where the dream could come off the screen and into real life?

It took a new breed of producers to pull all of this together. In their business skills, backgrounds and aspirations, they were ideal generators of the move west, for that involved a total transformation of themes, stars, and theaters after 1914. Unlike the American Protestants who first made films, these men began as small proprietors and entered the business not as inventors, filmmakers, or even entertainers. Rather, they were theater owners from immigrant backgrounds. A few came from Germany, most from eastern Europe, but virtually all were Jews who entered the country as part of the late nineteenth-century wave of immigration. They proceeded to set up nickelodeons in their own neighborhoods and went on to build store fronts and luxury theaters in better neighborhoods as the market expanded. By 1913, several had become so aware of the new desires of the viewers, as well as the opportunities available in this marginal industry, that they entered production themselves and moved to Los Angeles. In the process, they expanded and consolidated casting, filming, and exhibiting, until by 1920 they held the reins of the "Big Eight" companies, and virtually monopolized the market.[4]

Why were the Jews able to realize fully the potential in the third stage of the industry's growth, from 1914 to 1920? In the first place, these recent immigrants brought cultural baggage to America that gave them several advantages, in the film industry as well as in the process of upward mobility. A number of scholars have shown how this group experienced more movement up the social ladder than any of their fellow immigrants. The film moguls participated in this ethnic success story and benefited from the traditions and

[4]The assumption that they entered production after 1912 comes from their various biographies, cited below. Leo Rosten's sociological study, *Hollywood: The Movie Colony and the Movie Makers*, New York, 1941, p. 61, lists the "Big Eight." See also Norman Freedman, "Hollywood: The Jewish Experience and Popular Culture," *Judaism*, Fall 1970, pp. 482–87.

circumstances that fed into it. Paradoxically, it was their outsider status in Europe that gave rise to many of these advantages. Discriminatory policies in Russia and other countries had made land ownership difficult and encouraged these outsiders to enter commercial trades. For hundreds of years, they lived in towns and cities of the Pale or eastern European ghettos, serving as small merchants or craftsmen for a rural hinterland. When industrialization spread from western to eastern Europe in the late nineteenth century, Jews were affected in two ways. It disrupted their status as small property owners and stimulated violent pogroms. Acutely aware of the power arrayed against them and accustomed to gauging it for centuries, many immigrated to America. And unlike Italians, Greeks, or other Southern Europeans, they came in family groups and did not look back nostalgically to a homeland. While others went back and forth, the Jews settled permanently with their kin in American cities. To facilitate matters, their experiences as shopkeepers and skilled workers gave them trades that could be utilized in a rapidly urbanizing country. At a time when most other immigrants, and Americans for that matter, came from rural backgrounds, the Jews as literate urban entrepreneurs had a great advantage. They quickly compensated for their relative lack of capital and began to climb the economic ladder.[5]

For the Jews who entered the movies, there was another element in their experience that contributed to their success. Because they had been outsiders, they were conditioned to seize new commercial opportunities that were not already monopolized by people of the host culture who might discriminate against them. In eastern and central Europe the landless Jews functioned as tradesmen on the margins of an agrarian society. In addition, since they were occasionally subject to removal, often forced to leave their homes at a moment's notice, many found it in their interests to have occupations not tied to land or solid property. European Jews thus became skilled at meeting the secondary or consumption desires of the surrounding group and finding opportunities on the fringes of society. In America's expanding economy, particularly in eastern cities like New York, these immigrants used their former skills to succeed in ready-made clothing, entertainment, and other entrepreneurial endeavors. Little wonder that moguls like Adolph Zukor started by selling furs, Samuel Goldwyn made gloves, Louis B. Mayer owned a burlesque house, and Carl Laemmle often compared selling movies with his experiences selling clothes. The garment trades in particular required a sensitivity to current styles. Critically important in all these skills was the ability to suspend one's own tastes and calcu-

---

[5]On the uniqueness of the Jews, see Nathan Glazer, "The American Jew and the Attainment of Middle Class Rank: Some Trends and Explanations," in Marshall Sklare, ed., *The Jews: Social Patterns of an American Group*, Glencoe, Illinois, 1958, pp. 138–46. For their economic position, skills, and sexual demography, as well as their status in Europe, see Simon Kuznets, "Immigration of Russian Jews to the United States: Background and Structure," *Perspectives in American History* 10, 1976, pp. 35–124. On mobility compared to others, see Stephan Thernstrom, *The Other Bostonians: Poverty and Progress in the American Metropolis, 1880–1970*, Cambridge, Mass., 1973, pp. 136–37, 142–43, 162–65.

late the desires of others. These movie executives cultivated this art, giving them an advantage in a marginal industry which appealed to consumer styles. Since film was a product geared to subjective rather than material needs, the Jews moved into the field with ease. To sharpen his perceptions, Samuel Goldwyn would sit in the front of the audience with his back to the screen, watching the viewers' reactions to the celluloid image. He explained the methods this way:

> If the audience don't like a picture, they have a good reason. The public is never wrong. I don't go for all this thing that when I have a failure, it is because the audience doesn't have the taste or education or isn't sensitive enough. The public pays the money. It wants to be entertained. That's all I know.[6]

Using skills like these, the moguls gained spectacular success in the movies. But their rise was not merely the realization of American individualism. Rather, these leaders combined a strong sense of commercial opportunity with the realization that, as in the shtetl, they could only make it if they cooperated. Abraham Bisno, an organizer of garment unions in New York and Chicago, articulated this tendency. In the old country, he argued, the aristocracy lived for the past, the peasants for the present, and the Jews for future opportunities. That spirit carried in the new world as well. Nicholas Schenck, who became head of United Artists, admitted, "Yes, I've done all right for an immigrant boy, it could only happen in this country. . . . unfortunately it is not always greatness that takes a man to the top. It is a gambling spirit. I used every bit of my ability at dangerous times, while other men slowed down at the curves." Yet linked to this risk-taking drive was a strong sense of group cohesion. Even the reckless Schenck never abandoned his ethnic or family ties: he and his brother Joseph often worked together. Following the same pattern, Sam and Jack Warner were brothers and partners; Jesse Lasky and Samuel Goldwyn, Sam Katz and A. J. Balaban were brothers-in-law and partners, and Carl Laemmle became famous for what was probably typical, hiring scores of relatives to work in his Universal Studio.[7]

Each of these producers made films and statements filled with patriotism. Obviously this was good for business. But it also helps explain their rise, for America appeared to offer the full flowering of aspirations that were often thwarted in the old country. Perhaps the strongest impetus flowed from secularization and enlightenment. Late in the nineteenth century, a number of European countries granted civil rights to Jews, providing the

[6]On moveable trades, particularly clothing, see Kuznets, "Immigration," pp. 56–57, 104–13. *Today's Living*, August 9, 1959, p. 8, untitled clipping, Goldwyn File, MOMA.

[7]Abraham Bisno, *Bisno, Union Pioneer*, Madison, Wisconsin, 1967, pp. 5–45; Alan Hynd, "Interview with Nicholas Schenck," *Liberty Magazine*, June 28, 1941, p. 8. On Jesse Lasky and Samuel Goldwyn, see "Obituary," *Los Angeles Times*, February 1, 1974; on Balaban and Katz, see Carrie Balaban, *Continuous Performance: The Story of A. J. Balaban as Told to His Wife*, New York, 1942, p. 74; for Zukor and Loew see Adolph Zukor, *The Public Is Never Wrong*, New York, 1953, p. 237. On Laemmle's policy at Universal see undated clipping, Laemmle File, MOMA.

first step toward full participation in the host culture. When emancipation merged with the deep millennial traditions within Judaism, the result was a cultural renaissance that yielded a tremendous potential to change both Jewish life and the wider world. Some Jews responded to this promise through movements like Hassidism or reinvigorated orthodoxy. Other theological innovations involved a move toward liberal and conservative brands of the faith. Still others reached out for the secular world. In artistic circles, a flowering of rich poetry and literature occurred in Yiddish as well as the host cultures' tongues. Jews who saw a sharp contradiction between poverty and pogroms, and the promise of a new life, became Zionists, radicals, or enlightenment thinkers, in the new world as well as the old.

In America, all these tendencies would flourish, for those who wanted   10
an individualized secular millennium might see the promised land. Discrimination existed, but unlike Europe there were no strong anti-Semitic politics; and a separation of church and state encouraged Jews to enter the wider society. In addition, the religious structure of Judaism contributed to this process, for those who wished to make the choice. As one contemporary perceived, it was easier for these European pariahs to tap this opportunity than Catholic immigrants, accustomed to a hierarchical church and state, for "in its ecclesiastical institutions, no religion is more democratic than the Jews'. Among them there is no authority comparable to the Roman Catholic Pope, no denominational supervision, no ordained clergy. Any ten Jews can organize a synagogue or minyan, choose their own members and employ a rabbi." A decentralized structure also fostered assimilation into the expanding economy. Many had shed their Yiddish dialect, their distinctive clothes, and even their names in the process of Americanization and upward mobility. Every movie mogul went through at least part of this process. Some married Gentile women and retained their heritage not through orthodoxy but through liberal synagogues or charity organizations. Each might have agreed at one time or another with the highly assimilated hero of Abraham Cahan's brilliant novel, *The Rise of David Levinsky*, who saw that in the new country, provided one had the money, public equality at least appeared possible. Entering a dining car on a train where he joined a group of American businessmen, David remarked,

> But I was aware that it was "aristocratic" American food, that I was in the company of well-dressed American gentiles, eating and conversing with them, a nobleman among noblemen. I throbbed with love for America.[8]

---

[8]For a general study of the liberalizing trend, see Nathan Glazer, *American Judaism*, New York, 1957, and Harold Rosenberg, "Jewish Identity in an Open Society," in Harold Rosenberg, *Discovering the Present*, Chicago, 1973. Abraham Cahan, *The Rise of David Levinsky*, New York, 1917, pp. 329–30. For a similar drive among the moguls, see Samuel Goldwyn, *Behind the Silver Screen*, New York, 1923, pp. 1–35. Ray Stannard Baker, "The Disintegration of the Jews," *American Magazine*, October 1909, pp. 590–603, saw the Jews' religious structure similar to American values.

Optimism, however, only partially explains why Jews were so successful in the entertainment industry. Movies, after all, were not just another consumer product. They exemplified not just fun but the way the class order was changing. To seize this opportunity, the moguls combined business with their inherited traditions of expressiveness. In contrast to the dominant elements of nineteenth-century American culture, which were permeated with a code of self-denial, Jews were accustomed to a life that included a great deal of festivity. There is no question that Jewish tradition emphasizes a strong moral code and condemns hedonistic indulgence. Yet at the same time Yiddish folk culture encouraged celebrations distinctly different from the rituals of the Protestant middle classes and more in tune with their fellow immigrants. A rich tradition of humor formed a layer to soften the acute awareness of outsider status and was often used against the dominant group's pretensions and discrimination. Many religious holidays and Sabbath observances included music, singing, dancing, and did not forbid drinking — no small matter in a Victorian society often committed to blue laws and sobriety. Although Jews shared with Americans a taboo against premarital sex and a strong dedication to marital fidelity, women were considered sexual beings, a contrast to the ideals surrounding their Victorian sisters. Moreover, Jewish women of eastern Europe were never put on a pedestal; they functioned in the economy and participated in religious rituals in the home. Finally, Jews did not share the frugality of their Protestant peers. Money was not to be continually poured into business at the expense of enjoyment; rather, it was to provide the means for a life of comfort, even extravagance, when it could be afforded.

With this heritage, the Jewish film moguls were prepared to confront the changing moral values taking hold in the cities. The key to this process was timing. It was not enough that the Jews had skills in consumer trades and sensitivity to new trends or that they drew on a festive tradition. These advantages would have meant little fifty years earlier or later. But at the turn of the century, Jewish producers provided the missing link in the development of the motion picture industry. For the urban areas where the immigrants landed were soon to be the hotbeds of the revolution in manners and morals. Shrewd businessmen in the immigrant entertainment zones could see that as white-collar men and women incorporated the styles of foreigners and blacks, danced to ragtime, and patronized formerly working-class amusement parks, there was money to be made. As the press and vice reports asked whether this would lead to the disintegration of the home and the disorganization of the community, Jewish entrepreneurs could face this upheaval with optimism. According to the editor of the *Jewish Daily Forward*, the Lower East Side had become

a place where one descended in quest of esoteric types and local color; as well as for the purposes of philanthropy and uplift work. To spend an evening in some East Side cafe was regarded as something like spending a few hours at the Louvre; so much so that one such cafe, in the depths of

East Houston street, was making a fortune by purveying expensive wine dinners to people from uptown who came there ostensibly to see how the "other half lived" but who saw only one another eat and drink in freedom from restraint of manners.[9]

Cultural mixing also suggested the opening up of the class order and thereby drew on the Jews' millennial hopes in the new world. Formerly, middle-class values emanated from a Victorian heritage which in America was closely linked to a secularized, evangelical spirit. Newcomers from European countries who wanted to move up had a distinct advantage if they were also Anglo-Saxon Protestants, for their common background with the host culture provided few restrictions on assimilation. By the same token, Catholic or Eastern and Southern Europeans who wanted to rise had to shed many of their traditions, which the dominant group portrayed as vice-ridden and decadent. Only now, as modern Americans, symbolized by the movie stars, borrowed the dances, styles, and sports associated with immigrants, aspiring foreigners could elevate themselves without shedding all of their cultural past. In essence, as Anglo-Saxon city dwellers became more like their former "inferiors," it facilitated mobility from below. As this unfolded in the early stages of the motion picture industry, it could easily become linked to the utopian potential, the promise of a new America. . . .

In the Mediterranean climate, the twentieth-century quest for freedom from the past . . . took a romantic turn. Ever since the late nineteenth century, Americans coming into the area were struck by three things: the Spanish heritage, the climate, and the lack of industry. In this wide expanse of vacant land, evidences of the Spanish were visible all around. Besides the Mexican population, and the proximity of that Latin country, the Spanish-style architecture of haciendas and missions spread a romantic aura over the landscape. When this was coupled with the mild weather and proximity to beaches, mountains, and desert, the city offered a powerful drawing card to potential settlers. With no heavy manufacturing center or tenements, the population was less densely settled than in Eastern urban centers. Planners encouraged this through zoning and developing outlying tracts and linking them together with streetcar lines. In the unique urban-suburban mixture that resulted, developers lined the streets with imported palm trees. Boosters were careful to point out, however, that this romance and fair climate was "mediterranean" — the center of a sophisticated civilization — not "tropical" like savage lands.[10] As one of the city's major designers expressed

---

[9]On Jewish life and festivals in Europe, see Mark Zborowski and Elizabeth Herzog, *Life Is with People: The Culture of the Shtetl,* New York, 1952, especially pp. 409–30. Cahan, *Levinsky,* pp. 284–85.

[10]Fogelson, *Fragmented*; Warner, *Wilderness*, pp. 113–53; Gottleib and Wolt, *Thinking Big*, pp. 11–53. For a contemporary account of the romantic ambiance, with photographs and an analysis of Los Angeles architecture in the nineteenth and twentieth centuries, see Reyner Banham, *Los Angeles: The Architecture of Four Ecologies*, New York, 1971.

it, Los Angeles should not be dissipating, but "natural — for here nature and the trees are the thing. It should invite family outings, lovemaking, and a forgetfulness that cities are at hand."[11]

Given this vacationland potential, it is no wonder that the city's main   15 developer noted as early as 1909 that Los Angeles was "already the tourist metropolis of the country, the indirect profit through the attraction and retention of outsiders is certain and enormous."[12] No doubt the first testimony to this City Beautiful movement was in Pasadena, where wealthy Easterners built lavish winter homes. The crowning glory of this trend was Henry Huntington's Georgian palace, and its mammoth estate, complete with expansive lawns, statues, fountains, and dozens of gardens comprised of exotic plants from all over the world. As the homes in the city began to emulate this style in small with Spanish or Moorish motifs, a real estate developer, Abbot Kinney, took the next logical step. Near the Pacific Ocean he created an entire community modeled on Venice, Italy, complete with canals, gondolas, and a doge palace, surrounded with flamboyant homes he wished to sell to newcomers in search of fun and safe living. Developers then exploited this "site extraordinarily beautiful in topography and lavish in extent" by creating huge parks all over the city. Gradually, these elements combined to give Los Angeles the aura of a vacationland where families could settle in the sun, live, work, and play. Shrewd businessmen like Kenney were quick to capitalize on this: beach resorts, amusement parks, and restaurants proliferated. Movie houses cropped up everywhere — from none in 1900 to over five hundred by 1928. Finally, reformers in the Progressive era used vice laws to make these areas safe, so Los Angeles would become "the city most sought in the United States by pleasure lovers."[13]

Little wonder that movie makers were drawn to this "man-made, giant improvisation." If "there was never a region so unlikely to become a vast metropolitan area as Southern California," as its most perceptive historian, Carey McWilliams, noted, what better place for the movies? Besides the economic and political environment, it seemed an ideal locale where creative imaginations could flourish. Adolph Zukor led the way when in 1913 he brought his Famous Players in Famous Plays to Los Angeles. In his company was William de Mille, a noted Broadway producer and playwright who was captivated by the traditional imagery of the West. As de Mille crossed the Rockies, he found himself becoming "younger," for in the "new state" of

[11]Charles M. Robinson, *Los Angeles, The City Beautiful, Report of the Municipal Art Commission for the City of Los Angeles, California*, Los Angeles, 1909.

[12]Ibid.

[13]Ibid. For a brief account of Venice, built between 1905 and 1910, see Fred Basten, *Santa Monica Bay: The First Hundred Years*, Los Angeles, 1972. For the number of theaters in Los Angeles, seating capacity, and per-capita seats, see the elaborate listings in *The Film Daily Yearbook*, New York, 1927, pp. 100–105. In 1880 the city had only two theaters, seating six hundred each, and six concert halls. See Department of Commerce, Bureau of the Census, *Report on the Social Statistics of Cities*, Washington, D.C., 1886, p. 781. Charles Chaplin, *My Autobiography*, pp. 129–31. Robert O. Schad, *Henry E. Huntington*, San Marino, California, 1931.

California men could still escape the hierarchy and traditions of the East. In addition to "choosing one's inheritance," de Mille also saw that amid the sunshine and beauty, one could find a new life of freedom. Charles Chaplin, fresh from the slums of London in 1913, was even more enthralled. Los Angeles appeared truly the "land of the future, a paradise of sunshine, orange groves, vineyards, and palm trees. I was embued with it." Still another could link this new frontier to the old imagery, and see it now open to the children of immigrants like himself. As Jesse Lasky read a western tale on a train going to the land of sunshine, he wrote,

> I became again a child at my grandfather's knee....And every time I glanced out of the train window at the rolling prairies, the mountains, the desert, I saw the vast panorama of sky and earth forming a backdrop for those heroic souls whose first wagon train actually took much of the same route three-quarters of a century before . . . a migration but for which I myself would not have been born in my beloved California. Superimposing the past on the present . . . was an emotional, almost mystical experience.[14]

Film moguls brought this "mystical" atmosphere directly into their new studios, which differed dramatically from the ascetic and mundane production sites of the East. In New York, Chicago, Philadelphia, and Long Island, the studios sat primarily in downtown business sections or manufacturing areas. Producers used cheaply made warehouses and factories which were barren looking and almost indistinguishable from the surrounding commercial or industrial enterprises. Internal managements also reflected the strict Victorianism that tried to contain the dangerous potential of the movies. Griffith was not alone in his concern for propriety. At Vitagraph Studios in Brooklyn, the chief executive, Albert Smith, recalled that formality and full names were essential, for "this was part of a plan to exert every precaution in favor of our young actresses. While it may be regarded as unusual precaution on our part, we nevertheless ordered all couches removed from the dressing rooms and make-up areas."[15] In contrast to these entrepreneurial establishments, the modern corporate studios in Los Angeles created an atmosphere where moral experimentation could blossom.

Perhaps the best example of this was Universal City, built in 1913 by Carl Laemmle, the theater owner and former clothing salesman from Chicago. Surrounded by the hills and palm trees of the San Fernando Valley, the white, Spanish-styled studio buildings glowed in the sun. Touching

---

[14]McWilliams, *Southern California*; William de Mille, *Hollywood Saga*, New York, 1939, pp. 113–53. This is one of the best memoirs of the era; de Mille also saw land and labor as much cheaper than in the East, see pp. 44–45. Charles Chaplin, *My Autobiography*, pp. 130–31; Jesse Lasky, *I Blow My Own Horn*, New York, 1957, pp. 160–61.

[15]See "A History of Production in the East," pp. 25–32. An insightful view of the East Coast studios in the early days is in Chaplin, *My Autobiography*, pp. 170–77. See also "Essanay's New Studio in Chicago," *MPW*, July 11, 1914, p. 266. For the quote and studio policy of Vitagraph, see Smith, *Two Reels*, p. 212.

base with romanticism, the administration building followed the Spanish revival style. Yet it reflected a new America. Appropriately, Laemmle called his weekly column in the 1915 trade journal the "Melting Pot," for he glorified the Universal stars who rose up the ladder of success, shed their ethnic or Victorian pasts, and assumed a modern, healthy personality. Articles on current films hailed the sporty life. One starred Christy Mathewson, a pitcher for the New York Giants, who played a man bored with office work who turns to sports for fun and fortune. Other stories featured players having fun on the back lots, which included Roman, Athenian, Egyptian, or Parisian sets. Pictures showed the many exotic animals used in Universal films. In this cosmopolitan environment, as a studio flyer proclaimed, "Mexicans, Chinks, Indians and good Italians work, and such is the soothing climate of California that all these contrary entities live in harmony." All this rested on the high salaries and affluence that the new studios could provide, for the Los Angeles playland cost money. . . .

More than most industries, the studio also had a personnel turnover which suggested that the "new life" was open to youth and talent. Clearly, the studios existed in the corporate world, but they blended modern and traditional business styles. In other firms, upward mobility by no means ceased; but here, fame and success could happen quickly, without long apprenticeship or professional training. Film relied heavily on imagination, rather than heavy investments in elaborate machinery or scientific processes. After all, it took only a story, talent, and a camera to make a movie. But without the personal touch in advertising and selling, there could be no profits. Since the product also had to be in touch with the latest tastes and psychological needs, it was an ideal place for individuals to make it on their own ideas and talents. Then, with the children of immigrants in power, movie making appeared to offer a place where all newcomers could rise on ability, without having to face discriminatory employers or a rigid seniority system. Precisely because a volatile market encouraged mobility in the midst of bureaucratic hierarchy, one noted observer could describe the modern movie industry in nineteenth-century terms:

> the gold rush was probably the only other set up where so many people could hit the jackpot and the skids together. It has become a modern industry without losing that crazy feeling of a boom town.[16]

Yet this boom town opened to a much wider group of aspirants than   20
the older variety. For above all, Hollywood was an urban mobility ideal which had a much broader base than the traditional Protestant middle classes. Coming into the Los Angeles studios to create a modern life to

---

[16]In this regard the motion picture industry reflects more the type of organization prevalent in the clothing and cigar businesses than that of car production, flour milling, or steel. See Alfred Chandler, *The Visible Hand: The Managerial Revolution in American Business,* Cambridge, Massachusetts, 1977, pp. 209–39. Budd Schulberg, *What Makes Sammy Run?,* New York, 1941, pp. 213–14.

spread to the nation's cities were a new breed of people. The trade journals for the industry in 1920 list the personnel for the West Coast studios, and show that most of the movie creators came from those places where the film audience was largest. Over two-thirds of the American filmmakers were born in the 1890s in metropolitan areas, compared to less than one-third of their nonmovie peers. Over half of the writers, directors, editors, and players came from urban centers containing over 100,000 people in 1890, at a time when there were only twenty-eight such areas in the entire nation. The majority of the remainder came from Canadian or European cities. Thus, with five-sixths of the movie people coming from cities when most of the nation was still rural, they had a head start on their audience and were ideally qualified to create, propagate, and live a vision of modern urban life.[17]

It is well to keep in mind that this was a young cosmopolitan group. With the Jewish moguls on top and a large ethnic component among the rank and file, the creative personnel were already one step removed from the Victorian restraints holding earlier filmmakers. As the middle-class audience groped for ways to absorb foreign exoticism and youth, this collection of people was well suited to serve these needs as well. Those who created the aura — producers, directors, cinematographers, and set designers — came largely from European or Canadian backgrounds. Undoubtedly, this foreign contingent would appear larger if the trade journals had listed the parents' place of birth as well. Those who provided the models — actors and actresses — were overwhelmingly young. Two-thirds of them were under thirty-five. Moreover, three-fourths of the industry's female performers were under twenty-five. This suggests that the youth cult so necessary for uplifting "foreign" elements concentrated most heavily on women, who were responsible for making sensuality innocent.[18]

The industry's employees looked to Los Angeles for a vision of the new life, which included foreign touches filtered through an ever-widening Anglo-Saxon lens. One way to gauge this is to look at the writers who actually formulated the stories. Over 90 percent of them were born in America and had either higher education or journalism experience. This suggests an affluent group, since less than 10 percent of the population during the teens went to college, and publishing was not usually a commoner's trade. This was also the group most likely to include morally emancipated women, a factor also reflected in the industry. During the twenties, women comprised from one-third to one-half of the screenwriters. Although their numbers declined sharply in the following decades, they held prominent and influen-

---

[17] . . . The results of this study were gleaned from the *Motion Picture Directory and Trade Annual, 1920,* a source that gave the vital biographical information on the white-collar creative workers. This was compiled by Elaine Tyler May, "Who Put the Schmaltz on the Screen?" Master's thesis, UCLA, 1970. The comparison of 1890 comes from the listed birth places and dates in the *Directory,* then comparing them to city size as well as the urbanization of the nation in Bureau of the Census, *Population,* Washington, D.C., 1890.

[18] Ibid., Tables IV, V.

tial positions during the early Hollywood heyday.[19] In 1920, the forty top female writers were of middle-class Anglo-Saxon stock. None were of poor or worker origin. Like their male counterparts, most were college educated or had publishing backgrounds. Maturing in the Victorian twilight, they were captivated by urban life. From the memoirs of several, we can see that they were in the vanguard of moral experimentation, forging into dress reform, new sexual styles, and consumption. It is no accident that these forty females created over 70 percent of the stories written by women. Their plots overwhelmingly revolved around heroines like themselves.[20]

The movie personnel were thus well prepared to participate in one of the most striking features of modern filmdom. When the large contingent of urbanites, youthful players, foreigners, and women scenarists left studios like Universal, they went home to "Hollywood." Before 1916, Hollywood had been nothing more than a sleepy community of orange groves. But after the industry moved west, it came to symbolize the fruits of the screen and the Los Angeles paradise. It was not the locale of the studios; rather it was an almost mythic place where the movie folk spent money on personal expression. This consumption encouraged individual creativity and freedom, while it also served as a mark of success. A shrewd observer of the industry, producer William de Mille, saw that the movie people's "conspicuous consumption" gave status to an often routine job and reflected on the "company that paid you." As huge sums of money rolled in, the stars — who after all did not make a tangible product — used spending to validate their almost magical success. Mary Pickford saw her vast salary increases as the way to prove that she really had made it. Charles Chaplin had similar emotions but also envisaged extravagance as an exciting break from bourgeois restraints. He recalled that in 1914,

> I was reconciled to wealth but not to the use of it. The money I earned was legendary, a symbol in figures, for I had never actually seen it. I therefore had to do something to prove I had it. So I procured a secretary, a valet, a car, a chauffeur. Walking by the showroom one day, I noticed a seven-passenger Locomobile . . . the transaction was simple; it meant writing my name on a piece of paper. So I said wrap it up.[21]

[19]Ibid. In *The Directory*, editors and screen writers were listed together, and one-third were women. Since on the screen credits, editors were usually not women, we can assume that women writers in 1920 would constitute an even higher percentage. During the twenties, one-third of the screenwriters were women; see *The Film Daily Yearbook*, New York, 1925. The same source listed only one-sixth women screenwriters in 1940, one-twelfth in 1950 and 1960. In other words, the teens and twenties were the height of female involvement as screenwriters.

[20]The profile of the forty-one top screenwriters is from Daisann McLane, "Silent Sisters: Women Screenwriters in Hollywood, 1915–1929," Senior thesis, Princeton University, 1976. McLane drew on the writers' files in MOMAFL and LCPAL. That they focused on new women and consumption themes to the exclusion of others was gathered from a tabulation of listings in *The American Film Institute Catalogue*, in McLane, "Silent Sisters," pp. 60–96, Princeton University Library. Anita Loos, *A Girl Like I*, New York, 1960, pp. 1–100.

[21]"Movie Royalty Homes in California," *Photoplay*, June 1915, p. 23.

Because the consumption allure was the key to the Hollywood image, the star's life took on more than a private importance. In contrast to earlier stage personalities, film idols presented national models as leisure experts. As early as 1915, fan magazines showed how the star's domain reflected the Southern California style. In a city that contained few monuments or buildings reflecting the nineteenth-century Anglo-Saxon culture, there seemed to be a release from the restraint of tradition. Amid a virgin land of constant romance, it was easier to create a lifestyle frowned upon in the East. One tangible example was the expansion of domestic enjoyments and accoutrements far beyond their Victorian limitations. As Mary Pickford said of the estate that would soon be Pickfair, "Maybe this summer I will take a vacation, but if I do it will be right here in Los Angeles. I can't see why anyone would leave Los Angeles for a vacation." There were good reasons for this. Celebrity domiciles were located in the farthest reaches of this suburban city, removed from ethnic groups and business centers. The vague, mythic term "Hollywood" connoted a way of life unfolding in the exclusive neighborhoods of Beverly Hills, Santa Monica, and Brentwood. Freed from any nearby reminders of social responsibility, in areas cleansed through vice crusades, the stars could create a new, uplifted life without the inhibitions of the past. Usually homes drew on styles of European, African, or Asian aristocracy, reflecting not only high culture, but the quest for a more exotic life. Before the War, they were stately and classical. Always they were opulent, and mirrored cultivation and success. . . . [22]

Understanding the Text

1. What reasons have traditional film historians given for the fact that the movie industry centered in Southern California? How does May refute these explanations?

2. Why, according to May, were Jewish immigrants so well suited to founding the modern film industry?

3. How did Southern California become, in May's words, "a man-made, giant improvisation" (para. 16)?

4. How did the movie industry offer special opportunities for rapid social mobility to immigrants and nonimmigrants alike, in May's view?

5. How did Hollywood foster a new consumption-oriented culture free, in May's words, "from the restraint of tradition" (para. 24)?

---

[22]Pictures of these homes appear in Fred Basten, *Beverly Hills: Portrait of a Fabled City,* Los Angeles, 1975, pp. 61–66, 82–83. On the city free of vice and the suburban homes, see George Ade, "Answering Wild-Eyed Questions About the Movie Stars in Hollywood," *American Magazine,* May 1922, p. 52.

Exploring and Debating the Issues

1. Read or reread Denise S. Spooner's "A New Perspective on the Dream" (p. 22), and compare the reasons ordinary middle-class émigrés came to California with those of the film-industry insiders whom May describes.

2. Write an essay on the ways that Hollywood today continues to profit "by creating a modern utopia where the dream could come off the screen and into real life" (para. 4).

3. In the early years of Hollywood, Jewish actors and actresses tended to conceal their ethnic identities by changing their names. To what extent has this practice changed in contemporary Hollywood? How can you explain any changes?

4. May describes the ways in which the film industry encouraged a fantasy architecture that expressed romantic dreams and desires. Choose a well-known California theme park (such as Disneyland), and analyze the ways in which its architecture continues this tradition.

F. SCOTT FITZGERALD

FROM

The Last Tycoon

When he died suddenly of a heart attack in 1940, **F. Scott Fitzgerald** (1896–1940) had on his desk the manuscript of a novel that, even in its incomplete state, is considered one of the great Hollywood novels. By basing the characterization of its lead character, Monroe Stahr, on that of the legendary Hollywood studio czar Irving Thalberg, Fitzgerald — who was working in Hollywood at the time as a screenwriter — clearly intended to get at the heart of the new society growing up on the West Coast. Though unfinished, *The Last Tycoon* reveals the kind of human insight that Fitzgerald displays in *The Great Gatsby,* another American classic.

It was noon already and the conferees were entitled to exactly an hour of Stahr's time. No less, for such a conference could only be interrupted by a director who was held up in his shooting; seldom much more because every eight days the company must release a production as complex and costly as Reinhardt's "*Miracle.*"

Occasionally, less often than five years ago, Stahr would work all through the night on a single picture. But after such a spree he felt bad for days. If he could go from problem to problem there was a certain rebirth of vitality with each change. And like those sleepers who can wake whenever they wish, he had set his psychological clock to run one hour.

The cast assembled included, besides the writers Reinmund, one of the most favored of the supervisors, and John Broaca, the picture's director.

Broaca, on the surface, was an engineer — large and without nerves, quietly resolute, popular. He was an ignoramus and Stahr often caught him making the same scenes over and over — one scene about a rich young girl occurred in all his pictures with the same action, the same business. A bunch of large dogs entered the room and jumped around the girl. Later the girl went to a stable and slapped a horse on the rump. The explanation was probably not Freudian; more likely that at a drab moment in youth he had looked through a fence and seen a beautiful girl with dogs and horses. As a trademark for glamor it was stamped on his brain forever.

Reinmund was a handsome young opportunist, with a fairly good education. Originally a man of some character he was being daily forced by his anomalous position into devious ways of acting and thinking. He was a bad man now, as men go. At thirty he had none of the virtues which either native Americans or Jews are taught to think admirable. But he got his pictures out in time and by manifesting an almost homosexual fixation on Stahr, seemed to have dulled Stahr's usual acuteness. Stahr liked him — considered him a good all around man.

Wylie White, of course, would have been recognizable in any country as an intellectual of the second order. He was civilized and voluble, both simple and acute, half dazed half saturnine. His jealousy of Stahr showed only in unguarded flashes, and was mingled with admiration and even affection.

"The production date for this picture is two weeks from Saturday," said Stahr. "I think basically it's all right — much improved."

Reinmund and the two writers exchanged a glance of congratulation.

"Except for one thing," said Stahr, thoughtfully. "I don't see why it should be produced at all and I've decided to put it away."

There was a moment of shocked silence — and then murmurs of protest, stricken queries.

"It's not your fault," Stahr said. "I thought there was something there that wasn't there — that was all." He hesitated, looking regretfully at Reinmund: "It's too bad — it was a good play. We paid fifty thousand for it."

"What's the matter with it, Monroe?" asked Broaca bluntly.

"Well, it hardly seems worth while to go into it," said Stahr.

Reinmund and Wylie White were both thinking of the professional effect on them. Reinmund had two pictures to his account this year — but Wylie White needed a credit to start his comeback to the scene. Rose Meloney was watching Stahr closely from little skull-like eyes.

"Couldn't you give us some clue?" Reinmund asked. "This is a good deal of a blow, Monroe."

"I just wouldn't put Margaret Sullavan in it," said Stahr. "Or Colman either. I wouldn't advise them to play it — "

"Specifically, Monroe," begged Wylie White. "What didn't you like? The scenes? the dialogue? the humor? construction?"

Stahr picked up the script from his desk, let it fall as if it were physically, too heavy to handle.

5

10

15

"I don't like the people," he said. "I wouldn't like to meet them — if I knew they were going to be somewhere I'd go somewhere else."

Reinmund smiled but there was worry in his eyes.

20

"Well, that's a damning criticism," he said. "I thought the people were rather interesting."

"So did I," said Broaca. "I thought Em was very sympathetic."

"Did you?" asked Stahr sharply. "I could just barely believe she was alive. And when I came to the end I said to myself 'So what?'"

"There must be something to do," Reinmund said. "Naturally we feel bad about this. This is the structure we agreed on — "

"But it's not the story," said Stahr. "I've told you many times that the first thing I decide is the *kind* of story I want. We change in every other regard but once that is set we've got to work toward it with every line and movement. This is not the kind of a story I want. The story we bought had shine and glow — it was a happy story. This is all full of doubt and hesitation. The hero and heroine stop loving each other over trifles — then they start up again over trifles. After the first sequence you don't care if she never sees him again or he her."

25

"That's my fault," said Wylie suddenly. "You see, Monroe, I don't think stenographers have the same dumb admiration for their bosses they had in 1929. They've been laid off — they've seen their bosses jittery. The world has moved on, that's all."

Stahr looked at him impatiently, gave a short nod.

"That's not under discussion," he said. "The premise of this story is that the girl did have dumb admiration for her boss if you want to call it that. And there wasn't any evidence that he'd ever been jittery. When you make her doubt him in any way you have a different kind of story. Or rather you haven't anything at all. These people are extraverts — get that straight — and I want them to extravert all over the lot. When I want to do a Eugene O'Neill play I'll buy one."

Rose Meloney who had never taken her eyes off Stahr knew it was going to be all right now. If he had really been going to abandon the picture he wouldn't have gone at it like this. She had been in this game longer than any of them except Broaca with whom she had had a three day affair twenty years ago.

Stahr turned to Reinmund.

30

"You ought to have understood from the casting, Reiny, what kind of a picture I wanted. I started marking the lines that Carroll and MacMurray couldn't say and got tired of it. Remember this in the future — if I order a limousine I want that kind of car. And the fastest midget racer you ever saw wouldn't do. Now — " He looked around. " — Shall we go any farther? Now that I've told you I don't even like the kind of picture this is? Shall we go on? We've got two weeks. At the end of that time I'm going to put Carroll and MacMurray into this or something else — is it worth while?"

"Well, naturally," said Reinmund, "I think it is. I feel bad about this. I should have warned Wylie. I thought he had some good ideas."

"Monroe's right," said Broaca bluntly. "I felt this was wrong all the time but I couldn't put my finger on it."

Wylie and Rose looked at him contemptuously and exchanged a glance.

"Do you writers think you can get hot on it again?" asked Stahr, not un-   35
kindly. "Or shall I try somebody fresh?"

"I'd like another shot," said Wylie.

"How about you, Rose?"

She nodded briefly.

"What do you think of the girl?" asked Stahr.

"Well — naturally I'm prejudiced in her favor."   40

"You better forget it," said Stahr warningly. "Ten million Americans would put thumbs down on that girl if she walked on the screen. We've got an hour and twenty-five minutes on the screen — you show a woman being unfaithful to a man for one-third of that time and you've given the impression that she's one-third whore."

"Is that a big proportion?" asked Rose slyly, and they laughed.

"It is for me," said Stahr thoughtfully, "even if it wasn't for the Hays office. If you want to paint a scarlet letter on her back it's all right but that's another story. Not this story. This is a future wife and mother. However — *however —*"

He pointed his pencil at Wylie White.

" — this has as much passion as that Oscar on my desk."   45

"What the hell!" said Wylie. "She's full of it. Why she goes to — "

"She's loose enough," said Stahr, " — but that's all. There's one scene in the play better than all this you cooked up and you've left it out. When she's trying to make the time pass by changing her watch."

"It didn't seem to fit," Wylie apologized.

"Now," said Stahr, "I've got about fifty ideas. I'm going to call Miss Doolan." He pressed a button. " — And if there's anything you don't understand, speak up — "

Miss Doolan slid in almost imperceptibly. Pacing the floor swiftly Stahr   50
began. In the first place he wanted to tell them what kind of a girl she was — what kind of a girl he approved of here. She was a perfect girl with a few small faults as in the play but a perfect girl not because the public wanted her that way but because it was the kind of girl that he, Stahr, liked to see in this sort of picture. Was that clear? It was no character role. She stood for health, vitality, ambition and love. What gave the play its importance was entirely a situation in which she found herself. She became possessed of a secret that affected a great many lives. There was a right thing and a wrong thing to do — at first it was not plain which was which but when it was she went right away and did it. That was the kind of story this was — thin, clean and shining. No doubts.

"She has never heard the word labor troubles," he said with a sigh. "She might be living in 1929. Is it plain what kind of girl I want?"

"It's very plain, Monroe."

"Now about the things she does," said Stahr. "At all times, at all moments when she is on the screen in our sight she wants to sleep with Ken Willard. Is that plain, Wylie?"

"Passionately plain."

"Whatever she does it is in place of sleeping with Ken Willard. If she   55
walks down the street she is walking to sleep with Ken Willard, if she eats
her food it is to give her strength to sleep with Ken Willard. *But* at no time
do you give the impression that she would ever consider sleeping with Ken
Willard unless they were properly sanctified. I'm ashamed of having to tell
you these kindergarten facts but they have somehow leaked out of the
story."

He opened the script and began to go through it page by page.
Miss Doolan's notes would be typed in quintuplicate and given to them but
Rose Meloney made notes of her own. Broaca put his hand up to his half
closed eyes — he could remember "when a director was something out
here," when writers were gag men or eager and ashamed young reporters
full of whiskey — a director was all there was then. No supervisor — no
Stahr.

He started wide awake as he heard his name.

"It would be nice, John, if you could put the boy on a pointed roof and
let him walk around and keep the camera on him. You might get a nice
feeling — not danger, not suspense, not pointing for anything — a kid on
the roof in the morning."

Broaca brought himself back in the room.

"All right," he said, " — just an element of danger."   60

"Not exactly," said Stahr. "He doesn't start to fall off the roof. Break into
the next scene with it."

"Through the window," suggested Rose Meloney. "He could climb in
his sister's window."

"That's a good transition," said Stahr. "Right into the diary scene."

Broaca was wide awake now.

"I'll shoot up at him," he said. "Let him go away from the camera. Just a   65
fixed shot from quite a distance — let him go away from the camera. Don't
follow him. Pick him up in a close shot and let him go away again. No attention on him except against the whole roof and the sky." He liked the shot —
it was a director's shot that didn't come up on every page any more. He
might use a crane — it would be cheaper in the end than building the roof
on the ground with a process sky. That was one thing about Stahr — the literal sky was the limit. He had worked with Jews too long to believe legends
that they were small with money.

"In the third sequence have him hit the priest," Stahr said.

"What!" Wylie cried, " — and have the Catholics on our neck."

"I've talked to Joe Breen. Priests have been hit. It doesn't reflect on
them."

His quiet voice ran on — stopped abruptly as Miss Doolan glanced at
the clock.

"Is that too much to do before Monday?" he asked Wylie.   70

Wylie looked at Rose and she looked back not even bothering to nod.
He saw their week-end melting away, but he was a different man from
when he entered the room. When you were paid fifteen hundred a week

emergency work was one thing you did not skimp, nor when your picture was threatened. As a "free lance" writer Wylie had failed from lack of caring but here was Stahr to care, for all of them. The effect would not wear off when he left the office — not anywhere within the walls of the lot. He felt a great purposefulness. The mixture of common sense, wise sensibility, theatrical ingenuity, and a certain half naïve conception of the common weal which Stahr had just stated aloud, inspired him to do his part, to get his block of stone in place, even if the effort were foredoomed, the result as dull as a pyramid.

Out of the window Rose Meloney watched the trickle streaming toward the commissary. She would have her lunch in her office and knit a few rows while it came. The man was coming at one-fifteen with the French perfume smuggled over the Mexican border. That was no sin — it was like prohibition.

Broaca watched as Reinmund fawned upon Stahr. He sensed that Reinmund was on his way up—not yet. He received seven hundred and fifty a week for his partial authority over directors, writers and stars who got much more. He wore a cheap English shoe he had bought near the Beverly Wilshire, and Broaca hoped they hurt his feet, but soon now he would order his shoes from Peal's and put away his little green alpine hat with a feather. Broaca was years ahead of him. He had a fine record in the war but he had never felt quite the same with himself since he had let Ike Franklin strike him in the face with his open hand.

There was smoke in the room and behind it, behind his great desk Stahr was withdrawing further and further, in all courtesy, still giving Reinmund an ear and Miss Doolan an ear. The conference was over. . . .

"Mr. Stahr's Projection Room" was a miniature picture theatre with four rows   75
of overstuffed chairs. In front of the front row ran long tables with dim lamps, buzzers and telephones. Against the wall was an upright piano, left there since the early days of sound. The room had been redecorated and reupholstered only a year before but already it was ragged again with work and hours.

Here Stahr sat at two-thirty and again at six-thirty watching the lengths of film taken during the day. There was often a savage tensity about the occasion — he was dealing with *faits accomplis* — the net result of months of buying, planning, writing and rewriting, casting, constructing, lighting, rehearsing and shooting — the fruit alike of brilliant hunches or of counsels of despair, of lethargy, conspiracy and sweat. At this point the tortuous manœuvre was staged and in suspension — these were reports from the battle-line.

Besides Stahr there were present the representatives of all technical departments together with the supervisors and unit managers of the pictures concerned. The directors did not appear at these showings — officially because their work was considered done—actually because few punches were pulled here as money ran out in silver spools. There had evolved a delicate staying away.

The staff was already assembled. Stahr came in and took his place quickly and the murmur of conversation died away. As he sat back and drew his thin knee up beside him in the chair the lights in the room went out. There was the flare of a match in the back row — then silence.

On the screen a troop of French Canadians pushed their canoes up a rapids. The scene had been photographed in a studio tank and at the end of each take after the director's voice could be heard saying "Cut," the actors on the screen relaxed and wiped their brows and sometimes laughed hilariously — and the water in the tank stopped flowing and the illusion ceased. Except to name his choice from each set of takes and to remark that it was "a good process," Stahr made no comment.

The next scene, still in the rapids, called for dialogue between the Canadian girl (Claudette Colbert) and the *coureur du bois* (Ronald Colman), with her looking down at him from a canoe. After a few strips had run through Stahr spoke up suddenly.

"Has the tank been dismantled?"

"Yes, sir."

"Monroe — they needed it for — "

Stahr cut in peremptorily.

"Have it set up again right away. Let's have that second take again."

The lights went on momentarily. One of the unit managers left his chair and came and stood in front of Stahr.

"A beautifully acted scene thrown away," raged Stahr quietly. "It wasn't centered. The camera was set up so it caught the beautiful top of Claudette's head all the time she was talking. That's just what we want, isn't it? That's just what people go to see — the top of a beautiful girl's head. Tell Tim he could have saved wear and tear by using her stand-in."

The lights went out again. The unit manager squatted by Stahr's chair to be out of the way. The take was run again.

"Do you see now?" asked Stahr. "And there's a hair in the picture — there on the right, see it? Find out if it's in the projector or the film."

At the very end of the take Claudette Colbert slowly lifted her head revealing her great liquid eyes.

"That's what we should have had all the way," said Stahr. "She gave a fine performance too. See if you can fit it in tomorrow or late this afternoon."

— Pete Zavras would not have made a slip like that. There were not six camera men in the industry you could entirely trust.

The lights went on; the supervisor and unit manager for that picture went out.

"Monroe, this stuff was shot yesterday — it came through late last night."

The room darkened. On the screen appeared the head of Siva, immense and imperturbable, oblivious to the fact that in a few hours it was to be washed away in a flood. Around it milled a crowd of the faithful.

"When you take that scene again," said Stahr suddenly, "put a couple of little kids up on top. You better check about whether it's reverent or not, but I think it's all right. Kids'll do anything."

"Yes, Monroe."

A silver belt with stars cut out of it.... Smith, Jones or Brown.... Personal — will the woman with the silver belt who — ?

With another picture the scene shifted to New York, a gangster story, and suddenly Stahr became restive.

"That scene's trash," he called suddenly in the darkness. "It's badly   100 written, it's miscast, it accomplishes nothing. Those types aren't tough. They look like a lot of dressed up lollipops — what the hell is the matter, Mort?"

"The scene was written on the set this morning," said Mort Flieshacker. "Burton wanted to get all the stuff on Stage 6."

"Well — it's trash. And so is this one. There's no use printing stuff like that. She doesn't believe what she's saying — neither does Cary. 'I love you' in a close up — they'll cluck you out of the house! And the girl's over-dressed."

In the darkness a signal was given, the projector stopped, the lights went on. The room waited in utter silence. Stahr's face was expressionless.

"Who wrote the scene?" he asked after a minute.

"Wylie White."   105

"Is he sober?"

"Sure he is."

Stahr considered.

"Put about four writers on that scene tonight," he said. "See who we've got. Is Sidney Howard here yet?"

"He got in this morning."   110

"Talk to him about it. Explain to him what I want there. The girl is in deadly terror — she's stalling. It's as simple as that. People don't have three emotions at once. And Kapper — "

The art director leaned forward out of the second row.

"Yeah."

"There's something the matter with that set."

There were little glances exchanged all over the room.   115

"What is it, Monroe?"

"You tell *me*," said Stahr. "It's crowded. It doesn't carry your eye out. It looks cheap."

"It wasn't."

"I know it wasn't. There's not much the matter but there's something. Go over and take a look tonight. It may be too much furniture — or the wrong kind. Perhaps a window would help. Couldn't you force the perspective in that hall a little more?"

"I'll see what I can do." Kapper edged his way out of the row looking at   120 his watch.

"I'll have to get at it right away," he said. "I'll work tonight and we'll put it up in the morning."

"All right. Mort, you can shoot around those scenes, can't you?"

"I think so, Monroe."

"I take the blame for this. Have you got the fight stuff?"

"Coming up now."   125

Stahr nodded. Kapper hurried out and the room went dark again. On the screen four men staged a terrific socking match in a cellar. Stahr laughed.

"Look at Tracy," he said. "Look at him go down after that guy. I bet he's been in a few."

The men fought over and over. Always the same fight. Always at the end they faced each other smiling, sometimes touching the opponent in a friendly gesture on the shoulder. The only one in danger was the stunt man, a pug who could have murdered the other three. He was in danger only if they swung wild and didn't follow the blows he had taught them. Even so the youngest actor was afraid for his face and the director had covered his flinches with ingenious angles and interpositions.

And then two men met endlessly in a door, recognized each other and went on. They met, they started, they went on. They did it wrong. Again they met, they started, they went on.

Then a little girl read underneath a tree with a boy reading on a limb of   130
the tree above. The little girl was bored and wanted to talk to the boy. He would pay no attention. The core of the apple he was eating fell on the little girl's head.

A voice spoke up out of the darkness:

"It's pretty long, isn't it, Monroe?"

"Not a bit," said Stahr. "It's nice. It has nice feeling."

"I just thought it was long."

"Sometimes ten feet can be too long — sometimes a scene two hundred   135
feet long can be too short. I want to speak to the cutter before he touches this scene — this is something that'll be remembered in the picture."

The oracle had spoken. There was nothing to question or argue. Stahr must be right always, not most of the time, but always — or the structure would melt down like gradual butter.

Another hour passed. Dreams hung in fragments at the far end of the room, suffered analysis, passed — to be dreamed in crowds, or else discarded. The end was signalled by two tests, a character man and a girl. After the rushes, which had a tense rhythm of their own, the tests were smooth and finished — the observers settled in their chairs — Stahr's foot slipped to the floor. Opinions were welcome. One of the technical men let it be known that he would willingly cohabit with the girl — the rest were indifferent.

"Somebody sent up a test of that girl two years ago. She must be getting around — but she isn't getting any better. But the man's good. Can't we use him as the old Russian Prince in *"Steppes"*?"

"He *is* an old Russian Prince," said the casting director. "But he's ashamed of it. He's a Red. And that's one part he says he wouldn't play."

"It's the only part he could play," said Stahr.   140

The lights went on. Stahr rolled his gum into its wrapper and put it in an ash-tray. He turned questioningly to his secretary.

"The processes on Stage 2," she said.

Understanding the Text

1. How does Fitzgerald indicate the role of personal taste and judgment in Hollywood decision-making?

2. Describe the character of Stahr. What physical and linguistic details contribute to that characterization?

3. How does Fitzgerald illustrate the control of imagistic detail, down to camera work, in cinematic creation?

4. What does this selection reveal about the power of specific individuals in the film industry?

Exploring and Debating the Issues

1. Analyze the image of the Hollywood tycoon that Fitzgerald presents. Is it a sympathetic, neutral, or critical image?

2. Fitzgerald depicts how, after months of work by teams of writers, directors, camera crew, and performers, the personal impressions of one studio "oracle" can make or break an entire project. In class, discuss whether this process enhances or detracts from artistic creativity.

3. Write an essay explaining the extent to which Fitzgerald's fictional depiction of Hollywood reflects Lary May's historical account (see "The New Frontier: 'Hollywood,' 1914–1920," p. 301). Keep in mind that Stahr is based on the legendary Jewish studio chief Irving Thalberg.

4. Read *The Last Tycoon,* and write an extended analysis of its representation of the film industry.

JAMES J. FLINK

The Automobile Age in California

Although the American automobile industry was born in Detroit, California is the center of America's car culture. In this selection from his book *The Automobile Age* (1988), **James J. Flink** (b. 1932) shows how Los Angeles, the epicenter of American car culture, came to be shaped by the automobile. Already beginning to sprawl out along train and tram lines at the turn of the century, L.A. was destined to become a city without a center once the automobile arrived. A long-time student of American car culture, Flink is also the author of *America Adopts the Automobile, 1895–1910* (1970) and *The Car Culture* (1975).

California led the nation in 1929 as it had in 1910 in ratio of population to motor vehicle registrations. It remained true as well that the leading regions in motor vehicles per capita were still the Pacific and the West North Central states and that the South continued to lag behind the rest of the country in adopting the automobile. But the gaps among the various regions of the United States already had closed appreciably by 1920. During the decade 1910 to 1920 automobile registrations increased more rapidly in the Rocky Mountain states and in the South, the early laggards in adopting the automobile, than in the East North Central, Middle Atlantic, and New England states. Although the agricultural states of the trans-Mississippi West continued to be the largest market for new cars, and California remained known as a bottomless pit for automobile sales, regional differences in the diffusion of the motorcar were becoming less significant. With a United States average of 10.1 persons for every motor vehicle registered in 1921, California ranked first with a ratio of 5.2:1 and Mississippi last with 27.5:1. By 1929 the United States average was 4.5:1. California still led the states with 2.3:1, and Alabama ranked last with 9:1. Long-distance trucking and a new mobility of people were beginning to open up the Pacific Coast and the Southwest to commercial development, make specialized regional economies more interdependent, and lessen the distinctiveness of regional lifeways.

A lifestyle based on personal automobility first developed in Southern California, and nowhere in the world has mass motorization been more pervasive in its impact. "Mass motorization of the region was largely accomplished during the . . . span of the single decade following World War I," Ashleigh Brilliant relates. "Since the earliest days of motoring, Southern California, with its benevolent climate, attractive scenery, and relatively good roads, had been regarded as a 'motorist's paradise.' Until the postwar decade, however, the automobile was considered primarily as a means of recreation. For more practical purposes there was the Pacific Electric Railway, world famous for the efficiency of its service."[1]

Los Angeles has been called "a city built on transport." Its first population boom followed the completion of the Santa Fe Railroad line in 1885. Competition with the Southern Pacific reduced the railroad fare from Kansas City, Missouri, to only one dollar, bringing a flood of tourists and fortune seekers. Invalids and retired couples in particular sought the region's dry air and sunshine. Many came for a winter vacation and stayed on as permanent residents. Midwestern farmers relocated to become citrus growers.

In contrast with the immigrants to Eastern and Midwestern cities in the late nineteenth century, the immigrants to Southern California were older, overwhelmingly native-born and white, and relatively affluent. The largest proportion came from the rural Middle West, where a highly decentralized residential pattern was the norm. "Americans came to Los Angeles with a conception of the good community which was embodied in single-family houses, located on large lots, surrounded by landscaped lawns, and isolated from business activities," Robert Fogelson points out. "Their vision was

---

[1]Ashleigh E. Brilliant, "Some Aspects of Mass Motorization in Southern California, 1919–1929," *Southern California Quarterly* 47 (Oct. 1965): 191.

epitomized by the residential suburb — spacious, affluent, clean, decent, permanent, predictable, and homogeneous. . . . Here then was the basis for the extraordinary dispersal of Los Angeles."[2]

A decade prior to this first population boom, the Southern Pacific had   5
built five lines radiating out from Los Angeles to San Fernando, San Bernardino, Anaheim, Wilmington (near the San Pedro port), and Santa Monica. Reyner Banham observes that this rail system "constitutes the bones of the skeleton on which Greater Los Angeles was to be built, the fundamentals of the present city where each of these old lines is now duplicated by a freeway." He goes on to note that "subdivision of adjoining land proceeded as fast as the laying of rails" and that "commuting began almost as soon as the rails were down. . . . Before 1880 then, the railways had outlined the form of the city and sketched in the pattern of movement that was to characterize its peculiar pattern of life."[3]

Horse-drawn streetcars began to connect the Los Angeles business district with fashionable residential areas in 1876, then suburban development began in 1887 when an electric trolley line began to operate from downtown out Pico Street to serve the Electric Railway Homestead Association Tract. This was the first of a number of trolley lines built by real estate developers out to large tracts of land in outlying areas that they subdivided into homesites. Easy access to downtown by trolley was emphasized in advertising the lots. "Often mechanically unreliable, and even more often on unsound financial footings, the street railways rarely turned profits as transportation businesses, though they often contributed to huge speculative profits in real estate," Martin Wachs writes. Building street railways out to low-density population areas was feasible because of these huge profits and because "Los Angeles . . . was just growing to maturity as a city when street railways were introduced and it had never developed a significant commercial and industrial core."[4]

Between 1901 and 1911 some seventy-two separate street railways were merged, reorganized, consolidated, and extended into the Pacific Electric Railway by Henry Edmunds Huntington, the heir of Southern Pacific magnate Collis P. Huntington. By 1911 this constituted the largest electric interurban system in the United States. Pacific Electric served fifty-six communities within a one hundred-mile radius over 1,164 miles of standard-gauge track with its "Big Red Cars." The associated Los Angeles Railway Company operated streetcars over an additional 316 miles on narrow-gauge track within the city of Los Angeles. Proximity to streetcar lines, observes Mark Foster, "continued to be an important prerequisite for

---

[2]Robert M. Fogelson, *The Fragmented Metropolis: Los Angeles, 1850–1930* (Cambridge: Harvard UP, 1967) 144–45.

[3]Reyner Banham, *Los Angeles: The Architecture of Four Ecologies* (New York: Harper, 1971) 77–78.

[4]Martin Wachs, "Autos, Transit, and the Sprawl of Los Angeles," *American Planning Association Journal* 50 (Summer 1984): 298, 300.

successful development until the 1920s. City maps drawn in 1902 and as late as 1919 show few streets more than five or six blocks from streetcar lines."[5]

Critics of urban sprawl have erroneously blamed the Southern California freeway system for making Los Angeles not a city but a collection of suburbs in search of a city. The unchecked horizontal growth of Greater Los Angeles in fact preceded rather than followed from mass motorization in the 1920s. Wachs notes that by 1910, "largely because of the Pacific Electric System, Los Angeles was functionally integrated with Long Beach, Santa Monica, and San Bernardino. The extent of the metropolitan region has not grown substantially since then, and most of the recent growth has consisted instead of filling in the spaces between outlying areas associated with important stations on the Pacific Electric." The Southern California freeway system closely parallels the 1923 Pacific Electric route map, which, as Banham says, "pretty well defines Greater Los Angeles as it is today." The socioeconomic impact of the Big Red Cars has been most thoroughly examined by Spencer Crump. "Unquestionably," he writes, "it was the electric interurbans which distributed the population over the countryside during the century's first decade and patterned Southern California as a horizontal city rather than one of skyscrapers and slums."[6]

Southern California's second great population boom occurred during the 1920s, when the population of Los Angeles County grew from 1.2 million to 2.2 million. By 1930 only 20 percent of Angelinos had been born in California. At the time, C. Warren Thornwaite characterized this mass movement as "the greatest internal migration in the history of the American people." "Like earlier booms, it was fostered by speculators, bankers, and businessmen," Wachs relates. "In 1921, the 'All Weather Club' was formed to advertise the wonders of Southern California in the East and especially to promote tourism, in the belief that a substantial proportion of those who vacationed in Southern California would be 'sold' on the idea of staying permanently."[7]

Whereas earlier affluent vacationers generally had shipped their open touring cars out from the East by rail, the combined effect in the 1920s of improved roads, better tourist services, and the closed car was that increasingly people came to Southern California in their motorcars. Motorization proliferated much faster than population. Between 1919 and 1929, while the population of Los Angeles roughly doubled, automobile registrations increased 550 percent, from about 141,000 to 777,000. Remarked city

10

[5]Mark S. Foster, "The Model T, the Hard Sell, and Los Angeles's Urban Growth: the Decentralization of Los Angeles during the 1920s," *Pacific Historical Review* 4 (Nov. 1975): 476.

[6]Wachs, "Autos, Transit" 300; Banham, *Los Angeles* 82; Spencer Crump, *Ride the Big Red Cars: How Trolleys Helped Build Southern California* (Corona del Mar: Trans-Anglo, 1962) 100.

[7]C. Warren Thornwaite, *Internal Migration in the United States* (Philadelphia: U of Pennsylvania P, 1934) 18; Wachs; "Autos, Transit" 302.

planner Gordon Whitnall in 1930, "So prevalent is the use of the motor ve-hicle that it might be said that Southern Californians have added wheels to their anatomy."[8] Although ridership on the Pacific Electric System in-creased into the 1930s, it failed to expand proportionately with population growth as more and more riders switched to motorcars. Significantly, the level of mass motorization, as measured by the ratio of motor vehicles to people, has not greatly increased in over half a century. Los Angeles County had one motor vehicle for every 2.85 persons in 1929 and one motor vehicle for every 1.7 persons in 1979, to lead the nation in automobiles per capita at both dates.

Despite Southern California's highly decentralized settlement pattern, a 1931 traffic study showed that over twice as many motor vehicles entered the Los Angeles central business district (CBD) as entered the CBDs of other large American cities. During identical twelve-hour periods, some 277,000 motor vehicles entered the Los Angeles CBD, while among cities with roughly equal-sized CBDs 113,000 entered in Chicago, 66,000 in Boston, and only 49,000 in St. Louis. Moreover, despite the fact that Los Angeles de-veloped as a post-automobile city, its streets were the narrowest and most disconnected and it devoted the least land area to streets in its CBD of any large city in the United States. For example, in 1924 only 21.4 percent of the Los Angeles CBD was devoted to streets, compared with a range of 29 to 44 percent for other large American cities. This gave Los Angeles the most se-vere automobile traffic congestion in the world in the pre–World War II pe-riod. Downtown traffic snarls were already so bad during the 1919 Christ-mas shopping season that the city put into effect on April 10, 1920, a ban on street parking during business hours. Business dropped off so sharply that the ban was revised on April 26 to apply only during the evening rush hours.

Mass motorization fit hand in glove with a Southern California econ-omy that necessitated the dispersion of business locations. For good rea-sons, a commercial-industrial core never developed in Los Angeles. To begin with, fear of earthquake damage led after 1906 to a 150-foot limitation on the height of downtown buildings, which remained in effect until the mid-1950s. Citrus growing, the movie industry, and later the aircraft indus-try required large tracts of land available only in the suburbs. The petro-leum industry, central to the local economy, located facilities where oil was found or near the port from which it was shipped. As petroleum exports mounted, by 1930 the port of Los Angeles had come to rank third in total commerce and second in tonnage in the United States. The port facilities and related commercial activity were located along forty miles of waterfront in the Long Beach, San Pedro, and Wilmington areas, whose northern edge was about twenty miles distant from the traditional commercial core of the city. New residential communities sprang up between downtown Los An-geles and the port area. Wachs notes that although manufacturing indus-

[8]Quoted in Foster, "The Model T, the Hard Sell" 470.

tries grew, the segment of the workforce engaged in manufacturing declined from 28 percent in 1920 to 22 percent in 1930. "Los Angeles was increasingly described as a 'white-collar' town; real estate, finance, and tourism expanded most prominently."[9]

Thus, mass motorization neither caused the dispersion of economic activities nor changed the form of residential patterns in Southern California. However, the motor vehicle permitted decentralization that went well beyond what had been possible with electric traction. And this created a new urban lifestyle in Southern California that uniquely combined big-city amenities with low population density, single-family housing, and unparalleled individual mobility and access to outdoor recreation.

In areas close to the central business district that were served well by streetcars — such as Hawthorne, Inglewood, and Gardena in the South Bay area — mass motorization had little impact. There was a substantial increase, however, in the number of new subdivisions opened as mass motorization enabled real estate promoters to develop tracts of land remote from streetcar lines. The development of the San Fernando Valley was the prime example. The number of new subdivision maps recorded soared from 346 in 1920 to peak of 1,434 in 1923. With this new suburban construction, the amount of land converted to urban use in the Los Angeles area increased from 14.2 percent in 1924 to 24.4 percent a decade later. Construction of single-family residential dwellings accounted for 75 percent of this urban land use in the area between 8.6 and 10.3 miles from downtown Los Angeles.

The 1930 United States census revealed that 93.7 percent of the dwelling units in Los Angeles were single-family homes — the highest proportion of any American city — and that population density in the Greater Los Angeles area was only 2,812 persons per square mile. This contrasted with densities of over 23,000 persons per square mile in New York City, nearly 18,000 persons per square mile in Boston, and nearly 17,000 in Chicago. Single-family residences accounted for less than 53 percent of the dwelling units in all three of these cities.

The movement of population outward plus traffic congestion led to the rapid decline of downtown Los Angeles, as businesses and professional offices located outside the central business district. Between 1920 and 1930 the proportion of banks located outside the CBD increased from 45 percent to 89 percent, theaters from 26 percent to 80 percent, dentists' offices from 16 percent to 55 percent, and physicians' offices from 21 percent to 67 percent. The proportion of residents living within a ten-mile radius of the CBD who entered it daily declined from 68 percent in 1924 to 52 percent in 1931.

"The impact of the automobile upon Los Angeles's urbanization process compared to that in other cities is distinguished chiefly by its magnitude," Foster concludes. "Both critics and defenders of Los Angeles's

[9]Wachs, "Autos, Transit" 302–03.

decentralization generally concede that by 1930 the city was in many re-spects the prototype of the mid-twentieth-century metropolis."[10] This is most forcefully demonstrated by an examination of the parallel impact of the automobile on southern cities during the 1920s.

Understanding the Text

1. According to Flink, how did California lead the nation in the early develop-ment of America's car culture?

2. How, in Flink's view, did the characteristic suburban sprawl of Los Angeles develop prior to the automotive age?

3. How did the automobile contribute to the decline of downtown Los Angeles?

4. What effects did mass motorization have on Southern California communi-ties in general?

Exploring and Debating the Issues

1. In an essay, analyze how the image of Southern California car culture has been portrayed in popular culture. In addition to film or television depic-tions, you might review such pop tunes as the Beach Boys' "Little Deuce Coupe" and Jan and Dean's "Little Old Lady from Pasadena."

2. Flink claims "a lifestyle based on mass personal automobility first devel-oped in Southern California" (para. 2). In an essay, explain to what extent this observation applies to your region of the state.

3. Denise S. Spooner ("A New Perspective on the Dream," p. 22) suggests that one reason Midwesterners came to California was to escape the tightly knit communities in their home states. How, in your opinion, has California car culture contributed to dispersed communities, both socially and geograph-ically? Be sure to base your discussion on specific communities.

4. In your journal, reflect on your own attitudes toward automobiles. Do cars mean more than transportation to you and, if so, in what ways?

[10]Foster, "The Model T, the Hard Sell" 483.

JAMES D. HOUSTON

In Search of Oildorado

It's not easy living in the Central Valley if you have to put up with coastal California's almost complete neglect of you and your region. **James D. Houston** (b. 1933), a long-time writer and novelist on the California scene, went out to try to correct the problem by visiting Kern County, the fourth-largest oil-producing region in America and the eighteenth largest in the world. Making his way to Taft, California, home to the Oildorado festival and its court, the Maids of Petroleum, Houston found a place much more like Texas and Oklahoma than the California the rest of the world imagines. In fact, many of the Central Valley's residents can trace their family lines back to the Okies who emigrated in the 1930s. A writer, editor, and novelist, Houston has published many books, including *Continental Drift* (1978), *Californians: Searching for the Golden State* (1982), and *Farewell to Manzanar* (with Jeanne Wakatsuki Houston, 1973).

California's best-known exports nowadays are not things. They are images, composed of such unnatural resources as lifestyle frontiers and the shapes of leisure — not the bottled wine itself but the chilled chardonnay in the hot tub; the kid on the trail bike, on the rim of the bluff, at sunset. The images depict all varieties of the West Coast adventure in Life with a capital L, the Living and Exploring and Spending and Expanding and Exploding. They are exported on film, on record and tape, via the covers and inside pages of the *National Enquirer, Road and Track, TV Guide, People, Self,* and *Us.* Meanwhile, more traditional resources, such as timber, cotton, cattle, hogs and poultry, crude oil and natural gas, come to the public's attention when some feature of the environment has been violated or is about to be swamped. But for the most part, though they fuel and finance the rest of it, these tend to exist in the shadow of The Great Postindustrial Experiment, which dazzles us with such a blinding light.

To see this other part of California, the resource-full part, it helps to get away from the coast from time to time, and head inland, which is why I found myself on the road to Bakersfield again, over there in Kern County. About 7 percent of the cotton grown in the United States comes out of Kern County. According to Bill Rintoul, it is also the nation's fourth-largest oil-producing region.

"If Kern seceded from the rest of California," says Bill, "which of course it is not planning to do, at least not right away, but if it were separated off, this county all by itself would be running fourth in oil, after Texas, Alaska, and Louisiana. For that matter, it is the eighteenth-largest oil producer in the world."

Bill is a Kern County patriot. I do not mean he would defend his county's honor with guns and knives. But he likes the place, he has spent most of his life there, and takes its flaws along with its virtues. He actually prefers the unrelieved flatness of the landscape. We were talking once about the heavy groves and wooded canyons characteristic of the northern coast, and he said, "You know, it's funny, but there is something about that kind of country that just doesn't feel right. Those trees all around you. And the rain it takes for that kind of growth, the way it drips down through the trees. The way the mountains rise up. Half the time you can't see the sun. I suppose it's just what a person gets used to. You get used to a certain idea of what the world is supposed to look like. I'd just rather see the sun and know where I'm going."

Bill makes his living as a petroleum journalist. He writes columns for the *Bakersfield Californian* and the *Tulsa Daily World*. When I called and told him I might be heading his way, there was a pause. He is not a fast talker. He thinks things over. After a moment he said, "Well, if you time it for next weekend, you could be here for some of Oildorado. I am going to be the Grand Marshal in the parade this year. Maybe you could ride along with me in the limousine."

I had heard of Oildorado but didn't know much about it. The fact is, on the day I called him, everything I knew about oil in California could fit easily into the spare can I carry around in the back of my Mercedes, which has a diesel engine, by the way, an old 1960 190D. It will give me thirty-five miles to the gallon on a trip like this, where the roads are straight and flat.

Naively I asked, "Does the parade run through the oil fields?"

"No, it runs right through downtown Taft. On second thought, maybe you'd be better off watching from the sidewalk. That way you'll be sure to see all the floats and the Oildorado Queen and the Maids of Petroleum. If you want to see the fields themselves, my suggestion is to drive down Highway 33. There is no other road quite like it in the eleven western states."

In literature, Kern's finest moment comes in that scene midway through *The Grapes of Wrath,* when the Joad family stops at Tehachapi Pass to take a first long and thirsty look at this land they have struggled so hard to reach. Ruthie and Winfield, the youngest, are awestruck by the sight, "embarrassed before the great valley," is the way Steinbeck described it:

> The distance was thinned with haze, and the land grew softer and softer in the distance. A windmill flashed in the sun, and its turning blades were like a little heliograph, far away. Ruthie and Winfield looked at it, and Ruthie whispered, "It's California."

The vista Steinbeck chose, in 1939, to flesh out the dream these immigrants carried with them from Dust-Bowl Oklahoma is a long way from the world most Californians inhabit now. The largest cities, the densest networks of subdivisions, mobile home parks and retirement towns are found along a coastal strip, some forty miles wide, between Sonoma County and San Diego. By and large, this is where The Big Experiment is going on. It is also a zone of intense tourism. People living in or near the coastal communities often find themselves caught in that mind-boggle between how a place

once looked and felt and how its packaging looks once it has become mer-
chandise on the international travel circuit.

In Kern County you do not have to put up with much of this. In the 1979   10
Atlas of California, on the page where "Major Tourist Attractions" are
marked with circles and dots of various colors, Kern is blank. Gray Line
buses do not linger in Bakersfield or Oildale or Taft. Movie stars and sports
celebrities seldom buy homes there, though they might well invest in the
land. People don't visit, as a rule, unless they have business there, or relatives, or have come searching for Oildorado.

Heading east out of Paso Robles, I cross the county line halfway
through a lonesome dip in the Coast Range called Antelope Valley. The hills
along here are so dry and brown they shine in the sunlight as if ready to
burst into flame. Just as the county sign flashes past, I hear Conway Twitty
on the radio, station KUZZ out of Bakersfield coming in clear now. His voice
rich with stoic remorse, Conway tells some lost sweetheart she is standing
on a bridge that just won't burn. It seems perfect. This land could torment
you for years without ever quite killing you. And the road signs for what lies
up ahead don't seem to promise much relief: Bitterwater Valley, Devils Den,
Lost Hills.

The first blur of color is startling, almost uncanny, when this narrow
passage opens out into cotton fields, hundreds, perhaps thousands of acres,
with bolls white and ready for picking. A couple of miles go by, and one side
of the road turns from cotton into a long orchard of dusty almond trees. As
the last slopes level out, where Antelope Valley joins the broad San Joaquin,
the first grapevines appear, their leaves half green, half rusty brown after
harvest. To the south the rows look about a mile long, stretching across to
the base of the Temblor Range. To the north there is no telling how far the
rows extend, no limits visible up that way. Vines merge toward the horizon.

A few more miles go by, and the vines give way to another stand of almond trees, older and thicker, bearing well, and then a peach orchard, and
now, across this highway, facing the orchards you can see what all this land
looked like once, and would look like now without the aqueduct. The contrast is spectacular. In this landscape almost nothing grows naturally. No
shrubs, no trees, no houses. No people. Out this way there aren't even any
beer cans. Without the aqueduct that intersects this highway a few miles up
ahead, there would be nothing here but tumbleweed and sagebrush and the
diesel rigs powering past on their way to Interstate 5.

Water is one of three resources that have shaped Kern County. Oil and
country music are the other two. The water is imported from rivers farther
north. The music is what you might call a hybrid product, transplanted
southwestern and Okie energy finding new roots here, giving Bakersfield its
nickname, Nashville West. The oil, however, is indigenous. While the gui-
tars and the fiddles and the gospel quartets float through the airways a few
feet above the ground, and while the piped-in water taps the riches in the
first foot of earth, thousands and thousands of wells suck up the riches farther down, planted there fifty or sixty million years ago when uncountable

generations of plankton sifted downward through the fathoms of this one-time inland sea and left tiny skeletons behind to be transformed into crude.

When we talked on the phone Bill told me Kern County is now produc- 15 ing more oil than some of the OPEC nations. He said this with such genuine pride in his home region, I felt obliged to ask him which OPEC nations he was referring to.

Again there was a pause, as if he had forgotten. He had not forgotten. Bill is a living encyclopedia of petroleum lore, but he will hesitate like this, as if the facts are elusive and hard to pin down. "Oh, I think Qatar is one," he said. "Gabon is another. Ecuador is in there somewhere."

On the radio Willie Nelson is singing, "Whiskey River, don't run dry." Out here on Highway 46 the crops have disappeared for a while. Sand and sagebrush stretch away on both sides of the road. It's odd to be comparing this alkaline wasteland with Ecuador.

Standing all alone in the sand and the wind, where Highway 46 meets 33, there is a cafe with a couple of gas pumps called Blackwells Corner. I swing right, as Bill instructed me to do, heading south. Within a few miles I am surrounded by walking beams, steam generators, derricks, and fields of grimy pipe. No crops at all grow along this side of the San Joaquin. The soil is parched. Animals are scarce. The only movement in this moon-like realm comes from the pumps, their metal beams nodding with the motion and profile that has stirred several dozen writers to compare them to praying mantises. I now see why. This type of field pump resembles nothing in the world as much as a mantis on a string. What you see from the road are hundreds of praying heads, painted orange or yellow or black and connected by cable to something underground that seems to pull each one by the nose, so that they are all, on their various cycles, silently, ceaselessly bowing.

I will soon learn from Bill that if there was a Guinness book of financial records, this oil field would be in it. Late in 1979 Shell bought it for what was said at the time to be the largest sum ever to change hands in a corporate transaction. The field, called Kernridge, which now produces fifty thousand barrels each day, was sold for $3,653,272,000. Shell's geologists estimate 364 billion cubic feet of natural gas are waiting underground here, along with five to six hundred million barrels of oil, most of which had long been considered too expensive to get at or too viscous to pump. Soaring prices changed that view.

South of this field, and near the village of McKittrick, I enter a much larger 20 and more valuable oil field, a legendary field that has created five towns and numerous fortunes. It is called the Midway-Sunset. It is over twenty miles long. As Bill is soon to tell me, it is among the twelve largest fields in the United States. It was the fourth in the history of the country to deliver a billion barrels — as of 1967 — and they are still a long way from the bottom.

I have some trouble with figures like a billion barrels, or 364 billion cubic feet. I have some trouble with the scale of this whole business. It is almost too much to grasp. These fields and Bill's almanac memory are filled with numbers that simply bring the imagination to a standstill. Standard Oil of California grossed $42 billion in fiscal 1980. Kern County produces nearly four million barrels of oil per week. The United States still imports about five million barrels per day. A typical reason, or symptom: there are 5.1 million automobiles in Los Angeles. These cars alone burn fifteen million gallons of gasoline every day. There are forty-two gallons in a barrel. By 1967 this field I'm driving through produced a billion barrels. In other words, 42 billion gallons, 168 billion quarts. But where are they now? And how big a cavity does that leave below? Is it bigger or smaller than Carlsbad Caverns? And how much bigger can it get before the roof caves in?

I am beginning to wonder if it helps to drive out through these oil fields. Even here, right in the middle of it, along Highway 33, which displays the most elaborate collection of field equipment west of Oklahoma, there is not much to see, not much to hold to, nothing nearly as immediate as that vast field of cotton with its bolls like a field of white eyes along the roadside watching you pass.

I think it was easier in the old days, when they had gushers that would blow the tops off the derricks, puddle the earth with lakes of oil and fill the air for miles around here with an oily haze that would stain the laundry and cloud the sun. The most dramatic of these, Lakeview Number One, blew in on March 14, 1910, with such force and volume it could not be brought under control, and it was never brought under control. People still talk about the soaring column of oil and sand and rock. Unable to cap or channel it, they used timbers and sandbags to construct great dikes and holding sumps. Of the nine million barrels said to have come pouring forth during the year and a half it gushed and geysered, some four million were trapped and processed. The rest just ran free and seeped back into the earth from whence it came. This went on for 544 days without restraint. Then one day it stopped as suddenly as it had begun. The bottom fell in, due to some shift of underground pressure, and that was the end of the Lakeview Gusher, but the beginning of flush times in the Midway-Sunset, as well as the true launching of Taft, the largest town among these west-side fields. (The sign at the edge of town listing weekly luncheon times for Kiwanis, Lions, Optimists, and Rotary, claims a population of 18,500, but a plumbing contractor Bill introduced me to confessed that the true population is closer to twelve thousand. "People will throw these numbers around," he said. "They will try to rope in Fellows and Tupman and some of the outlying areas, but as long as I've been here, which is forty-four years, the population of the town itself hasn't changed that much one way or the other.")

Taft happened to incorporate in the same year Lakeview Number One burst forth, and it looks back upon that event as a grand and almost supernatural announcement of the town's arrival. Emblazoned across the 1980 souvenir T-shirts being sold in Taft, where Oildorado originated, is the phrase SEVENTY YEARS OF BLACK GOLD.

Seventy years. Even in the foreshortened history of California this place is very, very young. My house in Santa Cruz is older than any two-by-four in Taft. In this part of the world the coastal mission towns, like Santa Cruz, go

25

back as far as towns go. The central valley had to wait until after statehood. And Taft's side of the valley had to wait even longer. As late as 1900 there was still nothing here but sagebrush. In 1902 Southern Pacific ran a spur line out this far, to service the new wells. The end of that spur line gathered a dusty collection of shacks and tents and converted boxcars. The town is still built close to the ground, in a hollow between hills studded with producing wells. The view in all directions is of dry, oil-bearing hillsides, their bare slopes defined by a few wooden derricks that survive from the early days — the same kind of definition trees provide.

Hills like these are uncommon in the San Joaquin, which by nature is as flat as a football field and about the same shape. Geologists call them anticlines. Where they rise from the plain, oil from sand and shale layers farther down has been gathered upward, within easy reach of the surface. Just out of sight, a few miles east, there lies another low range called Elk Hills, an unassuming cluster of tawny ridges that offer almost nothing to the passing eye, yet Elk Hills happens to be California's number-one producing field. Since 1912 it has belonged to the federal government, as a naval petroleum reserve. For a while in the 1920s, it was famous for its role in the most notorious oil scandal of all time though never quite as famous as Wyoming's Teapot Dome field — another naval reserve — which gave the scandal its name.

In 1921 Albert Fall, then Secretary of the Interior, brought the control of these fields into his department and promptly leased them out to high-rolling cronies. Elk Hills went to Edward Doheny, the original California oil baron and L.A. entrepreneur, in exchange for "a personal loan" of $100,000. After the dealings were exposed, Fall became the first cabinet officer in American history to be convicted of a felony and sent to prison. Doheny was acquitted. Elk Hills spent the next fifty years rather quietly, as a low-production reserve administered by the navy. It was not until the Arab oil embargo of 1973, and the new pressure to develop domestic fuel supplies, that the idea of reopening Elk Hills for commercial use was seriously considered. Bill Rintoul says a hundred sixty thousand barrels a day come out of there now, and two hundred million cubic feet of gas.

At a small shop called Oildorado Headquarters, on the main street in downtown Taft, I pick up a couple of the black and gold T-shirts, an official program, and the special issue of the Taft *Daily Midway Driller*. In a back room, beyond the cash register, bright lights are shining. Life-size costume boards have been set up, with notches at the top for neck and chin. The costumes are old-time and turn-of-the-century Western. People are waiting in line to have their pictures taken standing behind these boards, as souvenirs of this festival which is already three days along. It started Wednesday with the queen contest and the official opening of the Westside Oil Museum. Things will begin to peak tomorrow with the big parade and hopefully climax with the World Championship Welding and Backhoe Races at Franklin Field.

Outside this shop, where I am meeting Rintoul, numerous sheriffs are passing by, numerous vests and cowboy hats, bonnets and gingham dresses. Bill is easy to spot. He is not in costume. A man of simple tastes, he never overplays his hand. As Grand Marshal of tomorrow's parade he could get away with almost anything, but he shows up in checkered slacks and a short-sleeved sport shirt. No string tie. No turquoise. He has a brand-new cowboy hat, which he has left in the car. He pretends to be worried that the parade committee might get the wrong idea.

"If they see that hat they might start talking about horses. Then I might   30 have to tell them to forget the whole thing." He grins a weathery grin, as if he is turning into a heavy wind to look at me. "I think the Grand Marshal deserves a limousine, don't you?"

Whatever they give him to ride, Bill is going to do well as Oildorado Marshal. His heart is in exactly the right place. He is an oil fields aficionado, a man fascinated with every feature of the way this business works. He grew up here in Taft, joined the army during World War II, came back for a few years in the fields before going off to Stanford for a degree in journalism. Secretly I suspect he writes his daily columns and his feature pieces for *Pacific Oil World, Well Servicing,* and *The Drilling Contractor* so he can continue to roam among these anticlines at will. He loves all of it, the mathematics, the geology, the look of a drilling rig, the lore of the roughneck, the gusher legends, the way a late sun tints steam plumes rising from the generators. He jumped at the chance to meander once again through his own home territory, to take me on a little tour, which now begins, in the Veterans Hall, where the Oildorado Civic Luncheon is being served, and where the Grand Marshal's attendance is expected.

We walk in moments before the invocation. Bill moves directly to the head table, while I find a spot, a vacant folding chair, at one of the long tables lined up in rows across the hall. Maybe two hundred people are here, merchants and their wives, the civic leaders of Taft, dressed as cowhands, schoolmarms, desperadoes. The brightest outfits are black and gold, worn by a dozen young girls dressed as saloon dancers, 1890s style, with high fringed skirts and high-heeled shoes. These are the girls who ran for queen, sponsored by such groups as the Taft Rotary, the Desk and Derrick Club, the Moose Lodge. The winner, sponsored by Veterans of World War I, Barracks 305, is a slim and pretty senior from Taft High. She wears a glossy beauty-contest banner that says OILDORADO QUEEN. The others each wear a banner saying MAID OF PETROLEUM. Later, two hours from now, after speeches by Oildorado presidents, mayors, and council members past and present, after all the testimonials to the community of Taft and the Oildorado tradition, these fourteen girls will dance a cancan routine to taped music, a high-stepping, side-kicking, skirt-lifting dance that will end with their backsides first to the speakers' table and then to the crowd. They are giddy with anticipation, jumping up and sitting down and hurrying out to the lobby. Now they all come to a temporary halt as the M.C. calms the room and asks us to stand while a portly minister intones the blessing.

Still standing, we put our hands over our hearts, face the flag, and say the pledge of allegiance. Then we sing "God Bless America." It has been a long time since I sang "God Bless America" before lunch. It feels good. One thing I will say about the people of Taft: they are not cynical. They do not intend the phrase "Maid of Petroleum" to have more than one meaning. They genuinely want America to be blessed by someone. And though relatively little of the profits from these mammoth oil reserves trickles into town, they are thankful when the fields come back to life, as they have in these past few years, because then Taft comes back to life. The mood on this particular afternoon in Veterans Hall is one of carefully nurtured prosperity.

During lunch — paper plates of fried chicken, potato salad, carrot-and-raisin salad, coffee or iced tea from pitchers — I talk to the plumbing contractor who moved here forty-four years ago. He wears a rodeo shirt and cowboy hat and has let his beard grow out for the whiskerino contest. Business has been good, but it is a mixed blessing. He complains about the hard time he has finding qualified help. "They all want to go work in the oil fields now. Out there they start at seven-fifty, and move up to nine, nine-fifty right away. Your best workers are going to head for the fields. So I've always got a new man to break in."

After lunch we drive out to the site of the Lakeview Gusher, south of town, on Petroleum Club Road. The distance is ten kilometers, a figure I remember from the program. Early Saturday morning there is to be a footrace, an event called "The Lakeview Gusher 10K" starting where the original derrick stood before the gush of oil and gas reduced it to splinters, and ending downtown.

The race is another tribute to that great explosion. The place where those racers will assemble, "The Site," is a built-up pit perhaps forty yards across. Its walls were originally made of timbers, sandbags, and dirt. A wetter climate would long ago have flattened these walls, but seventy years from now it will probably look pretty much the same. Sandbags can still be seen, tattered strips of burlap show through the dirt and the grimy boards. In the special edition of the *Midway Driller* there is a photo of two grinning, oil-stained men standing on an oil-encrusted wooden raft floating in a shiny lake of oil. They are poling from one side to the other. This caked and sandy pit Bill and I are standing in used to be that lake.

While we wander to the far side he is telling me the story, one he heard firsthand from an uncle who worked this field in the earliest years. Eventually both of us fall silent, kicking at the shards of oily sand. Something eerie hovers here, something reverent in the breeze across these scarred dunes, in the near-absence of motion or life where once there had been such a swarm, such frenzy.

Between the pit and roads stands a monument, with a plaque affixed, which says AMERICA'S MOST SPECTACULAR GUSHER. It's a California Registered Historical Landmark. If you squint, it could be a gravestone. Around here they talk about this gusher as if it had a life and an identity, the great creature who sprang forth, lived its wild existence for a year and a half, and suddenly died, of subterranean causes. Seventy years later there are photos every-where — in the Oildorado program, in the special issue of the *Driller,* in shop windows downtown, and on permanent display in the new Westside Oil Museum — the lakes and rivers of oil, the oily workers rafting through it, the shattered derrick, the black spurting geyser of oil. They commemorate the early time, which was also the time of wildness, before this piece of earth had been quite tamed, and the sky-high gusher who could not be con-tained burst forth, made a huge and glorious mess, then disappeared or perhaps just retreated back into its cave.

I don't know why, but when you're driving around in the central valley, the songs from these country and western stations always seem to be providing some ironic comment on the landscape or the general situation. As we pull away from the gusher site, Bill switches on KUZZ, and it's an old Buck Owens arrangement called "Today I Started Loving You Again."

Buck is singing it. Merle Haggard wrote it. They both happen to be Kern County heroes. As we near the oil field village of Maricopa, Bill says in pass-ing that he knows someone who went to high school with Merle in the days before he married Bonnie Owens. Everyone in Kern County seems to know someone who knows Buck Owens or Bonnie or Merle or all three. "She was married to both of 'em, you know. Of course, not at the same time."

By pure coincidence the one thriving business in Maricopa is called Buck's Steakhouse. No connection. "Best place to eat, for as long as I can re-member," says Bill. From the look of things, it is the only place to eat. Taft and Maricopa started even, back in 1910, when they both incorporated. By 1911 Maricopa had its own opera house. In the mid-1970s, when they were filming *Bound for Glory,* Woody Guthrie's life story, Maricopa was chosen as the location for some early scenes set in the wind-blown west Texas town of Pampa during the 1930s. Very little had to be changed. It still has that sanded, worn-down Western patina. Only the cars are new, and some of the pickups outside Buck's.

Maricopa sits near Midway-Sunset's southern edge. We head due east now, along the base of the Temblor Range, running almost parallel to the California Aqueduct, which also swings eastward here, with its long flow from the Delta passing through these lowlands before making the salmon's leap over the Tehachapis and down again, to water Southern California. Along here the aqueduct waters more cotton fields. A few miles out of Mari-copa we are driving through one of those tracts so vast your eyes burn try-ing to see the end of it. And right out in the middle of this small continent of cotton, about half a mile off the road, stands the drilling rig we have come looking for. With no pumps or derricks in view, the rig looks like some inter-galactic vehicle that has landed in the wrong place.

It's part of Bill's beat to see how they are doing, how deep the hole is, and whether they've had any show. This is a wildcat well, he says, in a part of the valley that hasn't been drilled before. "There's probably some oil down there, but ten years ago you wouldn't have found anybody drilling that deep."

He takes a side road, looking for access, finds it, and we are easing along a dirt track between cotton rows toward a clearing where maybe half an acre has been opened up to make room for the platform, the caravan of trailers.

Bill has two hard hats in the trunk. We don these and climb the metal   45
ladder. Everything is made of metal and painted battleship gray. The steel platform is thirty feet above the cotton, and rising a hundred thirty feet above the platform is the bolted network of struts and pulleys they call the mast. Climbing aboard you have the feeling of boarding a great vessel, anchored in the invisible waters of the inland sea.

Five men are working, the standard crew, all wearing hard hats and T-shirts, and smeared with grease and oil. Bill introduces me to Terry the tool pusher, the crew leader, who grins when I offer to shake his hand and shows me the palm thick with grease. Something about the way he stands would tell you he is in command, even if you hadn't been told in advance. His face is lean, his hair black and straight. He could be part Cherokee. Early thirties. He wears cowboy boots and jeans, no shirt. Without being muscular, his body looks powerful, whip-like. He stands with one foot forward, like a sailor on a rolling deck.

Bill mentions a man who died a couple of days ago, on another rig in some other part of the county. "I read in the paper that the cable crushed his chest."

Terry laughs and shakes his head, nods toward the draw works, the broad metal drum that winds and unwinds the cable that feeds up to the top of the mast, then down toward the center of the platform where the lengths of pipe are lowered or raised.

"I read that story," Terry says. "There is no way this cable is gonna crush your chest. If it breaks and comes whipping out of that drum it might knock you around some. It got me once. But it's not gonna crush your chest. What I figure is, they were pulling on the pipe, and it was the pipe broke loose and come free and swung out and got him. That pipe is what can crush you."

Any of this stuff could crush you. This is what Terry is ready to roll with,   50
not an ocean, but the great chunks of moving metal that surround him. The drilling pipe comes in thirty-foot sections. They are slung from the cable on a lobster-shaped hook the size of a VW bus, which hangs directly overhead. Next to us, another large piece of thick steel is hanging loose, about the size of a Harley-Davidson. When I ask Terry about it he says, "All this is here is a great big pipe wrench. We just clamp it onto the pipe there to tighten the fit."

He shrugs it off, makes it simple. And it is simple. You put a bit on the end of a pipe, and you start cutting a hole in the ground. After a while you screw on another length of pipe, and you cut a little deeper. It isn't the act that's impressive. Like everything else in the oil business, it's the magnitude. This rig down here at the absolute bottom edge of the San Joaquin Valley is running a pipe that is now twelve thousand feet into the ground, chipping and grinding through the next inch or foot of sand or shale or ancient fossil layer. What we have here is a brace and bit over two miles long, which is deep, Bill says. An average well in Kern County runs four to five thousand feet. Lakeview Number One came in at 2,225 in 1910.

Retracing our route through the rows of cotton we head back toward Taft, where I left my car. From there I follow Bill to Bakersfield and our final stop, a Basque place downtown called The Pyrenees, established in the days when Basque shepherds roamed the foothills east of here. The food is served family style, and the folks who run the place pile it on the table as if everyone who walks in is a shepherd just back from a month in the mountains or a roughneck coming off a seventy-two-hour shift.

This is Bill's favorite restaurant. The house beverage, Picon Punch, warms his county patriotism, stirs to life an epilogue for today, a prologue for tomorrow's parade.

"Kern is a kind of headquarters, you see. This is the biggest drilling year in the history of the state of California, and two-thirds of the new wells are here in this county — over two thousand wells. Meanwhile, oil people fan out from here in all directions. The contractor Terry works for has twenty-one rigs like that one we climbed. His main yard is outside town, but his rigs are trucked to Nevada, Wyoming, and into the Rockies where all the new exploration is going on. You take Terry himself. He grew up here in Bakersfield, started out as a roughneck, worked his way up to tool pusher. He just got back from Evanston, Wyoming. Couple of years ago he was working in Alaska. It's typical. Some of those fellows over in Taft, you would never know it to see them walking along the street, but they have been to Peru, to Arabia, Iran, and Venezuela, and they wind up right back home again."

The next morning we start out in separate cars, planning to meet at the reviewing stand. I am ten miles south of Bakersfield, whizzing along to Loretta Lynn's version of "I've Never Been This Far Before," and near the village of Pumpkin Center, when I smell the smell of warm rust, glance down and see my temperature needle heading off the gauge.

I pull over, pop the hood open, and gingerly ease the cap loose. Steam pours out but no water. There isn't much left. The top seam on my radiator has split. I make it to a phone and call the first place listed in the Yellow Pages that claims to be open on weekends. I cadge some water from a Freddy Fast-Gas and limp back to this radiator shop on the outskirts of Bakersfield, in the middle of a district that seems coated with rubber dust and filmed with oil, not from wells but from the generations of cars that have moved through its grimy jungle of transmission shops, upholstery parlors, abandoned service stations, warehouses, and wrecking yards.

I pull in with steam billowing around my hood and a trail of what could be diluted blood. The radiator man is sympathetic, a fellow in dark coveralls whose eyes cannot quite open, as if the lashes have been coated with honey. He says that since it is Saturday and he plans to close at 1:00 P.M. he will do the repairs only if I pull the radiator myself and install it again. I agree, making it clear that I am truly in a rush since my friend is going to be the Grand Marshal in the Oildorado parade. I emphasize this, figuring the local reference might enhance our relationship. He stops me right there.

"The what parade?"

"Oildorado."

"What the hell is that?"

Well, I think, this is curious. Here is a fellow whose entire livelihood depends on the internal-combustion engine, the heat it generates while burning gasoline, heat that must be cooled with water, which must circulate and sooner or later spring a leak, which he then is qualified to repair. And this fellow has never heard of the event I have driven halfway across the state to attend, the celebration of an industry that keeps not only this radiator man but a good part of California, if you will pardon the expression, solvent.

"You mean to tell me," I say, "that you work on cars all day long, every day, and you have never heard of Oildorado over there in Taft?"

Something in my tone unnerves him. We are both on edge. For a moment his eyelashes pull apart. I see indignation in there. "Hey," he says, "you want this goddamn radiator fixed?" Before I can reply he says, "Taft is thirty-five miles away. How the hell am I for Christ sake supposed to know what's going on over in Taft!"

I don't argue. It is important for the two of us to get along, at least for the next hour, which we do, working side by side, sometimes eyelash to eyelash, above and below the fittings.

By the time I reach Taft it is midafternoon. I have missed the parade. I have missed the Lakeview Gusher 10K Run. I have missed the Fly-in at Taft Airport and the barbecue at The Petroleum Club. Searching for Bill, I stop at Franklin Field, where the World's Championship Backhoe Contest is scheduled. It hasn't started yet. I happen to catch the most intense tug-of-war I have ever witnessed. These are not college kids pulling each other across a mudhole at the Spring Fling. These are some of the largest men in the state — truckers, hay-buckers, roustabouts, and derrick-men — thick men bursting through their T-shirts and playing for keeps.

One team is fully outfitted with matching blue and white jump suits, paratrooper boots for sure footing, and ball caps that say "Duval Sporting Goods." They have a coach, also in uniform, who paces back and forth in a half-crouch, muttering instructions before the match begins. They have some moves worked out, some hand and voice signals. They have prepared for this moment, and it is sad to watch those thick boot soles sliding through the sand as they are dragged across the line in less than thirty seconds by some ragtag group who have evidently organized at the last moment, who wear Adidas running shoes, whose T-shirts do not even match, but whose pecs and biceps would bring tears to the eyes of many regulars at Santa Monica's Muscle Beach. After a few rebel yells the winners swagger off toward the Budweiser truck, while the team from Duval Sporting Goods stand there frowning at each other, gazing at their shoes in bewilderment.

In the middle of the bare acreage called Franklin Field, sixty backhoes are lined up, their earth-scraping bulldozer blades drawn in low at the back, their crane-arms crooked high in front, scoops at the ready, waiting for the championship to begin. The cabs are empty. On one windshield a sticker says "Iran Sucks." In a half-circle a thousand fans wearing cowboy hats stand around sipping Budweiser and waiting too. This is where I finally find Bill. I recognize him by his bare head. He is carrying his hat. I still have not seen him wearing it.

He doesn't take my absence personally. When I explain what happened he laughs and says it reminds him of the old Merle Haggard tune "Radiator Man from Wasco," which is set in a Kern County town north of Bakersfield, up Highway 43.

"Sounds like you've been reliving Merle's song," he says.

I ask him if the parade committee had made him ride a horse.

"Nope, a fellow here in town provided a Cadillac, which would have been real comfortable if the top was down. It wasn't a convertible, though. The roof was so low I couldn't get my cowboy hat on. In that respect I guess I lucked out. My wife, Frankie Jo, was with me, so we all three sat hunched in the front. The fact is, I am weary. Waving to so many people, trying to keep a smile on for an hour and a half, and then not sure anybody can even see you, under a low roof like that."

Bill grins all through this account, amused by the parade, and narrows his eyes as if faced with heavy weather, which at the moment happens to be true. It is clouding up. Warm heavy clouds have filled the sky.

"I'm glad I don't have to do this again," he says. "Five years from now, it'll be somebody else's turn. They only have Oildorado every five years, you know. For a while it was annual. But people were running out of time for anything else."

I have a couple of beers and wait for the backhoe drivers to mount their rigs. I can only guzzle so much Bud, since I plan to start north this afternoon, sooner or later, and there are mountains to climb. I decide on sooner. It is looking more and more like rain, and the backhoes are still sitting like tanks on D day waiting for the signal from Eisenhower. Something has delayed the contest. No one is certain what, and no one much cares as long as the Bud holds out.

I say good-bye to Bill and start out 33 through the Midway-Sunset, making one last quick stop at Fellows, another oil-field village five miles away. Fellows reminds me of the pueblos in New Mexico, the ones you pass driving out of Albuquerque — no roadside billboards in any direction, no pitch to the motorist, no hotels or motels or fast-food neon, no Rotary lunch. It's just a village, a cluster of low buildings a mile or so off the road, out there all by itself in the high desert. Pumping wells dot the slopes beyond town, where the Temblor Range begins to rise. More wells decorate

70

75

the plains spreading south. There is no main street in Fellows, no grocery store. Where the houses stop, I find what I have left the highway for, another gusher site Bill has recommended, another monument stone, another plaque:

THE FIRST GUSHER

Midway Field 2-6, which made the Midway Oil Field famous. Blew in over the derrick top, November 27, 1909, and started the Great California Oil Boom. At its peak it produced 2000 barrels a day.

Lakeview was the biggest and wildest. Midway 2-6, coming four months sooner, gets credit for being first. The granite block stands by itself inside a low fence. The air and land nearby is strangely quiet under the lowering sky, punctuated by a faint creaking from the nearest well, where the cable rubs once in every cycle. No wind this day, no dogs, no cars. Perhaps everyone who lives in Fellows went off to Franklin Field. In the hills and plains around the monument where the first gusher blew in, nothing moves but the bowing pumps, the silent praying of a thousand mantises near and far across the western San Joaquin.

Understanding the Text

1. How, in Houston's descriptions, does Kern County differ from the traditional images of coastal California?

2. Houston is a visitor to Oildorado. How do his attitudes toward the Kern County oil fields evolve throughout his selection?

3. How does Kern County's population reflect the Okie migration depicted in *The Grapes of Wrath*?

4. How does Houston use humor to convey his descriptions of Kern County oil country?

Exploring and Debating the Issues

1. Both Houston and Joan Didion ("Notes of a Native Daughter," p. 51) begin their selections by dismissing the popular images of coastal California. Compare and contrast the tone and purpose of the two writers' essays on the Central Valley.

2. John Cassidy ("The Comeback," p. 274) identifies Silicon Valley's and Hollywood's "regional networks" as reasons for these area's success. In an essay, analyze whether the Kern County economy can claim such a basis for support.

3. Houston wrote this essay in the early 1980s. Visit your library or the Internet, and research the oil industry's current place in the California economy.

4. Write an essay arguing whether the people in Kern County are typically Californian or whether they resemble American Southerners or Midwesterners more.

CESAR CHAVEZ

The Organizer's Tale

The story of the United Farm Workers Union and its founder, the late **Cesar Chavez** (1927–1993), parallels, for California Chicanos, the story of Martin Luther King, Jr., and the civil rights movement. In this selection, Chavez tells his own story, describing his initiation as a union activist and the birth of his own National Farm Workers Union. His long struggle to ensure the civil rights of farm workers eventually culminated in the formation of the UFW. At the time of his death in 1993, Chavez was still working to improve the lives of California farm workers, concentrating on protecting workers from agricultural pesticides.

It really started for me sixteen years ago in San Jose, California, when I was working on an apricot farm. We figured he was just another social worker doing a study of farm conditions, and I kept refusing to meet with him. But he was persistent. Finally, I got together some of the rough element in San Jose. We were going to have a little reception for him to teach the *gringo* a little bit of how we felt. There were about thirty of us in the house, young guys mostly. I was supposed to give them a signal — change my cigarette from my right hand to my left — and then we were going to give him a lot of hell. But he started talking and the more he talked, the more wide-eyed I became and the less inclined I was to give the signal. A couple of guys who were pretty drunk at the time still wanted to give the *gringo* the business, but we got rid of them. This fellow was making a lot of sense, and I wanted to hear what he had to say.

His name was Fred Ross, and he was an organizer for the Community Service Organizations (CSO), which was working with Mexican Americans in the cities. I became immediately really involved. Before long I was heading a voter registration drive. All the time I was observing the things Fred did, secretly, because I wanted to learn how to organize, to see how it was done. I was impressed with his patience and understanding of people. I thought this was a tool, one of the greatest things he had.

It was pretty rough for me at first. I was changing and had to take a lot of ridicule from the kids my age, the rough characters I worked with in the fields. They would say, "Hey, big shot. Now that you're a *politico*, why are you working here for sixty-five cents an hour?" I might add that our neighborhood had the highest percentage of San Quentin graduates. It was a game among the *pachucos*[1] in the sense that we defended ourselves from outsiders, although inside the neighborhood there was not a lot of fighting.

After six months of working every night in San Jose, Fred assigned me to take over the CSO chapter in Decoto. It was a tough spot to fill. I would suggest something, and people would say, "No, let's wait till Fred gets back," or

[1]Mexican youths of the 1930s and 1940s who developed their own style and language living in American barrios. [Eds.]

"Fred wouldn't do it that way." This is pretty much a pattern with people, I discovered, whether I was put in Fred's position, or later, when someone else was put in my position. After the Decoto assignment I was sent to start a new chapter in Oakland. Before I left, Fred came to a place in San Jose called the Hole-in-the-Wall and we talked for half an hour over coffee. He was in a rush to leave, but I wanted to keep him talking; I was that scared of my assignment.

There were hard times in Oakland. First of all, it was a big city and I'd get lost every time I went anywhere. Then I arranged a series of house meetings. I would get to the meeting early and drive back and forth past the house, too nervous to go in and face the people. Finally I would force myself to go inside and sit in a corner. I was quite thin then, and young, and most of the people were middle-aged. Someone would say, "Where's the organizer?" And I would pipe up, "Here I am." Then they would say in Spanish — these were very poor people and we hardly spoke anything but Spanish — "Ha! This *kid*?" Most of them said they were interested, but the hardest part was to get them to start pushing themselves, on their own initiative.

The idea was to set up a meeting and then get each attending person to call his own house meeting, inviting new people — a sort of chain letter effect. After a house meeting I would lie awake going over the whole thing, playing the tape back, trying to see why people laughed at one point, or why they were for one thing and against another. I was also learning to read and write, those late evenings. I had left school in the seventh grade after attending sixty-seven different schools, and my reading wasn't the best.

At our first organizing meeting we had 368 people: I'll never forget it because it was very important to me. You eat your heart out; the meeting is called for seven o'clock and you start to worry about four. You wait. Will they show up? Then the first one arrives. By seven there are only twenty people, you have everything in order, you have to look calm. But little by little they filter in and at a certain point you know it will be a success.

After four months in Oakland, I was transferred. The chapter was beginning to move on its own, so Fred assigned me to organize the San Joaquin Valley. Over the months I developed what I used to call schemes or tricks — now I call them techniques — of making initial contacts. The main thing in convincing someone is to spend time with him. It doesn't matter if he can read, write, or even speak well. What is important is that he is a man and second, that he has shown some initial interest. One good way to develop leadership is to take a man with you in your car. And it works a lot better if you're doing the driving; that way you are in charge. You drive, he sits there, and you talk. These little things were very important to me; I was caught in a big game by then, figuring out what makes people work. I found that if you work hard enough you can usually shake people into working too, those who are concerned. You work harder and they work harder still, up to a point and then they pass you. Then, of course, they're on their own.

I also learned to keep away from the established groups and so-called leaders, and to guard against philosophizing. Working with low-income people is very different from working with the professionals, who like to sit around talking about how to play politics. When you're trying to recruit a farmworker, you have to paint a little picture, and then you have to color the picture in. We found out that the harder a guy is to convince, the better leader or member he becomes. When you exert yourself to convince him, you have his confidence and he has good motivation. A lot of people who say OK right away wind up hanging around the office, taking up the workers' time.

During the McCarthy era in one Valley town, I was subjected to a lot of red-baiting. We had been recruiting people for citizenship classes at the high school when we got into a quarrel with the naturalization examiner. He was rejecting people on the grounds that they were just parroting what they learned in citizenship class. One day we had a meeting about it in Fresno, and I took along some of the leaders of our local chapter. Some red-baiting official gave us a hard time, and the people got scared and took his side. They did it because it seemed easy at the moment, even though they knew that sticking with me was the right thing to do. It was disgusting. When we left the building they walked by themselves ahead of me as if I had some kind of communicable disease. I had been working with these people for three months and I was very sad to see that. It taught me a great lesson. 10

That night I learned that the chapter officers were holding a meeting to review my letters and printed materials to see if I really was a Communist. So I drove out there and walked right in on their meeting. I said, "I hear you've been discussing me, and I thought it would be nice if I was here to defend myself. Not that it matters that much to you or even to me, because as far as I'm concerned you are a bunch of cowards." At that they began to apologize. "Let's forget it," they said. "You're a nice guy." But I didn't want apologies. I wanted a full discussion. I told them I didn't give a damn, but that they had to learn to distinguish fact from what appeared to be a fact because of fear. I kept them there till two in the morning. Some of the women cried. I don't know if they investigated me any further, but I stayed on another few months and things worked out.

This was not an isolated case. Often when we'd leave people to themselves they would get frightened and draw back into their shells where they had been all the years. And I learned quickly that there is no real appreciation. Whatever you do, and no matter what reasons you may give to others, you do it because you want to see it done, or maybe because you want power. And there shouldn't be any appreciation, understandably. I know good organizers who were destroyed, washed out, because they expected people to appreciate what they'd done. Anyone who comes in with the idea that farmworkers are free of sin and that the growers are all bastards, either has never dealt with the situation or is an idealist of the first order. Things don't work that way.

For more than ten years I worked for the CSO. As the organization grew, we found ourselves meeting in fancier and fancier motels and holding expensive conventions. Doctors, lawyers, and politicians began joining. They would get elected to some office in the organization and then, for all practical purposes, leave. Intent on using the CSO for their own prestige purposes, these "leaders," many of them, lacked the urgency we had to have. When I became general director I began to press for a program to organize farmworkers into a union, an idea most of the leadership opposed. So I started a revolt within the CSO. I refused to sit at the head table at meetings, refused to wear a suit and tie, and finally I even refused to shave and cut my hair. It used to embarrass some of the professionals. At every meeting I got up and gave my standard speech: we shouldn't meet in fancy motels, we were getting away from the people, farmworkers had to be organized. But nothing happened. In March of 1962 I resigned and came to Delano to begin organizing the Valley on my own.

By hand I drew a map of all the towns between Arvin and Stockton — eighty-six of them, including farming camps — and decided to hit them all to get a small nucleus of people working in each. For six months I traveled around, planting an idea. We had a simple questionnaire, a little card with space for name, address, and how much the worker thought he ought to be paid. My wife, Helen, mimeographed them, and we took our kids for two- or three-day jaunts to these towns, distributing the cards door-to-door and to camps and groceries.

Some eighty thousand cards were sent back from eight Valley counties.   15
I got a lot of contacts that way, but I was shocked at the wages the people were asking. The growers were paying $1 and $1.15, and maybe 95 percent of the people thought they should be getting only $1.25. Sometimes people scribbled messages on the cards: "I hope to God we win" or "Do you think we can win?" or "I'd like to know more." So I separated the cards with the penciled notes, got in my car and went to those people.

We didn't have any money at all in those days, none for gas and hardly any for food. So I went to people and started asking for food. It turned out to be about the best thing I could have done, although at first it's hard on your pride. Some of our best members came in that way. If people give you their food, they'll give you their hearts. Several months and many meetings later we had a working organization, and this time the leaders were the people.

None of the farmworkers had collective bargaining contracts, and I thought it would take ten years before we got that first contract. I wanted desperately to get some color into the movement, to give people something they could identify with, like a flag. I was reading some books about how various leaders discovered what colors contrasted and stood out the best. The Egyptians had found that a red field with a white circle and a black emblem in the center crashed into your eyes like nothing else. I wanted to use the Aztec eagle in the center, as on the Mexican flag. So I told my cousin Manuel, "Draw an Aztec eagle," Manuel had a little trouble with it, so we modified the eagle to make it easier for people to draw.

The first big meeting of what we decided to call the National Farm Workers Association was held in September, 1962 at Fresno, with 287 people. We had our huge red flag on the wall, with paper tacked over it.

When the time came, Manuel pulled a cord ripping the paper off the flag and all of a sudden it hit the people. Some of them wondered if it was a Communist flag, and I said it probably looked more like a neo-Nazi emblem than anything else. But they wanted an explanation, so Manuel got up and said, "When that damn eagle flies — that's when the farmworkers' problems are going to be solved."

One of the first things I decided was that outside money wasn't going to organize people, at least not in the beginning. I even turned down a grant from a private group — $50,000 to go directly to organize farmworkers — for just this reason. Even when there are no strings attached, you are still compromised because you feel you have to produce immediate results. This is bad, because it takes a long time to build a movement, and your organization suffers if you get too far ahead of the people it belongs to. We set the dues at $42 a year per family, really a meaningful dues, but the 212 we got to pay, only 12 remained by June of 1963. We were discouraged at that, but not enough to make us quit.

Money was always a problem. Once we were facing a $180 gas bill on a 20 credit card I'd got a long time ago and was about to lose. And we *had* to keep that credit card. One day my wife and I were picking cotton, pulling bolls, to make a little money to live on. Helen said to me, "Do you put all this in the bag, or just the cotton?" I thought she was kidding and told her to throw the whole boll in so that she had nothing but a sack of bolls at the weighing. The man said, "Whose sack is this?" I said, well, my wife's, and he told us we were fired. "Look at all that crap you brought in," he said. Helen and I started laughing. We were going anyway. We took the $4 we had earned and spent it at a grocery store where they were giving away a $100 prize. Each time you shopped they'd give you one of the letters of M-O-N-E-Y or a flag: You had to have M-O-N-E-Y plus the flag to win. Helen had already collected the letters and just needed the flag. Anyway, they gave her the ticket. She screamed, "A flag? I don't believe it," ran in and got the $100. She said, "Now we're going to eat steak." But I said no, we're going to pay the gas bill. I don't know if she cried, but I think she did.

It was rough in those early years. Helen was having babies and I was not there when she was at the hospital. But if you haven't got your wife behind you, you can't do many things. There's got to be peace at home. So I did, I think, a fairly good job of organizing her. When we were kids, she lived in Delano and I came to town as a migrant. Once on a date we had a bad experience about segregation at a movie theater, and I put up a fight. We were together then, and still are. I think I'm more of a pacifist than she is. Her father, Fabela, was a colonel with Pancho Villa in the Mexican Revolution. Sometimes she gets angry and tells me, "These scabs — you should deal with them sternly," and I kid her, "It must be too much of that Fabela blood in you."

The movement really caught on in 1964. By August we had a thousand members. We'd had a beautiful ninety-day drive in Corcoran, where they had the Battle of the Corcoran Farm Camp thirty years ago, and by November we had assets of $25,000 in our credit union, which helped to stabilize the membership. I had gone without pay the whole of 1963. The next year the members voted me a $40 a week salary, after Helen had to quit working in the fields to manage the credit union.

Our first strike was in May of 1965, a small one but it prepared us for the big one. A farmworker from McFarland named Epifanio Camacho came to see me. He said he was sick and tired of how people working the roses were being treated, and he was willing to "go the limit." I assigned Manuel and Gilbert Padilla to hold meetings at Camacho's house. The people wanted union recognition, but the real issue, as in most cases when you begin, was wages. They were promised $9 a thousand, but they were actually getting $6.50 and $7 for grafting roses. Most of them signed cards giving us the right to bargain for them. We chose the biggest company, with about eighty-five employees, not counting the irrigators and supervisors, and we held a series of meetings to prepare the strike and call the vote. There would be no picket line; everyone pledged on their honor not to break the strike.

Early on the first morning of the strike, we sent out ten cars to check the people's homes. We found lights in five or six homes and knocked on the doors. The men were getting up and we'd say, "Where are you going?" They would dodge, "Oh, uh . . . I was just getting up, you know." We'd say, "Well, you're not going to work, are you?" And they'd say no. Dolores Huerta, who was driving the green panel truck, saw a light in one house where four rose-workers lived. They told her they were going to work, even after she reminded them of their pledge. So she moved the truck so it blocked their driveway, turned off the key, put it in her purse and sat there alone.

That morning the company foreman was madder than hell and refused   25
to talk to us. None of the grafters had shown up for work. At 10:30 we started to go to the company office, but it occurred to us that maybe a woman would have a better chance. So Dolores knocked on the office door, saying, "I'm Dolores Huerta from the National Farm Workers Association." "Get out!" the man said. "You Communist. Get out!" I guess they were expecting us, because as Dolores stood arguing with him the cops came and told her to leave. She left.

For two days the fields were idle. On Wednesday they recruited a group of Filipinos from out of town who knew nothing of the strike, maybe thirty-five of them. They drove through escorted by three sheriff's patrol cars, one in front, one in the middle, and one at the rear with a dog. We didn't have a picket line, but we parked across the street and just watched them go through, not saying a word. All but seven stopped working after half an hour, and the rest had quit by midafternoon.

The company made an offer the evening of the fourth day, a package deal that amounted to a 120 percent wage increase, but no contract. We wanted to hold out for a contract and more benefits, but a majority of the rose-workers wanted to accept the offer and go back. We are a democratic union so we had to support what they wanted to do. They had a meeting and voted to settle. Then we had a problem with a few militants who wanted to hold out. We had to convince them to go back to work as a united front, because otherwise they would be canned. So we worked — Tony Orendain and I, Dolores and Gilbert, Jim Drake and all the organizers — knocking on doors till two in the morning, telling people, "You have to go back or you'll lose your job." And they did. They worked.

Our second strike, and our last before the big one at Delano, was in the grapes at Martin's Ranch last summer. The people were getting a raw deal there, being pushed around pretty badly. Gilbert went out to the field, climbed out of a car, and took a strike vote. They voted unanimously to go out. Right away they started bringing in strikebreakers, so we launched a tough attack on the labor contractors, distributed leaflets portraying them as really low characters. We attacked one — Luis Campos — so badly that he just gave up the job, and he took twenty-seven of his men out with him. All he asked was that we distribute another leaflet reinstating him in the community. And we did. What was unusual was that the grower would talk to us. The grower kept saying, "I can't pay. I just haven't got the money." I guess he must have found the money somewhere, because we were asking $1.40 and we got it.

We had just finished the Martin strike when the Agricultural Workers Organizing Committee (AFL-CIO) started a strike against the grape-growers, DiGiorgio, Schenley liquors, and small growers, asking $1.40 an hour and 25 cents a box. There was a lot of pressure from our members for us to join the strike, but we had some misgivings. We didn't feel ready for a big strike like this one, one that was sure to last a long time. Having no money — just $87 in the strike fund — meant we'd have to depend on God knows who.

Eight days after the strike started — it takes time to get twelve hundred people together from all over the Valley — we held a meeting in Delano and voted to go out. I asked the membership to release us from the pledge not to accept outside money, because we'd need it now, a lot of it. The help came. It started because of the close, and I would say even beautiful, relationship that we've had with the Migrant Ministry for some years. They were the first to come to our rescue, financially and in every other way, and they spread the word to other benefactors. . . .

30

The people who took part in the strike and the march have something more than their material interest going for them. If it were only material, they wouldn't have stayed on the strike long enough to win. It is difficult to explain. But it flows out in the ordinary things they say. For instance, some of the younger guys are saying, "Where do you think's going to be the next strike?" I say, "Well, we have to win in Delano." They say, "We'll win, but where do we go next?" I say, "Maybe most of us will be working in the fields." They say, "No, I don't want to go and work in the fields. I want to organize. There are a lot of people that need our help." So I say, "You're going to be pretty poor then, because when you strike you don't have much money." They say they don't care about that.

And others are saying, "I have friends who are working in Texas. If we could only help them." It is bigger, certainly, than just a strike. And if this spirit grows within the farm labor movement, one day we can use the force that we have to help correct a lot of things that are wrong in this society. But that is for the future. Before you can run, you have to learn to walk.

There are vivid memories from my childhood — what we had to go through because of low wages and the conditions, basically because there was no union. I suppose if I wanted to be fair I could say that I'm trying to settle a personal score. I could dramatize it by saying that I want to bring social justice to farmworkers. But the truth is that I went through a lot of hell, and a lot of people did. If we can even the score a little for the workers then we are doing something. Besides, I don't know any other work I like to do better than this. I really don't, you know.

Understanding the Text

1. Why did Chavez initially have no interest in listening to Fred Ross?
2. Why did Chavez first become involved in the organized labor movement?
3. What strategies did Chavez use to recruit farm workers to the labor movement, and why?
4. Summarize in your own words the events surrounding the first National Farm Workers Association strike in 1965.

Exploring and Debating the Issues

1. In your journal, write an entry exploring whether you would be willing, at times, to work for no wages, sacrificing your family's needs, as Chavez did in his early years organizing farm workers. If you would be willing, what would your motivation be? If you would not be willing, why not?
2. The most famous strike by farm workers was the grape strike, which led to a secondary boycott of Gallo wines. In class, form teams and debate the use of strikes and boycotts as a means to achieve the goals of labor.
3. In class, stage a conversation between Chavez and a member of one of the old Sacramento families Joan Didion mentions ("Notes from a Native Daughter," p. 51) on the right of farm workers to organize.
4. Write an essay in which you explain whether Chavez's work organizing farm workers helped them to realize the California dream, even in part. To develop your ideas, you may want to consult the readings in Chapter 1, "California Dreaming: Myths of the Golden Land."
5. Compare the conditions of farm workers as described by Chavez with those of a later period: the immigrants described by William Langewiesche in "Invisible Men" (p. 99).

LUIS OMAR SALINAS

My Fifty-Plus Years Celebrate Spring

Writing from the perspective of a Central Valley farm worker, **Luis Omar Salinas** (b. 1937) writes here that if it is true that "hard work ennobles the spirit," then "the road to heaven must be crowded beyond belief." The life of a farm worker could not be better conveyed. Salinas is the author and editor of numerous works, including *Afternoon of the Unreal* (1980), *Prelude to Darkness* (1981), and *The Sadness of Days* (1987).

O n the road, the mountains
in the distance are at rest
in a wild blue silence.
On the sides of the highway
the grape orchards unfurl   5
deep and green again
like a pregnant woman
gathering strength
for the time to come.
And with the passing   10
of each season
human life knows little
change. Forty years
in this valley,
the wind, the sun   15
building its altars
of salt, the rain that
holds nothing back,
and with the crop
at its peak   20
packing houses burn
into morning,
their many diligent
Mexican workers stacking up
the trays and hard hours   25
that equal their living.

I've heard it said
hard work ennobles
the spirit —
If that is the case,   30
the road to heaven
must be crowded
beyond belief.

Understanding the Text

1. How does the imagery in this poem convey Salinas's attitudes toward the natural world?

2. What impressions of the lives of farm workers does this poem convey?

3. Beginning with the poem's title, describe Salinas's use of irony.

Exploring and Debating the Issues

1. The poem refers to a life of little change for California farm workers. Read or reread Cesar Chavez's "The Organizer's Tale" (p. 345), and discuss the ways in which the formation of the United Farm Workers Union attempted to improve farm workers' lives.

2. Compare and contrast Salinas's attitudes and tone with that of another farm worker, Ramón "Tianguis" Pérez ("Ripon," p. 108).

3. Compare Salinas's sensitivity to the natural cycle of the seasons with that of David Mas Masumoto ("As If the Farmer Died," p. 185). How would you account for any differences?

Researching the Issues

1. Tourism is one of California's leading industries. Conduct a research project in which you determine the most popular tourist sites in the state, and then write an analysis of how these sites correspond with conventional images of California. (You might read or reread James J. Rawls's "California: A People, A Place, A Dream," p. 8.)

2. Sports are big business in California, and its cities compete for professional teams by offering tax breaks and new facilities and stadiums. Research the recent history of one California sports franchise (for instance, the Oakland Raiders or the Anaheim Ducks), and support, challenge, or modify the proposition that taxpayer dollars should be used to lure new franchises or to maintain existing teams.

3. In 1991, California plunged into a recession that was deeper and longer than that experienced by most other regions of the country. The severity of the slump took most observers by surprise. Conduct research into the causes of the 1990s recession. Should observers have been surprised? What lessons can be drawn from the state's experiences?

4. Investigate the contributions of the entertainment industry — including film, television, music, theatre, and dance — to the California economy. What portion of the state's economy is fueled by entertainment?

5. Not everyone in the entertainment industry is a star. Research the professional opportunities offered in entertainment, and evaluate the best opportunities for college graduates.

CALIFORNIA ON THE NET

1. Use the Internet to research the proportion of small startup firms and large corporations in Silicon Valley. You might try http://www.silvalonline.com or http://www.svpal.org.

2. The Biotechnology Industry Organization, an international consortium of biotech concerns, maintains a web site at http://www.bio.org. Visit the site, and determine California's contribution to the biotechnology industry.

3. Critics charge that agriculture in California pays too little for water compared to business or residential users (see Gerald W. Haslam, "The Water Game," p. 191). Use the Internet to research both sides of this issue. You might try the California Department of Food and Agriculture site (http://www.cdfa.ca.gov), industry sites, or conservation sites (http://www.sierraclub.org). Use your findings as the basis of an argumentative essay on this issue.

6. While much of California has rebounded economically in the late 1990s, some regions have not. Investigate those regions that still suffer from high unemployment, and analyze the reasons for this.

7. The United Farm Workers Union was established in the 1960s, but its struggles did not end then. What are the current labor issues that the union is addressing today, and how are its members attempting to achieve their goals?

8. Economic development has taken its toll on the California coastline. Research some of the current threats to the California coast from pollution and the responses to those threats by such organizations as Heal the Bay and the Sierra Club.

Acknowledgments *(continued from p. iv)*

Ward Connerly, "Race Preferences Lose in Court— Again" from the *Los Angeles Times* (April 9, 1997). Copyright © 1997 by Ward Connerly. Reprinted with the permission of the author.

Margaret Leslie Davis, "Mulholland's Legacy" from *Rivers in the Desert* (New York: HarperCollins Publishers, 1993). Copyright © 1993 by Margaret Leslie Davis. Reprinted with the permission of Richard Curtis Associates, Inc.

Mike Davis, "Sunbelt Bolshevism" from *City of Quartz: Excavating the Future in Los Angeles.* Copyright © 1990 by Verso. Reprinted with the permission of the publishers.

Joan Didion, "Notes from a Native Daughter" from *Slouching Toward Bethlehem.* Copyright © 1965, 1968 by Joan Didion. Reprinted with the permission of Farrar, Straus, & Giroux, Inc.

Chitra Bannerjee Divakaruni, "Yuba City School" from *Black Candle: Poems About Women from India, Pakistan, Bangladesh.* Copyright © 1991 by Chitra Bannerjee Divakaruni. Reprinted with the permission of CALYX Books.

Sue Kunitomi Embrey, "Manzanar" from Arthur A. Hansen (ed.), *Japanese American World War II Evacuation Oral History Project/Part I: Internees* (Westport, CT: Meckler Publishing, 1990). Copyright © 1978 by The Oral History Program, California State University, Fullerton. Reprinted with the permission of the Oral History Program, California State University, Fullerton.

F. Scott Fitzgerald, excerpts from *The Last Tycoon.* Copyright 1941 by Charles Scribner's Sons, renewed © 1969 by Frances Scott Fitzgerald Smith. Reprinted with the permission of Scribner, a division of Simon & Schuster.

James J. Flink, "The Automobile Age in California" from *The Automobile Age.* Copyright © 1988 by The Massachusetts Institute of Technology. Reprinted with the permission of The MIT Press.

Sylvia S. Fox, "Teacher Shortage" from *California Journal* (March 1998). Copyright © 1998. Reprinted with the permission of the author and Information for Public Affairs, Inc.

Nathan Glazer, "Blacks Only" from *The New Republic* 216, no. 4 (January 27, 1997). Copyright © 1997 by The New Republic, Inc. Reprinted with the permission of *The New Republic.*

Gerald W. Haslam, "The Water Game" from *The Other California: The Great Central Valley in Life and Letters.* Copyright © 1993 by Gerald W. Haslam. Reprinted with the permission of the University of Nevada Press.

Chris Hayhurst, "Toxic Technology: Electronics and the Silicon Valley" from *E: The Environmental Magazine* (May–June 1997). Copyright © 1997 by the Earth Action Network, Inc. Reprinted with the permission of *E: The Environmental Magazine,* Subscription Department, P.O. Box 2047, Marion, OH 43306; Telephone (815) 734-1242. Subscriptions are $20 per year.

John D. Houston, "In Search of Oildorado" from *Californians: Searching for the Golden State* (New York: Alfred A. Knopf, 1982). Copyright © 1982 by John D. Houston. Reprinted with the permission of the author.

William Langewiesche, "Invisible Men" from *The New Yorker* (February 23 and March 2, 1998). Copyright © 1998 by William Langewiesche. Reprinted with the permission of Darhansoff & Verrill Literary Agency.

Yeh Ling-Ling, "The Welcome Mat Is Threadbare" from the *Los Angeles Times* (April 13, 1994). Reprinted with the permission of Population-Environment Balance.

Jack Lopez, "Of *Cholos* and Surfers" from *Cholos and Surfers: A Chicano Family Album.* Reprinted with the permission of Capra Press, P.O. Box 2068, Santa Barbara, CA 93120.

Michael J. Mandel, "Taking Its Place in the Pantheon: Silicon Valley's Starring Role in the Information Economy Isn't Likely to Be Eclipsed Any Time Soon" from *Business*

Week (August 25, 1997). Copyright © 1997 by The McGraw-Hill Companies. Reprinted with the permission of *Business Week.*

Malcolm Margolin, "Among Kin" from *News from Native California* (Spring 1992). Copyright © 1992. Reprinted with the permission of the publishers.

Al Martinez, "Can We All Get Along?" from *California Journal* (January 1998). Copyright © 1998. Reprinted with the permission of Information for Public Affairs, Inc.

Rubén Martinez, "Refine Immigration Policy to Reflect History and the Moment We Live In" from the *Los Angeles Times* (February 27, 1994). Copyright © 1994 by Rubén Martinez. Reprinted with the permission of the author.

David Mas Masumoto, "As If the Farmer Died" from *Epitaph for a Peach: Four Seasons on My Family Farm.* Copyright © 1995 by David Mas Masumoto. Reprinted with the permission of HarperCollins Publishers, Inc.

Lary May, "The New Frontier: 'Hollywood,' 1914–1920" from *Screening Out the Past: The Birth of Mass Culture and the Motion Picture Industry.* Copyright © 1980 by Lary May. Reprinted with the permission of Oxford University Press, New York.

Arthur F. McEvoy, "California Indians as Capable Resource Managers" from *The Fisherman's Problem: Ecology and the Law in California Fisheries, 1850–1980.* Copyright © 1986. Reprinted with the permission of Cambridge University Press.

Jack Miles, "Blacks vs. Browns" from *The Atlantic Monthly* (October 1992). Copyright © 1992 by Jack Miles. Reprinted with the permission of Georges Borchardt, Inc. for the author.

Ruben Navarrette, Jr., "Well, I Guess They Need Their Minority" [editors' title] from *A Darker Shade of Crimson.* Copyright © 1993 by Ruben Navarrette, Jr. Reprinted with the permission of Bantam Books, a division of Bantam Doubleday Dell Publishing Group, Inc.

Ramón "Tianguis" Pérez, "Ripon" from *Diary of an Undocumented Immigrant,* translated by Dick J. Reavis. Copyright © 1991 by Dick J. Reavis. Reprinted with the permission of Arte Publico Press.

Romesh Ratnesar, "The Next Big Divide? Blacks and Hispanics Square Off Over Bilingual Education" from *Time* (December 1, 1997). Copyright © 1997 by Time, Inc. Reprinted with the permission of *Time.*

James J. Rawls, "California: A Place, A People, A Dream" from Claudia K. Jurmain and James J. Rawls (eds.), *California: A Place, A People, A Dream* (San Francisco: Chronicle Books/The Oakland Museum, 1986). Reprinted with the permission of The Oakland Museum.

Marc Reisner, "Things Fall Apart" from *Cadillac Desert, Revised and Updated.* Copyright © 1986, 1993 by Marc P. Reisner. Reprinted with the permission of Viking Penguin, a division of Penguin Putnam, Inc.

James Richardson, "What Price Glory?" from *UCLA Magazine* (February 1997). Copyright © 1997 by the Regents of the University of California. Reprinted with the permission of *UCLA Magazine.*

Richard Rodriguez, "Proofs" from *To the Promised Land.* Copyright © 1988 by Richard Rodriguez. Reprinted with the permission of The Aperture Foundation.

Malcolm J. Rohrbough, "Days of Gold" from *Days of Gold: The California Gold Rush and the American Nation.* Copyright © 1997 by the Regents of the University of California. Reprinted with the permission of the University of California Press.

Mike Rose, "A Visit to Edwin Markham Intermediate School" from *Possible Lives: The Promise of Public Education in America.* Copyright © 1995 by Mike Rose. Reprinted with the permission of Houghton Mifflin Company. All rights reserved.

Jean Ross, "What Has Proposition 13 Meant for California?" from *California Voter* (Spring 1998). Reprinted with the permission of the author and the League of Women Voters of California.

Luis Omar Salinas, "My Fifty-Plus Years Celebrate Spring" from Gerald W. Haslam (ed.), *Many Californias: Literature from the Golden State* (Reno: University of Nevada Press, 1992). Reprinted with the permission of the author.

Peter Schrag, "California, Here We Come" from *The Atlantic Monthly* (March 1998). Copyright © 1998 by Peter Schrag. Reprinted with the permission of the author. "Language Barrier: California's Bilingualism Mess" from *The New Republic* (March 9, 1998). Copyright © 1998 by The New Republic, Inc. Reprinted with the permission of *The New Republic.*

Steve Scott, "Reality Votes" from *California Journal* (January 1998). Copyright © 1998. Reprinted with the permission of Information for Public Affairs, Inc.

Anna Deavere Smith, "The Unheard" from *Twilight Los Angeles: 1992 on the Road.* Copyright © 1994 by Anna Deavere Smith. Reprinted with the permission of Doubleday, a division of the Bantam Doubleday Dell Publishing Group, Inc.

Gary Snyder, "Cultivating Wildness" from *Audubon* (May–June 1995). Copyright © 1995 by the National Audubon Society. Reprinted with the permission of *Audubon.*

Gary Soto, "The First" from *New and Selected Poems.* Copyright © 1995 by Gary Soto. Reprinted with the permission of Chronicle Books, San Francisco.

Denise S. Spooner, "A New Perspective on the Dream: Midwestern Images of Southern California in the Post–World War II Decades" from *California History* (Spring 1997). Copyright © 1997. Reprinted with the permission of the California Historical Society.

Judith Stacey, "Land of Dreams and Disaster: Postindustrial Living in the Silicon Valley" from *Stories of Domestic Upheaval in Late Twentieth-Century America.* Copyright © 1990 by Judith Stacey. Reprinted with the permission of BasicBooks, a subsidiary of Perseus Books Group, LLC.

John Steinbeck, excerpt from *The Grapes of Wrath.* Copyright 1939 and renewed © 1967 by John Steinbeck. Reprinted with the permission of Viking Penguin, a division of Penguin Putnam, Inc.

Charlie Stoddard, "An Age of Limits and Definitions" from the *Los Angeles Times* (May 27, 1994). Copyright © 1994 by Charlie Stoddard. Reprinted with the permission of the author.

Richard Steven Street, "Battling Toxic Racism" from *Organizing for Our Lives.* Copyright © 1992. Reprinted with the permission of NewSage Press.

Nathanael West, excerpt from *Miss Lonelyhearts and the Day of the Locust.* Copyright 1939 by the Estate of Nathanael West. Reprinted with the permission of New Directions Publishing Corporation.

Nancy Wride, "Vietnamese Youths No Longer Look Homeward" from the *Los Angeles Times* (April 4, 1994). Copyright © 1994 by the *Los Angeles Times.* Reprinted with permission.

Connie Young Yu, "The World of Our Grandmothers" from Asian Women United of California (ed.), *Making Waves: An Anthology of Writings By and About Asian American Women* (Boston: Beacon Press, 1989). Copyright © 1989 by Asian Women United of California. Reprinted by permission.

Index of Authors and Titles